VITAL DIPLOMACY

Ethnography, Theory, Experiment

Series Editors:
Martin Holbraad, Department of Anthropology, University College London
Morten Axel Pedersen, Department of Anthropology, University of Copenhagen
Rane Willerslev, Museum of Cultural History, University of Oslo

In recent years, ethnography has been increasingly recognized as a core method for generating qualitative data within the social sciences and humanities. This series explores a more radical, methodological potential of ethnography: its role as an arena of theoretical experimentation. It includes volumes that call for a rethinking of the relationship between ethnography and theory in order to question, and experimentally transform, existing understandings of the contemporary world.

VITAL DIPLOMACY

The Ritual Everyday on a Dammed River in Amazonia

By Chloe Nahum-Claudel

berghahn
NEW YORK · OXFORD
www.berghahnbooks.com

First published in 2018 by
Berghahn Books
www.berghahnbooks.com

© 2018, 2024 Chloe Nahum-Claudel
First paperback edition published in 2024

Library of Congress Cataloging-in-Publication Data

A C.I.P. cataloging record is available from the Library of Congress

British Library Cataloguing in Publication Data

A catalogue record for this book is available from the British Library

ISBN 978-1-78533-406-1 hardback
ISBN 978-1-80539-125-8 paperback
ISBN 978-1-80539-384-9 epub
ISBN 978-1-78533-407-8 web pdf

https://doi.org/10.3167/9781785334061

CONTENTS

ILLUSTRATIONS

ACKNOWLEDGEMENTS

This book is based on sixteen months' fieldwork in the Enawenê-nawê village of Halataikwa, concentrated in 2008–2009 while I was a Ph.D. student in the Department of Social Anthropology at the University of Cambridge. The research was made possible by a grant from the Economic and Social Research Council (ESRC) in the UK. The book was written during three years spent as Trebilcock-Newton Research Fellow at Pembroke College, Cambridge, and one year spent as a research fellow at the EHESS in Paris. I am grateful to all these institutions.

Most of all I thank the Enawenê-nawê. While my stay was just a blip in time from the perspective of the community, for me it was the whole world – a break in time, the closure of my previous life, and an opening to the future. This book is dedicated to them. I hope that some of their wisdom is faithfully interpreted. In their remarkably solidary community I learnt from everyone, but various people also showed me particular love and compassion. In particular, the woman I called mother, Kawalinero-asero fed and comforted me daily; her daughters, Atolohe-neto, Kawalinero-neto, Yokwali-neto, Menakalose-neto, Maxiolo, Mamiro, and their children were constant companions. Their husbands helped me in many ways. Circling the village I would like to thank a few others into whose houses I ventured most often to ask questions or pass the time: Sotailiti and his household; Kawekwa-atokwe; Kamerose-atokwe and Kamerose-asero, and their daughters and sons-in-law.

My greatest intellectual and personal debt is to my Ph.D. supervisor Stephen Hugh-Jones for his clarity of thought as a teacher and writer, and his kindness and generosity as a person. In Cambridge I also thank Barbara Bodenhorn, Martin Holbraad, Marilyn Strathern,

Francoise Barbira-Freedman, Piers Vitebsky and Rupert Stasch for their mentorship over the years.

I lived for long periods between 2006 and 2010 in Rio de Janeiro, Brazil, and the people I met there had a major influence on my life and my anthropology, and supported me in many practical and emotional ways. My fieldwork would have been impossible without the support of Eduardo Viveiros de Castro. In 2006 he welcomed me into his seminars at the Museu Nacional and introduced me to students and colleagues who became my friends and interlocutors. My research authorisation would never have been granted by the National Counsel for Technological and Scientific Development (CNPq) and the Agency for Indigenous Affairs (FUNAI) if it had not been for his guidance and tenacity through the process. I also thank Marcio Silva, another ethnographer of the Enawenê, for his good advice; Aparecida Vilaça for her ongoing inspiration and support; Marcio Goldman and Tania Stolze-Lima for conversation and hospitality; and for friendship and anthropological stimulus I thank Flavio Gordon, Fernanda Chinelli, Jose-Antonio Kelly, Julia Sauma, Guillerme Orlandini Heurich, Antonia Walford, Luana Almeida, Laura Lowenkron, Luciana França and Eduardo Dullo.

In Mato Grosso I thank Ivar Busatto, the director of OPAN, for access to the library in Cuiabá to consult materials on the Enawenê. Antonio Carlos de Aquino, the head of FUNAI in Juína, was always judicious in negotiations that arose between myself and the Enawenê. At FUNAI in Brasilia Giovana Acácia Tempesta helped me to access archives held there on the Enawenê.

Specific chapters of the book have benefited from comments at various stages. The Introduction benefited from astute readings by Michael Scott, Taras Fedirko, Anthony Pickles and Sertaç Sehlikoglu. Chapter 1 has improved following input from Kenny Calderón-Corredor, the Magic Circle in Cambridge, and the Seminar of Americanist Anthropology in Paris. I developed Chapter 3 on the basis of a seminar presentation at the University of San Diego in 2011, where Joel Robbins provided important feedback and conversations with Rupert Stasch did much to further my thinking. Chapter 5 benefited from the engaged reading of Milena Estorniolo. Chapter 4 profited from comments received at the Social Anthropology seminar at Durham University and the Kinship and Relational Logics seminar of Klaus Hamberger at the EHESS. The whole book is better thanks to Jessica Johnson's careful reading of an earlier version of the manuscript. Morten Pedersen, one of the three editors of this book series, provided sharp editorial feedback, which helped restructure and orient the manuscript following peer review. I also thank the two anonymous reviewers for their useful appraisals.

Various parts of the book improved thanks to input from my Ph.D. examiners, Philippe Erikson and Marilyn Strathern, and to conversations with Cédric Yvinec, Olivier Allard, Johanna Gonçalvez-Martin, and Jeanne Pensard-Besson. For copy editing I thank Max Webster, Autumn Green, Caryl Williams, Gillian Nahum and Pia Spry-Marquez. In addition I give special thanks to my mother, Gillian Nahum, for her faithful snail-mail correspondence throughout my fieldwork and for her belief in me, which has given me courage.

Finally, to Anthony Pickles. I carried the memory of our meeting through fieldwork in 2008–2009, and returned to the UK in 2010 to find him again. I thank him for sharing his intelligence, love and humour and for all the joys of our life together.

A NOTE ON LANGUAGE

The field research on which this book is based was conducted in the Enawenê-nawê's Arawakan language, which I learned to speak at a basic level through immersion and without systematic teaching or linguistic analysis. Except for personal names all foreign terms are italicised and translated the first time they are used in each chapter but are not italicised in subsequent usage.

In the past, the ethnonym Enawenê-nawê has been written Enauenê-Nauê or Enawene-Nawe. The correct pronunciation is with the primary stress at the end of each word and a secondary stress on the very first syllable: (e.,na.we.'ne) (na'we) (Rezende 2006: 5). I opt not to capitalise the second word because -nawe is a collectivising suffix meaning 'people', which creates various noun classes. I exclude the - nawê suffix throughout the book, using the abbreviated form 'Enawenê', as people themselves often do. This makes for easier reading and allows me to use the form 'Enawenê people', Enawenê women (*Enawenê-nero*) or Enawenê men (*Enawenê-nawê*) in which a translation substitutes the suffix. Indeed, many nouns are gendered, -o endings are feminine and -e endings masculine (e.g. blessing shaman: *hoanaytalo/hoanaytale*).

In the rare cases that I use names these are people's actual names. In fact, Enawenê people accumulate names through the life course and are known by different names contextually. Enawenê adults are generally called by parental or grandparental teknonyms, usually after the first child born to a couple, or their first grandchild. The gender and generation of a person referred to in the book can thus be inferred from the suffix: *-ene* means father, *-eneto* mother, *-atokwe* grandfather, and *-asero* grandmother.

The orthography of the Enawenê-nawê language is not firmly established. Spelling variations abound among authors; for example, the name of the ritual that is the subject of this book has been represented in various ways: *Iyaõkwa* (Almeida 2011), *Yãkwa* (Mendes dos Santos 2006). I prefer the approximation *Yankwa* for its simplicity for the reader of English. In general I have tended to minimise use of accenting compared to my Portuguese-speaking colleagues. As such, my representation of the language is only loosely based on Rezende's (2006) phonology.

I use a broad phonemic transcription composed of the following symbols: a, b, d, e, h, i, k, kw, ky, l, m, n, ñ, o, r, s, t, w, x, y. Primary stress falls on one of the two final syllables of a word, and most often the last. Some of the main sound variations are as follows: b and w are variant sounds of the same phoneme at the beginning of words e.g. *bera*, *wera* (cooking hearth structure); *biyti*, *wayti* (dam). Between vowels, w and m are interchangeable e.g. *kawinalili*, *kaminalili* (clan name). d, l are variant sounds of the same phoneme at the beginning of words e.g. *lerohi*, *derohi* (name of ritual). l and r are allophones e.g. *Kawali*, *Kawari* (man's name), *halikale*, *harikare* (host). i and e are allophones e.g. *esewehe*, *esewehe* (salt), *awale*, *awali* (beautiful). The diphthong [aj] can be represented ai or ay.

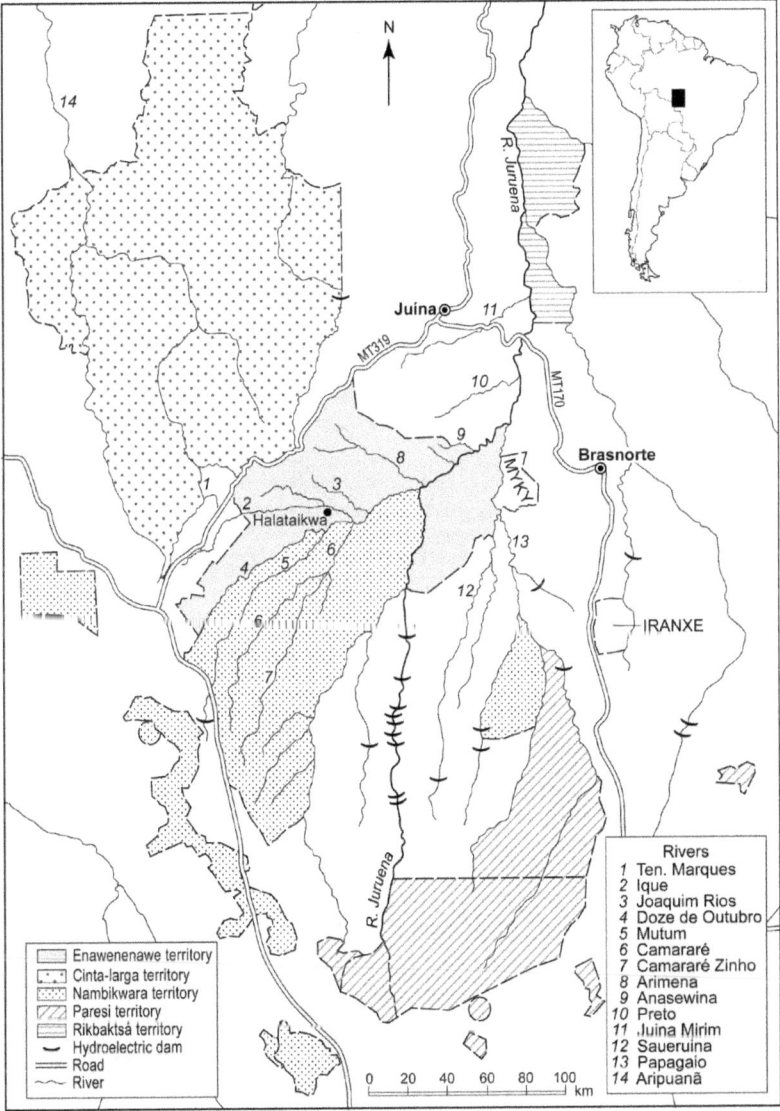

Map situating Enawenê-nawê territory in Brazil.
Map by Philip Stickler.

Introduction

The fish had not come. By the end of April 2009 the five teams of Enawenê-nawê fishermen had tended their fishing dams for nine weeks as opposed to the usual six. They had waited in vain for shoals of migrating fish to rush noisily into them. The dearth was due to the advancing construction of a string of hydroelectric dams on the upper reaches of the Juruena River, located in Mato Grosso state, an economic frontier region of Brazil. The Juruena flows north to feed the Tapajós and then the Amazon itself. It is one of many Amazonian rivers where the Brazilian government has incentivised the generation of hydropower. Living at this new resource frontier, in 2009 the Enawenê found themselves lacking sufficient fish for the ritual season's climactic feasts. In response, pioneering fishermen left their fishing dam to travel to the fast-growing town of Juína, the centre of the agribusiness and cattle industries that dominate the region, in order to buy fish from an aqua-farm. They persuaded agents from the government agency that assists the country's indigenous population to advance 12,000 reals for the purchase. The advance was taken from the 1.5 million real compensation agreement that Enawenê representatives had just signed, after fraught negotiations, in exchange for the building of eight hydroelectric dams.

At the bridge that carries the region's main road over the River Juruena, the fishermen took delivery of three tons of an artificially cross-bred fish from a refrigerated lorry. Located approximately 100 miles upstream of the Enawenê's single village on the small, winding, Iquê River, this bridge was a significant place on the Enawenê landscape. It was here that they mounted road blocks to make demands of government, and from here that they travelled by road to meetings in the local, regional and national capitals of Juína, Cuiabá and Brasilia. While the bridge was thus routinely a place for the negotiation of resources and recognition, this was the first time it had staged a handover of fish.

In a forest clearing near the bridge the fishermen arranged the fish in flattened baskets made from palm materials and smoked it on wooden racks, just as they would have done if the fish had been caught in their dams' traps. However, given the fishermen's already prolonged absence that year, they were in haste to return to the village. Instead of leaving the fish to smoke and cure gradually over weeks, they roasted it for just 24 hours before loading it into their outboard-powered aluminium boats for the seven hour journey home. By the time the fishermen greeted their wives, the strange-looking 'foreign fish' (*iñoti kohase*) – as women immediately took to calling it – already smelled pungent. Women spat on the floor and exclaimed with disgust that it was rotting. They urgently erected smoking racks and lit fires to prevent the fish from spoiling completely. When they tentatively tasted the foreign fish they commented on its oily texture. There were many complaints of aching stomachs in the following days. I had never received so many meals of fish coupled with manioc bread, since this foreign fish was said to be good for a 'foreign woman' (*iñoti-nero*) to eat. In the days of intense commerce that always followed the fishermen's return from their dams, women kept the slowly smoked fish that had been caught in the dams' traps separate from this oily foreign fish. They chose the former for the payments they busily distributed to their affines, to secure their children's betrothals and fix their patrilineal clan names.

That year I had accompanied a team of twelve fishermen to the most distant of the five dams constructed by the men of *Yankwa*, as the fishermen are known. As they tended empty traps and were denied the fortifying meals that should have followed the hard work of building a dam out of wood and vines in a rushing river, the team had struggled to keep up the light-hearted ribaldry that is supposed to characterise encampment sociality. Before I left them to return to the women in the village – I was dispirited, hungry and eager to escape the tense and frustrated atmosphere at the failing dam – I counted just forty-four flattened baskets of fish in the two watertight smokehouses the men had constructed in preparation for smoking a prodigious haul.

After the same period in 1981 there had been nearly a thousand such baskets at one dam, not including all that the men had unrestrainedly feasted upon. We know this because Vincent Cañas, the Jesuit missionary who lived with the Enawenê for a decade after contact in 1974, kept a careful record of the catch. In 1985 he gave up counting the fish by day ten when 'all along the dam there are shoals of fish who want to descend the river'. A decade later, in 1994, a biologist working with the mission's laicised successor NGO, Operação Amazônia Nativa (OPAN), weighed the returned fishermen's dry catch. He estimated a total production of 18 tons of fresh fish from three dams (Costa Júnior 1995b). This puts the three tons of farmed fish purchased in 2009 into perspective, and demonstrates that 2009 was a new and drastic low in what, by all accounts, had been a gradual reduction in fishing yields.

On a brief visit to the River Arimena's fishing dam in 2008 I had witnessed the riot of fecundity as the fish shoaled into the traps, and the elation and bodily vigour of men and their growing sons. As I took my leave from another dam in 2009 the dam's leader, who had been my host, confided to me his anxiety. He was faced with the prospect of returning to the ritual hosts in the village with a pitiful catch. He worried over the pairs of fish that he would have to hand to each one of the men of three hosting clans on the evening of the return, and then of the same number of the larger, flattened baskets he needed to distribute the following morning. However, the lack of fish was more than a lack of exchange currency. The success of dam fishing is at once a barometer for the quality of relations among the team of fishermen, their ability to realise the will of powerful ancestors, and to forge an alliance with the spirit masters of the fish. The dam's leader asked me a series of rhetorical questions that expressed this frustrated efficacy: had I noticed that all the men had finished weaving a second round of sieves for their wives? But had I heard him calling out for the men to 'fetch firewood!' 'Fetch palm leaves to make the smoking baskets!'? And had I seen him running into the encampment to motivate everyone to get to work gutting and smoking the fish? Crafting tools like manioc sieves and graters, and ornaments like bead-chains for their wives, was supposed to take up men's spare time, in between smoking the catch, but in the absence of fish it had become men's central occupation. The fishermen were in no doubt that the advancing construction of the concrete dams upstream of their wooden ones had disrupted the fish's migrations. Nonetheless the traps' emptiness implied their failure to channel ancestral power as they built the dam; to secure the alliance of the masters of the fish, the *Yakairiti*; and to animate their humanoid traps through mental and bodily discipline.

It was two weeks after I had returned to the village, as I was ensconced with the women of my household in preparations for the feasts that would welcome the returning fishermen, that I heard about the solution for the crisis. A man called Dalyamase, who consistently took up the task of 'solving problems' related to the foreign world on behalf of his community, called the new village payphone to inform the anxious hosts of the fleets' imminent return. The women of my household spoke excitedly about how a 'document had finally emerged' to liberate the compensation. The document had come down from Brasilia and onto the state capital of Cuiabá, before reaching the local office of the national agency for indigenous affairs, or 'FUNAI'. The success of this bureaucratic travail was an assurance of men's mastery of relations with powerful and resource-rich outsiders.

Mobilising such relations to buy farmed fish was an innovation upon an established pattern. The Enawenê had already sought gasoline and nautical oil to power the fleets' departure to the distant dam sites from the same hydroelectricity consortium whose developments threatened their fishing livelihood. Outboard-powered boats had gradually replaced canoe travel over the previous decade and the fleet had now become too large to be fuelled by maternity and pension benefits. In the context of this constant deficit of fuel and with the consortium's interest in securing the Enawenê's agreement to hydroelectricity developments, the enemy also became the readiest source of 'help for the ritual'. With the radical lack of fish in 2009 foreigners had become, for the first time, both the cause of a new insufficiency in the ritual economy and the source of goods with the potential to supplement and even expand it.

Alongside these resource-mediated frontier relations, cultural politics was in full swing. The delivery of farmed fish to the bridge was filmed by a Brazilian NGO called *Video nas Aldeias*, who were working on behalf of the government heritage agency to document the Enawenê's cultural resilience in the face of the damming threat. OPAN had initiated the documentation project hoping that high-level government recognition of the Enawenê's cultural vitality would bolster their resistance to the dams. Together with the London-based organisation Survival International, OPAN had also arranged for a journalist from *The Sunday Times* to visit the Enawenê in 2008 in order to write a feature about their assertive opposition. The Enawenê's spectacular ritual life has also attracted a steady stream of film crews. For example, in 2012 the community allowed the Brazilian media giant Globo to make a documentary about their dam-fishing ritual, Yankwa, for national prime time viewing – again in the hope that this would strengthen their position.

One of the reasons the Enawenê were successful in seeking help for their rituals was that they fitted pervasive ideals of Amerindian identity by virtue of being largely monolingual in their Arawakan dialect, having an active and spectacular ritual life, and taking a warrior stand to protect their territory. In October 2008 they had invaded and burned the construction site of one of the hydroelectric dams, causing significant financial loss to the consortium. The Enawenê's readiness to go to war to protect their own existential prerogatives posed an ongoing investment risk, both to the consortium and the Brazilian National Development Bank, which was financing the dams. The consortium and the government's joint commitment to assisting the Enawenê with the resources they needed for their ritual life was an attempt to mitigate that investment risk. Indirectly, it was also connected to the attention the Enawenê received as 'authentic Indians' from NGOs, government agencies, and the media, which was conditioned upon their seeking gasoline and fish 'for their rituals' – to build monumental wooden dams and feed threatening spirits. Of course as soon as they incorporated these resources, refuelling at the gas station and feasting on farmed fish, they were subject to accusations of culture loss, dependence and avarice – caught in a familiar trap in which the only 'real Indian' is a pure other with whom there is no relationship.

It was from online clips of the Globo Reporter documentary that I first discovered that farmed fish had either supplemented or entirely replaced the dams' catch over the three years subsequent to my leaving the village in July 2009. In 2010 the Enawenê had spent 80,000 reals from their completed 1.5 million compensation payout on fish; in 2011 fish was purchased with new funds provided by the hydroelectricity company; and in 2012 the government heritage agency provided funds for seven tons of fish in order to fulfil its responsibility to safeguard the Enawenê's ritual life after their dam-fishing ritual, Yankwa, had been inscribed as 'intangible cultural heritage in need of urgent safe-guarding' both by the Brazilian heritage agency and by UNESCO.[1] The government was offering cultural recognition of the Enawenê's ritual life and compensating their lost fishing livelihood while denying them meaningful participation in riverine resource developments.

This ethnography of the major ritual in the Enawenê's annual cycle of festivities, Yankwa, is situated in this fraught context. Nonetheless, its descriptive and analytical scope is not circumscribed by these global phenomena of resource-capture, environmental despoliation, and the transformation of life into heritage. These conditions frame the book just as they conditioned what I could learn about the Enawenê and their ritual life, but they do not define its contents, just as they do not define the totality of Enawenê life.

The construction of wooden dams and the fishermen's subsequent return to the village, disguised as dangerous spirits and laden with fish and gifts of basketry and beadwork, is the climactic moment of Yankwa's calendrical ritual process. Throughout the months of Yankwa the Enawenê share their harvests of corn, manioc and fish with one another and with invisible spirit masters, called Yakairiti, in order to assure the continued health and prosperity of their fast-growing population, which was 500 strong in 2009.[2] Abundant gardens are planted and harvested, wooden dams are constructed to entrap migrating fish; and a predictable, daily sequence of dance, flute music and ancestral song fills the village's central arena every day, punctuated by periodic events of clowning, feasting and exchanging. This everyday ritual activity is organised on the basis of patrilineal clanship, with two of the nine clans playing a major hosting role during each biennial.

Fishing expeditions organise the temporality of the ritual process, with music and feasting leading up to, and then on from, them. In order to succeed, the dams' construction must be timed to coincide with the downstream journey of shoal-living fish. The fish go upstream to spawn and feast in the flooded forest when the river level rises during the rains. As the rains slow and the river levels drop, they return to the major rivers. In 2008 and 2009 it was in mid February that the men of seven clans took their leave of the hosts and women in order to journey to five different rivers in the hope of catching and smoking whole shoals of fish. During their absence, the men of the two host clans and all the women of the village are allied in a busy and festive vigil for the fishermen. Men clean the village's sandy central arena, clear a special port of arrival and ceremonial pathway, and make adornments; while women clean gardens, stock up on manioc flour, distil ash salt, and gather firewood for the dramatic feasts and the months of routine ritualism that follow. Through such preparations the villagers orchestrate the peaceful return of both the fishermen and the predatory spirits with whom they are closely allied.

When the fleets finally dock, the incomers' fish is exchanged for hosts' garden foods, drinks and civilised body ornaments over a day and night of spectacular performance. This culminates when the flutes and their animating spirits are restored to their dedicated house at the centre of the village. Over the next two months, the fishermen play the flutes belonging to the two host clans, one after the other, and drink until the harvest from their collective manioc gardens has been exhausted. In order that hosting privileges may circulate among the nine clans, the final phase of the ritual process in June or July involves the preparation of new collective manioc gardens for a new pair of hosts. The harvest from these gardens, which are sited and felled in year one and then further cleared, burned and planted in year two, serve the fishermen and flute players of a subsequent biennial.

Yankwa is not simply the name of a ritual, although it can be used by Enawenê people as such (e.g. 'soon it will be Yankwa and we will leave for the fishing dams'). It is also a collective noun used in a contextual and relational way to designate 'the dancers', 'the men', 'the women', 'those who plant manioc', 'the flute players', or 'the fishermen'. More abstractly 'Yankwa' refers to the unity of the separate clans, whose members always play the flutes that belong to others and never their own. Throughout the book I will use 'Yankwa' in both the reified sense ('the ritual', 'the season') and as a collective noun that can mean the flutes, the men, the dancers or the fishermen depending on the context. Although this may be confusing at points for the reader, I do so in order to maintain something of the complex polysemy of this noun, whose every usage implies a linkage between flute, man and spirit on the one hand and, on the other hand, the interdependence between the single clan and the whole community that works, sings and fishes for it.

The word 'Yankwa' also evokes a whole series of resonances based on contrasts within an annual cycle of rituals. In relation to these other ritual seasons, Yankwa is thus a particular structure of experience and a collective persona. It generally prevails from at least December through to June, although in 2008 it began in October and extended into July of the following year. *Lerohi*, another clan-based flute ceremony, follows Yankwa each year, occupying the driest months of July and August. Yankwa and Lerohi are paired, both occupying the season of agriculture, with Yankwa planting manioc and Lerohi planting corn. As such, both are devoted to the Yakairiti, the dangerous subterranean spirits who are masters of riverine and agricultural resources. Whereas both Yankwa and Lerohi play flutes, oppose clans, and are devoted to agriculture, the other pair of rituals, *Saluma* and *Kateoko*, oppose men and women, and are devoted to a more mobile economy based on poison fishing, the gathering of honey and other forest foods. Men, as the warrior collective 'Saluma', and women, as perfected versions of ancestral womanhood known as 'Kateoko', relate not only to each other but also, via their gendered exchanges, to celestial ancestors called *Enole-nawe*. These are perfect, powerful and mainly – though not unambiguously – benevolent spirits, in sharp contrast to the perverse and predatory Yakairiti.

Each of these seasons and collective personae thus evokes contrasting mythic events and relationships; the sound and melody of a certain kind of vocal or instrumental music; specific economic prerogatives; a particular ceremonial and work routine; certain patterns of dance steps that condition the experience of village space; and a distinctive ceremonial relationship system that determines the circuits through which food and other wealth is distributed. There is also a less tangible mood or ethos that characterises each season. Yankwa is priestly in its gravitas though it has many carnival moments, while during Lerohi, when women dance arm in arm with men to circuit between the village's houses, the atmosphere is less formal and even a little flirtatious. Similarly, the women of Kateoko are always conscientious about their singing and dance steps and they are punctiliously decorated, whereas in the role of Saluma men are extravagantly flirtatious and disorderly. They charge Kateoko, breaking women's solemn dance line in order to cover their skirts with honey. On the other hand, in preparation for potentially dangerous political missions, when they have arrows and war clubs rather than honey in hand, Saluma becomes tensely focused on voicing songs evoking ancestral potency.

Further elaborating upon Yankwa's place in this annual cycle is beyond the scope of this book. Its aim is to seek a holistic understanding of Yankwa as a process that is at once economic, social, cosmological and political: a way of structuring a fisher-agricultural economy, of reconciling antagonistic spirits, of organising social divides of gender and clanship, and seeking recognition from powerful outsiders. This entails moving through activity sequences of monumental dam-building, carefully orchestrated performances, and festive gendered work, and between the different perspectives within Yankwa's relationship system: that Yankwa's fishermen, diplomatic emissaries and flute players; that of women, who provision community feasts and are the audience of men's performances; and that of the humble, servile hosts, who are the ritual's owners. I focus less on the esoteric and musical dimensions of performance (the content and form of chants, flute music, ceremonial dialogues, and poetic incantations) than on the *work* involved in sustaining a life of perpetual ritual. This work is always both mundane and extraordinary, practical and cosmogonic, productive and performative.

In the second half of the book, this processual analysis of Yankwa gives way to a series of ethnographically grounded arguments that develop the understanding of Yankwa as a project of vital diplomacy. By this I mean that Yankwa structures relations between different kinds of others – affines, spirits and foreigners – as the condition for political unity, health and material prosperity. Although the Enawenê's village, manioc gardens, extended family houses and fishing dams are the primary settings for this ethnography, it was in thinking about road blocks mounted at the bridge, and meetings about dam compensation held in urban conference centres, that I began to find a use for this concept of diplomacy. In these contexts Enawenê men encountered people whose interests were fundamentally opposed to their own, with whom they had to engage through the medium of unfamiliar bureaucratic structures, like meetings and document exchange, and with whom they had to communicate in a national language in which no Enawenê person had yet gained fluency in 2009. In other words, like many people living at resource frontiers or 'zones of friction' in Tsing's terms (2005), the Enawenê rapidly had to become sophisticated boundary-crossers. It appeared to me that this was a challenge for which their ritualised social relations and cosmological entanglements prepared them peculiarly well.

The rest of this Introduction is divided into four parts. I begin by making the connection between this book's two key concepts, ritual and diplomacy, in order to detail how the Enawenê's intensely ritualised life implies a diplomatic orientation in the cosmos, in social interaction and in political agency. Secondly, I situate the diplomatic orientation of the Enawenê within an Amazonian comparative horizon, presaging some of the lines of contrast among Amazonian peoples that I will return to throughout the book. I then present an account of Yankwa's endurance and transformation through a violent colonial history in order to demonstrate Yankwa's capacity to reconstitute prosperity, health and peace through the vicissitudes of history. Finally I reflect on the fieldwork on which this book is based. It was undertaken at a historical juncture when the Enawenê were beginning to think of anthropological research as necessarily exploitative and disempowering – very much like research conducted for hydropower viability studies. This gave my ethnographic research a politicised and highly gendered character in ways that condition the kind of ethnography I have written.

Ritual and Diplomacy

It may be jarring to hear the concept of diplomacy applied to an Amerindian population of just a few hundred, not least because in dominant popular and anthropological constructions of Amazonian societies they are represented as non-centralised or anti-state, hostile to the cementation of sovereignty, dominated by a factional politics, and cosmologically oriented to warfare and the capture of alterity.[3] But it was an essay by Claude Lévi-Strauss (1949), based on his fieldwork with the Enawenê's neighbours, the Nambikwara, during the Second World War, that prompted me to consider the Enawenê's practical diplomatic skills, honed through ritual practice, together with their interactions with those they call *iñoti* – a term I translate as 'foreigners' after Lévi-Strauss.[4] The Nambikwara reserved aggression of an artful and highly controlled kind for people with whom they sought alliance, whereas they avoided and fled from those considered beyond the ken of common humanity. There was a useful tension between aggression and cooperation in Nambikwara political life, which exercised and dissolved antagonisms. Lévi-Strauss contrasted this to the European morality in which there was a stark disjuncture between an impossible ideal of total peace, and a peril of total war (ibid.: 152).

In particular he was thinking of the marked, organised and stylised expression of aggression in gift exchange, marriage alliance, ceremonial dialogue and chiefly oratory, all of which were in evidence when Nambikwara bands met in the savannah (Lévi-Strauss 1949: 150). He argued that these ritual forms should be understood as the equivalents of European foreign affairs, because they were elaborate technologies for negotiating relative status and brokering peace. This points to collective, institutionalised and conventional ways for dealing with shifting and contested boundaries between a society and its outside, in a space that falls between common citizenship and total enmity.[5]

I suggest that anthropological theorisations of ritual may help us to approach diplomacy more rigorously as a dialogic, and more often collective, enterprise that occurs within a frame that is co-constructed by its participants. This allows us to get beyond the polarised definition of diplomacy as either an individualised social skill akin to tact or discretion; or a set of practices, laws and customs located in privileged institutions – archetypically in the embassies of sovereign nation states. It allows us to see diplomatic encounters as moments of incorporation, in which boundaries are crossed and affirmed at the same time, rather than as encounters that mediate a pre-existing condition of otherness. What most interests me here is that reading diplomacy into ritual allows me to highlight the commonalities and interpenetration between cosmological, social and foreign relations in Enawenê life.

I begin with the proposition that ritual and diplomacy are kindred orientations in the world. In both, action becomes artful and reflexive, is oriented to wider goals beyond the immediate interactive context, and is accommodating of psychological and social ambiguity. Unresolvable questions such as: what is our relationship? Is this aggression real or performed? Will my actions be effective? are posed through boundary-testing interactions. In making this argument I depend on Seligman et al.'s (2008) theorisation of ritual as a way of negotiating existence in a world whose order is never transparently accessible. A ritual orientation is based on the acceptance that living with social and cosmological others is an inherently uncertain and ambiguous enterprise, one not conducive to transparent knowledge, but which calls for the kinds of rhythmic, conventional, reiterative actions of ritual that allow life to be lived on the basis of the creation of temporary order (ibid.: 12).[6]

This view of ritual appeals to me because within it Yankwa's capacity to accommodate mercurial, unknowable spirits, as well as new forms of life-death ambiguity, appears not as something exceptional and separate – a world-ending crisis – but as ritual's business as usual. Whether or not farmed fish would prove to be an acceptable substitute for dam-caught fish was still unresolved when I last visited Halataikwa in 2013. The Yakairiti's dissatisfaction with the foreign fish had been blamed for several untimely deaths in the preceding years. Nonetheless farmed fish continued to be purchased for Yankwa's feasts and some men had even dug ponds and become fish farmers themselves. Yankwa accommodated such ambiguities without resolving them. In fact, as a sequence of activities devoted to regenerating the conditions for human life by coordinating several kinds of difficult relationships at once: between the living and their ancestors, between opposed individuals and clans, between humans and the species on which they depend for their livelihood, and between living people and more distant others – spirit masters and foreigners – Yankwa's vitalising project was always inevitably imperfect and unfinished. This was implied by the very fact that community members continued to be struck down by the Yakairiti and to sicken and die.

If the world were predictable, its order given, then it would not be necessary to assert and test it annually by such acts as the burning of the old flute house and the building of a new one, or by watching flowering grasses grow in order to follow the progress of the hydrological cycle and decide when best to depart for fishing dams. Every act in Yankwa's course tests the status of the human community, and of individuals within it, vis-à-vis others who escape transparent knowledge. It does this based on an 'as if' order (Seligman et al. (2008: 8), an understanding of how the world came to be that serves as the basis upon which to recreate it through cosmogonic chanting, sequences of work days that reproduce archetypal order, and the annual performance of originary acts such as the 'burial' of a mother of manioc, who will fecundate the rest of the garden. In Enawenê conceptions the knowledge that directs all of these activities is fragmented, hard to access, to hold onto, and to perform effectively. The relentless regularity of ritual is perhaps a means to mitigate this basic condition of deficit through restless rehearsal, reiteration and repetition.

The most obvious goal of Yankwa is to generate continuity between the past and future. Led by elders who master ancestral knowledge, men sing about the origin of the universe – the alternation between day and night, the origin of the sun and celestial bodies, the river system, the peopling of the earth, the reason for the fish's migrations, or for the clonal propagation of manioc. As they do so they regenerate a connection between past and future. Song masters who use their serialised knowledge to lead ceremonial life, and incantation specialists whose poetry is protective and propitiatory, are those who most fully incarnate this ancestral power-knowledge. They are the most highly valued members of Enawenê society because they alone can assure the connection between past and future. Their access to the past is a matter of lineage – of ancestral connection. They submitted themselves to the teaching of song masters who are now dead and who were trained, in turn, by an ascending line of predeceased song masters, each with specific competencies in a genre of chants. Lineal continuity is also reproduced in the performance of these chants by men who perform in birth order lines, echoing the elder song master, who walks at their head.

If Yankwa is a project of collecting and concentrating human vitality in order to stabilise an ancestrally grounded Enawenê identity, this is nonetheless a process that requires interpenetration between the living, as the Enawenê define themselves, and the Yakairiti, who are their Janus face. Through every phase of Yankwa these chants and the ordered musical ceremonial routines of rhythmic dance, gestural conventions and melodic flute-play accompany economic activities that take people out of the centre of their village and into a world that is owned by invisible others. Economic matters of transforming the landscape through the work of building villages, clearing gardens and constructing fishing dams thus not only realise ancestral knowledge and archetypal order, but entail cooperation and negotiation with predatory spirit owners of resources. As in other animist systems of thought, the idea that reflexive consciousness is a facet shared by humans and other beings in the cosmos implies that the taking of other lives always risks their vengeance. Thus life is a positional quality and a sliding scale, perennially threatened by predatory agencies who would appropriate human vitality and thus cause sickness and death.

The constraint that vitality or life force is shared with other beings and must be appropriated from them implies that economic activities entail care, negotiation and reciprocity. Ideally, they must promote the regeneration of not only Enawenê people but also the species from which they draw their energising substance – principally manioc and fish. During Yankwa the Enawenê domesticate their landscape to promote the growth and flourishing of their staple crop, manioc, and build fishing dams to harvest great quantities of fish at the time of their peak fertility just after spawning. The temporality of manioc, fish and human cycles of growth and regeneration are coordinated. This agricultural emphasis on regenerative cycles, through which vitality is accrued and channelled on the basis of care and control, contrasts with the predatory emphasis in many Amazonian 'symbolic economies of alterity' (Viveiros de Castro 1996).

Santos-Granero's argument in *Vital Enemies* (2009) allows me to draw this contrast most clearly. He argues that where vitality is conceived as a finite currency in the 'political economy of life' it must be accrued by means of capture. The taking of slaves by historical Arawakan populations was a means, he suggests, to augment a stock of finite vital resources. Of course, there is no reason why regenerative and predatory accrual of vitality could not coexist, but the concept of vital diplomacy allows me to highlight the specificity of the Enawenê's animist cosmology, which is a consensual, collaborative political economy of life; one based on the organisation of work to promote the fertility of humans together with the species on which they rely. These are the species endowed with blood and therefore life force, but only those the Enawenê have the knowledge and capacity to control. Their economy of life thus excludes the bloody meat of terrestrial game mammals, whose consumption is associated with loss of control and the dissolution of human identity.

For the Enawenê then, vitality is accrued through production, growth and regeneration as part of an effort to turn a potentially agonistic relationship with spirit masters (whose relationship with Enawenê people is always potentially one of vengeance) into a synergetic one. Thus Yakairiti are entreated to direct their shoals of fish into the dams' traps so that they may later share in the resultant smoked catch during village feasts. Manioc is fed with the dams' smoked catch, and the plant is nurtured and secluded in order to promote her robust good health. The success of the cultivators' nurture is later evidenced in the growth of large, fleshy tubers. In turn, expansive clean gardens and the harvest of manioc's milky tubers are the assurance of the community's health and prosperity.

Material plenty, which is brought in from fishing dams and gardens to be displayed in the open arena of the Enawenê's village, provides tangible evidence of the accrual of vitality. So too does the gathering of people in musical performance. In both cases, work itself – be it dancing or digging – creates strong, corpulent bodies and an energetic, wakeful village that hums with purposeful sounds and movements at predictable times of the day and night. In fact, Enawenê people often speak of activity and wakefulness as the first assurance of the interconnected values of productivity, health and plenty. Laziness is a backsliding into illness, listlessness and frailty. Additionally, in their most energised work, people consider themselves to be imbued with the spirit of Yakairiti. This implies that their actions both affirm a civilized identity and a position of mastery in the universe insofar as they are based on the performance of ancestral knowledge, the affirmation of a correct, invariant sequencing of time, and the regulation of human relationships with threatening enemies, and, at the same time, transcend stability and control to embrace disorderly, unpredictable forces.

The oscillation, in both economic work and musical performance, between action based on stability and control and that based on boundary-transcendence, is explored throughout the book. Men and women alternate between behavioural modes in which they imitate ambivalently super- and anti-human Yakairiti, and modes in which they serve these others as denizens of a separate underground dominion. There are men richly adorned and donning sun-diadem feather headdresses, playing harmonious flute music, dancing in birth order lines, and chanting correct sequences of verse; and there are men tooting and screeching on trumpets and whistles, running chaotically, ululating excitedly. In the latter guise they threaten to cross out of the frame of performance and sow disorder and violence. When the fishermen return to the village disguised as wild, voracious spirits one can never be certain to what degree man and mask are one – how dangerous these kinsmen may have become in their transformed state. The hosts ply them with heavy, warm drinks to mollify, satiate and calm them, and both hosts and incomers collaborate to unravel their wild disguise and to reveal the men beneath. When roles are based precisely on the partial relinquishing of self-control, what is reflexively performed is the boundary between role and self, 'the players may let the role run away with them' as Seligman et al. (2008: 83) put it. Unruly clowning may be a mask for ecstatic possession and this is a blurring of which captivated but circumspect spectators are mindful. It is also what makes performances memorable, exciting and enlivening. This ambiguity between role and self, present in all the performances in the central arena, is a crucial technology of ritual action in general, because through it people seek to control forces that they recognise to be partially intransigent and unknowable.

Such a play with boundaries, a dance with ambiguity, is an ineluctable part not only of dealing with ancestors, other species and spirits, but also of social relations. During Yankwa the dominant role oppositions, between hosts and Yankwa, women and men, are continually crossed, and then reaffirmed, and then reversed again in a reflexive play on positional identity. Because Yankwa takes place in a single village that is densely interconnected by ties of intermarriage, it is not a conventional 'ritual of diplomacy' in the manner of more common Amazonian visiting rites, in which ritualised acts help to accommodate the strangeness of parties who come together for the event. However, Enawenê people do relate to one another for much of the time as if they were others.

They routinely step out of their ego-centred kinship relations to engage in stylised and formulaic relations defined by conventionalised role oppositions. These oppositions stand for archetypal self-other relations. For example, when hosts face the returning fishermen they do so as representatives of the society of living; they have fashioned themselves with ornaments, body paint, accessories, offerings and postures so that they become emblems of civilized humanity, and they face not brothers-in-law but men disguised as Yakairiti.

Webb Keane (1995: 107) has eloquently described the ways that the aesthetic power and ancestral quality of performance rests on formality and abstraction, such that ritualised speech and behaviours help to create the social divides they project. Thus, even among co-residents, who have lived their whole lives together, opaque, esoteric forms of dialogue open up a space within face-to-face interactions, effecting temporary estrangement. This is the case every day when hosts distribute drinks to the decorated flute players, who personify 'Yankwa' – the merging of hosts' clan identity, spirits and flutes. Their transactions are marked by predictable gestures, distanced body language and formal dialogues, which suggest that the primary agents of the act of giving and receiving stand somewhere beyond, or between, the co-present men. What I am pointing to is the extent to which, in both mundane and climactic performances, Enawenê people are other to one another and to themselves. As such they are diplomats: representatives of abstract wider communities and lofty goals, consciously negotiating encompassing forces via their dyadic relationships, and aware of the world-making stakes of their gestures and words. In their double estrangement – from their interlocutors and from themselves – they are akin to the ideal-typical figure of the diplomat who is a pure representative, and for whom social distance is the positive foundation for dialogue.[7]

Stasch's (2011: 160) definition of ritual as action that brings wider world-making into an 'interactional here-now' to generate efficacious connection between microcosm and macrocosm crystallises the analogy I am drawing between ritual and diplomacy, both as forms of action that negotiate encompassing forces. I now want to suggest that the space in which the Enawenê live, which is precisely designed to connect micro- and macrocosm, village and universe, gives action a particularly powerful diplomatic quality in this sense.

Their circular village is both a model of the universe and of people's place within it, and a panoptic space for public sociality. Looking out from the cleared hilltop village surrounded by low-lying manioc gardens you can see far into the distance on all sides and have the impression of dominating the landscape. The roofs of the dwelling circle enclose the open sandy arena, which also seems to contain the sky, positioning those who live in the circle of dwellings as the guardians of the cosmos. As the sun arcs its way overhead it follows the cardinal architecture of the village, connecting the flute house at the western edge of the arena to the ceremonial pathway at its eastern edge. In this cosmically aligned space people's movements are coerced into participating in wider cosmic patterns. This is a potential that is mobilised at every phase during Yankwa when cardinal orientation is used to indicate progress through the world-making sequence. Thus when men leave to go dam fishing, their flutes and spirits move outwards from their central temple in an easterly direction to the waterways, and when they return they do so in a westerly movement back to the centre of the village.

Social experience in this space is defined by its panoptic quality. The arena draws the attention of every member of the community inwards, and every house's front door provides a clear view of the unfolding spectacles. No one can be unaware of their audience when they occupy this space. As other anthropologists who have worked in the circular villages of Central Brazil have noted, action in such a space has a thoroughly reflexive quality; speech and movement are aestheticized. The arena is designed to host respectful conduct, controlled sporting contests and the performance of generosity through public exchanges. In it, demonstrations of aggression or hostility should be suppressed.[8]

While sociality in a plaza village has a diplomatic quality particular to it, the ritualisation of social interaction is a theme that transcends these specificities. For sociologist Erving Goffman, in even the most apparently informal social encounters every move a person made was ritualised. He saw the subtle workings of discretion, deception and circumlocution that go into sustaining the position and identity of the self in relation to others as matters of diplomacy and social skill. Drawing on Goffman's *Interaction Ritual* (1967), Enfield (2009: 77) summarises what is at stake when he says that ritual may be 'both weapon and shield for handling the political and moral delicacy of social co-presence'. However, the effect of Goffman's microanalysis was to fuse everyday life and ritual and to render all interaction disconcertingly hyper-analytical. The Africanist Max Gluckman (1962), by contrast, saw ritual as a relational technology whose value lay in cutting through this Goffmanesque nightmare of social co-presence. Gluckman's analysis is pertinent, because it demonstrates ritual's capacity to effect a virtuous simplification in potentially complicated and fraught social relations.

Gluckman had in mind so-called 'segmentary' African societies in which two individuals always had various overlapping relationships that implied contradictory obligations and behaviours. In such settings rituals were a necessity. Within a ritual's frame these contradictory relationships were substituted by a single, well-defined dialogic one. This is what occurs at Yankwa when the whole male population is divided into two unequal halves – the single host clan and all the rest, who oppose them as Yankwa – and they interact on the basis of predictable exchanges of goods and services and archetypal behavioural codes. The multitude (up to 80 men) who share the identity of Yankwa are inevitably romantic adversaries, respected in-laws and awkward new allies. The structured nature of their collective activity and its orientation to hyperbolic affines (the hosts) allows them nonetheless to coexist in public space. Indeed, Enawenê men say that Yankwa is pleasurable because it motivates them to leave the enclosure of their separate houses to drink, laugh and talk together. So while the panoptic plaza gives a potentially painfully reflexive quality to action (and this is why men stride purposefully through it and into their front doors when they return from fishing expeditions with their catch, and why women use perimeter paths to bathe, access gardens, and visit kin) it also provides the setting and structure for successful diplomacy based on unconstrained co presence, mixing and circulation. Rituals create social situations in which diplomacy becomes possible.

This at once social and cosmological opposition between Yankwa and host is totalising at any one point in time, but the oppositions are reversed when hosts who formerly served drinks and lit fires become the dancers, flutes players, drinkers, and fishermen of 'Yankwa'. There is thus a constitutive tension between the contingency and solidity of the current order, whose basic forms – the relationship between fish and manioc, men and women, Yankwa and hosts, human and Yakairiti – are eternal, and whose configuration is ever-changing. That this overriding social boundary is made in order to be 'crossed, violated, blurred, and then, in an oscillating way, reaffirmed, re-established, and strengthened' returns us to Seligman et al.'s characterisation of ritual as a subjunctive universe that allows us to live by creating temporary order (2008: 12). Each year the Yakairiti are fed and satisfied, the flutes are put to rest, and then new gardens are planted so that the whole process may begin again about five months later. The ritual's repetition and its restless intensity implicitly show that the world-making task is ever incomplete.

This opening reflection on the interpenetrating temporal, cosmological and social dimensions of Yankwa's ritualised diplomacy will be fleshed out ethnographically in the chapters of this book. In the final chapter I consider how these ritual dynamics played into the Enawenê negotiations with the hydroelectricity consortium and the government in 2008–2009, at a time when Yankwa's values of growth, plenty and productivity implied the accelerating incorporation of foreign resources. These resources were consistently sought to enable and expand Yankwa's economic work and, in line with this goal, their distribution was egalitarian and collectivist. Demands made of the government and consortium were therefore persistently made in the name of the Enawenê people as a whole, and they were justified by ritual prerogatives – in particular the need to fish and feast for the Yakairiti. Satisfying the Yakairiti now implies an ambivalently antagonistic and cooperative relationship with those who exploit the Yakairiti's riverine dominion without care or reciprocity. In turn, this incorporation of resources, which has become necessary for Yankwa's successful orchestration every year, depends on an equal and opposite move: defiant opposition and political warfare. The Enawenê have to force their opponents to treat them as significant, powerful and necessary interlocutors, because the latter assume that they are powerless subjects. It is this alternating dynamic and the tension it generates between aggression and cooperation – a tension whose diplomatic efficacy Lévi-Strauss also noticed – that is the focus of my analysis in the final chapter of this book.

Amazonian Comparative Horizons

Meditations on otherness have been a central focus of Amazonian anthropology. In this section I want to clarify how ritualised ways of generating and reconciling difference fit within the theoretical landscape of Amazonian anthropology. The most influential anthropologists of the region, Philippe Descola and Eduardo Viveiros de Castro, have both argued that Amerindian social philosophies are 'cannibalistic' (Descola 1992; Viveiros de Castro 2014). They mean that Amazonians are oriented to the capture and incorporation of alterity, both literally by means of hunting and warfare, and symbolically through shamanic and other ritual modes of drawing in foreign potencies, such as names, songs and capacities, for the purposes of social reproduction and regeneration. The argument has even gone so far as stating that, since human identity is intrinsically positional or perspectival, predatory agency defines the human subject position (Viveiros de Castro 1998a; 2010: 47). Over the last decade debate in Amazonian anthropology has been organised around the expansion and contestation of this model of Amazonian personhood and cosmology, on ethnographic, theoretical and political grounds.[9] This effort to arrive at an understanding of what distinguishes the ontologies of the indigenous people of Amazonia has gone hand in hand with a countervailing tendency to extend theorisations derived from Amazonian ethnographic cases to other parts of the world as part of a renewed interest in animism. This latter move has demonstrated that themes of predation, vengeance and the reversibility of the opposition between the living and the dead are prominent in many animist contexts worldwide, just as they are in Enawenê cosmology and mythology.[10] However, as I have already argued by drawing a distinction between the Enawenê's consensual and regenerative political economy of life, and the regime of capture explored by Santos-Granero, there is room to explore and expand upon alternatives to the predatory model of Amazonian ontology.

In this book I draw attention to productive contrasts among Amazonian societies. Some of the intersecting contrasts I consider are between people who hunt and eat terrestrial game, and others who base their livelihoods on fishing and agricultural production; people who drink fermented beer, and those who reject it; people who actively wage war, and those who stage rituals; people who live in small, undifferentiated settlements, and those who live in large, heterogeneous villages. These contrasts do not map onto one another or correspond in a stable way to societies on the ground, and they can even coexist within single societies during different seasons of the year, or historical epochs. We do not need, therefore, to espouse a view of peoples as bounded populations with a common culture in order to observe patterns that are the outcome of histories of interaction, hybridity and oppositional identity formation.[11] Thus the Arawak-speaking Enawenê no doubt forged their pescatarian, teetotal identity in opposition to the cannibal, bacchanalian habits of their most deadly recent enemies, the Tupi-mondé-speaking Cinta-Larga. Although the Enawenê are today reduced to a single village polity, their ancestors would have been part of far-reaching exchange networks that connected them to other hierarchical, settled, riverine agricultural polities across the Southern Amazon fringe (Heckenberger 2005). This history of connection is suggested by the many commonalities that endure between the Enawenê and the Arawak-speaking or Arawak-influenced peoples of the upper Xingu River. These commonalities include a manioc and fish oriented economy, an ambivalence towards terrestrial predation, gift-like exchange systems, ideologies of descent, primogeniture and hierarchy; and ritual systems based on unequally distributed esoteric knowledge, conventional codes of speech and the structured use of space (Andrello, Guerreiro and Hugh-Jones 2015). These values and institutions still underpin open-ended social systems, both in the Xingu and in Northwest Amazonia, and they are also the basis on which people within those systems contrast themselves to predatory others who live at their periphery.

I am by no means the first to draw attention to divergences in orientation between Amazonian peoples; there has been a long tradition of exploiting salient lines of contrast for the purposes of theorisation.[12] Particularly useful, I find, is Stephen Hugh-Jones' (1996: 15) adoption of Mary Helms' contrast between 'superordinate societies', who seek to expand outwards from an ordered centre by defensively controlling external powers that threaten their integrity, and 'acquisitional polities', which seek to dominate the outside in order to strengthen their political centre. Together with the better-studied peoples of the Xingu and Northwest Amazonia, the Enawenê are an example of the first. For them, manifestations of ancestral power like ornaments, songs, dances and ritual are located within the politico-ideological centre, rather than imported from outside the social realm. In turn, relations within the community are characterised by the positive valuation of affinal sociality. Archetypal social relations are those civil and civic-minded ones between affines; relationships conducted across lines of difference that people strive to maintain through the exchange of careful speech, reciprocal services and vital wealth – precisely the kind of social relations that I characterise as diplomatic. This contrasts with the model of 'typical Amazonian social organisation in which, internal differences are effaced by an overriding opposition between inside and outside such that affinity is suppressed within the local group'.[13]

Without reducing Amazonian societies to a play of simplistic counterpositions between warlike and peaceful, hunting and fishing, small and complex, hierarchical and egalitarian, settled and mobile, it therefore seems timely to develop alternative coherences in the ethnographic record. My theoretical focus on ritualisation and diplomacy, and my effort to reflect more widely on what this ethnography may reveal about other fisher-agricultural societies of Amazonia, are an attempt to do this. Successive theorisations in this book around themes such as the symbolic and practical linkage between fishing and agricultural harvests; the structuring of space and sound in ritual performance; the celebration of productivity and abundance; the civilising and curative potentials of cuisine and teetotalism; and indigenous responses to hydropower developments, each seek to combine insights on the basis of both coherences and contrasts across Amazonia.

In addition to taking inspiration from regional debates, this book also draws upon previous research with the Enawenê. This research has generally been undertaken by Brazilian scholars associated with the NGO

OPAN, which prided itself on providing anthropologically informed and culturally sensitive assistance. For example, researchers associated with OPAN produced the only existing descriptions of the Enawenê language (Rezende 2003); studied the process of introducing writing as a new technology for expression in the indigenous language in the 1990s (Zorthêa 2006); profiled the population's health status (Vieira Weiss 1998); and outlined the basics of Enawenê social organisation, cosmology and subsistence strategies (Busatto et al. 1995).

The research that has been most useful to me was conducted by anthropologists Marcio Silva and Gilton Mendes dos Santos, and was mainly undertaken in the 1990s. Silva (1995) provided an initial sketch of the Enawenê's patrilineal clan system, their Iroquois kinship terminology, uxorilocal residence norm and clan exogamous marriage patterns. He subsequently undertook a rigorous analysis of genealogical and demographic data, focusing on processes of marriage alliance (Silva 2012). In terms of my focus in this book on the social and cosmological organisation of Yankwa, the most relevant works are those by Silva on Enawenê ceremonial organisation and gender dynamics (Silva 1998, 2001). Silva's work is concerned with characterising the structure of the Enawenê cosmos, and the structural contrasts between rituals in the annual cycle. As such it is abstracted from everyday material and relational processes, which are my focus. Silva's former student Gilton Mendes dos Santos (2001, 2006; Mendes dos Santos and Mendes dos Santos 2008) expanded upon Silva's descriptions of the annual calendar of agricultural and fishing activities, concentrating on the intersection between Enawenê ecological knowledge and animist cosmology. His work on the mythic and cosmological dimensions of economic life covers some of the same ground as this book. Again, my account differs from his by following Yankwa's unfolding at the micro level of day-to-day activity, and insofar as I connect material and relational work to wider symbolic processes. For example Santos and Santos (2008) showed that building fishing dams was not only a means to capture a huge amount of protein food but also a crucial technology for mediating the Enawenê's relationship with the spirit masters of the fish. Mendes dos Santos (2001) also saw commonalities between dam fishing and agriculture at the level of myth (2001). However he did not bring together the mythic, technical social and cosmological levels of analysis in the way that I have sought to do.

Other OPAN-affiliated scholars, Jakubaszko (2003) and Almeida (2011), have focused on contact and inter-ethnic relations. In Chapter 6 I draw on Almeida's perceptive and detailed account of Enawenê negotiations with the hydroelectric dam consortium, as well as making use of a fine sociological investigation of the corporate and government structures behind the Juruena Complex (Galvão 2016). However, in line with the Brazilian division between 'indigenism' and 'ethnology' (Viveiros de Castro 1999); ritual and cosmology on the one hand, and on the other hand, interethic relations and contact, have tended to be treated separately by researchers among the Enawenê. It became obvious to me during my first stay with the Enawenê in 2006 that my research would have to connect them and, furthermore, that what I would be able to learn about ritual would be conditioned by political tensions surrounding hydroelectricity developments. Before I characterise how my research was shaped by the broader political context in which it took place, I want to look back in time to the Enawenê's mixed ancestry and to the transformations of Yankwa over the course of a turbulent history. I want to suggest that this is a history of efforts to reconstitute a prosperous, healthy and peaceful polity in response to colonial violence. As such, the challenge of responding to the vicissitudes of history probably characterised Yankwa well before the era of hydroelectricity.

Yankwa and the Tumults of Enawenê History

In 1973 a pilot flying from Mato Grosso's capital Cuiabá to the new frontier town of Juína reported sighting a large indigenous village to Jesuit missionaries, whose priority it was to establish peaceful contact with indigenous groups before conflicts erupted with rubber gatherers, gold miners and land picketers. Because of the village's proximity to areas inhabited by the Nambikwara, the Jesuit-led contact party thought it likely that the Indians would be speakers of a Nambikwara dialect. As soon as they entered the village in June 1974 the presence of hammocks told them that this was not the case (the Nambikwara sleep on the ground). The large and elongated houses, the quantity of clay pots, the flute house and then the accent of the men who came out to greet them, all suggested that these people were instead related to the Paresi, speakers of an Arawak dialect.[14] The missionaries thus returned with a Paresi family on their second visit. As they had hoped, their dialect was roughly comprehensible to the Enawenê. The Paresi even identified the isolated group as the Salumã, a lost subgroup of their own people (Lisbôa 2010: 24).[15]

The presence of two Paresi groups on the left margin of the River Juruena had been noted before, in 1909, by General Rondon. He had emancipated the Paresi from rubber gathering and enlisted their labour in the glorious national project of building a long-distance telegraph line. The two groups were described as having contrasting habits; the Salomá were said to hunt and eat game like other Paresi, while the Oazané restricted their diet to fish and a few species of fowl and were also marked out by their Jatobá bark canoes. Both of these latter distinctions matched the newly contacted group. Nonetheless, it is likely that the Enawenê's ancestry is more complex and mixed than their identification with one pescatarian, canoe-building Paresi subgroup suggests. This complexity is indicated by the Paresi's error when they named the Enawenê, 'Salumã'. As we know, Saluma is the name of a ritual season and the warrior persona of the men who perform in it. It is also the name of the ancestors of one of the nine Enawenê clans, Kaholase, who are said to have been eaters of terrestrial game. This ancestral people only adopted the pescatarian eating habits of the dominant clans when they joined a mixed village. It is likely that the ancestors of today's Enawenê include both the lost Salomá and Oazané, as well as other groups with their own dietary, territorial and linguistic distinctions, but it is also likely that all were once enmeshed in a more complex regional polity in the past.

The descriptions of the German explorer and ethnographer Max Schmidt, from his time among two Paresi subgroups in 1910, reveal the degree of shared culture between the Enawenê and Paresi. There are many commonalities in settlement choice, architecture, body ornamentation, religion and material culture. Just like the Enawenê's current village of Halataikwa, Paresi villages were 'without exception, immediately adjacent to a stream, never in the shadow of a hill but always in an open area with clear views all around' (Schmidt 1943: 15) and they contained a conical flute house in addition to the long, narrow dwelling houses that encircled an open arena. Enawenê and Paresi men used woven cotton garters at their ankles and below the knees, and tied their foreskins with buruti palm fibre (ibid.: 23); women used the same tight cotton miniskirts, dyed red with annatto, and wore moulded and dyed bands of rubber wedged between their calf muscles and knees (Schmidt 1943: 24). The Paresi also invoked celestial deities called *enole* to cure illness (ibid.: 28), and had an ensemble of bamboo flutes and gourd trumpets that matched those of the Enawenê. In both cases the most ubiquitous of these was a bamboo recorder with four stops. This is the instrument that produces Yankwa's melodic baseline. In contrast to the instruments of Yankwa, which were kept in the central flute house, the panpipes (called Lerohi by the Enawenê) were kept in dwellings (Schmidt 1943: 41–42).

In addition to this inventory of material culture, Schmidt made some telling observations about aspects of what we might call habitus and ethos that struck him as significant. He noticed that the Paresi never sat directly on the ground but always on stools; he was also impressed that 'there was never a lack of big square structures on which to bake in Paresi houses' (ibid.: 17), and that provisions of meat and discs of compacted manioc flour were dried for preservation (Schmidt 1943: 40). Indeed, large, thriving manioc gardens are the prime focus of collective and individual pride for both peoples (Mendes dos Santos 1994: 74; 2006: 188), a preference that is characteristic of Arawakan speakers more generally (Lathrap 1970). These are the same diacritical features to which both Enawenê and Paresi draw attention when they judge their mutual neighbours, the Nambikwara, to be of lowly status, because they lack enthusiasm for agriculture (and surplus production) and sit and sleep on the floor rather than raised up in hammocks.

When Schmidt made these observations in 1910 the Paresi population had declined to just 340 Paresi individuals (Schmidt 1943:13–14). However, from the reports of a Portuguese-Brazilian slaver called Antonio Pires dos Campos, who passed through the Paresi Plateau in 1728, we get some impression of a formerly large scale, regional civilisation – what Campos called the 'Kingdom of the Paresi' or 'Great Paresi Nation' (Pires de Campos 1862). Campos was from São Paolo, one of the many men known as *bandeirantes*, who penetrated unmapped regions of Brazil to enslave native inhabitants, find gold and extend Portuguese influence westwards against the claims of the Spanish. He wrote lyrically of passing ten or twelve large villages in a day's march through the Paresi Plateau,[16] each composed of up to thirty large communal longhouses, and he celebrated the peaceful and industrious nature of their inhabitants.[17] His report matches the emerging archaeological picture of the Amazon's major southern tributaries, which were densely populated by Arawakan-speaking fisher-agriculturalist folk, whose circular plaza communities were interlinked by road systems, organised into regional polities and integrated through public ritual (Heckenberger 2013). Even by the time Campos discovered this complex Paresi polity, its population would have been reduced by disease. And by advertising the Paresi's civility and their settled life, Campos opened the way for slavers to follow a decade later, when a gold rush brought hordes of men up from Mato Grosso state's capital Cuiabá (Price 1983: 131). The massive depopulation that followed was a version of what occurred all over Lowland South America after the New World's colonisation in 1492. One effect of demographic collapse was to reduce ethnically and linguistically complex regional polities to territorially discrete 'tribes' (Ferguson and Whitehead 1992).[18] It seems likely that the divergences between Enawenê and Paresi identity, dialect and ritual life began to be forged in the wake of gold mining, slave raiding, massacres and disease from the eighteenth century onwards.

The Enawenê emphasise the heterogeneity of their ancestry, which they say is composed of peoples with contrasting territorial origins and languages, diets and habits of dress, who came together in response to a violent history to form a common polity by adopting a shared language and culture. In Chapter 4 I connect Enawenê narratives about this unification of heterogeneous peoples with an analysis of Yankwa's ceremonial organisation in which cross-cutting dualisms based on divisions of clanship and gender are mobilised to sustain egalitarian political unity. This dynamic, which conjoins separate people in a compressed, singular polity, contrasts with the visiting festivities of other Amazonians, including the Paresi, in which rituals bring together separate but allied settlements. Visitors with whom relations are initially of exaggerated hostility are invited in, gradually familiarised and temporarily incorporated.[19] Thus, among the Paresi in the 1980s the flutes of Yankwa were played when allied settlements cooperated to make manioc beer and hunt, in order to invite those from more distant settlements. They tamed these incomers with insistent offers of beer. At nightfall the guests played first the aggressive flutes of *Iohoho* (Ioho) then those of *Yamaka* (Yankwa), which women feared, and finally other flutes, which came inside dwelling houses and danced along with women.[20] The strangers departed after two nights, having been familiarised through shared feminine work, and sporting contests in which male guests and villagers were mixed.

Among the Enawenê, it is co-resident affines who are reincorporated after a period of deliberate exile and estrangement. It is kinsmen who receive insistent offerings of drinks from hosts. The members of exogamous clans act as host and guests, servers and drinkers, for one another in turn. We cannot know in what form Yankwa existed in the more populous and interconnected past landscape glimpsed by Campos, but the endurance of Yankwa, Ioho and Lerohi through the turbulent history that separates the Paresi and Enawenê indicates these rituals' capacity to create conditions for peaceful alliance, in forms transfigured to fit the circumstances.

We know that Enawenê ritual life has been fairly stable at least since the Jesuit contact mission arrived in their village in 1974, because Vincent Cañas carefully diarised the ceremonial rhythms of the village's arena during the decade in which he lived among the Enawenê (1977–1987). He noted the time each night when the ritual commenced; the number of fires lit by hosts; the names of the hosts and of the dancers; dance formations; the quantity and types of foods and drinks distributed; and the subsistence activities and movements through territory that intercalated with the life of the arena (Cañas 1977–1987).[21] Another Jesuit priest, with some training in anthropology and linguistics, was so struck by the constancy of their ritual life when he visited that he dubbed the Enawenê the 'Benedictine order of the forest' (Lisbôa 2010: 50).

However, we also know that the orderly sequence of reciprocal hosting obligations that Cañas diarised, and the demographic recovery he helped to ensure after 1974, had been recently restored after a period of repeated ruptures. When elder community members talked about the time immediately preceding Cañas and Lisbôa's arrival, they narrated an effort to sustain Yankwa that was persistently thwarted by deadly village ambushes by the Cinta-Larga. These enemy attacks claimed eighteen lives between about 1940 and 1960, out of a population that was certainly less than 100 strong. These attacks occurred in the region Iquê and Joaquim Rios rivers to where the Enawenê were able to return in the 1980s once they could be convinced by the mission of their former enemies' pacification.[22]

The penultimate Cinta-Larga attack is said to have occurred during Lerohi, after the return of dam-fishing expeditions for Aweresese and Kairoli clans. In its wake, the population had fled, but because Kairoli clansmen were loath to leave behind their manioc garden (whose harvest was destined to provision Yankwa and Lerohi in the second year of their biennial as hosts) they had not fled very far. From this new but nearby village the fishermen again departed to build fishing dams the following year, and upon return they played the flutes of Yankwa and drank the second year's harvest from Kairoli clan's manioc garden. But when the dry season returned and as the village danced Lerohi, the Cinta-Larga attacked again, killing seven people. Elder men who narrated these events timed them according to Yankwa's calendar in this way, recognising that it was their attachment to Yankwa – to their fishing dams, manioc gardens and centralised village life – that had rendered them easy prey.

After this devastating last attack the remainder of the community abandoned these ties, leaving behind village life, agriculture and even navigation in a desperate flight for safety. They migrated southwards on foot, constructing bridges to cross the rivers Doze de Outubro and Mutum and then destroying them to conceal their location. This exodus is remembered as the lowest ebb in Enawenê history, a time when they thought they would be annihilated as a people. Two elderly women died of thirst on the journey and everyone was reduced to nakedness – men without penis ties and women without their red cotton skirts.

A civilised village life and Yankwa being impossible without manioc to drink, the survivors lived dispersed in encampments. Eventually, they raided manioc stems from Nambikwara gardens and founded a new village on the River Camararé. From this time on, elder people could once again recall the sequence of gardens planted and fishing dams constructed for Yankwa's successive hosts. It was soon after this that the mission encountered this apparently 'isolated' and 'monastic' group in the middle course of the River Camararé.

With Vincent Cañas on site, the mission protected the group from outsiders' incursions, arranged peace-making encounters with their former enemies, provided medical assistance, and developed a proposal for territorial demarcation (Busatto et al. 1995).[23] In this new era of peace and with an abundance of metal tools, larger gardens have been cleared and planted and, since 1998, access to boats with outboard engines has sped the progress of fishing, honey gathering, and corn-harvest expeditions, allowing for an even greater centralisation and intensification of life within the arena.

In these conditions of relative peace and plenty, with predatory enemies pacified, relations with iñoti and with predatory spirits have become paramount. By 2008, when I began my fieldwork, the protective role of the mission's successor NGO, OPAN, together with the isolation they had deliberately fostered for the Enawenê since 1974, was no longer tenable. The fleet of motor boats at the village port had multiplied rapidly since the first boats were introduced as bribes from unscrupulous farmers in 1998. Adult men in particular travelled frequently to and from urban centres to attend meetings about hydroelectric dam compensation, as well as events related to health care provision and land use reform. But although they lived at a fast-encroaching energy and agro-industrial frontier, surrounded by new towns, soya fields, cattle farms and hydroelectricity plants, and although they were avidly engaging with many different Brazilian institutions, they were still largely monolingual in their Arawak dialect.

Politicised and Gendered Fieldwork

In August 2006 I spent three weeks in the Enawenê's village on the Iquê River. I had met some twenty Enawenê men in the town of Brasnorte in a house maintained by OPAN, the NGO that had succeeded the Jesuit mission in providing assistance to the community after the assassination of Vincent Cañas in 1987. I arrived at a picket fence and explained my wish to make a short visit to the village, with a view to returning to conduct proper research in the future. My three week stay coincided with Lerohi and also with a visit by the OPAN team. During Lerohi two lines of men and women zigzag across the arena with their arms inter-linked, entering the houses of the dwelling circle to dance around their hearths and be served refreshments by their occupants. In one line the men play a shrill-sounding trumpet called *yalinya*, while in the other line panpipes called Lerohi are played. After a couple of days' stay in the village and surely frustrated by the lack of pause in the ritual in which he might host a meeting, OPAN's director dramatised his organisation's long relationship with the Enawenê to a rather small audience of men. Most of the village was too occupied with dancing to listen. He drew a boat in the sand to illustrate the thrust of his speech: the Enawenê would have to navigate their future and determine what role OPAN would have in it, given their increasing involvement with other outsiders. He asked one of the audience to fetch a very worn axe head – the first the Enawenê had received from Cañas and Lisbôa in 1974. Next to it he laid out gifts of new axes and fish hooks to symbolise the longevity of the community's relationship with his organisation. From this meeting I understood that there was a judicial process to reclaim the land around the River Preto, which was rapidly being deforested and settled, as part of Enawenê territory, and that there were several hydroelectric dams planned for the upper reaches of the Juruena River. From the way that Lerohi was allowed to drown out the Director's speech, I also understood that OPAN's importance had declined with the Enawenê's frequent trips to town and the multiplication of their relationships with outsiders.

To give some idea of the landscape, after my preliminary 2006 visit, as I was applying for my research permissions from the Brazilian Ministry of Science and Technology and the National Indian Foundation (FUNAI), I received a steady stream of 'Google alerts' about Enawenê foreign affairs. In May 2007 the Enawenê were blocking the main road through the region to protest the onset of construction of five hydroelec-tric dams on the Juruena River that had begun without their consent. A few months later, Greenpeace posted a short film of their visit to Juína to meet a group of Enawenê men. Their intention was to visit the River Preto in order to document the loss and deforestation of this portion of the Enawenê's ancestral territory. The clip showed a motorcade of trucks besieging the hotel in which Greenpeace and OPAN represen-tatives had taken refuge, as well as footage of a subsequent meeting of mayoral authorities, called to resolve the crisis. The mayor tells the visitors that 'the land and the Indians are ours' and that foreigners and NGOs are not welcome.[24] A few months later it was reported that the newly constructed village of Halataikwa had been reduced to ashes following a cooking accident and that the military police would make a helicopter drop of hammocks, pans, machetes, axes and food relief.[25] Two months on the Enawenê again blocked the road to protest the lack of information about the hydroelectric dams. This time they forced a high-level meeting, took five hostages and entered negotiations with the President of FUNAI to receive a greater share of the compensation promised for the dams.[26] Having followed these events, I was acutely aware of the politicised setting into which I was stepping when I began my doctoral research. Fittingly, arriving in Juína in January 2008, I met twenty Enawenê men who had come to secure funds for the gasoline and engine oil they needed for Yankwa's dam-fishing expeditions, which required up to 10,000 litres of fuel.

I would live in Halataikwa for sixteen months between January 2008 and July 2009 and return for short visits in the summers of 2010 and 2013. During this time, the community's well-founded distrust of the iñoti world from which I came often overrode the familiarity and friendship that grew based on cohabitation, shared work and linguistic apprenticeship. Most of the time there was an uneasy balance between familiarisation and mistrust. The Portuguese word for 'research', *pesquisa*, had entered the Enawenê lexicon to evoke betrayal, dishonesty and the delegation of powers to foreigners bent on exploitation. This made sense in a context in which appeals to pesquisa were recurrently made by Consortium representatives to support their claim that the Juruena Complex of dams would have a negligible environmental impact while the Enawenê saw the river polluted and fishing yields decline. If they had any doubt that research went hand in hand with exploitation this was confirmed in 2009 when community representatives were urged to admit researchers inside their territory to conduct viability studies for further hydropower installations. By this point they knew such research was a formality – a first step to inevitable licensing. In the context of both hydroelectricity developments and an ongoing territorial claim, anthropological research was considered risky as well. The Enawenê expressed their fears that my work could be misappropriated to justify hydroelectricity developments, or used by farmers to contest their claim to the River Preto region.[27] Because Brazilian Indians remain officially wards of the state, and Brazilian bureaucracy depends on expert mediators to speak on their behalf (Ramos 1998; 2009), this understanding of research, as something that allows outsiders to bypass them in decisions of direct concern, is well-founded.

My presence in Halataikwa was accepted, but always provisionally, as long as I responded well to Enawenê requests for assistance, left off researching valuable and sensitive esoteric knowledge, avoided politicised subjects such as territory and history, stayed out of foreign affairs (which did not concern me as a foreigner), and concentrated my research on uncontentious matters. In practice this meant that I spent most of my time with women engaged in everyday subsistence tasks such as harvesting, processing and cooking manioc; and taking trips to more distant gardens to gather medicinal plants, edible insects and whatever occasional food crops were in season – yams, sweet potatoes, araruta, corn, taro, arrowroot, lima beans, common beans and tropical green peas. I also spent a good deal of time working with women to craft items of material culture, such as drinking gourds, clay pots and the rubber bands that women wear under their knees.

At the time, it was a source of agonising frustration to me that the specialist knowledge held by male song masters was largely off-limits to me. I was sure that the deepest truths about Enawenê cosmology were contained within the chants that men voiced every night in the arena, whose form and content I could only glimpse without system-atic recording and transcription. Song masters, who were senior and venerable men, were not prepared to commit to an enduring relation-ship of apprenticeship with me, since this would have required great commitment on their part, and would have constituted an impossible admission of alliance with the anthropologist. However, the gendered and politicised nature of my fieldwork had positive as well as limiting implications.

Although the arena's musical performance is exclusively male at Yankwa, I quickly learned that the chants were addressed to the audi-ence of women, who listen and watch from the houses around it, and that men considered manioc work to be of equal importance to their immaterial labours of chanting and dancing in the arena. In a sense they sang and danced for women and for manioc. Enawenê people were also quite explicit that Yankwa was not only about cosmogonic chant-ing but about getting work done, assuring the community's health and unity by planting and harvesting manioc gardens, dam fishing, cooking large quantities of food and drinks to serve in the arena, and making beautiful things. Musical performances were just one among these dif-ferent kinds of work. It is these connections between gendered labour and public performance, and the relationship system that organises it, that were accessible to me, best fitted my interests, and also suited the level of linguistic fluency I was able to attain without doing systematic transcription work.

The gendered nature of this fieldwork also gave it a particular epis-temological character. I learned 'on the job' with women, acquiring contextual and embodied knowledge, whereas with men there was a split between distanced observation (e.g. watching performances) and discourse-focused engagement (e.g. interviews).[28] Men tended to emphasise my outsider status while women experimented with integrating me into their daily rounds; schooling me only when and if they fancied in some mythic snippet related to our shared task, some historical legend, or a piece of recent gossip about a betrothal alliance. They rarely tolerating my note-taking for long. In retrospect this oscillation between the contextual, embodied knowledge I gained with women and the abstract theory I gained by stepping back and interviewing men – often approaching them with a question that had emerged in the course of my feminine activities – was a productive one. It has allowed me to connect work and performance, ritual and economy, practice and knowledge.

From the perspective of my hosts, however, it also made me an inconstant character. One man struck a chord when he said my research was 'like fish soup, all mixed together'. Made from fish caught by men and manioc harvested by women, fish soup was a good metaphor for this alternation between male and female activities and perspectives in my research. Some men expressed the same view more critically: if I was really a researcher I should stop working manioc and start paying song masters for long informant sessions in which I would transcribe recordings of chants. But later, in order to defer impossible negotiations about what kind of ritual knowledge I could be taught and how much I should pay to learn it, the same man might tell me to go back to working manioc.[29] Since I was always potentially three people: a woman like other Enawenê women (*Enawenê-nêro*), a markedly female outsider (iño-ti-nero) and a researcher (pesquisador), my behaviour could always be found lacking according to one or the other identification. For example, as a researcher I was encouraged to enter the flute house because men considered it an excellent place to discuss Yankwa (although it was normally a space women only approached with food or drinks to offer). I would also be called out to exclusively male dawn and dusk political meetings in the central arena; and I was invited to go to the usually all-male dam-fishing encampments because they were considered the place for Yankwa-research par excellence.

Of course I was also subject to mild censorship from women for all these deviations from my female role. Although women accepted that as a researcher I should go to the dam, once I returned to the village my female status was foregrounded and I discovered that women and hosts were certain that I must have had sexual relations with some of the fishermen. Since Enawenê women travel to their husbands' dams 'seeking fish and penis' it was logical that this, and not research, should have been my prime motive for accompanying the men to the dam as well. It took some effort of persuasion from me and from the fishermen from Maxikyawina's dam to dispel these suspicions. In the meantime, one of the men with whom I shared a house in the village had formalised this accusation at the FUNAI office in Juína so that my research permit was in threat. Again, people judged his rash accusation to be motivated more by sexual jealousy than by a condemnation of my professional ethics. They said that it was because I had chosen to sleep with men other than my sisters' husbands (who were 'my husbands' by extension). This experiment with the efficacy of documents to make things happen had to be overturned by another document in which the community stated its support for my research and gave assurances about my professionalism.

At other times my ambiguous Enawenê-nêro/iñoti-nero status was problematic in the opposite direction. When the community's opposition to hydroelectric damming was at its height in September 2008, it was the feminine, participatory aspect of my fieldwork that was considered potentially exploitative. My effort to weave a cotton skirt, my daily fetching of water from the stream, and even my habit of sleeping by a fire (iñoti should use sleeping bags) were decried as an appropriation of Enawenê culture. During this period, when my very presence and participation was contested in this way, I retreated to my household and visited, circulated and occupied public space less often, counting on the continued support and companionship of my co-residents.

Of the fifteen longhouses in Halataikwa, the one in which I lived was average in size and unremarkable. The senior man of the house was a quiet, kind and dutiful man, one of the eldest in the village but neither an important member of his large clan, Kairoli, nor a specialist of any kind. His wife, who had taken me under her wing, was a woman of about fifty years of age called Kawalinero-asero by one of the various teknonyms that connected her to her many grandchildren. She was the mother of nine children, all but two of whom were already married with children of their own at the time of my fieldwork. She was a wry, witty, intelligent and affectionate woman, who oversaw my sisters' gardening schedules, swung and sang to her youngest grandchildren in her hammock when their mothers were busy working, and kept a beady eye on food stores in the eaves of the house. I joined in the gardening and cooking work of this couple's four married daughters, who filled the other sleeping compartments in the house. It was from their vantage point that I learnt about the mesh of alliances that knitted and knotted the village together.

Other women soon discovered that I liked to work, especially to go on long walks to the distant gardens, so, early in the mornings, a child would often come to my hammock to invite me to join another household's excursion. It was through such feminine harvesting and gathering trips that I gradually came to know the whole community, and it was generally from women that I learned about myth, shamanism and the spirit world, as well as gardens, cooking and kinship. In particular, my proximity to three women who dealt intensely with the unseen world exposed me to Enawenê care of the body, medicine and eschatology on a daily basis. Kawalinero-asero suffered from what I translate as a manioc 'allergy', a chronic condition requiring constant care that I consider in Chapter 5. This required her to avoid manioc gardens, processing work and food. This is no mean feat when manioc is the staple food and working it is a daily feminine duty. During my stay, she sought treatment from shamans who work by sucking pathogens from the body or channelling spirit auxiliaries to discover the cause of malady. One of these was her eldest daughter, a widow who lived next door and was one of two female shamans practising in the village at the time. She also sought help from her elderly widowed mother, who lived in the abutting sleeping compartment and who was a respected blessing shaman. By the end of my fieldwork Kawalinero-asero was also beginning to practise blessing shamanism, having learned from her mother in the course of her own treatment.

As a result of my immersion in feminine work inside the house and in the gardens, this ethnography approaches cosmology via its embedding in economy: the content and form of Enawenê ancestral knowledge – its musicality, its serialised, formalised conventions of knowledge and its ceremonial discourses – are in the background while the material, sensory and performative aspects of Yankwa's work, both male and female, are in the foreground. This emphasis on the symbolic entailments of agriculture and fishing is important for theoretical reasons as well. In Amazonia it has been male hunting practices that have received the most attention. Given that the Enawenê are not hunters, but rather masters of aquaculture and agriculture, it is fitting that the predominant perspective in this book is a female one – that of the harvest.

Chapter Outline

This book is divided into two parts. Part 1 follows Yankwa's process through dam-fishing expeditions, the fishermen's dramatic return, and then the ample feasts and intensive collective labour with which Yankwa culminates each year. Each chapter takes a detailed description of a particular activity sequence as the basis for theorisation. Thus Chapter

1 outlines the construction of a fishing weir and its humanoid traps, followed by men's anticipation of the descent of shoals of fish. Drawing upon comparative research in kindred fisher-agricultural societies of Amazonia, it demonstrates that dam fishing supports a life based on agricultural values of plenty and fertility. Beyond its economic importance, this technology shapes several kinds of relationships at once: that among the team of fishermen; that between men, fish and spirit masters; and that between men and absent hosts and women. All of these relationships entail forms of bodily and mental discipline akin to those observed by men and women during menstrual and post-partum seclusions. The result of this annual collective seclusion and monumental predatory endeavour is that men return to the village vitalised and changed.

Chapter 2 follows the practical and performative preparations made by hosts and women to stage the fishermen's return, and then analyses the structured performances by which the fishermen are reincorporated over twenty-four sleepless hours. The theoretical emphasis is on the playoff between visibility and invisibility, concealment and revelation, mask and man. This dynamic is revealing of the content of that mysterious word 'Yankwa', which refers at once to flutes, men and spirits, and to the whole season in which they are conjoined. The return of men who are said to be like enemy spirits – although they are also husbands, brothers-in-law and friends – invites this emphasis on the constitutively ambiguous relationship between persons and the roles they play as decorated and masked performers.

Chapter 3 begins after this dramatic return is complete, at the point when the fishermen take up the flutes of the first of two host clans, to play them night, afternoon and evening in an exacting musical routine. It would seem that the roles of performer and producer are straightforwardly divided between men and women in this gendered division of labour: men playing flutes, and women engaged in laborious gardening and cookery work to provision them. In fact, I show that women's daily manioc processing round is musical and dance like, the female equivalent of men's flute playing. I develop this argument through an analysis of the culmination of the returning sequence, during which there is a reflexive play upon the parallels between performance and production, and a switching of their gendered referents. Both kinds of work are revealed to be simultaneously arduous and pleasurable. This leads into a theorisation of the role of sexual desire in Yankwa's economy.

In Part 2 I take a thematic rather than a processual approach in order to further the proposition that Yankwa is a project of vital diplomacy that structures relations between affines, spirits and foreigners. These are aspects I approach in turn in three chapters on social, cosmological and foreign diplomacy. In Chapter 4 I analyse the complex ceremonial relationship system that structures the activity in the village arena, and its inscription in the dualistic space of the circular village. The village arena stages acts of social diplomacy such as exchanges of food, speeches and performances between clans and individuals, men and women, who are alternately opposed and allied in Yankwa's dualistic organisation. I present this dynamic through a description of the relational organisation of Yankwa's fundamental acts: the planting of clan manioc gardens for hosts, the public service of drinks made from their harvest, and the playing of the hosting clan's flutes that accompanies the drinking of their garden's harvest. I seek to understand this dynamic in the light of oral history accounts of the foundation of the Enawenê's society. This allows me to show that by uniting heterogeneous peoples as intermarrying clans in a single village, and rendering them dependent on one another for the expression of their identity, Yankwa is both the expression of, and condition for, the continued existence of a united, egalitarian polity.

In Chapter 5 I move from relations with social others to relations with invisible spirits, in particular the spirit masters of riverine and agricultural resources, the Yakairiti, and the animate manioc plant. The Yakairiti feature throughout Part 1 as the invisible motivators of Enawenê activity throughout Yankwa. It is for them that the Enawenê cook and feast on a daily basis. In this chapter I concentrate on the subsistence strategies, food processing methods and preferred recipes for this public commensal diplomacy. I place the analysis of cookery in the broader context of the material mediation of Enawenê relations with spirits, which includes not only cuisine but also craftwork, bodily care, shamanic treatments and food restrictions that protect and fortify vulnerable bodies. I argue that all of these processes of constituting the body and the material world are 'curative' in an expansive sense, as the means to turn relationships of predatory antagonism into consensual, enlivening ones. This is a mundane, materially mediated micro-diplomacy, which takes place in the gardens and houses of Enawenê people.

In Chapter 6 I come to the Enawenê's negotiations with the hydroelectric dam consortium and the government for a stake in riverine resources, bringing some of what we have learnt about Yankwa's internal dynamics to bear on these foreign relations of ambivalent enmity and alliance. I argue that Enawenê representatives' relative success in negotiations held in distant meeting rooms and in a foreign language rely on the maintenance of an adversarial positioning, which is sustained through an alternating dynamic of confrontation and approximation. By emphasising the temporality of Enawenê foreign diplomacy, which is grounded in the contrasting ritual seasons of Yankwa and Saluma, this analysis complements that which I pursued in two previous publications about the Enawenê's incorporation of foreign resources (Nahum-Claudel 2012), and their use of document exchange in negotiations (Nahum-Claudel 2016a). Through this dynamic the Enawenê succeed in transforming a depoliticised, pecuniary matter of compensation into a diplomatic affair between rival sovereignties.

Notes

1. 'Yaokwa, the Enawene Nawe people's ritual for the maintenance of social and cosmic order' was registered by IPHAN in 2010 and then by UNESCO in 2011.
2. Silva (2012: 65) provides accurate data on Enawenê population growth. As an indication of the speed of recent population growth, in 2009 three fifths of the population were under 14 years old.
3. I am referring to Clastres' famous argument in *Society Against the State* (1977) and to the characterisation of Amazonian societies in terms of a 'symbolic economy of alterity' (Viveiros de Castro 1996).
4. The choice of translation, which I prefer to the Amazonianist convention of 'white men' because it clarifies the political and positional significance of the term, is not meant to imply that the Enawenê consider themselves to be non-citizens, that their demarcated indigenous territory is uncomplicatedly sovereign, or that they consider non-indigenous Brazilians to be radically alien. Rather, I intend it to suggest a relationship of relative externality and committed engagement.
5. This argument speaks to contemporary scholarship in international relations that seeks to break out of a definition of diplomacy as the official practice of international relations conducted by the delegates of sovereign nation states. This narrow definition is out of step with the contemporary reality in which NGOs, social movements, corporations and indigenous peoples (to name but a few) may all be engaged in diplomacy. In this context, more open definitions of diplomacy are being embraced and explored; for example, as 'a way of knowing and dealing with otherness' (Cornago 2013: 1). See also Constantinou (1996). This is a move to which anthropologists have sought to respond, see Marsden, Ibañez-Tirado and David (2016).
6. Seligman et al.'s definition of ritual is a conventional one associated with a Durkheimian legacy in which 'ritual creates and recreates a world of social convention and authority beyond the inner will of any individual' (2008: 12), but they invest this understanding with new and particular force through a contrast with sincerity, which they pose as an alternative frame for action with which ritual always exists in tension. Sincerity characterises an abiding concern with a feeling, thinking self who is motivated by an effort to relate authentically to a world as it really is, and to relate to others on the basis of a search for truth and coherence – both in the self and in the world. While sincere orientations seek to reduce and overcome social and psychological ambiguity, ritual accommodates it (ibid.: 8–10).
7. This idea of the positive value of estrangement, both from the self and from others, is taken from Sofer (1997), who draws on Georg Simmel.

8. Based on work in the Upper Xingu, Gregor (1970, 1977, 1994) has demonstrated that the arena promotes civic values of peace, harmony and generosity, and Basso has analysed the extensive use of special linguistic registers for civility in the arena in addition to predictable gestural and postural codes that signal respectful interpersonal alignment (2007, 2009).

9. Works by Vilaça (1992), Stolze-Lima (2005) and Fausto (2012) were instrumental in the development of the theory of perspectivism, which was nonetheless given a particular critical force by Viveiros de Castro, on the basis of a sustained contrast between Amazonian people's forms of knowledge, and those of the discipline of anthropology (e.g. Viveiros de Castro 2004). Outside of regional scholarship and thematic interest in animism, it has been this aspect of perspectivism – that most distanced from Amazonian myth and shamanism – that has gained most fame in wider anthropology, by virtue of its association with the 'ontological turn' (see Holbraad and Pedersen 2017). Elaborations and critiques of perspectivism from within Amazonian anthropology are too diverse to chart in full. I will mention but a few trends: Santos-Granero (2002) and Heckenberger (2005) explore Arawak-speakers' divergence from the perspectival model. Bonilla (2016) and Walker (2012, 2013) are among the authors who demonstrate Amazonian people's association of humanity with the position of prey, rather than predator, in the context of histories of subjection to powerful masters. In addition to these interventions, which push us to variegate and nuance our understandings of Amazonia, several authors attack perspectivism on political grounds for representing Amazonian people as ontologically alter in ways that, they claim, do concrete harm (Ramos 2012; Bond and Bessire 2014; Bessire 2014a, 2014b).

10. On animism see Bird David (1999), and on the limits and possibilities of perspectivism's extension to other regions see Descola (2001); Fausto (2007); Brightman, Grotti and Ulturgasheva (2012); and Praet (2013).

11. See Hornborg (2005) and Hill and Hornborg (2011) on the relational construction of ethnicity in Amazonia.

12. I include only the most important precedents for my thinking here. Viveiros de Castro (1992) grounds his ethnography of the Araweté in a contrast between Gê sociological dialecticism and Tupi cosmological dualism. Viveiros de Castro and Fausto (1993) compare the semi-complex alliance systems of Central Brazil to the Dravidian terminologies and restricted exchange systems of Amazonia. Fausto's (2012) study of two estranged parts of a single ethnic group, the Parakana, shows that apparently radical contrasts in cultural orientation and social structure can be developed in the course of a few generations, in response to divergent historical conditions and political choices.

13. This model of 'typical' Amazonian social organisation was developed by Rivière (1984) and Overing (1975) for Guiana, and later generalised by Viveiros de Castro (1998b, 2001, 2009).

14. Details of this expedition were recorded by Thomas de Aquino Lisbôa in his published diary (Lisbôa 2010: 13–17).

15. Paresi and Enawenê dialects are both part of the southern branch of the Arawakan language diaspora (Aïkhenvald 1999), which is the most widely distributed of the Amazon's four major language families: Arawak, Tupi-Guarani, Gê and Carib (see Epps 2009). Various Paresi grammars exist (e.g. Brandão 2014), although for the Enawenê language only a phonological study has so far been made (Rezende 2003),

and, as yet, there has been no analysis of the degree of divergence between the two dialects.

16. The Paresi Plateau refers to the rolling plateau that rises from the Amazon rainforest near the Bolivian border. From its northern and western slopes spring the Juruena and Guaporé rivers, tributaries of the Amazon; and from its southern side come the headwaters of the Paraguay River, which flows south to Argentina. In other words, this plateau divides the drainages of the two great rivers of South America, the Amazon and the Rio de la Plata.

17. Campos contrasted the Paresi to the cannibalistic 'Cavihis', who he encountered when he reached the western limit of 'the kingdom of the Parecis' at the Juruena River. According to Dal Poz (1991: 53), these were probably the ancestors of the Enawenê's former enemies, who are known in the region today as the Cinta-Larga. Such a division between 'tame' and 'wild' Indians is found in many other colonial reports (see Price 1983).

18. The Paresi are exemplary of the drastic depopulation of Amazonia as a whole. It has been estimated that a population of five million in 1492 was reduced to just hundreds of thousands by the middle of the last century (Denevan 1992). For the Paresi, from the uncountable population found by Pires dos Campos in 1728, the population was estimated at 1,150 by 1848, and by Rondon's count in 1907 there remained just 340 individuals (Schmidt 1943: 13–14).

19. On Amazonian drinking festivities see Erikson (2004a); Goldman (1963); Sztutman (2008); Vilaça (1992, 2010).

20. This review of Paresi social organisation and ritual is taken from Ramos Costa's (1985) ethnography, based on research she undertook in the early 1980s. See pages 52–62 on history; 116–124 on social organisation and 177–192 on inter-village visiting rites and the flute cult. From Ramos Costa's description it is clear that the flutes that dance with the women are the panpipes Schmidt transcribed as *Zero*, and which correspond to the Enawenê's Lerohi.

21. His aim was not to convert the Enawenê but to follow an ethic of 'incarnation' himself and, through shared living and the study of language and culture, to build an anthropological foundation for the mission's future assistance to the Enawenê.

22. Mendes dos Santos (2001) provides a fuller story of the Enawenê's migrations in response to enemy attack over the course of the twentieth century. The Cinta-Larga were being pushed southwards towards the Juruena's headwaters because of an invasion of rubber gatherers and gold panners in their territory on the River Aripuanã (Arruda 1984).

23. The Enawenê indigenous territory was formally established in 1996 and covers 742,000 hectares. However the delay in demarcating this land left it vulnerable to settlers and loggers throughout the 1980s. Determined to protect its integrity from incursion, the Enawenê followed trails forged inside their territory, raided camps for tools and ambushed settlers. Enawenê warriors killed two men in 1984, and in 1986 a whole family (Arruda et al. 1987). In reprisal, Cañas was murdered in 1987 by landowners hostile to the demarcation of Enawenê territory.

24. Greenpeace Brasil. 'Amazônia, uma região de poucos'. YouTube. https://www.you tube.com/watch?feature=player_embedded&v=q9esNX7bzHY (accessed 14 March, 2017).

25. Rodrigo Vargas. 'Índios Enawenê vão receber mantimentos'. Diario de Cuiabá 20/10/2007. http://www.diariodecuiaba.com.br/detalhe.php?cod=300939 (accessed 14 March, 2017)

26. Keity Roma. 'Índios mantêm rodovia bloqueada'. Diario de Cuiabá 07/12/2007. https://pib.socioambiental.org/es/noticias?id=51312 (accessed 14 March, 2017).
27. In July 2009, the community was convinced that Placido Costa Júnior had intentionally betrayed them because his research on the Enawenê's fishing practices (e.g. 1995) had been cynically misapplied by the hydroelectricity consortium.
28. See Ardener (1975) and Golde (1986) for classic discussions of gendered fieldwork.
29. This concern with payment struck me in my very first week of fieldwork, when I was given a fish to cook and eat by a man in the house next door. I was immediately informed of the size and quantity of fish hooks he expected in return. I had anticipated generalised sharing with my hosts, but payment (*etoli*) and calculation had a prominent place in Enawenê life. The challenge of establishing acceptable standards of value equivalence, especially for the gathering of sacred, esoteric knowledge, is a fairly common one in anthropological experience. Fausto (2016: 133) opens an article entitled 'how much for a song' with Gertrude Dole's observation that the Kuikuro of the Xingu were constantly concerned with balancing accounts so that 'virtually every gift or service requires a return. Sharing and pure gift-giving are almost non-existent'. In the case of teaching songs, among the Kuikuro as among the Enawenê, payment is usually made in luxury items and is the means by which an apprenticeship is established, even if the student is a kin member. This is based on the idea that payment is necessary in order for songs to become lodged in the apprentice's mind (see also Allard and De Vienne 2005: 133). The Enawenê are quite clear that without payment the apprentice forgets, the blessing shaman errs in his rendition of the incantations, and the curer is lazy in his pursuit of his patient's missing pulse. Efficacious payment is thus strongly positively valued by the Enawenê in ways that contradicted my expectation that it implied a commodification of relationships that was best avoided.

Figure 1.1 On 18 February 2008 women look on as Yankwa's fleets prepare for departure to the fishing dams.

1

Mastery and Subjection at the Fishing Dams

I was a month into fieldwork in 2008 when I stood on the bank at Halataikwa's port with most of the women of the village, watching men load their cargo: huge baskets of dry manioc breads and flour to sustain them through their two month absence, drums of gasoline, bundles of calabashes, machetes, axes, tarpaulins and other tools. In a party mood, men and children in forty or so powered launches zoomed off down the River Iquê one by one, voicing euphoric ululations and throwing goodies like T-shirts, sweets, bags of rice, packets of biscuits, soaps and bead necklaces to the women and children on the bank, before disappearing around the river's bend. We all climbed back up the sandy path that links the port to the village. It felt oddly quiet after the buzz of the morning's final preparations and the sense of expectation that had grown over previous days and weeks.

Women had been amassing manioc breads and flour over the preceding weeks and then hosts had distributed some of them to Yankwa's dancers, so that calabashes full of dry bread and flour had cluttered the arena on successive mornings. Finally, there had been a four day countdown to departure, orchestrated by Yankwa's paramount leader, who called for the fishermen to make the baskets in which to transport their breads and flour to the dams (day 4); for the women to gather the waxy banana leaves with which to waterproof these baskets (day 3); for the women to fill the baskets (day 2); and finally, on the morning of departure, for the fishermen to pack up their hammocks and get down to the port. These instructions came each day at dawn and fulfilling them made the village hum with coordinated activities, as all around the dwelling circle baskets were woven, leaves gathered and baskets lined and conscientiously filled. Women loaded their husbands' and sons-in-laws' baskets with breads they had made themselves, as well as with those the men had received from hosts, and others brought over to the house by their female betrothal partners. In two months' time the village would be crisscrossed again by laden hands, as returning fishermen carried gifts of smoked fish to their female betrothal partners, in recompense for this sustenance.

The guiding question in this chapter is why a collective, male dam-fishing expedition should be the central phase of Yankwa's process? The economic answer is valid but insufficient: men need to capture a great quantity of protein food in order to feed months of feasting and musical ceremonialism that will follow their return, as well as to repay women's efforts in harvesting great quantities of garden foods. The complementarity between fish and manioc is certainly an important theme throughout Yankwa, which marshals a double plenty of these two vital resources. Indeed, I will show that dam fishing is both practically and symbolically modelled on manioc agriculture: only farmers would think to domesticate the riverine landscape in such a way as to enable a massive and seasonal harvest of fish. And, in turn, only fish farmers would plant their manioc gardens early, as the Enawenê do, in order to ensure that their most plentiful manioc harvest comes once they are laden with their catch of migrating fish. While these arguments, with which I begin the chapter, are important for understanding Yankwa's annual calendar, they tell us nothing about the significance of the dam as a technology or the reason why it must be the men of Yankwa who dam – even hosts become 'a 'little bit Yankwa' when they tend the village dam. We can get to this by analysing the mythological, technological and social aspects of the dams' construction, which – like other crucial activities during Yankwa's course – follows a charter myth starring the cultural hero Datamale, who made the world as it is today in the origin times, and his son Dokowyi. As Enawenê people always point out, this origin story is an essential frame of intelligibility for the technology of dam fishing, and also, I will add, for its temporality and ethos.

Just as the myth is a drama of two acts, the dam is a dual technology composed of Datamale's weir of wood and vine, which forms a barricade across the river and slows its current, and then the many traps that are later inserted into it and that will actually do the work of capturing the fish. Whereas the dam is an artifice designed by Datamale, these traps are said to be resurrections of Dokowyi's body – today they are crafted by men in his image. The construction of the weir and the tending of the traps form two opposed phases of the expedition, which the Enawenê gloss as a first and second moon (although construction and fabrication tasks take only two weeks). The first phase, that of construction, is upright and vigorous and follows an archetypal series of tasks upheld by a leader in order to realise Datamale's heroic will, by ensuring that the weir withholds the river's force and blocks the fish's downriver passage. This is therefore a phase defined by mastery – knowledge, skill and physical dominion focused on the boundary between land and water, the domains of men and fish. Once the weir is built and the traps are made, the trapping of fish necessitates a completely opposing attitude from the team of fishermen, as well as contrasting orientation to space and time.

Where before the men were ordered behind the leader, now they are in undifferentiated fellowship; where before time was sequenced, now it is amorphous; where before they spent their time exerting themselves at the weir and in the water, now they sit in their hammocks in the dry encampment, where fires constantly burn and they rest, engage in craft-work and abandon their serious labours for ribald banter, talk of dreams and quiet contemplation. This new orientation is justified by the 'traps' desires' and the risk of the 'traps' paralysis'. Men effectively live for their traps and in the process they engage in a self-conscious individual and collective self-fashioning that is likened to, and shares many features with, the techniques of self-care observed during the lifecycle seclusions, which Enawenê men observe at several points in their lives: after they have sex for the first time as youths, upon the birth of their children and during their wife's menstruation. Why does this form of predation entail men in seclusion akin to that to which they are subjected by the shedding of women's blood? The answer to this question hinges on the equation between the blood of prey and that of women and the close identification between men and their phallic and humanoid traps in which the fish's blood is shed. The outcome of these lived analogies are that dam fishing is not only a prodigious predatory endeavour but one that elaborates and collectivises an ethics of predation to such an extent (including asceticism, self-care, fasting and forms of propitiation) that it becomes – and is to some degree explicitly conceived by Enawenê fishermen as – an annual collective male seclusion that assimilates prodigious fishermen to teenage boys. Of course teenage boys are at once at a peak of vulnerability and a peak of potential vitality, growth, fertility and attractiveness. So too, the fishermen's seclusion assures that they will return to the village filled with a fertilising vitality, the outcome of their having been transformed by their self-care, their connection to ancestors and their alliance with the spirit masters of the fish. These are the many reasons why dam fishing is at the heart of Yankwa.

The Dam Sites

Whereas in 2008 I remained in the village to accompany the women and hosts' vigil for the fishermen's return, which I describe in Chapter 2, on the 21 February 2009 I sat in a laden launch bound for the most distant of the five dams built by Yankwa's fishermen. I had been invited to Maxikyawina (a tributary of the River Doze de Outubro) by this dam's leader and thus accompanied twelve adult men, their many boy children and one wilful four-year-old girl, who had insisted upon joining her father rather than staying behind with her mother. Except for the fleet bound for Hoyakawina (the River Nambikwara), which sped off directly upriver from the port, the rest of the fleets of departing fishermen went downstream and gathered at a sandbank at the confluence of the Iquê and Camararé rivers. There, in a cacophony of dyadic exchanges, the men announced to one another which river they intended to dam, performing a decision that they had made over the previous weeks. The pull between men's contrary desires for familiarity and novelty ensures that the social makeup of encampments changes slightly, but not radically, each year. There is a family tradition of going to this or that dam, so that at dams fathers and their sons are united, and also reunited with other fishing companions of previous years. On the other hand men also like to explore forgotten parts of their territory.

Biologist Costa Júnior (1995a: 132), who conducted research on Enawenê fishing in the early 1990s, mapped twenty four past dam sites, most of which had been occupied in successive generations. However, in recent years the same set of six sites had been preferred, including one just upstream of the village on the River Iquê. This dam was tended by the hosts alongside the heavy workload involved in preparing for the return of the fishermen from the distant dams. The members of each dam site are collectively known as the owners of the river whose current they dam and in whose waters they bath. Each dam has a particular character, given not only by its members but by its surrounding vegetation, the species of fish that predominate there, and the dam's position in the river system and regional geography. The two largest fleets of boats, each composed of twenty adult men and many more children, went to the River Arimena (Olowina) and the River Preto (Andowina). Yankwa's principle leaders were at Olowina, which is also considered the original and archetypal place for dam fishing, and it was from there that

messengers liaised with the other fleets to coordinate the return to the village. The dam at which I was hosted, Maxikyawina, was renowned for the strength of the river's current, which meant that the dam was trickier to build and liable to break in the middle of the fishing period. This lent a certain hard-core status to its fishermen. One recompense was that plenty of a fragrant pink-fleshed river salmon were caught in the dam's traps. Another advantage of this dam was its proximity to Nambikwara villages, which could be reached by navigating upriver to the first rapid and taking a long day's walk through the savanna. Maxikyawina and Hoyakawina dam sites were both referred to jokingly as 'Nambikwara women's bathing pools' because of their location inside Nambikwara territory. Such visits yielded one of the Enawenê's most important valuables – shiny, black, delicate bead chains that are made from buruti palm nuts. Among the Nambikwara these are made by women, whereas among Enawenê the painstaking work is undertaken by men exclusively while they are away at the fishing dams. Getting hold of extra bead chains meant having extra gifts to bring home for wives and lovers.

The River Preto was the adventurers' choice for different reasons. Settler farmers who have cleared land along this river want to prevent the Enawenê from fishing there and thereby staking their claim to the land on the basis of traditional usufruct. In 2008, in a deliberate attempt to intimidate the Enawenê, gun-wielding farmers arrived at the encampment, which terrified the children, who were alone while their fathers checked their fish traps. The River Preto's tropical rainforest environment also abounds in Brazil nut groves and genipap trees, resources that are absent inside the territory demarcated for the Enawenê in 1996. Fishermen at this dam thus bring scarce and valued goods back to the village. Both the River Preto and the River Arimena are also close to the bridge where the region's main road crosses the River Juruena, joining the region's two main towns, Brasnorte and Juína, so it was from these dams that diplomatic affairs with the Brazilian state were conducted through the fishing period. This diplomacy was particularly necessary in 2009, when representatives from all six dams travelled to Juína for a meeting about hydroelectric dam compensation. Finally, the River Joaquim Rios (Tinoliwina) was the site of the smallest dam, which could be built and tended by just two adult men – as it was in 2008. It attracted those seeking a quiet life because they were recently bereaved or were otherwise seeking a break from society. It also had the advantage of being within easy reach of the village. Both its cosy size and its proximity made it easy for fishermen's wives to visit.

With outboard motors, the fishermen's journeys to these separate tributaries of the Rivers Camararé and Juruena take hours rather than days or weeks as they did before the Enawenê acquired outboard motors in 1998. The fishermen return to sites occupied in previous years, clear the overgrown encampment grounds and banish snakes and spiders from disused longhouses. These dam sites are tried and tested, the riverbed is rocky and good for grounding a weir, and each team of fishermen immediately sets to work collectively constructing a weir, which is a grid-like structure made by sinking tree trunks vertically into the riverbed and lashing them together with horizontals. Once the weir is built, each man makes his own set of conical basket traps. All of these – up to 100 of them – are inserted into the weir's underwater grid, their mouths opening upriver, ready to pull in the migrating fish. Once the weir is fortified with palm fronds and bark to resist the current, the stream finds a path through the mouths of the traps, creating whirling eddies on the water's surface. Elder men who are too frail to manhandle the heavy traps instead weave nets and suspend them above the weir to catch jumping fish. All of this collective and individual work to build the weir and then make the traps takes about two weeks. The result is that the river is entirely closed off, so that no fish can evade capture on their migration downstream after spawning. If the dam's construction is timed right, and all being well with the hydrological cycle and the fish's reproduction, shoals and shoals of fish are captured in the traps. This

Figure 1.2 Harvesting fish from the dam's traps.

monumental construction effort and its massive fish harvest are at the heart of Yankwa and in this chapter I shall explain why.

The Fish Harvest

Through the weeks leading up their departure, Yankwa sing about the sociable fish-people *(kohase-nawe)*, who are busy becoming fattened on fruits and berries, which ripen then fall into the flooded forest where they prefer to spawn. They refer especially to the habits of herbivorous, migratory and shoal-living fish, notably leporinus, river salmon and pacu species, which are most commonly caught in the traps.[1] In fact, about 80 per cent of the fish captured are Leporinus frederici (Costa Júnior 1995b: 155), a shoal-living, migratory species who are family guardians, feed on fruits, seeds and termites and have a taste for manioc. It is the vegetarian diet and sociable habits these species share with Enawenê people that allow them to be trapped in dams. The fish go upriver to eat the tree fruits and nuts that fall abundantly into the flooded forest during the rainy season, and once the river level begins to fall they travel back downstream in shoals. In Enawenê mythology it is this seasonal feasting behaviour that defines the sociability of these fish, who are imagined as aquatic counterparts to their agriculturally minded captors. These are fish who bite hooks that Enawenê fishermen have baited with their own favourite foods: cooked manioc bread or creamy queen leafcutter ants. In mythology and in the many chants about fish that are inspired by it, as well as in everyday decision-making about fishing strategies, these affinities between fish and Enawenê people are elaborated. For example, fishermen track the maturation of a species of flowering grass that begins to grown in the savanna at the onset of the rains.[2] They seek out the grass periodically, especially through January and February, to observe its stage of development in order to predict the timing of the fish's migration back downstream and thus to plan a timely departure for the dams. Called 'the fish's gardens', these grasses act as a barometer of the hydrological cycle and thus stand as a visible index of the movements of fish, who are hidden underwater. Once at the dams, anxious fishermen seek out the grasses again to help them predict the descent of the shoals of fish. They say that by the time the grasses' flower buds are swelling, so that they are 'pregnant with the rain', the traps need to be ready for the fish's arrival, since, once they have flowered, the fish will have passed downstream and the opportunity to trap them will have been missed.

These affinities between agriculturally minded fish and people make these prey the ideal food for Enawenê people, who are more ambivalent about eating carnivorous fish species, and who exclude terrestrial game from their diet entirely. Indeed, dam fishing is in no way a hunt, the symbolic and practical emphasis is on the harvest of a 'crop' of fish. This struck me when I saw men at the dam weaving baskets that were the same as those they usually only wove for their wives to use for transporting manioc. It struck me again when I saw how the traps were emptied. The action of pulling up the traps from deep underwater and then gathering the fish was very similar to the way women dug and pulled manioc tubers out from individual mounds, gathered them all together in a single basket and then poured them in a heap for sorting and scraping. When the fishermen check their traps, which they do twice or thrice daily, they take hold of a beam across the mouth of the trap, brace their legs against the weir and haul it out of the water. They then rest on the structure of the weir to pass the fish (which have usually died of asphyxia) up to a helper who is perched on the weir above and has the basket ready. Once a man has checked all his traps and passed up the fish, he pours the basket's contents onto a leaf matting on the bank. Then, much as manioc is elaborately processed and then shaped into discs for smoking and drying above the hearth, so that its starch and fibre can be stored for months, the fish are elaborately prepared and carefully smoked so that they too can be preserved for the hosts and women who wait in the village.

Building fishing dams in order to harvest and preserve great quantities of fish thus parallels the production of a storable surplus of garden produce. Over its eight month duration Yankwa stages a double plenty of manioc and fish: the fishermen go to the dams in February laden with durable manioc breads and must return in April or May weighed down with smoked fish. During the months after their return the manioc gardens yield most abundantly and everyone feasts on fish paired with manioc breads and drinks. That Enawenê manioc gardens reach their peak yield after the fishermen's return is not simply dictated by the seasons. Rather, the Enawenê have harmonised their agricultural calendar with the annual migration of fish by planting their gardens at the onset of the dry season in June and July (while the ground retains enough residual moisture for the stems to sprout) rather than at the start of the rains, which usually occurs around October time in central Brazil.[3] The Enawenê's manioc tubers are therefore biggest and juiciest in April and May, ready for the fishermen's return and the intense season of musical ceremonialism and feasting, rather than peaking between July and September as they do for most of the Enawenê's neighbours, by which time the Enawenê have moved on to planting their corn gardens and celebrating Lerohi.

A synchronous surplus of fish and manioc is also achieved through the rhythm in which gardens are planted and harvested. Manioc is a plastic crop that can be harvested anytime from eight to twenty-four months after planting (Dufour 1999) and that can therefore be depended upon to provide an even living all year round. Manioc stems are usually replanted in freshly turned soil mounds on the day they are harvested. Thus a manioc garden can be harvested gradually over many months and in that case its plants' maturation will be staggered the next year. In contrast, after the fishermen's return hosts' wives harvest intensively from the host clan's collective manioc field over three weeks. These are the gardens planted expressly to feed the returning fishermen. With the field's rapid replanting over about three weeks of intensive harvest and cookery in year one, the next year's harvest will again peak ready to meet Yankwa's return.

Dam Fishing and Manioc Agriculture in Amazonia

Other Amazonianist scholars have also noted the affinities between dam fishing and agriculture. Dam fishing is a highly technologically mediated, distanced and relatively bloodless form of predation and it yields a hefty harvest all at once. Nowhere else in Amazonia today are dams as monumental as those of the Enawenê still made, but we know that other Arawak speakers, or peoples historically influenced by them, in the Upper Xingu, the Baures region of Bolivia and in Northwest Amazonia either do or did build weirs, manipulate water courses and trap fish. As well as sharing the Enawenê's dietary preference for aquatic prey, these fisher-folk are also manioc farmers, who store surplus and elaborate myriad food stuffs from the highly versatile crop. Anthropologists and archaeologists working with these peoples, or with their ancestors' traces on the landscape, have commented on the equivalence and complementarity between dam fishing and intensive manioc agriculture. Gregor notes the analogy made by the Mehinaku between fishing and harvesting manioc (1985: 81); Heckenberger (2005: 196) comments that fishing dams seem to be rooted in the profoundly agricultural mindset of Upper Xingu peoples, who are 'fish farmers'; Erickson (2000) describes a pre-Columbian 'aquatic farm' in Baures that covered 500km^2 and allowed fish to be controlled and harvested; and Chernela (1993: 100–102) concludes that the various fixed facilities built by the Tukano-speaking Wanano allowed for 'dramatically high' yields of fish to be 'harvested easily'.[4] The areas where this fish-farming bent is found – the Xingu, the Baures region of the Bolivian lowlands and Northwest

Amazonia (NWA) – are all inhabited by Arawak-speaking peoples or others who have been historically influenced by them. Indeed, such features as the extensive exploitation of riverine resources, canoe navigation and intensive agriculture are known to be characteristic of Arawak speakers across their vast South American and Caribbean diaspora (Santos-Granero 2002).

Fish trapping is a highly mediated and distanced form of predation more akin to an agricultural harvest than to a hunt. Nonetheless, in NWA and to a lesser extent among the Enawenê, the theme of vengeance between fish and humans is prominent in the cosmology of dam fishing. In NWA people attack fish at their time of greatest fertility, as they ascend the river before spawning, and fish-people take revenge by attacking human fertility (see Cabalzar 2005: 51). Thus when the Wanano (or Cotiria) go to empty their traps of fish they go armed. Their arrows or machetes are not used to kill the fish, which are left to die by asphyxia, but to counter the fish's invisible aggressions against people (Calderón-Corredor personal communication and see 2011). In the Enawenê charter myth of dam fishing, which I turn to in the next section, the first dam was ingeniously devised by a father to take vengeance on the fish for the murder of his son. However, as I will show in the course of the chapter, these origins in vengeance are suppressed in the practice of dam fishing and the myth itself has a peaceful, consensual conclusion: the remaining fish are said to ascend to celestial rivers to recoup their numbers in order to return to populate the rivers and give themselves as food to Enawenê people – for whom fish are the only suitable prey.

The suppression of vengeance in dam fishing is clearest when we contrast it with collective expeditions to fish with vegetal poison (*aikyona*), which take place when the river level is low. This is the form of fishing that predominates during the season of Saluma in tandem with musical performances that emphasise warriorhood. Costa Júnior (1995: 124–26) witnessed one of these expeditions to a large lake called Honé in the early 1990s. The major emphasis is on catching the non-migratory and voraciously predatory peacock bass (*halira*, Cichla sp.), which pursues all moving prey (including young of its own species) to the death once it has gone into attack. Incarnating the warrior values of Saluma, the Enawenê are similarly relentless in their pursuit. They block the channel that links the oxbow lake to the River Juruena and erect fences across the lake to create manageable transects. Beginning with the transect nearest to the channel in order to drive the fish away from their escape route, they macerate plant toxins in the water and stir up the lake's sediment. The toxins concentrate the fish, which desperately follow the current in search of an outlet. Men line up their canoes on the far side of the outermost fence, standing atop them with bows and arrows and letting their arrows fly at the drowning fish who desperately seek escape. They work inwards towards the outer side of the lake, on one transect each day, so as to corner and kill these predatory fish. This, and not dam fishing, is surely the paradigm of a war on fish.

Dam fishing is not entirely bloodless: the captured fish often bear a bloody mark where they have been thumped by the bar that dissects the mouth of the trap, and this bar is also said to become stained with blood after many fish shoal into a trap. Nonetheless, almost all the fish die by asphyxia in the absence of men. Once they have built the dam, and once the traps are in place, fishermen are supposed to lie down to rest. As we shall see 'lying down to rest' is a euphemism for lifecycle seclusions and it signals the vulnerability of Enawenê fishermen, who are subjected to the blood of fish as it is shed by the traps.

The First Dam

In the lead up to departure for the dams in January and February, and then during the fishing period through March and April, I was told the charter myth for dam fishing many times, as though the significance of the technology was contained within its narrative. Following this cue, the myth provides the starting point for my analysis of the dialectical technology of Enawenê fishing dams, which are composed of the enabling weir and the deadly traps. The weir is the work of Datamale, the creator, and the first traps are said to be made from his murdered son's ribcage. The work of building the weir, fabricating the traps and then harvesting the fish composed distinct phases of the fishermen's approximately two month-long absence in 2009, just as they form two halves of the origin myth. A first moon was devoted to erecting the uprights and a second, beginning once the traps entered the weir, was referred to as the time in which the fishermen would finally 'lie down' (*aoxikya*) to rest in the encampment as Dokowyi's body trap worked to capture the fish. As they built the weir during the first moon, fishermen explicitly said they were like the creator Datamale.

> Dokowyi had a magic net with which he caught many fish with great ease. He alone controlled the net and when his father's trickster brother Wadaleoko took it he became ensnared. His intestines would have been squeezed out of him completely if Dokowyi had not rescued him from its stranglehold in time. Wadaleoko then told Dokowyi he had seen a spotted pacu fish very close to the river bank, and he urged Dokowyi to go and spear

it with an arrow. He specifically told him not to use his net. It was a trick; Wadaleoko had made the fish himself by throwing a sieve spotted with red dye into the water. When Dokowyi speared the magical fish, he entered the underwater world and was immediately surrounded by shoals of angry fish.

These fish (Leporinus, Brycon, Myleus) complained about the devastation his net had wrought: their villages had been decimated and their dance patios were almost empty. They asked Dokowyi who his father was, taunting him to admit that he was the son of the creator Datamale. Dokowyi bluffed that he was an orphan: a boy from the water, a child of the driftwood, of the sand of the river's beaches, and the leaves which floated on its current. As he spoke, he floated down the Juruena River as though he were indeed part of it. Faced with these evasions the fish called his bluff by asking him: 'who will avenge your death?'

Dokowyi answered by boasting of the vengeance he would take once he was dead and his body parts were transformed into an arsenal of weapons deadly to fish:

My veins, poison vines will avenge me;
My testicles, poison seeds will avenge me;
My snot, boggy shallows will avenge me;
My eye lashes, small fish traps will avenge me.
My ribcage, the giant fish traps that belong to the dam will avenge me.

With each deadly weapon Dokowyi listed, the fish rebutted with the warning: 'if any one of you should be with blood, your weapons shall be ineffective'. But when Dokowyi mentioned the final weapon, the giant fish traps, the fish trembled with fear and the Pike Characin Fish lanced Dokowyi through his middle with his spear-like nose, killing him. Fearing Datamale's revenge, all the fish then fled downriver.

Soon Datamale saw that his son was missing and he took to the river in the form of a river salmon to search for him. When he encountered a minnow nibbling on flesh-stripped bones, he knew that the fish had murdered his son. Datamale thought about what he would do before setting to work.

Along the river banks he planted fruiting trees and put worms in the earth so that the fish could feast when they entered the flooded forest. Then he swam downriver to tell the fish about the tasty abundance upriver. Irresistibly tempted, they followed him upstream. Once he had led the fish to their upriver feast, Datamale jumped back onto land and got to work constructing a dam and a smokehouse. He did this magically; throwing pieces of wood and vine into the water, the weir rose up by itself and the weir's cylindrical traps formed themselves from Dokowyi's skeletal ribcage.

Having prepared for the arrival of the fish, Datamale swam upriver to warn the fish that the water level was falling and the cold setting in; it was time they made their way downriver. He persuaded them by proposing that they gather baskets full of fruits, berries and worms to take downriver to their grandfather the Giant Catfish. Once again, despite their suspicions, the fish followed the beautiful fish downstream. Swimming at the head of the shoal, Datamale jumped out of the water just before he reached the weir. The fate of the shoals of fish was sealed; all of them drowned in the traps.

In the myth Datamale is master transformer, surmounting the frontier between earth and water, creating the ecology of the river banks and thus motivating the up and downstream migrations of the fish. Like Datamale, as they built the weir, fishermen alternated between terrestrial and aquatic activities, searching out vines and felling trees in the forest and then diving down to the riverbed to anchor them. In a more abstract sense I suggest that in their Datamale aspect the fishermen were manipulating the boundary between the terrestrial world of men and the aquatic world of fish, which allowed them, once the traps were inserted into the weir, to create a hinge between the levels of the universe so that the fish would 'drown in the traps' *(kohase aona mata enain)*, in the fishermen's own tantalising idiom.

One day Xayu-ene, who was the leader at Maxikyawina and the man who had invited me to come along to his dam, took me with him to watch the fish approaching the dam from upriver. Together we climbed the ladder to a lookout post some ten metres high up in a tree, which provided a view upstream of the dam. It was camouflaged with leaves so that the scouts who used it several times a day remained unseen by the fish. Xayu-ene pointed out a lone fish that was swimming around close to the traps but turning back upstream again. By this time his smoking rack was a little fuller than anyone else's and he explained to me that he and his father, who was a renowned blessing shaman, were alone in knowing the incantations to utter to the traps. I recorded these incantations with old Xayu-atokwe. They derive from the charter myth and are uttered in a whispered, densely metaphorical poetic language in which the true nature of things is at once revealed and masked. The incantation that propitiates the traps evokes the sun's rays, which blind the fish; likens the fish to buoyant palm leaves that are carried with the current; and repeats the warnings with which Datamale encouraged the fish to go downstream: the descent of the waters, the coming of icy-cold mornings, and the bird-calls that mark the end of the rainy season. In Enawenê epistemology such formulae move the cosmos by participating in and mastering its language of hidden names and thus tap into Datamale's ability to control transformation, rendering the fish susceptible to the traps – blind, weak and unable to resist the force of the current.

Where Datamale controls transformation and masters the boundary between land and water, Dokowyi plays the opposite role. He blurs the boundary, occupying a risky but powerful medial position. Lying to his inquisitors, he claims to be born of sand, leaves and flotsam, all elements that mediate between land and water. Then he boasts that death will transform him into a set of tools and techniques that ensnare fish also by transgressing the boundary between the terrestrial and the aquatic worlds of men and fish.

Where Enawenê fishermen said that they were "like" Datamale as they built the dam, they said that their traps "were" Dokowyi's body. Both are metaphors of sorts but there is an important distinction between enactment in the first case and actualisation in the second. The fishermen's task was to craft the traps in the image of Dokowyi and then, for the whole of the second moon, to animate these avatars by controlling their own thoughts and actions. While building a weir is a physical ordeal, animating traps involves individual and social technologies of the self. The vigorous, vertical collective work of weir-building gives way to the contemplative, individual handiwork involved in fabricating traps. Through this detailed, seated work, men's identification with the traps they craft begins. When all the fishermen have readied their traps, they insert them into the weir. The fishermen explicitly said that when the traps penetrated the weir, they became like teenage boys who had had sex for the first time and were subject to their female partner's blood at her next bleed. During the period of approximately one month through which the traps captured fish, the interdependence between the traps and the bodies and dispositions of their owners involved the fishermen in a series of special practices, like fasting, sexual abstinence, body purification, precise cooking methods and shamanic cures, which were akin to those observed by girls and boys during puberty seclusion and by parents following the birth of a child. Indeed, this second moon of the dam-fishing expedition is suggestively referred to as 'lying down to rest' in the same way as all of these seclusions.

In the origin myth, blood features as the fish's defence to Dokowyi's arsenal. The fish rebut Dokowyi's threats with the warning that his weapons will all be rendered ineffective by the presence of blood. There is a widespread conception in Amazonia that menstrual blood spoils fishing and hunting poisons; in its presence 'tools, materials, shotguns, baskets and fish traps become useless'.[5] Hunting and fishing are therefore usually proscribed for men whose wives are menstruating or have recently given birth. This is exemplified in an Enawenê morality tale about a hungry young man called Alame who went hunting birds while his wife bled. Alame was transformed into an ogreish tree being (a class of supernatural being called *atahale wayate*) and never returned to his human kin. Instead, he became a superlative predator, living in the forest and effortlessly capturing birds, which flocked to him as though he were an attractive tree and stuck to his branches. Although the link was never suggested by the Enawenê, it occurred to me that Alame's fate recalled Dokowyi's unnatural success with his magic fishing net; as well as his predator-prey brinkmanship; and his unstable and medial subjectivity. Dokowyi's position, like Alame's blood-induced one, is of propitious but risky openness.

As I have come to understand it, the traps embody this dangerous, medial quality – the merging of man and fish in Dokowyi's body trap – so that Enawenê fishermen do not have to. First, the organisation of space, divided between the encampment and the dam, is such that entrapment occurs in the absence of men, who are protected by the physical separations they have forged. Second, various behavioural and moral proscriptions around how the fish are cooked and eaten seem to be about boundary maintenance. As much effort goes into ensuring separations are maintained between men and their traps as goes into propitiating the traps directly (uttering invocations to the traps, making offerings to the masters of the fish) and indirectly, as men strive to generate a fertile mood and atmosphere through humorous banter, good dreams and food-sharing. Through men's risky identification with their traps – and through them with Dokowyi and with the fish themselves – dam fishing becomes not only a monumental predatory endeavour but also a collectivised and magnified version of puberty and postpartum seclusions, from which the fishermen will return to the village not only laden with gifts of smoked fish, but also themselves transformed.

The subjective journey men take over the two moons (first as Datamale and then as Dokowyi) represents a transformation from the mastery of exerted construction work to subjection to the wills and desires of their traps. This contrast is expressed in the dam's origin mythology, embedded in its dialectical technology (Datamale's weir and Dokowyi's traps), and evident in the changing ethos of encampment life. I will begin to evidence this now by turning to a description of the weir's construction, which is intended to be both technically accurate and revealing of the social relationships that underpin the construction effort of 'the first moon' dedicated to erecting the uprights.

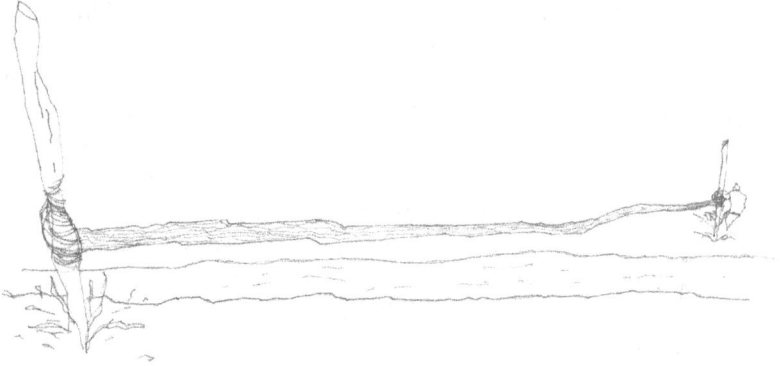

Step 1: *Inihi*, pulling taut the vine.

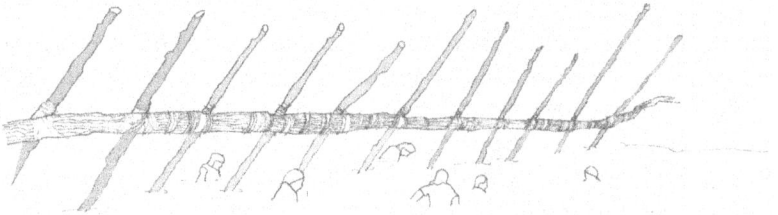

Step 2: *Etonola*, sinking the supporting uprights.

Step 3: *Mata heho*, measuring the trap positions.

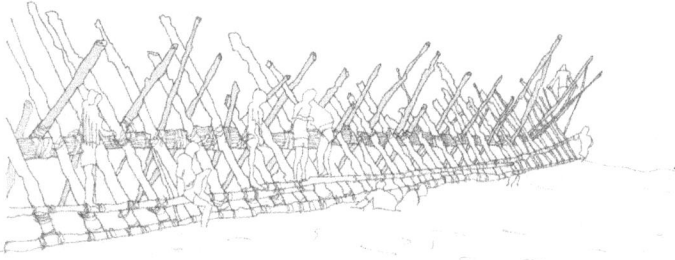

Step 4: *Etokokwayti*, laying down the horizontals.

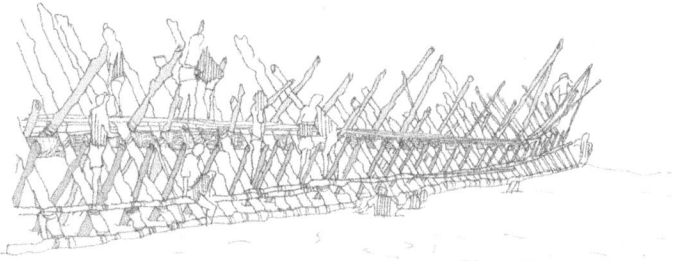

Step 5: *Ekase*, sinking thinner uprights; and Step 6, *Ikixiti mahe*, laying down a walkway.

Finally a mat woven from palm fronds (*ataikwa*) is placed on the weir's upriver face.

Figure 1.3 Building a fishing dam (*wayti*) in six archetypal steps. Illustration by Kate Altman.

Bounding Land from Water

Arriving at Maxikyawina mid morning, after a night spent fishing on the way, the first task was to clean the encampment of the long grass and scrub that had grown in the intervening year and to survey the remnants of last year's weir, pushing accumulated flotsam through to escape downstream. Weirs are built anew each year and then the vines that hold their structure together are cut when the fishermen leave, but the skeleton of old weirs remain, pushed downstream and disfigured by the current. Each day men awoke to a metaphorical injunction uttered by the leader that defined the day's work by referring to its key task. Before our departure from the village, when I asked men to explain how fishing dams were built they always systematically listed this sequence of construction tasks. This reveals the archetypal quality of the work, which it is the leader's task to reaffirm through his early morning injunctions and through the example he sets by going to work first.

In fact, such a concern with order and sequencing is a general feature of Enawenê epistemology, and the building of the dam through successive work days, which were formally announced by the leader at dawn each day, continued the pattern established by the 'countdown' of named task days before the fishermen's departure. Furthermore, during the construction phase the relationships among the team of men are very similar to those that prevail during Yankwa's village phases, where leaders orchestrate ceremonial life and economic activities. For example, during daily chanting, flute-playing and dancing in the village arena, each of the three or four groups of flute players follows a song master. The latter intones the chants at the head of the line, ensuring that they are uttered correctly and in sequence. In the same way, at the dam, a leader is responsible for coordinating the sequence of technical and ritual actions through which the weir and traps come into existence. At Maxikyawina the leadership role was shared by a father and son. The dawn calls were made by old Xayu-atokwe, who was a song master and blessing shaman and the eldest man of his clan. But he was too old to lead the heavy work of sinking tree trunks, or to be wholly absorbed in worldly politics, and so his son Xayu-ene was recognised publically as the dam's leader (*iwñerekaiti*) – it was he who had gathered allies to dam Maxikyawina with him before leaving.

On the first day after our afternoon arrival at the encampment, Xayu-atokwe woke us with a call that alluded to the vine (*inihi*) that had to be pulled taut and lashed to posts on the near and far banks of the river. In this case the vine was provided by a piece of thick steel cord, which had been salvaged from the defunct telegraph line that had once passed through Nambikwara land nearby. The cord was disentangled from the skeleton of last year's weir and anchored at each bank. Then it was reinforced with saplings (*mirihiru*) along its length, so that this central beam could be used as a precarious walkway during subsequent construction. At Maxikyawina this happened in the afternoon, after a morning spent gathering three boat loads of thick vines, which would be needed to lash together all the parts of the weir.

The second day's task was the sinking of the supporting uprights (*etonola*). Tree trunks were felled and trimmed so that they had a forked top, and were carried along the central beam on men's shoulders. They were dropped down on the downstream side of the beam, which then rested on the many forked uprights. Men dived down to ensure the uprights were wedged into the riverbed and then they used vines to lash them to the central beam.

The nature of leadership and collectivity in vigour during the construction phase is well illustrated by the third stage of construction, which involves the division of the upriver face of the weir into vertical transects and their distribution among the fishermen. It is called *hihatene*, which refers to the 'measurement' of these transects, which would eventually become 'trap positions' (*mata heko*). Xayu-ene used a neatly trimmed measuring stick about 50cm in length and walked along the central beam, measuring the intervals. As he did so all the men were lined up along the beam behind him, and they claimed and marked their positions with leaf or bark ties they had in their hands. As I watched from the bank the process seemed to me both formal and unceremonious. Xayu-ene sometimes named someone and sometimes agreed to the calls of 'it's mine' from his followers. Each man ended up with two, three or four positions depending on his willingness to have them.[6]

Like Yankwa's collective clan gardens, which are planted as one whole but subdivided for each clan member for the purposes of subsequent weeding and harvest, weirs are initiated by collective work but then maintained and harvested by the owners of each transect. The men continued to work together on the weir, and their trap positions were distributed along its length (rather than grouped), so that each man was dependent on his neighbours' construction efforts as much as his own. However, once the trap positions had been marked out on day three, men were now responsible for making sure the uprights were correctly spaced at their own trap positions. Once this measurement was done, the thick, heavy tree trunks (called *ese*, which means 'seed') that form the upriver face of the weir were floated downriver, lashed alongside the hulls of boats and then levered upright to rest against the beam. Their weight obliged three men to work together to lever each one into position. These uprights were positioned according to the measurements made that morning and lashed both to the horizontal beam and to the first uprights, which acted as counterbalancing supports to them.

Day four dawned with the call to lay down horizontals (*etokokwayti*). Tall, thin trunks were felled and lashed horizontally at three levels (at water level, and approximately one metre above and one metre below

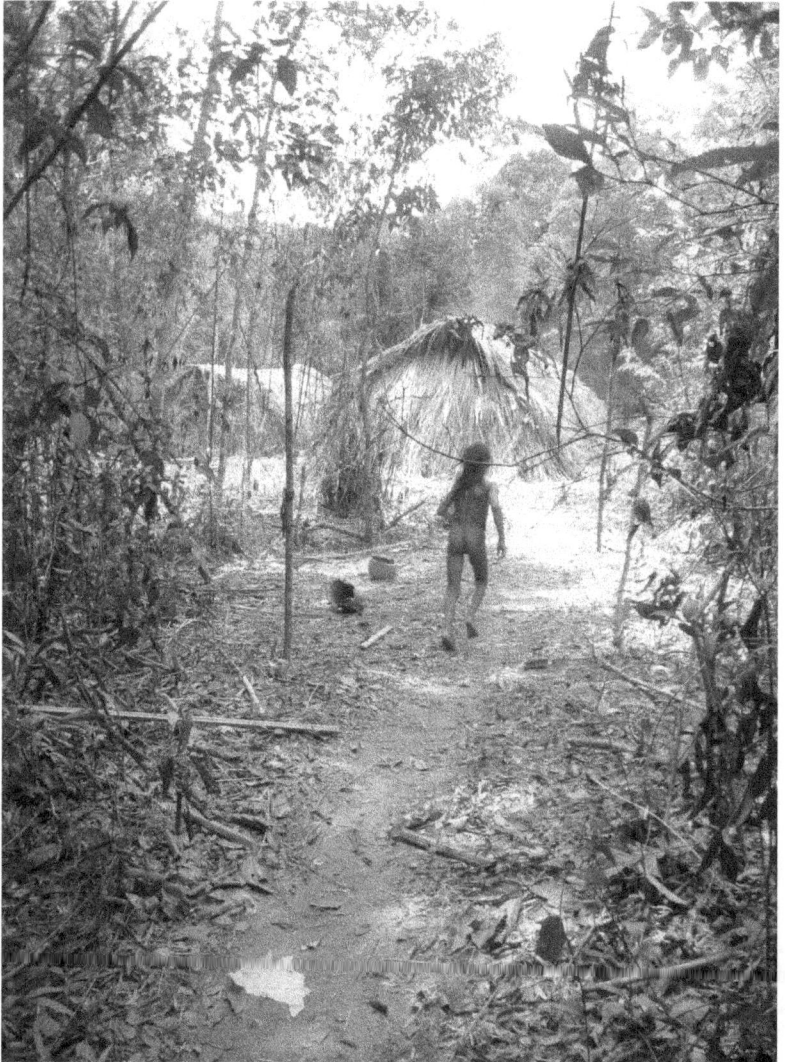

Figure 1.4 The encampment downstream of Maxikyawina's dam.

water level) to form a grid with the thick seed uprights. On day five a second pair of uprights (both seed and counterbalance) was added in the box-like positions created by the two horizontals that ran the length of the weir. This stage was not mentioned in the archetypal sequence narrated to me back in the village and it is possible that this was an extra measure, taken to account for the legendary force of the current at Maxikyawina. Each man was then responsible for creating the exact interval in which his traps would sit, by sinking thinner uprights called *ekase* ('legs') between the thick seed uprights that were reserved for him.

At the end of this day the penultimate task of the sequence was fulfilled by the laying of a wide and sturdy log 'walkway' (*ikixiti-mahe*) in the forty-five degree angle created between the uprights. This would enable men and children to move easily along the dam carrying baskets of fish. The final task, achieved on day six at Maxikyawina, was the laying of a mat of fine saplings and vines (*ataykwa*) over the underwater, upriver face of the weir. This mat generates resistance to the current and it will be pierced by the traps when they are inserted, so that the current flows strongly through the mouths of the traps. The day after this, first thing in the morning before the men sat down to make the traps, they added palm fronds and bark to this mat to gradually increase the weir's resistance to the river's current.

The Encampment

The separation between land and water, men and fish, is also one between the action of fire, which reigns supreme in the encampment and its smokehouses, and that of rushing water at the weir. This essential separation is inscribed in space. At Maxikyawina the encampment was about a hundred metres downstream of the weir, connected to it by a path that ran parallel to the river's course. This was far enough for the men to be inaudible and invisible to the weir but close enough that they would hear if the weir broke (as it did one night) and could hasten to repair it. The fishermen filed up to the weir together two or three times a day when they went to empty the traps, at dawn, noon and dusk, but otherwise no one passed by the weir casually on their way to gather materials in the forest. Rather, a designated scout was sent every hour or so to climb to the treetop lookout and secretly survey the fish as they approached the weir and to report sightings back to the encampment. All these scruples implied that the fish should remain oblivious to the men who awaited them downstream.

The day the weir was finished, the sagging central beam of the old house, left over from the previous year, gave way and we had to evacuate to a tarpaulin shelter before the roof fell in completely. Men would gradually begin building two new houses (over days 10 to 25 after our arrival) as soon as they had returned from their expedition to gather the all-important bark with which they would make the traps. These houses were not makeshift encampment huts; their architecture was the same as that of longhouses inhabited in the village, only on a slightly reduced scale to suit the smaller numbers they housed. But these houses were primarily hot, dry smokehouses rather than dwellings. The spaces for clusters of hammocks for a man, his father and his children, or a man and his son-in-law, or a group of friends (in the case of young men), were squeezed between the huge smoking racks that bisected the house. Taking up a third of the area of the house, the racks were built from logs that were thicker even than those forming the house's central pillars. The top shelf of these mega-hearths was reserved for the baskets of manioc flour and bread, which we had taken pains to keep dry as the houses were built; the bottom shelf would be for smoking the new catch; and the middle shelf for the continuation of the drying and preservation process. As I watched the men build the house they told me that when yields of fish were at their peak the smoking fires would make the house unbearably hot, so we would decamp to sleep outside. In addition to their sturdiness, the houses were thatched punctiliously with palm leaves, with all leaks stopped, so that it would remain dry through this often rainy period.

The careful control of fire has both practical and cosmological dimensions in the encampment, as it does in the village. In the village the emphasis is on fire's role in detoxifying manioc. I noticed that the care taken in the preparation of fish was akin to that with which women formed manioc loaves for drying and storage and packaged the fishermen's manioc breads in lined, watertight baskets. This similarity reflects the common destiny of fish and manioc to serve as durable wealth. Once caught, the cleaned, gutted fish would not be placed directly onto the wooden hearth racks but first arrayed in baskets made from woven strips of palm bark, which were flattened and held between a long green stick, split lengthways and tied. Around ten fish would be splayed out in each basket (*ekwa*), in a symmetrical pattern, pair of fish after pair of fish. In another arrangement called *halahahwala* and used for bigger fish, two fish were lashed together nose to nose and tummy to tummy. Each of these flattened baskets had its own handle, which . made it easy to turn during smoking and later facilitated stacking into baskets, transporting back to the village, exchanging and then hanging from the eaves of the hosts' houses. As well as being aesthetically pleasing and practical, these smoking baskets would become units of currency once fishermen returned to the exchange circuits of the village. Each phase of exchange with hosts, and each gift to betrothal partners, requires a conventional quantity of fish, which is measured in numbers of ekwa or halakakwale.

In addition to promoting the creation of durable stores of smoked and dried fish, there is a strict segregation of fire and water that exceeds this function and seems to be about upholding the boundary between land and water once the traps have been inserted and are transgressing it. Until the traps were in place, while men fished with hook and line to sustain themselves through weir-building, their cookery was of a devil-may-care kind: a whole fish laid directly on hot embers or a glowing ember pressed onto some fatty fish intestines so that its oils seeped into the manioc bread placed beneath it, making a smoky sandwich; or a whole fish poached in water and then its cooked flesh simply picked out by everyone with sharpened sticks. Once the traps entered the water and men began to fish with the hosts in mind, this rough and ready cookery was replaced by not only the careful preparation of fish for smoking but also the scrupulous attention to one crucial detail: no water should be allowed to drip into any of the fires. My hosts warned me about this very early on and explained the reason for it as follows: the 'tzzz' sound of water falling onto hot coals would anger the traps, which only liked to hear the 'tzzz' sound of fat dripping from roasting fish. This meant that pans of fish soup, or drinks made from boiling manioc flour and water, had to be stirred with caution to avoid overspill. When fishermen returned shivering from their dawn bath to check the fish traps, they squatted at a distance from the fire rather than standing over it to warm themselves. And whenever rain tested the new thatch everyone rushed to realign fronds in order to stop leaks.

Since the aim of weir fishing is to return to the hosts with smoked and durable fish, and since the fishermen are in such a wet environment, anxiety about 'the rot setting in' makes perfect sense. Beyond this, smoking the fish in such an elaborate way and obsessing over the mixture of fire and water may be a means to uphold the boundary between land and water as the fish 'drown' in the traps. One narrator of the dam's origin myth told me that when Datamale had emptied the full traps onto the river bank his haul had been so plentiful that it had rotted uneaten. He implied that the rotting fish was poetic retribution for Dokowyi's murder, but others said that Datamale had simply been overcome by the size of his catch. Nonetheless, the architecture, techniques and cuisine of the smokehouse seem designed to ensure against the spectre of baskets of rotting fish and to sustain the boundary between land and water, even as Dokowyi's body trap transgresses it.

From Leadership to Fellowship

As men embarked upon this bounding, which entailed different dominions, or layers of the universe, and different species (men and fish), social divisions were put on hold. The team of fishermen lived in fellowship with one another, united in opposition to the hosts whom they had left behind, along with the affinal obligations characteristic of village life. Men explicitly contrasted encampment and village life. They joked that the village was 'the hungry place' (*yeraitikwa*) because there they handed their catch over to their mothers-in-law and wives and ate just small pieces of fish themselves, whereas here they would soon be able to eat whole fish. On our first day I was schooled in this new regime: 'We don't feel shame here, you understand, here we are a "community" [he used the Portuguese *comunidade*] because we are few'. Another man added that women were stingy and hid honey from others, whereas, within the encampment, the men would freely take from one another's pots of gathered honey. In fact, men generally kept to their own honey pots but this normative discourse did reflect the many ways in which sharing was institutionalised at the dam.

This fellowship depended above all on the maintenance of a strict segregation between fishermen and the hosts, dam and village. The fishermen were united in their common orientation to the hyperbolic affines they had left behind in the village. In advance of my return to the village ten days in advance of the fishermen in May I was warned that hosts would press me insistently to tell them how much fish was stacked on the smoking racks but that I must not answer however much they probed. I should simply say that the smoking racks were empty. Since fish are the medium through which hosts and Yankwa will once again be reunited, it makes sense that secrecy surrounding fish should stand in for their estrangement, which is ideally total. The fishermen called themselves 'those ashamed in the face of the hosts' (*Kawali yeyaltaka*) and they were prompt to school me as soon as we arrived at the encampment: today we do not talk to the hosts unless they bring news that our children are unwell; today the hosts are like our enemies – we have left them behind our backs'. Another of the young men at Maxikyawina added to the lesson, telling me 'it's tough, next year I and my clansmen will host, and I will not talk to these people [referring to the men present who had been his fellows, year after year, at Maxikyawina] here and they won't talk to me either'. He motioned to his mother's brother Xayu-ene and the latter's children, who belonged to a different patrilineal clan. The absolute imperative was therefore that communication with hosts and women in the village should cease. But beyond this shared oppositional stance, encampment fellows were also united by their common construction task, ordered according to an archetypal sequence that they all knew to pat. If there was any doubt, they were united behind the dam's leader. The fishermen's unity was also strengthened by the assembling of fathers and their adult sons who lived dispersed in separate dwellings in the village, where uxorilocal residence is the norm.[7]

Throughout the fabrication of the fish traps (*mata*) the leader continued to provide the stimulus to work by issuing instructions at dawn. These instructions continued to follow an exemplary sequence as follows: first, gathering bark (mata) for the body of the trap; second, collecting fine vines (*teha*) to lash the parts of the trap together; third, seeking out buruti palms and extracting the stiff ribs (*ixohi*) from the fronds; fourth, affixing these to the bark cylinder; and fifth, and finally, fixing a reinforcing belt (*eoko*) around the trap.[8] Gathering the materials for these traps was perhaps even more arduous than weir-building. Whereas strong tree trunks abounded in the forest immediately adjacent to the weir, buruti palm groves were confined to pockets of the forest; the fine vines needed for lashing the parts of the trap together were harder to find than the abundant thick ones used for the weir; and, above all, the mata was sparsely distributed in patches of dark-soiled forest preferred for corn cultivation. And even when the men successfully located a tree the bark had then to be scored and then prised delicately off so that a cylinder remained intact.

Once all the elements had been assembled, the spirit of vigorous teamwork that had dominated since the men's arrival gradually transformed into one of undifferentiated fellowship; men sat together, chatted and joked, always with their hands occupied. This approximately week-long period spent making the traps was referred to as 'sitting down with the traps', which evokes the seated posture of the handiwork and implies the transition from the 'first moon' of vertical construction work to the 'second moon' spent 'lying down to rest'. Just as social differentiation between leaders and followers fell from importance after the weir was complete, so the sequencing of tasks ceased to order time. Once this second moon was underway there would be no more specific collective tasks to fulfil, beyond checking the traps and smoking the fish, and instead of waking to specific dawn injunctions, the men would stir each morning to the same simple call – 'let's bathe' (*bakuha*).

The traps were finished by the twelfth day after our arrival at Maxikyawina, each wrapped with a thick reinforcing belt around the middle of their bark ribcages and then transversally pierced with a bar that would impale the fish as they were sucked into the trap. This bar would also serve as a handle for the fishermen pulling the traps out from their underwater positions. The traps were stacked carefully under the shade of trees so as to remain cool and invisible until the next morning. And so at 5AM on our thirteenth day at Maxikyawina, old Xayu-atokwe evoked the transition to seclusion that men would undergo that day: 'we are dawning, the edible ones' captors will penetrate for the first time and then we will lie down to rest'. Upon waking, each man carried his own traps to the bank next to the weir. One trap at a time, he carried them along the weir's walkway, climbed down into the water to the first trap position and pierced the woven mat to forcefully push the trap into the opening. Immediately upon the traps' penetration the fishermen entered a new phase: they would finally lie down to rest in the encampment as the traps did their work autonomously at the weir.

Figure 1.5 On the day the traps penetrate, men carry their newly crafted traps to their positions.

The Traps Penetrate and the Fishermen 'Lie down to Rest'

The men explained to me that the trap entered the weir 'like a penis penetrating for the first time' and 'like a virgin having sex for the first time'. It was for this reason that all the trap owners were now 'heating up' (*wiwatatena*), or 'with blood' (*kadena*). They were, they told me, in the same state as teenage boys are after they have lost their virginity and their sexual partner has subsequently bled. Connecting the Enawenê's own simile of penetration and their self-identification with the traps: it is as if men's traps were their own penises, since the traps' penetration thrusts their owners into a seclusion state. Observing lifecycle seclusions ensures people's health in the future, and failure to observe them is blamed for frailty and loss of vigour. Here it was not the men themselves but their traps that risked becoming listless and lazy and failing to actively capture fish if their owners were careless about observing seclusion mores. The fishermen made the analogy with adolescent seclusion explicitly. They said that it was because they were 'heating up' following the traps' insertion that they would fast for the first three days, refraining from eating any of the fish that were caught in the traps. The analogy between men's subjection to the blood of fish and to the blood of women was also implicit in myriad practices that received no explicit commentary and which continued throughout the second moon, as the fishermen acted on their own bodies, thoughts and moods in order to propitiate the traps. I shall now explore both the explicit and tacit aspects of the fishermen's seclusion for and from the traps.

Recall that fishermen said the traps were Dokowyi's body. Dokowyi's body is present in the trap's morphology, notably in the bark cylinder, which is said to be his ribcage. As fishermen pushed the traps through the mesh they addressed Dokowyi, making a 'Brrrrr!' sound with their lips and then speaking to the trap. Being out of earshot on the bank I afterwards asked what had been said. The men told me that they exhorted their traps: 'be sure to capture your prey and not merely to look idly on'. Since fishermen explicitly likened themselves to Datamale, it follows that their relationship with the traps should be paternal, a bond of substance existing between the traps and the men who were their makers. This is indeed suggested by the imperative that each trap owner should make and then handle only his own traps, and then in the ways the fishermen's bodily and affective states are held responsible for their own traps' efficacy. The fishermen now called themselves 'trap owners' (*mata wayate nawe*), self-consciously defining themselves by their relationship with their traps. Inside the group, this self-designation largely replaced the previous one, *Maxikyawina wayate nawe*, which emphasised their collective belonging at the river they dammed together. Indeed, men now lived for their traps: warnings of the traps' 'paralysis' (*makanase*) became a constant refrain in the encampment as men fasted, purified their bodies, observed the taboo on water hitting hot embers and participated in blessings, offerings and exchange conventions to propitiate the traps.

Returning to events on the day of the traps' insertion now, by 9AM the traps had all been inserted and the trap owners returned to the encampment where their sons and nephews had been busy making small pans of a bland drink. This was a special drink, made just once during our stay and never in the village and described as a 'substitute' (*ketera ewene-kole* or *katadale*) for the hot manioc and corn porridge called *ketera*, which is drunk nightly in the village. The boys who accompanied their fathers, maternal uncles (in the case of fatherless children) or their future fathers-in-law, ranged from toddlerhood to puberty. These boys would only become trap owners once they had been initiated into Yankwa, following puberty. Men made sure they were accompanied to the dam by a son, son-in-law or nephew who was just shy of puberty and thus, while not strong enough to be a trap owner himself, was capable of taking charge of the domestic tasks involved in encampment life. These helpers gathered the fish handed up to them on the weir, collected firewood, cared for younger siblings and masticated manioc bread to make the everyday drink, a weakly fermented manioc-based drink called *oloniti*. They boasted that their oloniti would be almost as sweet as that made by their mothers. Indeed, because these boys took on typical feminine tasks unselfconsciously and with zeal, they looked to me like stand-in wives as they responded swiftly to their elders' calls for 'oloniti!' when the latter returned thirsty from the dam, or instructed their younger brothers to 'stoke the fire under the oloniti!' or chided them 'wear your flip-flops, the bees will sting you!'.

The substitute ketera that the boys had readied for the trap owner's return was just manioc flour added to boiling water. It was bland, grey, granular, lumpy and very unappetising – nothing like true ketera, which is smooth, viscous and intensely sweet. Almost none of this deliberately ersatz drink was actually imbibed by men. Rather, it passed between the men of separate clans, who are deliberately mixed at the dam, as an offering to the spirit masters of the fish (*Yakairiti*). All the trap owners gathered within a few metres of one another in front of the single house that had already been built, and each man offered a calabash of this drink to every other man in turn, excluding those of his own clan.

In the dialogues exchanged as calabashes passed between them, men promised to transport their catch to the village in order to share it with the Yakairiti.

The Yakairiti, who are the masters of fish and other resources, were said to 'hold onto/hold back' (*otokone*) the fish, preventing them from entering the traps if they were not satisfied by such offerings. Token offerings of manioc drinks, salt and fish were a taste of the abundant feasts that were promised to Yakairiti upon their return to the village with the fishermen. These promises persuaded these covetous spirits to guide the shoals of fish towards the traps. Upon our arrival at the encampment two weeks earlier, the elderly leader Xayu-atokwe had offered parcels of potassium salt to the Yakairiti in whispered tones of convocation. Now this substitute ketera was offered. The final offering would be made when the fast was broken with the sharing of the traps' catch, three days later. At this point the fishermen acknowledged the alliance with the Yakairiti that was crucial to their endeavour. All of these exchanges between men, of manioc, fish and salt, were described as *hesayliti*, which is the same word used to describe offerings that are made to the Yakairiti for the release of the stolen vitality of a kin member who is gravely ill. As we will see in Chapter 5, offerings of food are the major medium for the Enawenê's constant cosmic diplomacy with Yakairiti, on which both prosperity and health depend. These offerings create an alliance between fishermen and Yakairiti through the promise of future feasts. In the next chapter I will return to the particular character of the fishermen's alliance with the Yakairiti during the dam-fishing period, but for now I will continue with the sequence of activities that follows the traps' insertion.

At 5:30AM the next morning men awoke to the call 'let's bathe!' (bakuha). They picked fresh-smelling leaves on their way to the weir and when they pulled up each of their traps to check for fish and to knock out accumulated flotsam, they rubbed these leaves around the lip of the traps and whispered their encouragements to Dokowyi again. Although the traps do exert suction, fish could be seen getting close to the traps only to swim back upstream, especially, men said, in the first days when their fear of the traps was strongest. The fish had to desire to enter the traps in order to be captured. This was why the trap owners rubbed the traps' openings with leaves whose smell was said to be attractive to the fish. The leaves they used were the kind women wear to cover their pelvic region when they bathe, tucking a few of them under the palm nut bead chains they always wear around their hips. Perhaps these fragrant leaves are chosen, both for women's modesty and traps' deadly mouths, because of their ability to neutralise the smell of blood, vagina, semen and fish, which are said to share the same 'bloody' smell (*ede*). Or perhaps the point is to liken the trap to a seductive vagina that gains the capacity to lure the fish-penis?[9] What is clear is the androgynous and highly sexed symbolic character of the traps and in turn the necessity for human sexuality to be absent in order to favour the coupling of fish and trap. That afternoon Xayu-atokwe instructed his teenage grandson, a lad called Xayu whose wife was then heavily pregnant with their first child, to seek out and dig up the root of a purifying vine called *mehkali* so that the trap owners could wash their bodies with it. In the village, the juice of this vine is used to bathe teenagers and new mothers before they emerge from seclusion. The trap owners who liken themselves to teenage boys in seclusion during the first three days after the traps' insertion also bathed in mehkali before entering the water to check the traps, in the afternoon of the day they were first inserted. They each macerated a piece of vine with water to create a lather, which they rubbed into their hair, faces and whole bodies, in order, they said, to get rid of the smell of vagina, which lingered on them from sexual encounters prior to leaving the village. This suggests that once the traps enter the weir, their owners must purify their bodies in order to establish a state of abstinence or neo-virginity, which favours the coupling of fish and trap.

Indeed, in line with the absence of sex but the explosion of virtual sexuality, women and sex were absent presences in the encampment: they were omnipresent in banter, in dream analysis, in symbolic acts undertaken to fertilise the traps, in the feminine domestic work that men and boys undertook, and in men's craftwork, which kept them busy, contemplatively making things for women back home. Together, this generated an overwhelming emphasis on fertility. Let me take dream analysis first, which it seemed to me was more avidly practised at the dam than was usual in the village. When one man reported to us all that he had dreamed about helping a woman to carry her manioc basket back from the garden – an act immediately understood by everyone to imply a covert sexual liaison – the dream was said to augur the imminent capture of shoals of fish. This dream, which connected sex and harvest, was therefore taken to be a virtual experience that the traps would consummate physically, by capturing fish.

Masculine banter revolving around themes of women and sex was also a stated ideal. Men said that the 'traps desired' (*mata esane*) talk of sex and women, as well as happiness and high spirits in general. As men gathered honey they joked about the different shapes of women's vaginas and their girlfriends' particular tastes for specific honey varieties.[10] On other occasions, femininity was evoked by men's necessary adoption of feminine tasks. When men wanted to drink their fish soup thickened with corn flour, they had to pound the seed themselves. Three men pounded corn seed together in a miniature standing hollow log mortar (a portable version of the mortars used by women in the village). The mortar was comically small and the men's technique hilariously clumsy as they tried to move their hips up and down as women do in an exaggerated version of the gyrating rhythm, which men always identify as inherently sexual. Most of the ingredients flew up in the air and ended up scattered over the ground as the men laughed at their inadequate performance of femininity.

After the traps' insertion men also spent much of their time crafting tools and bead chains that were destined for their wives and lovers back in the village. They crafted flat baskets (*tohe*), fine sieves (*atwa*), manioc graters (*timale*) and buruti palm nut bead chains (*hoxiru*), as well as doing some feather work for themselves. Craftwork joined the adult fishermen in contemplative co-presence and provided ample opportunity for boys' approaching puberty to be apprenticed in the skills required of married men, among which basketry and bead-making are paramount. If ideologically speaking, men 'lie down to rest' after the traps penetrate, in fact, they sit down to craft. While their bodies may be passive compared to the hefty work of construction, their hands are busy feeling their way through intricate work. As well as keeping absent women in mind, the fishermen's absorption in craftwork is consistent with their seclusion for the traps, since craftwork is a major pastime during lifecycle seclusions in the village. Young Enawenê people are expected to sit and silently make the body ornaments that they will don on emergence from seclusion, having discarded those they previously wore. Ethnographers working in Northwest Amazonia and the Xingu have noted that repetitive and meditative forms of handiwork like bead-making and weaving are valued as intellectual practices. As such they play a central role in the self-education and moral cultivation of young people, which is a major goal of seclusion.[11]

Since men stressed the importance of abstinence and purification and reintroduced women and sex as objects of talk and contemplation, it surprised me, then, that men's wives could also decide to take up their paddles and journey to their husbands' encampments 'seeking fish and seeking penis' (*kohase atawene, talaseti atawene*) as they said. Indeed, as I would realise too late, the conventional nature of such women's visits was one of the justifications for the appropriateness of my travelling to the dam along with twelve men. The reason I held onto was that everyone recognised the dam as the place of Enawenê culture par excellence, and thus it was a necessary site for an anthropologist's research, but it was naive of me to be shocked when I returned to the village and was suspected of having had sex with some of the men. Most Enawenê men and women thought this was simply inevitable. It took me and my hosts at Maxikyawina some time to quash the rumours after our return in May. In fact, one of the reasons I had returned early to the village was that I was exhausted, not only by hunger due to the lack of fish and the strains this placed on my relationship with my hosts, who were obliged to share scarce food with me, but by the bantering male sociality for which I served as resident sex object.

Putting my own position aside, fishermen freely recognised that women's visits broke with the imperative of abstinence for the traps. But such visits were nonetheless quite routine. In both 2008 and 2009 the men damming the rivers Joaquim Rios and Nambikwara received long visits from their wives and people's commentaries suggested that such cheeky expeditions had long been part of dam tradition.[12] If women's desire for fish and for their husbands was such that they had the determination to make the journey then they had the freedom to take up their paddles. For the fishermen the slippage between the ideal of abstinence and that of consummated desire did not seem to cause disquiet either. Perhaps this affirms the emphasis on fertility during this time, which conforms to certain boundaries but also overspills them.

Through the initial communal fast, simultaneous baths in mehkali, hours spent in seated craftwork in quiet co-presence and ribald banter, the fishermen became a community of substance. The men were unified by their shared diet, mores and the cultivation of a harmonious and convivial mood. This is a collective seclusion. When one man had a bad dream everyone joined him in the morning to wash with the purifying vine; and when one man's toddler whinged, whoever was nearest the child pacified him with a piece of fish. The traps were said to desire exchange and conviviality, and to be paralysed by vexation and stinginess. The traps' susceptibility to the society of men effectively compelled openness among fellow fishermen.

When the traps were inserted into the weir, having felled and carried trees to construct the weir, and then trekked the forest in search of bark, men were looking thin. They told me they would soon be filling out as they finally lay down to rest. As well as implying all the prescriptions associated with seclusion, lying down was about the regeneration and hearty eating that would build up men's bodies and make children grow to the subsequent wonderment of their mothers. The simple imperative 'let's bathe!' served as the everyday euphemism for emptying the traps, since, like hunters worldwide, the fishermen never presume the presence of their prey and avoid any direct mention of them. But bathing is more than a convenient euphemism; it is recognised as a defining feature of encampment life, which has vitalising and regenerative qualities of its own. This was clear in the fishermen's jokes that their early morning baths likened them to teenage girls, who always rally their friends to bathe in the cold streams surrounding the Enawenê's hilltop village before the dawn mists have cleared. They remarked that just as teenage girls grew vigorous by bathing in the cold, so their own frequent baths in the waters by the weir would strengthen them.

While the fishermen lived a different kind of life together from that of hosts and women back home, and ate different foods, their bodies changed and in some real way they became strange to hosts and women back in the village. The men commented most of all on their attainment of an ideal of strength and corpulence, but they also deliberately lost the body ornaments that men in the village never go without. Garters that usually defined their biceps and calf muscles were said to be carried away by the river's current during the rigours of weir-building. These garters are woven by women and so the fishermen had to wait for their return to the village to replace them. The fishermen also stopped decorating their bodies with annatto dye, trimming their fringes or shaving their sideburns. Again, these were women's grooming tasks. Their shaggy fringes and sideburns would distinguish their bodies from those of the hosts. But these superficial changes to the body are indexical of deeper changes, which are harder to fathom. Like teenage boys and girls and new parents, who are secluded within the village's longhouses, the fishermen are excluded by their temporary exile from the routine elements that characterise village life: public performances, gardening work, reciprocal conjugal services and general affinal civility in and outside of the house. Anticipating return, young Xayu told me 'when first we return to the village and we drink ketera, it tastes bitter to us; it is too sweet for our palate'. Agreeing that ketera was bitter-sweet, other men chimed in that it would also take some time before they understood the rapid speech of women. These comments about the ephemeral difficulties of readapting to village life can be taken as affirmations about the transformative nature of seclusion, which is harnessed for its social and cosmological efficacy in most Amazonian societies.[13]

Fasting and Feasting

Fasting and feasting scruples suffused the whole fishing endeavour. As I have already mentioned, when they inserted the traps, the fishermen likened themselves to teenage boys who were 'heating up' after sexual intercourse had rendered them vulnerable to a woman's blood. A major aspect of any seclusion is the exclusion of fish from the diet. Indeed, fishermen said that it was because they were like teenage boys who were 'with blood' that they would not eat the first fish caught in the traps. This taboo on eating fish lasted three days at Maxikyawina in 2009. During these three days, instead of being the property of the man whose traps had caught them, the fish were threaded onto a stick and passed – quite deliberately and publicly – between several hands until they reached old Xayu-atokwe, who in turn gave them publicly to the other elderly man in the encampment, Kamikye-atokwe, who was the one to carefully smoke them. These fish were systematically shared out at the breaking of the fast on day three. This ended the three day 'heating up' phase, during which the fishermen explicitly likened themselves to teenage boys.

There were only three fish to share at the breaking of the fast in 2009, but the rule was that every man and child present (and even I) had to taste a small piece of each species. The mood was bombastically celebratory, as if we were performing the way fish should be shared thereafter and celebrating the plentiful meals that were to come. Once broken, the fast did not give way to unburdened feasting. This was what I had come to expect from all the talk before we left the village of the bliss of resting, eating plenty and returning to the village fattened on fish. On a brief visit to Olowina's weir in 2008 while the fish were shoaling into the traps, as they should, I saw men's meals of whole fish, and the fishermen and their children did return to the village healthily fattened. However, fish yields from the dams have diminished since the 1990s, and in 2009 there was an unprecedented dearth. We ate no fish at all on many days and on most days someone would economise by making one pan of thin fish soup from which everyone received a small calabash. As I revealed in the Introduction, the solution found by the leaders at Olowina and Andowina was to buy fish from an aquafarm in Juína. In Chapter 6 I will discuss the implications of the fishing dams' failure in the era of hydroelectric damming. Here I merely want to note that 2009 turned out to be a year of dramatic change, although the men could not know this until weeks after the traps had gone in. Day after day they expected the shoals to descend and worried about the Yakairiti's disposition towards them and attempted to work against the traps' paralysis, even replacing perfectly good traps in which little to no fish had been captured with ones they newly crafted. All I want to note at this point is that when there is plenty, as there should be, countervailing ideals of restraint and hearty eating are not in conflict, people can eat well and also smoke many fish for the hosts every day. This is how it should be at the fishing dams and in 2009 men somehow managed to retain their joviality, banter and generosity despite a mounting undercurrent of uncertainty and unease.

After the breaking of the fast the consumption of fish followed a particular sharing regime. Trap owners swapped fish like for like: a fat fish of one kind with someone else's similarly fat fish of the same species. When a man's trap yielded, the fish was passed up to a young helper stood atop the weir with his basket poised. Then the trap owner would empty the basket out onto a bed of leaves on the bank and give his helper a couple of fish to swap with others immediately. The fish swapped were those destined for the family's meal; the majority of the fish, which was destined to be smoked for the hosts, was kept by the owners of the traps in which it was caught. There were, therefore, disparities in the amounts of smoked fish accumulated by each trap owner, depending on the number of trap positions he had taken on and the efficacy of his traps, but because of the swapping regime there were no such disparities in the fishermen's and their children's meals, because the obligation to swap implied that it was only possible to eat whole fish on days when some had been caught in traps belonging to more than one man. This simple swapping therefore institutionalised commensality and a morality based on self-restraint by asserting that fish is always destined for others.[14] This is also affirmed by the collective nickname, 'eaters of entrails' (*enaxi hwale*), which the fishermen used self-consciously once fish-trapping was underway. This expressed the ideal that fishermen should live off the sweet, smoky cakes made by rubbing the fish's oily entrails into manioc flour and compacting the mixture inside a leaf wrapping before baking it in the ashes of the fire. This was hardly an ascetic diet, since the cakes are rich, sweet and highly appreciated. Nonetheless, by repeating this nickname the fishermen seemed to remind themselves that fish were to be saved for others.

Conclusion

Dam fishing is a form of alimentary predation that has deep affinities with agriculture. At the simplest level this is because dam fishing captures migratory, herbivorous species whose habits are in tune with the hydrological cycle, which must also prevail over agriculture. The Enawenê elaborate and refine this basic affinity in various ways: by planting their manioc gardens early so that the greatest fish and manioc surpluses come into step; by employing the same material culture for fishing and agriculture and through the kindred habits and routines of manioc and fish harvests; finally there is the matching care with which fish and manioc are smoke-dried and stored for future consumption by others. The Enawenê are not unique in elaborating on the complementarity between intensive agriculture and damming and other trapping techniques that bring in a plentiful fish harvest. It is from Tukano-speaking groups that the most detailed information on fish trapping and its symbolism comes and there we find an elaborate mythological trope centring on a war with fish. I have explored the extent to which Enawenê dam fishing could be understood in these terms, which certainly fit with their origin story in which a grieving father builds a dam to avenge the murder of his son and then tricks the fish towards their demise. Nonetheless I argued that vengeance is suppressed in the practice of dam fishing, both by the Enawenê's confidence that fish are fated to serve as their prey, and in the whole suite of practices designed to prepare and seduce the fish into giving themselves up to the swirling current. Further, if vengeance is linked to aggression, then the fishermen's whole ethos and attitude is the obverse of vengeful: it is based socially on humour and openness, individually on contemplativeness, self-awareness and restraint, and on attentiveness and even indulgence towards the traps and their prey.

The question of the ethos of dam fishing has been central to this chapter, which I entitled 'from mastery to subjection' to draw attention to the set of contrasts that prevail over the two moons through which Enawenê fishermen first build the weir and make the traps and then put their dual technology to work. In the first moon, the fishermen enact the mastery of their cultural hero, Datamale, by following an archetypal series of construction acts. They throw their whole bodies into this task of forging the separation between land and water and then making the traps that will breach it. This construction phase is rigorously segmented and sequenced, just as ceremonial activities are in the village. Following the sequence established by their leader but known to all mature men, the team of fishermen are also differentiated, with young men taking their lead from those with longer experience.

Once the traps are in place, on the other hand, mastery gives way to an attitude that I gloss as subjection. The idiom 'lying down to rest' emphasises men's physical passivity and they now spend their time in the encampment, which is at a remove from the dam. Instead of engineering a physical technology, they embrace a set of mental and social techniques in order to generate the convivial and fertile atmosphere that is desired by the traps. These technologies of the self are intangible but they require no less sustained effort than the onerous construction work. Like the dam's structure, which may break in the current, this individual and communal cultivation of mood, atmosphere and attitude may also fall short. If the traps become 'paralysed', new ones will need to be made. Generating a positive cast of mind through craftwork, creating joyous and energetic communication through banter, achieving self-restraint and generating sociability through swapping and sharing all become the major tasks of communal life. Time, where before it was sequenced, becomes amorphous: defined merely by the morning, noon and nightly bath, the imperative to prepare the fish for smoking and then to continue with one's open-ended craftwork oriented to faraway women.

Enawenê dam fishing, in sum, is a predatory endeavour involving an exceptional degree of mastery. The building of the veritable 'technopolis' – the stalwart dam and the sturdy smokehouses – which becomes the infrastructure for the relationship between men and traps, whose channels are propitious moods, talk and corporeal dispositions, and whose failure – a backsliding into inertia and inanimacy – is perennially threatened. Humanoid, androgynous traps are the nexus for a meeting between men and fish, water and land, humans and their heroic ancestors, and fishermen and their spirit allies the Yakairiti. What the Enawenê told me was that weirs and traps were built through direct contact with ancestral power, a power that they appropriated to themselves by following an archetypal sequence of construction acts defined by Datamale in the origin times, and which they also drew upon in their efficacious incantations. While the fishermen were very explicit about the translation of myth into life at the dam, the shifting references to blood, menstruation and seclusion were often implicit, and how they occurred to men as they rubbed leaves over the rims of traps or washed their bodies with the foam of a purifying vine remained inherently mercurial and mysterious. Was Dokowyi, the day he was murdered by the fish-people, a teenage boy flouting seclusion and thus liable to be taken by his prey? The myth does not say this and it is probably futile to seek confirmation in myth for associations between fishermen and fertile women, or teenage boys who are for the first time thrust into the presence of blood. Nonetheless what emerges from my analysis is that the man-fish-trap nexus enchains abstinence to fertility, vulnerability to vitality, propitious openness to exerted boundary maintenance, and danger to predatory prowess. That is why annual dam-fishing expeditions imply an annual collective male seclusion.

At their dams, Enawenê fishermen live a version of the widespread philosophy that taking life implies 'the risk, and almost the necessity of giving oneself as a return, of falling prey' (Valeri 2000: 320). For the Enawenê, this paradox between mastery and subjection is embodied by Dokowyi, the masterful fisherman who himself falls prey – or is he martyred to originate the technologies that will avenge him? Dokowyi's dangerous and propitious position is shared by living fishermen once their traps are in place. This is a position akin to that of the shaman, who mediates between levels of the universe in a cosmos in which human vitality is perpetually at risk of depredation by other animate beings. This is also the position of patients in the presence of blood. In my analysis, it is in order to negate Dokowyi's fate that fishermen forge and strenuously maintain separations between the dam and the encampment, between water and fire, and between men and fish. Visual, olfactory and tactile contact is limited to the greatest degree possible: fish must not see or smell their real human predators, only their attractive stand-ins, the pleasantly scented, seductive traps, and men seem to avoid touching the fish, threading it onto sticks, into baskets and onto leaf mats and manipulating it during cookery via elaborate flattened baskets.

Predation is probably never a tale of unalloyed heroism and mastery. Hunting ethics commonly include elements of asceticism, such as linguistic discretion, alimentary restraint and sexual abstinence, which are all in evidence in the Enawenê's fishing encampments.[15] Eating entrails and abstaining from the first prey are particularly widespread hunting mores. What is exceptional about Enawenê dam fishing is the scale and intensity with which predation ethics are elaborated and collectivised. This matches, quite simply, the monumental scale of this predatory endeavour. The second exceptional quality is the thoroughgoing parallel established between dam fishing and lifecycle seclusions – the bleeding of fish and of women. This points to a basic recognition of the interdependence of human, manioc and fish fertility, which is also evident in Yankwa's temporal unfolding over the annual cycle, which coordinates the rhythms of these species' regeneration.

Seclusion always exists in dialectic with performance and display.[16] In seclusion the body and subjectivity are moulded. Inner capacities can later be dramatically revealed. For the Enawenê this happens when the fishermen return to the village. Back in the central arena their decorated bodies will once again perform for, and exchange with, hosts and women. We will see in the next chapter that the fishermen's return with Datamale's smoked catch inaugurates a riot of fecundity – the coming together of families of fish and manioc, and of people and their flutes. The hosts, women and children who have remained in the village eagerly await the fishermen. The latter boast that as soon as they return, women will leave aside the hosts (their erstwhile lovers) to take up with the exotic, strong fishermen, who come laden with fish and additional gifts of bead chains, basketry and manioc graters, which women value very highly. Indeed the buruti palm nut bead belts fishermen craft at the weir were often called 'vagina payment' (*akoseti toli*), since they were men's most seductive gifts and women's most valued possessions. As we will now see, the fishermen's return is a fecund reunification of spouses and lovers, and manioc and fish, which is life-increasing in every register.

Notes

1. These three fish the Enawenê call *balako* (Leporinus frederici), *hoxikya* (Brycon sp) and *kayale* (Myleus sp).
2. Called *ohã* by the Enawenê-nawe, Costa Júnior identified this grass as *Gymnopogo foliosus* (Costa Júnior 1995a: 128).
3. This applies at least to the Paresi (Mendes dos Santos 1994: 55), Nambikwara, Kamayura (Oberg 1953: 19–20, 91), Kuikuro (Carneiro 1983: 81–88), Mehinaku (Gregor 1977: 15–16), Kayapó (Dreyfus 1963: 27) and Aweti (Vanzolini Figueiredo 2010: 204). Mendes dos Santos (2001: 103) also commented on the Enawenê's 'premature' planting of manioc and corn, which he also understands as responding to the exigencies of their fishing calendar.
4. Baure people constructed wooden weirs erected atop an earthwork base to trap fish in the inundated savannahs when the floodwaters receded. Outlets funnelled into artificial ponds allowed the fish to be stored live until they were wanted (Erickson 2000). Heckenberger mentions a Kuikuru weir that sounds remarkably similar to an Enawenê dam: 'a tall (3-6 m) community-built weir several hundred metres in length and containing over 40 conical itaka traps. During high-water fish runs, hundreds of kilogrammes of fish could be harvested in a single day' (Heckenberger 1998 cit. Carneiro 1986). In the Xingu region, Basso (1975: 38) and Gregor (1985: 76) also mention the use of large funnel-shaped baskets held in small weirs built across streams by the Kalapalo and Mehinaku. Unfortunately there has been no detailed documentation of these Upper Xingu dams' construction or their significance. By contrast, in Northwest Amazonia a whole suite of trapping methods have been documented in great detail by anthropologists and native peoples (e.g. Cabalzar 2005; Calderón-Corredor 2011; Cabalzar and Candotti 2013). The most impressive are labyrinth fish fences, known in the region's Tukanoan lingua franca as *cacuri*, which captivated the Europeans who first explored its waterways 150 years ago (Calderón-Corredor 2011: 27). These traps are built above waterfalls in fast flowing rivers and have their openings downstream. They slow the river's current directly below them to guide the fish towards a V-shaped fence, which opens into an enclosure behind. The fish approach the fence as they migrate upstream and are imprisoned in the enclosure, from which the force of the current prevents their escape (see Cabalzar 2005: 309–10). Peoples of the region also build dams like the Enawenê's, in which conical basket traps are inserted into a weir structure (see S. Hugh-Jones 1979: 86; Reichel-Dolmatoff 1985; Chernela 1993:100–102; Cabalzar 2005: 310–11;). Although structurally similar, there remains a crucial difference: whereas the Enawenê capture fish on their way downstream after spawning, NWA traps usually capture fish as they travel upstream, on their way to spawn.
5. Belaunde (2006: 218–19); see also Brown (1985: 65) and Rivas (2004: 15). For the same reason, menstruation is incompatible with shamanism, because, like hunting,

it entails a risky openness to other beings in the cosmos (see S. Hugh-Jones 1979: 125–26; Clastres 1998: 10–13; Fausto 2007: 505).

6. It will be difficult for inexperienced men to make enough traps to have more than two positions, while a more senior man will probably want three or four. This all depends as much on a man's keenness and disposition as on his age. Bear in mind that each transect contains trap positions at three underwater levels. Making twelve traps will be impossible for a young, inexperienced man.

7. In all these ways the encampment resembles a form of social organisation that is very common in the small, predominantly patrilocal and internally cohesive settlements that predominate in so-called 'Dravidian Amazonia', where co-residents are united vis-à-vis surrounding foreigners. This kind of organisation precisely contrasts with the populous, internally differentiated villages that the Enawenê, like other central Brazilians, choose to live in most of the time (see Viveiros de Castro and Fausto 1993).

8. The traps are named after the tree from whose bark their body is made (Amaioua guianensis Aubl., according to Costa Júnior 1995a: 140). Each fisherman made between six and twelve traps, enough to fill the two to four positions he had been allotted at three underwater levels.

9. Northwest Amazonians are explicit about the seductiveness of their labyrinth fish fences; they say that they appear to fish as women with their legs open, which is why the fish are eager to touch, explore and enter them (Calderón-Corredor 2011: 89, 99). Mehinaku also liken fish traps to vaginas, which capture the penis-fish (Gregor 1985: 75–76).

10. On the eroticism of honey in Amazonia, see Viveiros de Castro (1986: 353) and Lévi-Strauss (1966: 42).

11. For example, learning basketry, bead-making and feather work was a major feature of Barasana youths' education, and like Enawenê fishermen, Barasana neophytes were explicitly compared to menstruating women during the seclusion phase of Yurupary rites. They bathed in cold water and observed a diet designed to purify and strengthen their bodies; their food intake was controlled by shamans and they observed prohibitions around contact with fire and water (Hugh-Jones 1979: 86–93). On the role of craftwork in seclusion see also S. Hugh-Jones (2009: 49) and Gregor (1977: 231).

12. As I have said, hosts also built a weir immediately upstream of the village, becoming thereby 'a little bit Yankwa as well' (see Chapter 2) and as such beholden to the ideal of sexual abstinence for the traps. This sat alongside the convention that hosts would take advantage of the absence of the majority of men to 'steal' (*ahakaha*, which has a playful more than pejorative connotation) sexual encounters with others' wives.

13. This point has been made in Amazonian contexts by S. Hugh-Jones (2009); Viveiros de Castro (2002); Roscoe (2001: 292) and Conklin (2001: 151–52), among others.

14. There may also be a cosmological dimension to the obligation to swap, although I admit that this is a speculative leap. It obviously meant that neither men nor their children ever ate fish that were caught in their own traps. Might this be an avoidance of the self-closure implied in eating from the trap with which a man is so closely identified? In a more abstract sense, like the taboo on water hitting hot coals, might this prescription be understood as another means of managing the risky identification between men and their traps and the blurring of aquatic and terrestrial dominions?

15. See, for example, Baldus (1952); Lizot (1976: 191); Lévi-Strauss (1966: 121); Valeri and Hoskins (2002: 287); Stolze-Lima (1999). All of these authors refer to terrestrial hunting, which dominates the literature on forest peoples. There are no doubt myriad other parallels to Enawenê fishing mores to be drawn with sea-faring hunters.
16. See Gregor (1970, 1977: 211); Journet (1995: 266–67); Viveiros de Casto (2002: 77) for other Amazonianist elaborations of this point.

Figure 2.1 Yankwa's fishermen returning from the dams decked out in fresh palm fronds and mud.

2

The Fishermen Return 'Like Yakairiti'

In 2008 I had been in Halataikwa for only three months when I witnessed Yankwa's return. I had already seen the excellent ethnographic film made about Yankwa, *The Spirits' Banquet* (Valadão 1995), and so I knew the fishermen would return disguised as Yakairiti and that there would be a dramatic confrontation. Nonetheless, I asked people what I could expect to happen, because I wanted to hear what people had to say about this climactic event's significance. Frustratingly, I was simply told that I would soon see for myself. Rather than a typical reluctance in the face of the anthropologist's tiresome requests for explanation, this seemed to be an insistence that this was to be a fundamentally visual spectacle. Indeed, in this chapter I will show that this return involves weeks of 'backstage' planning and preparation by the hosts and women to prepare the spatial architecture of the village for the fishermen's arrival, as well as last minute costume and make-up sessions by both residents and incomers. The village arena has to be made into a stage set to receive the fishermen, and ornaments and props have to be fabricated. Hosts also rehearsed for the fishermen's arrival over a month with a daily warm-up spectacle that helped to prime the audience of women and children for the arrival, which was increasingly eagerly anticipated.

Yankwa's return is compelling theatre for spectating women, children and anthropologists, and makes good cinema for outsiders too. The theatrical quality of the scenes of return makes for a vivid narrative, but they are much better viewed on film. Indeed these scenes compose the climax of all the films made about Yankwa to date.[1] Apart from making this single day in Yankwa's extended process irresistible to film-makers, the importance of visuality and first-hand experience also reflects what many anthropologists have singled out as the essence of ritual; namely, that its potency lies in action – in what happens, rather than what may be said or signified about the events.[2] Anthropologists working in villages like those of the Enawenê, with their open central arenas to which every encircling house has 'a front row seat' (Heckenberger 2005: 294), have often resorted to theatrical metaphors.[3] Thomas Gregor was so impressed by the spectacular and staged nature of Mehinaku life that he entitled his first ethnography *The Drama of Everyday Life* (1977) and explored the ways people met the challenge of forging spaces of concealment, privacy and intimacy in this panoptic space.

Why are film-makers so captivated by the fishermen's return and why was I similarly told that visioning the spectacle would provide all the answers I needed? I think the explanation has to do with the self-evident quality of the unfolding action. One need not understand the songs and dialogues, or even know anything much about the Enawenê, to appreciate a plot that is revealed through an aesthetic process. As we watch on film or in person, what we see is the fishermen docking at the port with blackened, clay-smeared bodies and wild green palm frond cloaks. Everything about their appearance and behaviour suggests that they are potentially dangerous to their hosts. Gradually their threatening appearance and odd bodily affects – strange cries, hunched posture, and slow, eerie style of motion – are muted as they come to resemble the hosts. This occurs as they are guided through a cosmically aligned space and as they are lavished first with a warm, heavy drink called *ketera* and later with a cool, refreshing drink called *oloniti*, along with potassium salt and mountains of manioc breads. Wild, bodily and affectively transfigured men come up from the water and out of the night, to be heated by an intense fire and given copious quantities of cooked foods. Any observer could grasp that this is a process of gradual taming and, if the observer knew that these incomers were said to be 'like Yakairiti' – perverse subterranean spirits who are masters of the fish with which men's boats are loaded – and that to see the Yakairiti with one's own eyes is to have a brush with death, then they would also understand that the lethal agency of these spirits was being domesticated in a risky and highly charged cosmic drama. While this is no doubt a fair overview of the plot, this interpretation does not account for the complex temporal structure of the fishermen's return, which is defined by repetition and variation. In order to see how the metamorphosis of the incoming spirit-men is achieved, it is necessary to look closely at action sequences.

I will start by asking what it means to say that the returning fishermen are 'like Yakairiti', which is how they were described by other members of the community. This is not a simple claim about men embodying, and thus making visible, spirits who are normally invisible. In fact, I will show that it is more accurately a claim about disembodiment; the disguise that fishermen add to their bodies begins a process of extroversion of a Yakairiti part, which they fully embody as they trap fish faraway at the dam. Both Enawenê discourse and the action sequences that occur upon return suggest that a trinity made up of flutes, men and spirits, and called Yankwa, is fused at the dam, where men neither play flutes nor serve the spirits, and that, upon return, the hosts' chief task is to separate this trinity so that men can again take up flutes to play and share weeks of feasts with the Yakairiti. There is thus a play between the visible and the invisible, concealment and revelation, auditory and visual sensory domains, as well as a progression between different kinds of sound: cries and onomatopoeia, dissonant whistles and trumpets, tightly constrained formal speech, singing, and finally the playing of melodic flutes. The returnees move through these different modalities as they perform the return of not only their physical bodies and the fish they carry, but also of two classes of flutes, which must be fed and restored to their central flute house one after the other. Yankwa's return is thus, on closer inspection, a series of returns made over a twenty-four hour period. Temporal transitions between darkness and light, night and day, work in tandem with a fundamental spatial axis that runs from west to east, river to land, water to fire, and Yakairiti to human. During Yankwa's absence, hosts and women are allied in the task of moulding this space, garnering resources, and readying themselves for these multiple returns.

'Like Yakairiti'

On the first evening after Yankwa docked at the port in 2009, I watched the masked fishermen stalk and spin in the half-light around the huge bonfire along with Maitoa, an elderly man of Kairoli clan. He said: 'You see them and you are dead, they are the Yakairiti, the very same'. I moved around the edge of the arena to sit with some women who were spectating from just in front of their doorways – at a safe distance. I asked them if they were afraid of these 'Yakairiti'. One woman responded, 'No, these are just Enawenê. They are only *like* Yakairiti. Only shamans can see the

Yakairiti themselves'. In a separate conversation with another huddle of spectating women I asked again and was told, 'The men are *really* Yakairiti when they are away at the dam, now they are just *like* Yakairiti'. I was intrigued by these statements about the identity of the disguised men, so the following day I went to find a middle-aged man called Kaweka-atokwe, who was often patient in answering my questions. I asked him if the men had been 'like Yakairiti' on the previous night. First he responded exactly as the women had by repeating the conventional line that Yakairiti were invisible except to shamans, but later on in our conversation he gave a revealing explanation, which has informed my analysis of the dynamics of the fishermen's return:

> When we are at the dam, Yankwa are with us, we go with Yankwa, we are Yankwa; we are not Enawenê, we are purely Yankwa. Today, here in the village, it is women's Yankwa. We have put them down and we are true Enawenê once more, we only take them up to dance with them now.

He used a phrasing that lacked a definite object, but he was obviously referring to flutes, which the returning fishermen would return to playing now after their silence during the dam-fishing period. However he also seemed to imply something more abstract; namely, the merging and parting of flutes, men and spirits. He seemed to be saying that a flute-man-spirit 'trinity' called Yankwa had been fused at the dam, whereas now that men performed for women, this trinity was dis-united – men would play flutes but they would no longer embody their spirits; it was as if flutes and spirits could be ejected from the bodies of the fishermen with which they had been one. Women's com-ments had suggested another dimension to this. For them, the men were self-evidently no longer Yakairiti, since they recognised them as husbands and kinsmen, but during their estrangement, while they had been invisible, they may truly have become unknowable, unpredictable Yakairiti.

Kawekwa-atokwe's explanation sheds light not only on the signif-icance of the flutes' silence during the period when men live for the traps but also on the absence of talk about the Yakairiti in the encamp-ments. I had seen offerings of salt, drinks and then fish made to assure the alliance of the masters of the fish in conducting the shoals into the traps, but the Yakairiti had otherwise been largely absent from men's talk, which all turned around the traps' likes and dislikes. Since I asso-ciated flute-playing with village life, it had not occurred to me to ask the fishermen why the flutes were not played at the dam, even though some flutes were among the cargo men took with them. In light of Kawekwa-atokwe's explanation, these silences now became evidence of the incorporation of flutes and Yakairiti by the fishermen, who lived 'Yankwa' wholly as they tended their traps. When the weir and the traps are destroyed at the end of the fishing period, the Yakairiti immediately become the focus of men's attention again and, at the same point, the flutes begin to be played. I never witnessed the fishermen's destruction of the dam, because I returned to the village ahead of the fishermen, but I inquired about the procedure for destroying the dam before I left. I was told that once they were ready to depart, the fishermen would throw the traps downstream of the weir, cut the dam's vine bindings and then begin to play the flutes. The leader then 'awakened' (*akasene*) the accompanying Yakairiti with the message 'we are going up onto the land, back to your owners'. The 'owners' are the hosts in the village, to whose clans the Yakairiti who accompany the fishermen – who are the men of all the other clans – belong. What all of this suggests is that after the initial offerings of salt, manioc drink and fish, the fishermen are silently assimilated to Yakairiti, via their traps. [4]

Recall that at the dam, the fishermen ceased to modify the surface of their bodies, concerning themselves instead with the internal state of their minds and bodies. This is suggestive of an internalisation of their relationship to the spirit world and contrasts with the emphasis on display and performance as the fishermen prepare to return. The returning fishermen stop to disguise themselves with genipap, mud, clay and palm frond masks and capes just before they reach Halataikwa's port and the hosts who await them. In so doing they make an internal relationship with the Yakairiti strikingly manifest on their skins. Although the skin idiom is foreign to the Enawenê, the interplay between the internalisation of a relationship with spirits and then its revelation in a visually striking display fits with the dynamic of the fishermen's seclusion and then sudden exposure. This idiom is borrowed from Melanesian ethnography, where secrecy and concealment are prominent themes of initiation cults, just as they are at this moment in Yankwa's process, when in anticipation of the gaze of hosts and women the fishermen turn themselves inside out, making the skin the site where their inner capacities are revealed. [5] So it was as women told me: their returning husbands and sons were now only men who 'looked like' Yakairiti. The returning fishermen are thus neither Yakairiti nor yet entirely Enawenê; this will only occur gradually, as they move through space, exchanging ornaments, affects, words and appetites; and as they take up the flutes in a series of phased movements inwards towards the flute house. The work of hosts and women to ensure this progression begins a month in advance of the fishermen's return.

Figure 2.2 The hosts, known as *Halokwayti*, re-enter the flute house at the end of their entertaining afternoon circuit.

Halokwayti: The Hosts' Vigil

Halataikwa felt empty and quiet in the days following the fishermen's departure in February 2008, when I was just a month into my doctoral fieldwork. The men of the two hosting clans, Aweresese and Lolahese were busy building their own fishing dam a little way up the Iquê River and the empty arena echoed with the absence of Yankwa's night-time musical routines, its noisy dawn men's meetings and its afternoon sporting sessions, when either football or the traditional ball game *haira* were played in the arena. We ate a meagre diet too, since women had taken a break from harvesting manioc after filling the fishermen's baskets with breads and flour. Instead of the daily harvest of manioc from nearby gardens, women took longer walks to visit distant gardens where gourds, yams, arrowroot and taro grew and they profited from these to gather edible insects and fungi. Rather than purposefully striding towards the manioc gardens, on most mornings small groups of women set off together at a leisurely pace to gather firewood before the day got hot, taking over a major male provisioning task. Just as the absence of men broke with the usual manioc provisioning routine, it also changed the shape of female households. With all but one husband absent from our house, the rest of the women took down the screens that usually separated their sleeping compartments and moved their hammocks together so that they and their children would have one another's company at night. Although during the fishermen's absence the male hosts (the men belonging to two out of the nine clans) remained dispersed in their separate houses around the dwelling circle, they would call out to one another from their hammocks after dark, raising their voices to chat and joke together through the thatch; and in the mornings they again called out to rally one another to start work on their common projects. It was as if the whole village now belonged to them.

However, this calm and slightly listless pace of life during which there was no activity in the central arena, lasted only two weeks. Then a new daily rhythm was set by hosts who sang and drank ketera served by women nightly inside the flute house and every afternoon came out into the arena to perform a brief but entertaining clowning circuit. This new routine, which replaced the dancing and flute-playing of the now departed fishermen, was called Halokwayti and it allied women and hosts in their vigil for the fishermen's return. I made the error of referring to this daily ceremonial routine as 'Yankwa' and was corrected: 'Yankwa' had gone away fishing, this was 'Halokwayti'. Just like 'Yankwa', it referred to flutes, spirits and men together, as well as to the phase in which they reigned, with its distinctive characteristics and temporality.

Halokwayti began in the hour before dawn when the unadorned men entered the flute house, chatted quietly and lit a small fire of twigs for light, before announcing themselves with toots on trumpets called *hok-watero* and with shrill cries made by blowing on the small gourd whistle called *kuyeyata*. These two kinds of aerophones, known as Yankwa's pet flutes (*ehola* or *Yankwa hola*), had previously been played to announce the orchestral music of the melodic flutes (*Yankwa ehaylia*), but now they alone were intoned, and only briefly, to punctuate the songs men chanted. Blowing on these shrill, tuneless instruments the men filed out of the flute house, crossed the sandy expanse of the arena and walked a little way down the path at its opposite, eastern edge. This was the path down which Yankwa's flutes and spirits had departed for the dams and it led to the port at which the fishermen would eventually arrive, so that Halokwayti gestured to the event that they awaited. They then filed back into the flute house and sat to sing in a low-toned unison. They were interrupted briefly when the women of the village served them calabashes full of the warm, sweet manioc and corn porridge, ketera. Men sang short verses in unison, marking the end of each verse with the screechy, brittle vibration of the voice distorted through the bamboo trumpets or with a scream from the whistle. They sang refrains in which they asked women to assist their vigil, by listening out for Yankwa's cries and for the hum of engine noise, and to look out for men with bodies covered in clay and genipap dye. They also said 'let me eat fish, rather than drinking only ketera' and 'let Yankwa return so that I may put away the pet flutes'. When Yankwa's arrival was imminent, Halokwayti asked all the women of the village, whom they addressed as daughters-in-law, to make manioc bread ready for the arrival. Halokwayti's chant sessions were short, lasting about half an hour, unlike Yankwa's two to three hour-long pre-dawn musical sessions before their departure for the weirs. Hosts said that this was because they had to be off scouting downriver before dawn for signs of the fleets' return.

Flute players are always served drinks and it is women who prepare this nourishment for the flutes and the Yakairiti they harbour. Every clan has its own pantheon of Yakairiti but they never incarnate the spirits of their own clan, but rather those of other clans. Thus the hosts are accompanied by the spirits and flutes belonging to the seven clans of the fishermen, while the fishermen are accompanied to the dams by the spirits and flutes belonging to the two host clans. The same principle applies to those who serve drinks to these men-spirits-flutes. During Yankwa, hosts' wives prepare drinks for flute players so that in distributing these drinks hosts nourish their own clan spirits; at Halokwayti it is the fishermen's wives who serve the flutes directly, nourishing their husbands' spirits by placing calabashes on the ground just outside the flute house and naming individual spirit recipients to come and receive their drinks. The men within the flute house respond with grateful toots and screeches and also make bawdy remarks, speaking through their bamboo trumpets to disguise their voices. This jovial, close relationship between women and Halokwayti, who are allied in the vigil for the distant and strange fishermen, is characteristic of the afternoon's diversions as well.

In the middle of the day, hosts would tend their own dam, as well as occupying themselves with their practical preparations for the fishermen's return, which I detail in the next section. When this work was done for the day and everyone had bathed off their exertions, the hosts began to adorn themselves for the afternoon session of Halokwayti. Instead of remaining seated in darkness, singing and drinking ketera, 'Halokwayti' – as the hosts were now known – now emerged painted with annatto dye, adorned with new palm silks and, as the time of Yankwa's return drew nearer, with feather diadems as well. All these adornments would be transferred to the bodies of the returning fishermen, who would wear them during their daily and nightly musical routines over the following months, but for now the hosts wore them, conscientiously perfecting themselves as paragons of true humanity. Decked-out in this perfect cer-emonial garb, they paraded out of the flute house, spinning on their heels in mock threat as they circled around anticlockwise, before filing a little way down the easterly pathway leading to the port where Yankwa would arrive. Then they looped back towards the flute house on the western edge of the arena. They re-entered the flute house with great fanfare, one by one: uttering euphoric ululations, they leapt up high and then squat-ted down low to re-enter the low door of the flute house (see Figure 2.2).

Women and children always made sure they were back from bathing in the stream in time to huddle inside their front doorways and watch this entertaining spectacle. They would comment on the quality of the hosts' adornment and the vivacity of their performance, which was per-fected gradually. Day after day men jumped higher, cried out louder, spun more gregariously and adorned themselves more beautifully. Hosts said that Halokwayti danced because it was happy and adorned, and danced more and more beautifully when the return drew near in expec-tation of the fish that would soon arrive. This is why I have called it a rite of vigil. In expectation of return, there is a gradual build-up in the intensity of practical preparations, accompanied by the continuous aggrandisement of Halokwayti's rousing afternoon performances, which fortified and energised the men, women and children of the village in an excited expectation for the fishermen's return.

Hosts' and Women's Practical Work

Between tending their dam in the morning and evening and adorning and parading themselves in the arena in the afternoon, the hosts had a window of time in the middle of the day during which to make practical preparations for Yankwa's return. They went into the forest to gather buruti palm fronds, which they boiled, pummelled, hung up to dry in the sun and then plaited or separated into fine, silky yellow strands. These were the new silks, which the returning fishermen would wear to dance. Additionally, they cleaned the sandy arena of accumulated debris; felled trees to gradually build up stockpiles of logs with which to feed the fires around which Yankwa would dance on their return; prepared the port at which the fishermen's fleets would land; and cleared a straight causeway joining the port to the village arena. This was the all-important path (called *xirewekwa*), which would guide the incomers to the village arena. In 2008 Yankwa took place at Halataikwa for the first time, after the move had been made from the former village of Matokodakwa in 2007, so that hosts had more to do than usual; creating the path for the first time, bridging streams and paving sections of it with logs to make it a veritable causeway.

This causeway slopes down from the hill on which the village is sited, taking as straight a line as possible from west to east until it reaches the bank of the Iquê River. The circular village is oriented so that the flute house sits at the western edge of the arena, its front door opening out to the east and thus facing both the river and the rising sun. The pathway enters the arena at its eastern side, directly opposite the front door of the flute house. This east-west axis of orientation of both path and flute house means that the passage of the sun each day draws a line that connects water to land. The sun appears to rise out of the river-path at dawn and to set behind the flute house at dusk. Enawenê villages are always circular; they always have their flute house either in the centre of the arena or at its western edge and they are always sited on hilltops near a river bend to allow for the construction of an east-west ceremonial pathway. It is Yankwa's hosts who are responsible for siting villages (every 5 to 10 years, historically) so that villages are part of Yankwa; their spatial architecture is conceived with Yankwa's realisation in mind. As other anthropologists working in circular villages have noted, they are models of the universe that place people and flutes in the centre of a landscape and a cosmos. The roofs of the dwelling circle seem to contain the dome-like sky, positioning those inside the dome at the centre of the cosmos, with the sun and the stars arcing their way overhead as if they were performing on a celestial stage. Geographically too the inhabitants of such a village have the impression of dominating the landscape that they survey: looking out from the cleared, hilltop place of the village surrounded by low-lying manioc gardens, you can see far into the distance on all sides. The paramount significance of the layout and orientation of villages has been a major topic in the ethnography of Gê- and Bororo-speaking peoples, who live to the east of the Enawenê; their villages, like those of the Enawenê, are 'arenas of cosmic significance'.[6] Upon arrival, the fishermen will move through a space that has been carefully designed to move them and to imbue them with a certain kind of 'cosmic habitus' to borrow Kapferer's phrase (2004: 42). Indeed, everything about the hosts' preparations and the fishermen's arrival suggests that spatial arrangements have the capacity to align person and cosmos.

Every phase of Yankwa is anchored in a particular orientation within this cosmically aligned village space. The task of both founding villages and then renewing this alignment year after year during Yankwa's absence falls to hosts. This special pathway and the port to which it led were only used when Yankwa returned; otherwise people used the narrow, steep and winding path that descended to the river where it came closest to the village, on its northeastern side. But the east-west axis that the causeway inscribed on the ground was crucial to every phase of Yankwa, structuring not only space but also time. Before Yankwa left for the dams, flute players ended each morning's session by proceeding towards the path, where they fell silent, gesturing to their own and the flutes' and spirits' approaching departure to the water. During Halokwayti the pet flutes dance out to the path and back into the flute house, drawing an elliptical path on the ground to elicit Yankwa's return. Upon the fishermen's arrival, they move up the path and then anticlockwise around the arena, with each circuit coming further inwards towards the flute house, until they eventually come to its door, at which point the flutes are symbolically returned to their house at the centre of the village and the men become able, once again, to take them up and play them. During the weeks of routine musicality that would follow, the flutes would re-emerge each night and afternoon to be played in the arena. During this returning phase, flute players would fall silent facing west and looking into the door of the flute house. This signalled their anticipation of the end of Yankwa, when the flutes would be laid to rest inside the flute house until the following year.

Hosts also embellished the space, anticipating Yankwa's needs on their trajectory from port to village. The hosts thought of everything that would please and accommodate both the fishermen and their accompanying Yakairiti, so that the whole space was set up to invite a gradual, measured and peaceful arrival. By the riverside they created a large clearing (called *dotakalaytikwa*) and erected hammock posts in it at convenient intervals so that the returning fishermen could take their rest there prior to climbing the path to the village. They built sturdy wooden platforms by the port as well, so that baskets of fish could be temporarily stored off the ground. Further up the path they erected shelters in which pots of a lightly fermented drink called oloniti sat. The pots of drink were supposed to sit there and become sour, since this was how the Yakairiti were said to appreciate the drink most. These pots were accompanied by wooden effigies of fish (*kohase edaotaka*), which were hung to please the incoming Yakairiti. Where the path met the arena the hosts made another clearing and filled it with lines of upright leaning posts, each with a small hollow at their base. These were devised to support the incomers' heavy baskets of fish, which they would set down prior to entering the arena to meet their hosts unencumbered.

Beyond gathering firewood, making ornaments and preparing the physical infrastructure for the return, the task that hosts themselves considered paramount was the making of potassium salt from various species of palm (*esewehe*).[7] This was the substance most fervently desired by Yakairiti and the only payment they would accept from the hosts for the fish, which they had helped to capture. Enawenê often described esewehe as 'just like money', using both the Enawenê word for payment, *etoli*, and the Portuguese *dinhero*.[8] As we shall shortly see, on the night after the fishermen return, when they are disguised as dangerous Yakairiti, they will kneel to lick this salt from hosts' palms, and will be tamed in the process.

The final crucial ingredients for the fishermen's return, and the months that will follow it, is the preparation of the manioc gardens for the subsequent months of intensive harvesting. During the latter half of the fishermen's absence, women went off most mornings to thoroughly clean and weed their manioc gardens, uprooting invading plants, piling them up with dead manioc stalks and the remnants of dead wood before burning the piles. Rather than dig up the manioc tubers to return home as early as possible, as they had done before Yankwa departed and as they would do after Yankwa's return, they remained in the gardens weeding until the sun had climbed high. This arduous, sweaty work was said to be necessary to make the manioc tubers grow well, since lazy weeding was said to cause manioc to grow lazily. Women tended to call on daughters and sisters-in-law to help them, expanding their work groups beyond the usual group of three sisters or a mother and two daughters. In order to animate and speed the tiring work, women took turns to visit each other's gardens in groups as big as ten to fifteen women. As a result, during Yankwa's absence, manioc gardens all around the village became sandy expanses of neat and evenly spaced mounds, each with tall stems protruding up to three metres into the air. After the return, women would just dig the tubers and hurry home as soon as their baskets were full; they would no longer have time to clean the gardens.

Anticipating the busy period that was to come, women also spring cleaned their houses, made bundles of new calabashes to contain Yankwa's drinks, and gathered stores of manioc starch and fibre to smoke and slowly dry above their hearths. Women also amassed great piles of firewood, which they stacked up against the outside wall of their houses. This stockpile would lighten their husbands' workloads during the weeks after their return. Finally, like their husbands at the dam, women were keeping their loved ones in mind by weaving new white cotton garters for the ankles, knees and upper arms of their husbands and sons, who would lose their old adornments in the current. All of these labours to prepare for the fishermen's return absorbed and unified the women and hosts in the village. And as the return drew nearer, as Halokwayti's afternoon performances were perfected, so the mood of excitement and expectation grew.

Imminent Arrival and Initial Confrontations

It was the hosts' and women's responsibility to ensure that Yankwa made an anticipated return rather than a surprise invasion and an air of risk

Figure 2.3 The hosts gather in the flute house in readiness to meet the incoming fishermen in the village arena.

signalled the tension between these two alternatives. In both 2008 and 2009 one of the two female shamans (*sotaloti*) practising in the village at the time predicted Yankwa's return – correctly in 2008 when Yankwa returned on the 14 April and prematurely in 2009 when the return occurred significantly later on 27 April. Their predictions set women about grating manioc in order to prepare ketera in a hum of energetic wakefulness in the middle of the night, and sent hosts to camp out at the port ready to meet Yankwa. Since hosts and women were always interpreting signs, false alarms of imminent return were inevitable. This was especially the case in 2009 due to Yankwa's prolonged absence. Women were on high alert for a fortnight, often harvesting manioc before dusk and keeping baskets of raw tubers behind the house ready to process urgently if some sign of approach should come in the night. Even with a payphone newly installed in the village, which allowed Olowina's fishermen to call from Juína when they had arranged the delivery of farmed fish and to tell the hosts that they expected to arrive in two days' time, women prepared their pans of ketera a day too early. When I commented on the waste of resources and energy that this occasioned, women brushed off my objections. It seemed that this was part of a show of indomitable preparedness.

Hosts said that Yankwa were unpredictable and unknowable and they restlessly went out scouting, listening for motor noise at the confluence downriver and hoping to make encounters with Yankwa to learn of their intended arrival. Ideally they would intercept messengers who were travelling between dam sites in order to coordinate the different fleets' return. Failing that they looked to see whether drums of gasoline, which Yankwa had stashed to fuel their return journeys, had been retrieved from the usual hiding places. While the hosts were brazenly eager to meet with Yankwa, the latter were said to be ashamed (*yeyale*) and to want to avoid the hosts' encounters. When parties from the two sides did meet, hosts were as solicitous as Yankwa were reticent and restrained. Hosts always took manioc drinks and breads on these scouting missions to give to fishermen and, if they succeeded in meeting, they would receive smoked fish in return, which they could show to the rest of the village as evidence. If they failed, they would leave the manioc breads and drinks on the bank at the confluence of the Iquê and Camararé rivers and they would return the next day to see if they had been taken. If so, they would know Yankwa had passed by and would surmise that return was in progress.

At 5AM on the morning of 27 April 2009 the hosts emerged from their pre-dawn chanting in the flute house and they split between downriver scouting and waiting at the port. At 7AM, one group returned from a scouting mission to say that Yankwa were silent and nowhere in sight, but half an hour later a dense hum of engine noise was incontrovertible evidence that all five fleets were approaching at once. Women thickened pans of boiled manioc juice with corn and manioc flour, having waited until the last moment to ready this ketera (to avoid wasting precious corn seed in case of another false alarm). Convinced beyond doubt of Yankwa's approach, hosts carried 125 litre pans of the ketera down to the port. I was with them as they stopped halfway down the path to adorn themselves with palm silks, annatto dye and feather armbands. Since the engine noise had stopped, they knew that Yankwa had also stopped at the same moment, and would be adding the final touches to their adornments, which are designed to contrast with their own. Yankwa would be painting with genipap; smearing themselves in mud and clay; tying wet, green vines around their wrists and ankles; and cloaking and masking themselves in 'raw', 'living' (*makone, kaseta*) buruti fibre. The hosts pointed out that these were exactly the same materials that the hosts were now winding around their arms, except that they had boiled, pummelled and then dried their palm fronds to separate them into silky straw-coloured strands. The contrast between the wild, raw Yakairiti-like incomers and the properly human hosts could not have been more explicit.

At 9:50AM the engine noise returned even louder, so that the hosts knew Yankwa were now ascending the Iquê River in their final approach. Down at the port they formed a line facing the river about twenty metres back from the bank. The fleet from the River Preto was the first to land and their leaders disembarked ahead of the others. As they stepped onto the land uttering shrill cries, the hosts stood firm allowing Yankwa to come forward and strike them with the long fish-topped sticks they carried. The two lines soon disaggregated into a mêlée in which several of the hosts allowed themselves to be knocked to the ground. Later people would comment on the excessive aggression of the encounter that year, which was considered a settling of accounts after details of hosts' sexual conquests with the women of the village had reached Yankwa's ears at the meeting about hydroelectric dam compensation, which had taken place a month previously in Juína. Despite the respectful distance hosts and Yankwa had kept from each other, the reunion had provided much opportunity for gossip to circulate. After this first clash, Yankwa dropped their fish-spears, leaving them for hosts to take, and began to unravel palm silks from hosts' arms. These they would use to replace their own raw bindings. Hosts then retreated to their pans of ketera, which stood ready. Now it was their turn to approach the incomers and they did so holding out calabashes full of sweet ketera – the drink of which the fishermen had been deprived for two months. Leaving the fishermen to drink, the hosts then hurried back to the village to prepare for a second encounter, which would take place in the arena itself.[9]

During this time down at the port, women had bathed, collected water, set out their calabashes, dressed in their brightest skirts, and painted their bodies and faces with annatto dye. The wives of hosts carried pans of ketera and bundles of calabashes out into the arena so they would be near at hand for their husbands to take from. It was 10:25AM when the hosts came running back into the flute house to replace the items of dress that had been stripped from them by the returnees, affix their headdresses, and take hold of sharpened, forked sticks called *tolohi* with which they would meet Yankwa in the centre of the arena (see Figure 2.3). At this point I was in the flute house and I heard the hosts' strategy discussion. Kawali, the leader of Aweresese clan, and the man universally regarded as the most knowledgeable and judicious leader of the village, would go out first. He advised that the others should come out swiftly after him, because, he said, in the previous year the clash between hosts and Yankwa had happened too close to the flute house so that the thatch had been damaged by the blows.

Whereas at the port side the hosts had passively and silently met the fishermen, who had the benefit of surprise, the hosts now had the upper hand. They were hidden in the flute house from where they had a view towards the path and could see Yankwa coming, while remaining concealed. This arrangement reinforced one of the differences in the appearance of the two parties: while the hosts' faces were framed with annatto and their fringes cut short so that they had clear vision, Yankwa's eyes were covered by long palm frond fringes, giving an impression of blindness, which was exacerbated by their crouching and hunched posture (a posture called *anolokwana*). Whereas at the port the fishermen arrived with noisy ululations, now they stalked slowly and silently in single file. As before, each incomer carried a pair of fish held in place in the flattened basket at the end of a long handle, so that it looked like a fish-spear. These were held angled downwards towards the ground in keeping with the crouching position of the men.

The loaded hush was suddenly broken when the hosts ran out of the flute house, and this time it was they, and not the incomers, who cried out. They emerged with the same cries, adornments and ostentation that they had perfected through the weeks of Halokwayti's afternoon performances. They had been practising and preparing for this moment for over a month. As soon as the vanguards had come together, the tail end of Yankwa's procession flooded in to join the fray. At this point, women who had been watching from inside their doorways or from

Figure 2.4 My adoptive younger brother Salika (left) and his nephew and co-resident playmate Anowlie are happily reunited after Salika's absence at the fishing dam. Anowlie looks 'hostly' like his father, while Salika's fringe has grown long and he is covered in black genipap.

behind stacks of wood broke their cover and their silence to become noisy commentators. They watched as each of the hosts was led away from the flute house by a pair of fishermen, who took him by either arm and divested him of his palm silks as they walked him out towards the pathway, where their baskets of fish were parked against the convenient leaning posts. Some women followed Yankwa and their hostages at a run, eager to see the baskets of fish.

Returning with some fish in hand – but not weighed down by whole baskets as I had seen in 2008 – hosts ran to the pans of ketera that their wives had placed ready for them. They filled calabashes and came back towards Yankwa, proffering the same sweet and filling drink they had offered down at the port. The hosts, who no longer had much of their silk garb left on their bodies, darted about addressing all the incomers in rushed formal dialogues as they deposited the drinks at the incomers' feet. The arena was soon littered with hundreds of calabashes so that the returnees had to pick a careful path through them in order to carry their baskets of fish back into their houses. Hosts persistently assailed them to accept more ketera. Once they had stowed the fish with their wives and mothers-in-law, groups of fishermen sat and drank ketera in the arena. Since there were three host clans in 2009 and since the wives or mothers-in-law of every host clansman had made a 125 litre pan for this encounter, I estimate that four thousand litres of ketera were prepared for this return. This was an intimidating plenty designed to domesticate and subjugate the incomers and the spirits they harboured.

Family Reunions

A mere half hour after the fishermen had docked, the collective encounter was over and the incomers concentrated on greeting their familes and then getting some rest. While the incomers relaxed, the hosts indefatigably entered each house in the dwelling circle to address a conventional welcome to each of the returnees, addressing them in kinship terms (e.g. 'have you returned brother-in-law?'). Once the clatter of the calabash washing was done with, women inspected their returned children, wondering at their being strong and tall and tying on the new garters they had made for them. Some of the boys strode around imperiously, shy of their mothers' attentions after so long away. Everyone ate fish with manioc bread. Through the middle part of the day, gifts passed between betrothed parties in greater frequency than at any other time. Full to brimming calabashes of oloniti were placed down by the hammock posts of returning future sons-in-law by women, and gifts of fish came back soon after. In one house I watched a couple count up stacks of the flattened baskets, which had first been used to smoke the fish, but which now became units of currency. Each stack of four baskets was destined for the future mother-in-law of one of the couple's unmarried sons. These women had sent their sons-in-law off to the dam with plenty of dried manioc bread and flour and the fish was a return for this sustenance. Men also handed over manioc sieves and graters to their wives and bead chains were said to be designed to adorn women's hips during lovers' reunions in the afternoon.

Husbands and wives, pairs of lovers and betrothal partners bestowed foods and other desired gifts on one another. In anticipation of this reunion, women had talked about their desire to eat fish and they had assumed that fishermen's desire for ketera was an important motive for their timely return. Manioc had flourished through women's careful weeding, just as fish had been caught in the body-trap with which men were intimately tied, and ornaments had been crafted through absorbing handiwork on both sides. Women eagerly grasped the new basketry that hung on their husbands' backs as soon as they entered the house and during family reunions women tied on their husbands' and sons' new garters. Men and women had turned their love and nurture into material form and now gave one another the products of their gendered labour, in the form of tools that enable gendered productive tasks and body ornaments that constitute gendered bodies. Among Enawenê, the exchange of fish for manioc foods and drinks is the archetypal act of gender complementarity in married life, in the betrothal partnerships that establish marriage alliances, and also between hosts and fishermen during Yankwa. When the fishermen return, all these cross-sex relationships are activated at once.

While the visual evidence suggests that people are constituting one another as gendered persons by bestowing tangible gifts and elements of attire, there is also a hidden dimension to the public dyadic exchanges between hosts and Yankwa. In the formal addresses, which precede every transfer of ketera between them, hosts addressed the incomers as *Itioda hwale*, which translates as 'eater of manioc' or 'eater of blood', since *Tiolero*, the mythic name of manioc, derives from the word for blood – *tiolaiti*. I was told that this was a way of addressing 'all the Yakairiti together' and also that the name 'belonged to manioc's flutes/spirits'. Like all formal dialogues made during Yankwa, these were uttered in a poetic linguistic register, which was sometimes referred to as 'Yakairiti language' (*Yakairiti wale*). The fullest versions of these formulae were the preserve of song masters, while young men used truncated versions. During these addresses, giver and receiver always adopted a distanciated body language, standing side on to one another and avoiding eye contact by looking downwards or into space. Hosts also marked the ground with their heel (a gesture called *ahotikixini*) before they handed each calabash over to indicate that the food contained was to be shared with the Yakairiti. Giver and receiver's remoteness to one another, coupled with the formal dialogues, indicates that these encounters between men are the mask for effects on a deeper, virtual plane (Kapferer 2004).[10] In the evening the returnees again disguise themselves in fresh green palm fringes and cloaks, so that they again look and act like dangerous Yakairiti.

Ioho, Masked and Cloaked around the Bonfire

After the period of rest, reunion, eating, grooming, bathing and gifting through the middle of the day, everyone prepared for Ioho. All of the returnees had spent the latter part of the afternoon making their own green palm fringe masks (*dosetayti*) and cloaks (*heseti*) by twisting together lengths of dry and wet palm fibres to serve as a headband, and then looping long lengths of fresh buruti palm leaves over the band to make a floor-length cloak. A fringe was then cut at the front just below the eyes, while around the side and back of the person the cloak brushed the ground. Ioho, which was the name of the returnees for now, also crafted a pretend version of a bow and arrow called *osole*, which perhaps added to the figure of otherworldly fierceness they cut, while also underscoring its performative nature.[11] Ioho effects the return of the pet flutes belonging to the host clan, which have been away at the dams. They replace those belonging to the clans of the departed fishermen, which have been played throughout Halokwayti. At the end of Ioho these returning pet flutes sit down to chant throughout the night during a phase called *hokwatero tokena*, which refers to the seated position of the men who play a trumpet called hokwatero and rehearse chants in a night-long marathon. At dawn, once this rehearsal is complete, the pets can re-enter the flute house – they have returned. This opens the way for the return of the melodic flutes and their restoration to the central house.

At this point it will be helpful to reiterate the dual distinction that is at play between two classes of flutes (which I gloss as pet and melodic) and between two opposed groups of men (hosts and fishermen), each of which plays the flutes belonging to the clans in the opposite group. The host clans' flutes and spirits have accompanied Yankwa's fishing endeav-our, helping to convey the shoals of fish into the traps. In parallel, during Halokwayti, the spirits and flutes belonging to the fishermen have remained behind to accompany all the hosts' activities. During Halokwayti the hosts limited themselves to playing the pet flutes of the departed clans, leaving all the melodic flutes hanging silently in the flute house. As the name indicates, there is a hierarchical relationship between these two classes of flutes, with the pet flutes (ehola) described as birds that accompany the melodic flutes, or as their 'workers' or 'employees' (ewakanale, or empregado in Portuguese). Unlike the civilised flutes, the pets are harsh-sounding trumpets and shrill whistles, which are said to 'lack understanding' (masemakalale) and to be capable only of emitting cries.

I was told that the pets were at their most 'aggressive' (hwerena) at Ioho but that once they had spilled oloniti, they 'calmed down' or 'became good' (awetakwale). This was also described as their 'coming to kneel' (tokwekwale) – which they literally did as they stooped to accept potassium salt from hosts' cupped hands. This transformation is again guided by the space that hosts set up, this time inside the village arena itself. In one hour, Ioho come inwards towards the light and heat of a huge bonfire and go from an aggressive stance through a supplicant one, to passively sitting to receive manioc breads. In other words, they are tamed. The most striking thing about Ioho is this staging around a huge bonfire situated in the centre of the arena. By paying close attention to the choreography of Ioho, which turns around this bonfire with a ring of torches arranged around it, we shall see how it paves the way for the emergence of the melodic flutes at dawn the next day and the months of routinised and sequenced musical ceremonialism that this emergence inaugurates.

The hosts had felled trees in the preceding weeks for this bonfire and they brought them into the arena during the late afternoon while Ioho were preparing their costumes. By 6:30PM hosts had also erected posts in a ring around the fire. There was one post for each host and these served as bearers for resin torches and also as the hosts' positions for the evening. The hosts readied themselves by setting a pan of refreshing oloniti down beside their post ready. One of Yankwa's leaders walked around the edge of the arena making the invitation to the incomers in kin terms; for example, 'Nephew! Let us rehearse our flutes!' All of the newly masked incomers thus gathered in a tight group in the darkness at the point where the path met the arena at its eastern edge. The men who had been leaders at the dams were bunched tightly in the middle, while all the followers were huddled around them. At the leaders' instigation they began, in chorus, to make an onomatopoeic sound with very elongated vowels and a rising and then falling pitch and volume:

'Ioowhoooo'. Interspersed they made strange ululations, different from the staccato cries of Yankwa or Halokwayti. Ioho also stamped their feet, and the tiny gourd whistle kuyeyata, which some of the men held, screamed piercingly. Ioho began to move slowly in an anticlockwise direction, in the outer ring between the hosts' circle of torches and the circle of dwellings. From just outside their houses women and children watched at a safe distance, since Ioho were said to be dangerous, *kiwini*, – like Yakairiti. Hunched forward, all the incomers stalked around the arena, all the while spinning on their heels in slow motion with every other step as they continued to make their eerie sounds. Halokwayti had taken the same course and they too had spun around on their heels, but they had moved more quickly, had been smiling and glowing red and yellow in the bright sunlight. In contrast, Ioho circled in the outer edges of the light cast by the blazing bonfire, casting sinister shadows.

At some point in their circuits, Ioho invaded the circle of hosts' torches, took calabashes of oloniti from the hosts, drank a gulp and threw the rest to the ground. Now they circled inside the ring of torches and were brightly lit by the bonfire. After this, Ioho went to fetch flattened baskets of pairs of fish (*halakakwale*) and brought these to the hosts (only leaders gave to every host) who accepted them at their posts, so that they gathered smaller or larger piles there, depending on their seniority. Ioho then gathered together with their backs to the bonfire and facing the entrance path and awaited the hosts who would bring them potassium salt. They knelt down and cried out – more quietly now – to receive it into their cupped hands. Next, the hosts brought logs, and Ioho were seated to receive manioc breads from all the hosts. Yankwa's leaders received so many that tall piles of breads grew in front of them, reaching higher than their heads, and threatening to topple over. These were expendable breads, made of poor quality manioc fibre – the kind of breads that are rarely eaten but that the Yakairiti are said to particularly appreciate because of their pungent smell.

At 8:10PM there was an interlude in which hosts and Ioho briefly swapped roles: hosts received cloaks from Ioho and circled around inside the ring of torches with the borrowed masks superposed on their 'hostly' annatto-painted bodies. They were self-consciously 'dressed up' and their cries were a muted version of those uttered by Ioho just previously. The returnees also took up their role as temporary hosts and ran back to their houses to fetch oloniti, which they proffered to the ersatz Ioho, followed by a fish accompanied with a whole manioc bread. Instead of the salt fed to Ioho and then the mass of inedible breads designed to overwhelm them, the disguised hosts were given a perfect meal consisting of high quality manioc bread topped with fish. The hosts sat down to eat, their work more or less done for the evening, since all that remained was to listen to the pets' songs, which would continue throughout the night.

The swap that I have just described was a performance of a rite of intercession and reversal called *Amamaneda-hwale*, which marks all the important transitions within Yankwa's ceremonial sequence. Struggling to find the right words, I asked Enawenê people if Amamaneda-hwale was 'funny or not serious', as these interludes always felt to me like the light-hearted scenes that punctuate Shakespearean plays, providing comic relief through mimicry and subversion. People told me not to be deceived by the appearance of a charade; Yankwa would not be 'correct' or 'complete' without Amamaneda-hwale. It is clearly import-ant as a marker of the completion of one phase and the transition to the next, but Amamaneda-hwale also works to relativise the opposition between hosts and Ioho or Yankwa, by revealing it to be contingent, temporary and perspectival, a point I return to below. This perfor-mance indicated that, at 8:30PM, Ioho was over. When the returnees again gathered together by the path at the eastern edge of the arena they now did so as 'Yankwa'. The fishermen had come up onto the land and they had entered the village and their houses. The pet flutes had returned in a frightful spectacle, but only now would Yankwa truly return as, for the first time, men found their voice in order to address the hosts in song.

The men of Yankwa circled inside the ring of torches, coming to face the front door of the flute house in order to symbolically restore a mythic first flute called *matakalo* to its home at the centre of the village.[12] The symbolic entrance of this flute was marked by loud ululations. The huddle then moved towards the house of the leading host, which stood at this point for Aweresese clan as a whole. They crowded in at the house's front door and began to sing, directly addressing the hosts as owners of the fish for the first time since they had left the village two months earlier. This first song is an expression of humility directed to the hosts. Whatever the yield of fish with which the incomers return, they express in song the same conventional shame at their pathetic catch. The resident host in my house, Kawalinero-ene, glossed some of its metaphors in a colloquial translation for my benefit:

> I have come into my owners' arena to lick potassium salt, but, my patron, I am afraid that there was not much fish at the dam. I went so hungry that I had to gather mushrooms and ants to eat. It was not only you people in the village who went hungry, I went hungry too. There was so little fish that every day we merely bathed in empty waters. I am ashamed.

Beyond the content of this song, it is significant that the incomers – who are now 'Yankwa' rather than 'Ioho' – had begun to sing. Since their arrival, incomers and hosts had communicated by means of ululations, feigned and sometimes real blows, exaggerated gestures of distanced respect, repeated exchanges of food and ornaments, and brief, formal dialogues. In other words, verbal communication had been subordinated to action. Now Yankwa stood still and sang slowly, conveying a simple message directly to hosts at their front doors. This was surely an indication that these were now men, detached from the Yakairiti part, which had moved them at Ioho earlier in the evening. Indeed, once this song was over, the men of Yankwa sat down with their backs to the fire, facing eastward, and they were crowned by hosts with feather headdresses called *daweriyti*, which are insignias of humanity. This is the ultimate symbol that man and spirit have become detached, since these headdresses are iconic of all the qualities that oppose the Enawenê to their predatory spirit alter egos (see Chapter 5). Yankwa would continue to wear these bestowed headdresses every day and night over the coming two to three weeks as they sang, danced and played the flutes of the first host clan, Aweresese, following an exacting daily routine of musical ceremonialism.

Before that routine could begin, on the following night, there was the long night ahead in which song masters would sit down with the pet flutes and sing. As hosts rested and ate nearby, periodically stoking the fire, song masters led the way through many chants. I was told that this was one of the longest sequences of chants in Yankwa's eight-month duration, and I saw as I stayed up to accompany it that it was a test of endurance for the returned fishermen, for whom this was the third near-sleepless night. Indeed, it was an explicit ethos that sleeplessness was part of Yankwa's resilient character at this time. Men sat with their heads between their legs, their temples resting on their fists as they tried to remain awake and to voice the chants, which became increasingly slurred and croaky as the Milky Way arced overhead.[13] The sighting of the morning star, anticipating dawn, would signal the end of the marathon and men looked for it well before it rose above the dwelling circle. When it did come into view the singing stopped abruptly and all the stalwarts who had remained through the night (many had already retired to their hammocks) walked to the eastern edge of the arena where the pets cried out a final time and then were silent.

Now, in a brief and chaotic cacophony, the melodic flutes would return. Men who had gone to bed roused themselves. Hosts brought out oloniti to refresh Yankwa and they also carried away the smouldering logs that remained of the bonfire in order to clear the arena for the expansive stomping of men, which would follow. At 6AM Yankwa, who were now greater in number and dressed in palm silks, many of them with their headdresses in place, took up the flutes they played for the leading host clan, Aweresese. In the usual routine, men in four instrumental groups rotate around separate hearths in the arena. However, on this day, the flutes danced in a formation called *danekwana*, which implies travel. Beginning at the eastern side of the arena, each flute group formed a line facing the flute house and stomped forwards towards it side by side. The other three groups were lined up behind, so that each line was close on the heels of the one in front. They swept around the patch of hot earth where the bonfire had been, coming close to the flute house, and then fanned around back towards the path. The men played their flutes' characteristic melody as they took small, quick steps. The same process was immediately repeated for the other two hosting clans' sets of instruments, so that all of Yankwa symbolically entered the flute house.

All of this music and movement was punctuated by exchanges as the flute players were approached by hosts bearing oloniti, salt and manioc bread – just as Ioho had been on the previous night. They were forced to drink and spill oloniti as they attempted not to fall out of step with the other dancers and, in return, they brought more fish for the hosts.[14] With this sequence of exchanges over, the flutes were silent. The men hung them up inside the flute house and went to rest. In retrospect, all the other action sequences had been leading to this moment, which passed in such haste.

'A Riot of Repetition'

After the flutes' entrance in the morning, the village had been quiet through the middle of the day until the hosting clans began to dress for a second performance of Amamaneda-hwale. Together, the men belonging to the three host clans played the flutes belonging to the remaining six clans, one after the other. Each clan's set of flutes was brought towards the flute house in the same rapid and stomping movement. The dancers received oloniti from the men of each clan in turn, at the moment when their flutes were being played. Clansmen rushed forward so as not to miss their oloniti slot and the arena was noisy and chaotic, the sequence of clans and their separate sets of instruments barely discernible in the rush of bodies. Lévi-Strauss observed that ritual speech, gesture and acts are typically fragmented and repetitious, and he commented that with such a 'riot of repetition' and with such 'infinite attention to detail' (1990: 673) differences tended to diminish until they dissolved altogether (ibid.: 673). This is a fitting description of the second performance of Amamaneda-hwale, in which all of Yankwa's clans were singularised momentarily and men had to switch between acting as host and Yankwa in a matter of seconds. The reversibility of the host-Yankwa opposition is thus foregrounded and performed as contingent: I am host whenever I face others who play my clan flutes. There is a tension between the long-term momentum in which a clan hosts the central phases of Yankwa for two years in every six to ten, but is also 'a little bit of a host' every time his clan makes a distribution of soup because they have a large catch of fish or a sick relative. Amamaneda-hwale seems to be a reminder of the temporariness and reversibility of the fundamental opposition between host and Yankwa, which is dramatised throughout these rites of return.

In fact, Enawenê frequently talk about their duality as Yankwa and as hosts. As we already know, in recent years hosts have also built a dam during Yankwa's absence and I often heard them say 'We are Yankwa as well, since we too have built a dam'. In 2008, during the period of family reunion around midday, hosts had gone to check the traps of their dam, which they had yet to destroy. When they re-entered the arena with their catch, they did so covered in mud and green palm fronds, making ululations characteristic of Yankwa. Instead of dropping fish however, they dropped only the green leaves they wore. The true fishermen responded immediately by treating this as the occasion for an impromptu role swap, bringing ketera out and deferentially handing it to 'Yankwa'. This role reversal was a great joke for everyone.

This dynamic of role swapping suffuses all of Yankwa, and it is tempting to see it as a sort of fundamental grammar, from which inventive dialectical twists are generated. One of the ways this is institutionalised is in the possibility – described in more detail in Chapter 4 – for an additional clan to put themselves forward as an extra host. Kairoli clan had done this in 2009. All except one of Kairoli's men had decided to go away fishing, which suggested that their prior obligation to fish for the true hosts (the owners of the collective manioc fields) trumped their new hosting role, but Yankwa had also danced for Kairoli clan, who had distributed their own ketera, manioc breads and flour before departure to the dams. Their position was thus asymmetrically dual. This had implications that I have so far ignored in my simplified description of the fishermen's return. For example, having clashed with the hosts upon first entering the arena, and having accepted ketera from them, Kairoli's returnees had hastened to their wives to start distributing their own calabashes of ketera, turning back towards the path 'as hosts' to intercept the other fishermen. Even as they did so they were approached by the other hosts who pushed ketera on them. This was a confusing but entertaining scene and some of Kairoli's members played this double role in a sustained way, delighting in telling me 'I am a host!' *(halikali nato!)* while, masked and genipap-dyed, they carried calabashes of drink out. Over the subsequent exchanges not everyone worked so hard at playing this dual role, preventing the complex sequence of exchanges I have described from being perpetually interrupted and subverted.

By the time of Amamaneda-hwale on the afternoon of the second day, I was exhausted trying to follow these repeated sequences and switches and so was everyone else. The nervous energy that had preceded Yankwa's arrival had been spent. Even by the time preparations for Ioho were made it was with the expectation attendant to a shared undertaking, rather than with the urgency of the initial encounters. Exhaustion had played its part in eroding the opposition between hosts and Yankwa, which had been so acute, and so had repetition. Over the preceding day and night, the distance between the hosts and the incomers had thus worn thin as if the magnitude of avoidance and shame had been halved every time some substance passed between them.

Conclusion

In this chapter we have seen the material and expressive life of the village completely absorbed in a vigil for the fishermen, with clownish afternoon parades and days spent engaged in the many tasks that are necessary to prepare the arena, path and port for the fishermen, and to ready all the elements that will ensure their peaceful reincorporation. Central to this effort is the creation of a cosmically aligned space, which guides the fishermen, compelling them to follow a certain trajectory after they step onto land as well as persuading them to be well disposed to their hosts, who have anticipated all their wants. With all of this practical work on top of the host's nightly singing and afternoon parades, the anticipated event of Yankwa's return is never far from the villagers' minds and, as time goes on, expectation grows to a fever pitch of hyperactive scouting missions and overzealous manioc cookery.

When Yankwa actually do return, the initial confrontations are over quickly, giving way to joyful family reunions, romantic encounters and preparation of the bonfire and cloaks for the evening's all-important performance. The men who arrive at port and those who dance in the evening are disguised as Yakairiti and, although they are not to be feared too greatly, they nonetheless have a reputation for aggression and should be treated with circumspection – one never quite knows if man and mask are one. The spears of fish they carry, like another element of their disguise, materialise their alliance with the Yakairiti, as do their black genipap body designs featuring fish, and their raw, wild cloaks. A Yakairiti side eclipses their opposed human side so that these spirit-men must undergo metamorphosis by means of the action of an immense bonfire and the presentation of intensely cooked foods – salt, oloniti and manioc breads – which quench the Yakairiti's and men's thirst and pay the spirit masters for their fish. With Ioho sated and the pet flutes returned to the flute house, 'Yankwa' returns, embodied by the melodic flutes. As Ioho the spirit-men uttered only onomatopoeic noises but they are now a measure more human as they master words and address their hosts before receiving headdresses and sitting down to sing.

In this fashion, each return sets the stage for another, as if each aspect of Yankwa's divided totality had to be restored separately in order to separate and rearticulate the complex whole of men, spirits and flute. The return is therefore gradual and phased, involving the repetition of equivalent action sequences in the course of which the reunion between hosts and fishermen becomes an intricate play of perspectives between opposed aspects of a divided self – between the human aspect of every person and their Yakairiti aspect. The drama of interrelationship between human and Yakairiti, as opposed classes, and between the living and dead aspect of every person, is realised over these two days as an absorbing aesthetic process. To shift to a socio-logical idiom, I have suggested that one effect of the combination of repetition and variation over twenty-four hours is to expend nervous energy and to blur and mix the separate identities of a divided community: men on both sides swap items of attire, words and goods from the moment they meet.

Now we enter the phase of routinised musical ceremonialism that follows these multiple returns. The climactic character of the encounters described above are deceptive, because the dancers of Yankwa will keep returning; they will return first for Aweresese clan, then for Lolaheses clan and finally for Kairoli clan, dancing for approximately three weeks for each of these hosts. Over these long weeks of feasting and musical ceremonialism the aim is to definitively quench the Yakairiti's prodigious thirst as well as to finish a sequence of cos-mogonic chants. This extended return started at about 4AM on the night after the melodic flutes had been restored to their central house. What does it mean to move between dramatic events and ceremonial routines?

Notes

1. Valadão (1995); Carelli and Campoli (2009); Francisco (2012).
2. For example, V. Turner (1977); Lévi-Strauss (1971); Kapferer (2004).
3. It is no accident that over the last twenty-five years Central Brazilian peoples like the Kayapó, Xavante, Karajá and Kuikuro, who all share this theatrical public life, have avidly embraced cinema and theatre as the most appropriate means of representing their cultures to outsiders. See T. Turner (1992); Nahum-Claudel et al. (2017); Graham (2012); Fausto et al. (2011).
4. The mutual exclusivity of flutes and traps suggests a deeper equivalence between them. Indeed, Enawenê flutes are androgynously gendered and humanoid in a similar way to traps. In a suggestive parallel, S. Hugh-Jones (1979: 217) notes that Yurupary (the name given to Tukano-speakers' sacred flutes and trumpets) translates directly into the image of a man with a fish trap in his mouth – a condensed image of power, abundance and fertility.
5. See O'Hanlon (1989); Strathern and Strathern (1971); Strathern (1988).
6. Maybury-Lewis (2009: 907) and see, for example, DaMatta (1982); Ewart (2013: 907); T. Turner (1979).
7. The palms are felled, left to dry and then burned in situ. Their ashes are transported to the village once cool. They are then piled into a conical basket, which has been specially made by hosts, and then lined with banana leaves by post-menopausal women, whom hosts call upon to take charge of the next phase of salt-making. The conical baskets are hung from the rafters of the house and water is poured into the top and left to filter down through the ashes and drip into a collecting basin placed underneath. The solution is then ferociously boiled, a little at a time, in a small ceramic pot kept especially for the purpose. Once most of the water has evaporated, the potassium salts are dripped onto a plate where a precious grey mountain forms. Among the Enawenê, as among other Amazonian salt-makers such as the Witoto (see Echeverri and Román-Jitdutjaño 2011: 497), this task is considered dangerous for women of fertile age to undertake or even to witness. When the fishermen return, hosts will pay these elder women with fish for these important services.
8. Salt's role as the pre-eminent currency of transaction between humans and spirits is an interesting twist on the role salt plays as a sort of high denomination currency in some regional exchange systems in Papua New Guinea (e.g. Godelier 1969: 26 n.1). Enawenê people's insistence on their salt's equivalence to cash struck me, because the salt was only used in tiny quantities as a condiment. Its value appeared to lie in its ubiquitous circulation. Each time Yankwa received some from hosts into their cupped hands (held just beneath their lips to give the impression that they were 'licking' it) they returned home to stash the salt in little parcels tied with string. In this way, a finite quantity of salt remained in circulation for months, throughout the season of Lerohi.
9. In 2008 the fleets' arrival from each dam was staggered through the early morning, so that this encounter was repeated and hosts had to repeatedly run up and down between village and port.
10. Linguistic analysis of these formal addresses, which is beyond my competence, would yield a much more nuanced understanding of the relationship between men and spirits, which are being negotiated both in these quietly muttered words and subtle gestures, as well as in the more accessible visual and affective domains.

11. Osole belonged to a mythical figure called Taxikanaway, a hybrid jaguar-boy who is the originator of hunting and warfare technologies. Osole seems to reference his toy bow, made from the flimsy spines of palm leaves and with which he shot at falling leaves before he became a man fit to hunt jaguars with a hardwood bow.

12. This moment is called *matakalo ixwana*, a reference to the very first Yankwa, performed by the Yakairiti themselves in mythic times. I will summarise this myth, because it was narrated to present the dangers that attend to Yankwa's return. When Yankwa first returned, the chief Yakairiti host (called Kaynwale, a name also adopted by the hosts during Halokwayti) ignored his brother-in-law's warning and sent women out to meet the returnees instead of going himself. The women were massacred by the incomers and a flute called matakalo, which was made by the Yakairiti from a human arm bone, was broken. Mayuwa-hwale, the man who was holding the flute when it broke, fled in fear of revenge and journeyed upriver. Along the way he met several helpers, acquiring a new flute made from a monkey's arm bone, as well as annatto seeds with which to decorate himself. The helpers urged him to return to the village decorated with the dye and playing this flute. So, he walked up the long, straight path that the Yakairiti had made in order to better see and kill him upon his arrival. It was a success. The hosts emerged from the flute house happy and everyone drank the Yakairiti's favourite kinds of oloniti (which are made from earth, clay and palm fruits rather than manioc). This 'raw' oloniti gives its name to Yankwa's chants during the returning phase: *Kayukolala*. Episodes from Mayuwa-hwale's curative journey form the central and often-repeated chants of Halokwayti, as the hosts make their own anxious preparations to ensure Yankwa's peaceful return. The bone flute matakalo is referred to as 'Yankwa's elder sister' because of its originary status.

13. Although I never tested the theory, it occurs to me that this might be a rehearsal for the song masters, who, after the months of silence, must bring to mind all the chants that will accompany the melodic flutes in the weeks to follow.

14. The host now received larger flattened baskets (*ekwa*), each containing about ten leporinus fish. As on the night before, senior men of the host clans received significantly more fish than their sons and younger brothers. To give an example from 2008, among one group of brothers (none of whom were song masters or leaders of their clan) the eldest received about 30 ekwa, the second 25, the third 12, and the last 9. In 2008 there was an additional transfer of fish to hosts at this point. Yankwa entered the two leading hosts' houses in turn, each man carrying a racket of fish with a charm, such as a child's plastic toy or a miniature calabash attached to it. These were called *Kohase kanola* and were hung in the rafters of hosts' houses, separate from the other fish received. At intervals over the next three months, they would be brought out and laid in lines on the arena, topped by high-quality manioc breads made by hosts' wives and, recognised by the charms attached to them, they would be reclaimed by their original donors. The very low yields of fish in 2009 excluded the giving of kanola.

3

Routine Ritualism and a Festival of Abundance

Grabbing his headdress and palm fibre silks from their hanging place by the front door, Yokwali-ene turned to me with a smile and said: 'I am the ritual, I am off to work' (*ritual nato, notrabalhana*). He was on his way out to the flute house where he would dress for the afternoon's flute-playing session. His joke self-consciously incorporated the Portuguese words 'work' and 'ritual' into an Enawenê syntax. From spending time in the town of Juína, Yokwali-ene had plenty of experience of administrative staff and shopkeepers having set hours and distinct spaces demarcated for work. His parting comment therefore indicated the similarly routin-ised nature of Yankwa's musical ceremonialism in the flute house and central arena. As he bathed, dressed in palm silks and painted with annatto dye ready to begin his daily ceremonial routine, Yokwali-ene did look much like an office worker getting 'suited and booted' for work. In 2009 he purchased a digital alarm clock as a practical accessory to this routine. He set it to wake him at 3AM every night, since he was among Yankwa's leadership and wanted to ensure he was among the first to arrive in the flute house. I loathed to hear the robotic voice in the dead of night repeating 'it's time to get up, it's three o'clock in the morning' until he switched it off. It awoke a nagging feeling that a better anthro-pologist would leave the warmth of their sleeping bag and go outside to transcribe men's chants with a willing informant. I was more comfort-able in a female role, allowing the music to wash over me in half-sleep before getting up to help serve manioc porridge at around 4AM, when the dancers paused to drink and chat.

Figure 3.1 Men's nightly flute playing winds down after dawn in February 2009 as Yankwa prepare to depart for the fishing dams.

It was not only Yokwali-ene who thought of dancing as work to be punctually attended and stoically pursued; men often complained that their limbs ached from dancing during the seasons of Yankwa and Lerohi, and women grumbled about their aches and pains when they danced alongside men during Lerohi, and without them at Kateoko. I experienced this myself when I danced with Lerohi every day for three weeks. This freed me from harvesting and processing manioc but was much more exhausting than stooping to dig up heavy tubers in the dirt or carrying a heavy basket. My legs, back and head ached from the small controlled steps I had to make in time with the rest of the line of dancers while the hot sun beat down on my head and the itchy feather ornaments clung to my sweaty chest. When Enawenê people complained of fatigue they generally followed up with a comment 'it's tough but that's the way Yankwa is; that is the way we Enawenê are'. In short, industriousness, sleeplessness and eagerness, both to sing and dance and to tackle all the essential labours that go on around the arena, are values in and of themselves.

This chapter is about the highly routinised dimension of Enawenênawe ceremonial life and its simultaneously eventful nature. It describes a festive phase during Yankwa's sequence in order to complicate the relationship between 'work' and 'ritual' and, by re-thinking the mutual involvement between these two categories, it comes to a complex understanding of Enawenê gender relations. We are used to thinking of economic activities like harvesting, cooking, gathering firewood and laying ritual fires going on in the background to sustain and enable ritual activities, like singing and dancing, exchanging surplus and feasting. I put this division between profane and sacred activities; between economy and art, and necessity and luxury, into question. On the one hand, chopping firewood and processing manioc are rhythmic and musical performances and, on the other hand, playing flutes at predictable times of the day and night is laborious. As such, there is a reflexive play on the boundary between gendered activities, and between what may be considered functional or pleasurable. How can music be understood as work, and work as music? And how does sexuality link the two? In order to explore these questions, the chapter focuses in on a forty-eight hour period that occurs towards the end of the seventeen-day sequence through which Yankwa 'returns' for each of the host clans. Over two days the relationship between public musical ceremonialism and domestic subsistence work is inverted and economic activities like chopping firewood and pounding manioc are brought into the village's central arena. During these 'work events', as I call them, energetic labour becomes a social and subjective stimulant that aligns men and women with spirits, so that a carnival mood grips the village.

This argument has implications for the way we approach Enawenê gender relations, because only men dance and play flutes at Yankwa while only women harvest, process and cook food. Meanwhile, the men of the host clan mediate between women and Yankwa; they serve the food and drinks that women produce and they convey Yankwa's fish and other products back out from the central arena to the doors of women's houses. However, this gendered division of labour is not an immutable fact of Enawenê life, but is one among several alternative patterns of gender complementarity that succeed one another through the contrasting seasons of the Enawenê year. Although women never play flutes, at Kateoko they decorate with the same palm silks and feather headdresses worn by Yankwa and they sing and dance while men provision them with drinks made from honey they have gathered, and with fish they have caught. This chapter is therefore about the particular model of gender complementarity that prevails during Yankwa, when women's work is defined by the tending and harvesting of manioc gardens and the making of manioc-based foods and drinks for Yankwa's consumption, and when, in turn, Yankwa are defined by their role as the players of flutes – some of which have an aggressive character that threatens but also excites the women, who are the principle audience of men's performances.

In Chapter 1 I showed that dam fishing is akin to harvesting manioc and that men are, in a sense, feminised in their fishing endeavour in a way that challenges a stereotypical distinction between masculine bellicose predation and peaceful feminine harvest. Here we approach a comparable assimilation between flute playing and manioc work. Both involve dance-like repetitive gestures and rhythmic breath and both have the capacity to take people out of the ordinary frame of human social relationships. In Chapter 2 we saw the fishermen return from the dams 'like Yakairiti' and gradually exchange their otherworldly habits for those of Enawenê people, as they prepared to receive headdresses and to play the melodic flutes. In this chapter we will see that this transformation is reversible; the orderly and civilised regime proper to the playing of 'melodic flutes' (*Yankwa ehaylia*) is subverted by the clownish, chaotic, dissonant persona of the 'pet flutes' (*ehola* or *Yankwa hola*), who have the appearance and affects of Yakairiti and whose playing by disguised and energised men brings a carnival mood to the village.

In terms of the sequential narrative I am presenting in Part 1 of this book, this chapter follows from the previous one after the climax of the fishermen's arrival, when all the energy of expectation has been released and exhausted and both the pet and melodic flutes have been returned to their house at the centre of the village. This climax is not an end but rather a beginning; it is the precondition for the melodic flutes' emergence every night and afternoon as Yankwa 'returns' for each of the host clans in turn. Over these two months Yankwa is at its most vital and all-consuming, with feasting, music, exchanging and clowning absorbing everyone's attention every day. The ultimate aim of the returning phase is to finish all the chants and to drink until there is nothing left in the hosts' manioc gardens so that the thirst of the Yakairiti is assured to be totally sated. As the pace of expenditure accelerates, Yankwa's pet flutes – chaotic and ludic characters who toot and whistle, rampage and spill food – increasingly take centre stage, interrupting and subverting the civilised and ordered musical routines of the melodic flutes, bringing women and men into risky and flirtatious contact, and assimilating Enawenê people to the spirits whom their performances are intended to satisfy. This is a festival of abundance in which what is on show is as much vigour in work – work modelled on sexual intercourse and the excitation of men for women and women for men – as it is labour's plentiful products. In order to demonstrate the interplay between routine and its festive acceleration and interruption, I must first describe the gendered daily round, with its characteristic rhythm, soundscape and modes of relationship, varying on a common theme through the different phases of Yankwa's extended sequence.

Variations upon the Daily Round

Each year Yankwa begins with the building of a new flute house and the brief rehearsal of all the wind instruments belonging to each of the nine clans, accompanied by the drinking of a sweet corn drink called *olxiwala*, from the corn gardens' early harvest. After this inauguration, Yankwa is composed of three central phases during which one pair of clans host the men of the remaining seven, who sing, dance and fish for them. These are the men of 'Yankwa' and they 'leave' (*tekwana*), are 'away' (*iytikini*) and then 'return' (*takwata*) for these two clans, each phase lasting approximately two months. There is the build-up to departure of most of the men of the village on dam-fishing expeditions, the period of their absence when hosts and women prepare the village for their return, and then the period of most intense musical ceremonialism and feasting, which follows their return. Once the return is complete, attention turns to the preparation of new collective gardens, which will allow a new pair of clans to host Yankwa over the following two years, generating an unbroken cycle of hosting obligations over the decades. In order to enable this the planting of gardens is staggered: at the end of Yankwa's return in the first year new manioc gardens are sited and their trees felled, while after the second year's return this land is further cleared, burned and planted.

During each phase (fresh corn, leaving, vigil, returning, burning/ planting) the twenty-four hour routine varies on a common theme, but a constant feature is the playing of flutes in the hours before dawn, accompanied by the drinking of ketera. Women's daily work routine is conditioned by the provisioning of this nightly drink; co-resident mothers and daughters, or teams of sisters, pool their labour to harvest the manioc crop in the hours after dawn, grate and sieve the tubers in the morning, and thicken the boiled juice with corn and manioc starch in the late afternoon. When the hosts carry out calabashes full of this warm drink the dancers break off and sit down to drink and banter close to their fire. The flutes are played most intensively after this ketera break and until dawn. Flute playing then gradually melds into a rising cacophony of talk and laughter as morning men's meetings supersede musical performance.

The rest of men's day varies through Yankwa's different phases. Before Yankwa leaves for the dams, the flutes are only played in the hours before dawn by men wearing their palm silks but not yet crowned with feather headdresses. Afternoons are taken up with playing a traditional ball game called *haira*, or football in the arena.[1] Hook and line fishing and trips to town to organise gasoline provision for the fleet of boats are also a major preoccupation. As we know from the previous chapter, during Halokwayti there are brief nightly song sessions and afternoon parades that accompany work to prepare the village for the fishermen's return. During Yankwa's returning phase, which concerns us here, musical ceremonialism is doubly intense compared to the leaving phase. The headdress-crowned returnees sing and dance in the arena not only before dawn (from between 2 and 4AM until 6 to 9AM) but also for an equivalent period in the afternoon and evening (from between 2 and 3PM until 6 to 9PM). Each day begins in the predawn session, when new chants are added cumulatively to a sequence. In the afternoon the flute groups take turns to rehearse the chants inside the flute house, turning around its central post. At dusk the hosts light three or four fires in the arena and all the flute groups then emerge from the flute house to perfect and complete the chants around their separate fires. All the women of the village watch and listen and the men of the host clan stand by to tend the fires.

During this intensive phase of return there is thus very little time to do anything but dance and men take most of their meals publically in the arena, where they are served by hosts.[2] Men return to their houses for little more than to catch up on sleep and they try to find snatches of time to clear and plant their manioc gardens with their wives. Thus there is an overarching intensification as Yankwa progresses through leaving, returning and gardening phases, as well as an intensification within each phase, with musical ceremonialism becoming increasingly absorbing in the course of each phase. This is not only audible in the hours of flute play, which begin earlier in the night and encroach increasingly into the middle of the day, but also in the lines of dancing men at each hearth, which get longer day by day, as adolescents and even young boys join their responsible elders towards the culmination of a phase. As we saw in Chapters 1 and 2, the end of both the departing phase and Halokwayti see a flurry of activity. During Yankwa's return the intensification takes on a different character; whereas before the emphasis was on amassing surplus and quickening preparedness, now the aim is to expend surplus and to finish chants so that the host clan's flutes can be safely put to rest. Towards the end of the returning phase not only were chanting and flute playing unbroken from before dawn until after dusk, but gluts of perishable food were served in excess, and libations of oloniti were repeatedly offered to the Yakairiti – this was a period of sumptuary dissipation.

While each phase may be talked about as a whole – leaving, away, returning, clearing or burning – in fact, except for the period when the fishermen are away and the paired host clans become a single unit called 'Halokwayti', each of the other phases is segmented so that this intensification occurs for each of the two or three host clans in turn. For example, in 2009 the two month phase of Yankwa's return spanned from 27 April to 23 June and was divided into equivalent sequences of approximately seventeen days duration for the three clans who were hosting that year: first Aweresese, second Lolahese and third Kairoli. Each clan's sequence was the same, involving successive days during which particular cosmogonic chants took precedence, giving their name to the day in the same way that construction tasks did at the dam. Since this sequence is archetypal, what I define as 'events' are breaks with routine, not because they are unexpected or accidental but because they push people out of a predictable daily round. Moments of transition, such as the fishermen's actual day of departure and return, are therefore events by definition because they force people to transfigure the pattern of their daily lives to accommodate their new social circumstances. Other events cluster at the culmination of each sequence as part of a momentum of acceleration and intensification.

In summary, over the course of Yankwa there are phases of energetic build-up and of exhaustion, dissipation and release, and these dynamics are matched by contrasting emphases in economic life, where amassing surplus allows for lavish display and expenditure at a later time. There is thus an overarching intensification over Yankwa's eight month process, within which time is segmented, not only into distinct phases but also into separate clan sequences within each phase. In each sequence there is a predictable daily round with habitual timings of flute play, ball games or gardening work; a characteristic orientation in village space; subtle variations in dress; and specific genres of cosmogonic chants. This routine is broken on certain days that have particular symbolic importance and come towards the end of each clan's sequence. These events seem to be about accelerating productive activity and exchange to make a public performance and display of abundance.

A Festival of Abundance

'There will be no "ritual" tonight, the women will pound in their mortars' one of the men in my house told me the first time I took part in the culminating days of Aweresese clan's returning sequence in 2008. The event was sometimes referred to as 'women's ritual' in Portuguese but was usually called *Batatakwayti* in onomatopoetic reference to the rhythmic pounding of pestles in mortars – *ba-ta-ta-kway-ti*. It was also referred to as *Yakaloti-nero* ('spirit-woman') in allusion to women's other-worldly transformation through their virile work. Effectively, Yankwa's wives led teams of women to make oloniti (the drink Enawenê people consume everyday like water) for hosts in an extraordinary way (at an accelerated pace, at night and in others' houses) and received food from hosts in payment for their work. This inverted the usual pattern in which hosts' wives made drinks to sustain and nourish Yankwa and did not receive any payment for this routine duty. This pounding ritual was the central event in a series of dramatised role reversals between men and women; Yankwa and hosts; Yankwa's wives and hosts' wives; and pestles and flutes.

The sequence of events begins the night before Batatakwayti, when men chant dangerous songs said to belong to the Yakairiti themselves, and continues up to the end of the clan's returning sequence. These chants are said to have been learnt by an Enawenê man called Bailiterese, who was taken to the Yakairiti's village and returned to transmit the songs to his human kin before dying. One of their themes is the Yakairiti's fermented beer, which swells the belly and potentially kills its drinkers. Although this was never spelled out to me by anyone, following directly after a night of Yakairiti-song, Batatakwayti in some sense enacts its themes, since Yakairiti women make oloniti, which they leave to sour instead of reboiling it to prevent its fermentation as they would ordinarily do. Over subsequent days the boisterous and lusty pet flutes (the same pets who took centre stage at Halokwayti and then at Ioho) would raid women's hearths to spill this oloniti into the Yakairiti's underground pans. As they did so they would behave suspiciously like Yakairiti themselves.

By 7AM Yankwa's dancing and Yakairiti song was winding down, but rather than giving way to a men's meeting, as it usually did, on this day the dancers headed straight for the port, where teams of men set off in boats. They went to fell saplings and strip them of their bark in order to make the two metre long pestles (*anase*) that women used every day for all kinds of food processing. When they returned at about 9AM, the men were referred to as 'pestle-bringing people' (*anase weku nawe*) by the women, who excitedly looked on from their doorways, taking a break from their manioc grating. The pestle-bringers walked in single file towards the flutes house, each man bearing six to eight of the new pestles on his shoulders. Upon hearing the hum of engines approaching, the hosts had already gathered in the flute house with oloniti to serve to their thirsty benefactors. Just a few minutes later, the hosts emerged from the flute house, each carrying a heavy load of pestles, which they took back into their own houses. After the heat of the day had passed, the sound of axes falling on wood filled the village as Yankwa split tree trunks that they had felled and gathered over the preceding days. They cut the firewood into handy lengths, divided it into equal-sized piles and tied each up into a neat bundle using bark fibre string. These bundles were destined for the hosts. Men counted their bundles repeatedly, naming each of the twenty-three adult members of the host clan to ensure they had accounted for everyone. Then they piled the firewood bundles by the sides of their houses, ready for distribution the next day.

Watching this, my hypothesis was that the pestles were a form of repayment for hosts' wives, who had been pounding the ingredients for Yankwa's drinks over the preceding days, weeks and months. By the same logic, the firewood would repay the hosts' equally constant work feeding the fires around which Yankwa danced every night and day. I proposed this theory that Yankwa were repaying the routine ritual services of hosts and their wives 'in one fell swoop' to one of the men as he split firewood, but it was briskly negated. Hosts, I was told, had already received fish upon Yankwa's return from the dams and that was why they tended the fires. This was something different. Tomorrow I would see; hosts would receive the firewood and then they would pay for it with fish soup. Had I not noticed that there were no hosts about because they had all gone fishing? As for hosts' wives, although the new pestles would remain in their houses for their use in the long term, it would not be them but Yankwa's wives who would be the first to pound with them that night.

Indeed, at dusk, after gathering in discussion in the arena, each of the men of the host clan, Aweresese, approached the doorway of one of Yankwa's leaders, the senior men who guided Yankwa's work on the host clan's behalf. The leaders' wives knew the hosts were coming and were waiting inside their doorways to see which host would issue the invitation, to 'make oloniti for "the dangerous ones" to drink'. 'The dangerous ones' is the conventional way Yakairiti are referred to in formal addresses. Over the course of the evening these leading women, who had just been summoned, invited women from other houses to join them at their host's mortar that night. Usually, women invited their betrothal partners (*enatunawenero*) – that is, the women who would become their children's mothers-in-law when they were old enough to marry. These were women whom they usually respectfully avoided except in the context of giving or receiving formal gifts. Leading women were thus preparing to head teams made up of their affines in manioc work that would take place outside of their household and under the cover of darkness. This contrasted absolutely with the everyday pattern in which women worked with their sisters, inside their extended uxorilocal households, in the hours of daylight. Indeed Batatakwayti was an opportunity to activate betrothal relationships and to publicly observe the evidence of others' affinal relations. Men, who were so used to mixing with their affines in the arena at night, would remain asleep in their separate houses while women mixed and made music. Women looked forward to this exciting and exceptional night and everyone was 'eager and willing' (*kainyawalo*) to participate.

On most nights men awaken and go to the flute house when they hear the leaders sound the flutes. As more and more men file in the sound gradually swells and diversifies. The same was true on this night. The wake-up call was provided by the wife of Yankwa's paramount leader, who pounded a pestle hard into an empty mortar at 3:30AM, as if she were drumming a rhythmic baseline. Women quickly dressed in their newest and brightest red skirts and hurried to the mortars to which they had been assigned the evening before. The leader at each mortar was the woman who had personally been invited by one of the seventeen male hosts of Aweresese clan. Each lead woman arrived at her host's house with two aluminium basins, one filled with dried manioc odds and ends and the other with dry corn seed. These were the raw materials that her team would pound to make the two kinds of flour that are used to make oloniti. Hosts had erected torches (posts to which a burning resin called *doti* was bound) next to the mortars in order to illuminate women's pounding. As more and more women arrived at their assigned mortars, the sound intensified until a syncopated galloping rhythm was generated by all the women pounding in mortars throughout the dwelling circle. The ground shook perceptibly.

As well as being exceptional in taking place under cover of darkness and joining a group of affines, the pounding technique and rhythm was distinct from the everyday norm. Women chose the narrower and lighter among the new pestles so that five, six or even seven women could pound together in one mortar. As I learnt through my own incompetence, this required a precise technique: a light grip on the pestle, an upright stance, a steady angle at the elbow and a springy bend in the knees. All of this allowed one – in theory – to bounce off the hardwood mortar bringing the pestle up straight and swift without clashing with the others before timing the next downward motion. Mature women set the pace for teenagers, while girls as young as five who had excitedly followed their mothers joined in for short bursts. Teenage girls practised this technique in groups in the run up to Batatakwayti, pounding flour at an accelerated pace, striving conscientiously at first but usually speeding up to the point of chaos and dissolving into laughter.

With this accelerated and intensified method, many pestles made quick and light work and the overall miraculous impression was that the ingredients powdered themselves. Only the usual ingredients needed to make the mildly fermented watery drink called oloniti were pounded, and the oloniti that would result was just the ordinary 'black stuff' (*kiyalo*) drunk everyday (rather than one of the various kinds of special, extra sweet oloniti that are sometimes prepared). What was exceptional was this method. On most days, one of the women of a household makes a new pan of oloniti, while the rest occupy themselves with harvesting fresh manioc for the day's pan of ketera. Alone, or with a young helpmate, she pounds corn seed and dried manioc bits, using a thick and weighty pestle. She puts about half a kilo of corn seed in the mortar, pounds it for several minutes, then passes it through a sieve, and then re-pounds and re-sieves the mass over and again until all the corn passes through the sieve. This takes her at least an hour.

By contrast, on this night, the pounding was a gallop compared to the usual trot and up to six women pounded together. Because only a handful of corn seed or manioc was placed in the mortar at once the ingredients were reduced to a fine powder in under a minute and could be scooped directly into a basin without the need for sieving. Like people all over the world the Enawenê hark back to a mythic golden age of ease and plenty in which today's burdensome work was effortlessly achieved. In the Enawenê version of this Edenic trope, a Star-woman descends from the heavens to become the cultural hero Datamale's wife whose full baskets of manioc walk by themselves; who drops one of her magic stones into a pool and it dries up so that the fish can be simply picked up; who slings her magic rope around the forest and pulls gently to clear the land for planting; and whose pans of drink are self-replenishing so that Yankwa's thirst is always quenched.[3] Although nobody ever connected these stories to women's pounding, it appeared to me that when women coordinated and accelerated their work, it took on a similarly miraculous quality. The next phase of this festival of abundance would take place in the daylight. The products of women's invisible but musical labour were revealed as each of the teams set up public hearths to finish the preparation of their oloniti in the central arena.

The pounding ended just before dawn and there was a flurry of simultaneous activity: teenage girls went to fetch water while leading women set up 125 litre aluminium pans on clay blocks in front of host's houses, and stoked plenty of firewood beneath them. Many such hearths were set up, forming a ring inside the arena. As this was going

on, Yankwa emerged from the flute house dressed in T-shirts and shorts
rather than their flute-playing attire and carrying the firewood they had
split and bundled the day before.[4] The hosts knew this moment was
coming and they were stood outside their houses ready with a small
pan of oloniti and some calabashes. The mass of firewood-bearers –
some eighty men – came towards two or three hosts at a time, littering
the ground at their feet with their bundles and waiting impatiently to
receive oloniti to quench their exaggerated thirst. Young men were most
unruly, dropping their bundles of wood noisily to the floor, stamping
on them and calling out to be brought refreshment. Once approached
by the host, they drank a gulp, made ostentatious ululations as they
spilled the rest to the ground, and then handed back the calabash. Hosts
rushed to serve all of the men who approach them and were theatrically
overwhelmed and extravagantly servile. They stood side on and gazed
down as they handed over the calabashes of drink, then turned and ran
back to the pan, only to turn again on their heels, in order to respond to
someone else's call to pick up firewood. As hosts played-up their good
servant role, Yankwa behaved with jocular aggression.

Women had bathed hurriedly, applied annatto to their faces and put
on their best skirts again in order to miss as little as possible of these
antics as they waited for their pans of water to reach simmering point.
Then they stirred in the corn and manioc flours at their public hearths.
Meanwhile Yankwa were rigging up a line between two posts in the
centre of the arena and hanging the flutes from it before proceeding to
decorate and dress them like dancers in feathers, annatto dye and palm
silks.[5] At about 9AM women returned to their hosts' mortars to pound
more manioc and corn in order to make the toasted breads that they
would masticate throughout the morning, using the enzymes in their
saliva to convert starch into sugar in order to sweeten the oloniti. After
this second round of pounding at the hosts' mortars, leading women
received a payment of dam-caught fish coupled with manioc bread from
their hosts and they shared out this ample meal among their team.

As I had been reliably informed, most of the hosts had been fishing
on the previous day. Consequently, hosts' wives had been quietly making
fish soup and griddling corn and manioc breads at their central heaths
while the pounding had taken over the open areas of the house. This
soup was referred to as a 'firewood-getting payment' (*tikwayti toli*). In
the middle of the day, hosts brought out pots of fish soup, each attrac-
tively topped by a pair of breads of contrasting colour (a yellow corn
bread and grey-white manioc one), and placed them in arced lines on
the arena. When Aweresese clan were hosting in 2009, twelve of the
hosts each brought out thirty to forty pots of fish soup each, amounting

Figure 3.2 Women arrange themselves around the heap of tubers to grate manioc together. They have straight backs and straight legs and pivot from the hips.

to a total of around 1,500 litres, which they invited the eighty men of Yankwa to receive. All of the recipients made several trips back and forth from their houses, ferrying calabashes or clay pots full of soup. Inside the house, their wives poured these into one big receptacle so that their husbands could return the pots to the hosts. In our household, the pan full of mixed soups, which were brought in by five men of the house, amounted to only slightly less than our co-resident host had just given out. Given that many of the women had already drunk the hosts' ketera in the early morning and eaten their payment of fish and manioc bread just previously, no one was very hungry and much of this soup was still uneaten at nightfall, by which time it had begun to bubble and rot.

At four in the afternoon, a few hours after the masticated toasts had been added, the oloniti-making culminated. The teams of women reconvened at their public hearths to pass the oloniti through a sieve, pressing the liquid out of the swollen corn and manioc fibres, which were then discarded. Oloniti is usually not sieved until the dregs are reached, in order to eke out the last quarter of the pan. On this day, however, immediate sieving makes a full to brimming pan of ideal, consumable oloniti. The oloniti had reached an ideal state of separation, sweetness and coolness. A mundane process that would usually take two days had been rendered public, musical and spectacular, as one part of a festival of abundance, which involved Yankwa's bounty of new pestles; the hosts' distribution of ample firewood; more fish soup than anyone could eat; the spectacle of beautified flutes and women; and of memorably energised men.

The Choreography of Work

During this exceptional long day the musicality inherent to mundane activities of pounding, cooking and chopping firewood is heightened and made public in a choreographed performance of everyday provisioning tasks. Women pound under the cover of darkness, which magnifies the musical character of their work, and the village auditorium is filled with their vibrations. The work of boiling, sweetening and sieving the oloniti, which is usually both silent and hidden inside individual dwellings, is displayed as a public spectacle. Simultaneously, silent flutes are publicly beautified and displayed in the middle of the day. There is therefore a thoroughgoing play of contrasts between the visual and acoustic dimensions of shared experience. This altered patterning of sound and vision creates a palpable break from routine and introduces a non-discursive reflexivity into the daily round. Reflexivity is also introduced through the manipulation of time and through role reversal. The acceleration of the pounding technique and of the whole oloniti-making process, and the sudden windfall of firewood, pestles and fish soup, are accomplished within altered relations of production: women receive food from hosts rather than offering it and hosts receive firewood from Yankwa rather than provisioning it. The effect of all these reversals is to mark all activities as exceptional events. To employ terms developed by Victor Turner (1977) to describe ritual processes, it is as if the village were flipped into an 'anti-structural' and carnivalesque mode of production: super-production in super-time, in which work is achieved miraculously under the cover of night, so that its fruits could be revealed and celebrated in the light of day.

At Batatakwayti the action of pounding becomes overtly a dance; the dance with the pestles, which produces the 'song of the mortar'. This is my idiom but it fits what men say about listening to women's pounding rather than awaking to play flutes themselves, as well as the onomatopoeic 'drumming' in the name itself. What I want now to emphasise is that this musicality is not unique to this extraordinary event but is rather a facet of women's everyday manioc work. Christine

Hugh-Jones was probably the first to observe that Amerindian women's manioc work was highly ritualistic such that it could be considered a female counterpart to male flute playing (1979: 181–82), but while it is well established that unified dance and chanting generate the experience of communion and pleasure, manioc work has commonly been understood as merely hard labour.[6] I want to show that women's coordinated manioc work stimulates the senses in a similar way to dancing and chanting.

Enawenê women's daily labours with manioc tubers are markedly dance-like if we follow a simple definition of dance as highly patterned activity combining controlled, rhythmic movements (Kaeppler 1978). And insofar as the sound of pounding all around the dwelling circle already fills the village at predictable times each day, Batatakwayti only dramatises the poetic qualities of everyday work. Although it would never occur to Enawenê women to look at it this way, their daily manioc round stretches and exercises the body holistically in a staged, gestural dance as women proceed through the tasks of digging, washing, rasping, grating, sieving and pounding in turn, each of which involves repeated, rhythmic gestures, which must be produced in their given order. From gardens to mortar, the sequence of tasks proceeds from low to high so that the body that is bent double in the early morning is brought increasingly upright. To uproot manioc, which grows deep underground, Enawenê women sit or kneel in the dirt, they plunge their hands deep into the ground and they wear cotton shorts and T-shirts, which are brown from habitual garden wear. However, once they have peeled and washed the tubers and piled them ready for grating, they leave a neat pile of naked white tubers in the house and go to bathe. Then they paint with annatto and change into their tightly woven red cotton skirts – the same ones they wear for marked ceremonial occasions. These skirts unyieldingly bind the hips, so that one's legs must be kept close together. Wearing them, women grate manioc standing up, with the bottom of the grater resting in a basin before their feet and its top resting on their thighs. They bend forward over their graters and, keeping legs straight and knees softly locked, they use the hips as a pivot to rhythmically and vigorously push the tubers down the grater and lift them up again with the whole upper body (see Figure 3.2). The next stage is sieving the wet pulp to gather the juice and press the fibre into compacted discs for drying. This requires a more upright position in which legs and back are perpendicular. The final action of pounding the odds and ends of tubers – the leftovers that are too small to grate – brings women to standing with their arms raised high above their heads before they bring the pestle downwards.

Each morning and all over the village, knots of women make these same patterns with their bodies at the same time, just as men can also predictably be found chopping up firewood at the back of their houses every evening before dusk. As a result of this tendency for simultaneity in provisioning tasks, every phase of Yankwa has its distinctive daily soundscape made up of economic as well as musical labour, as well as its defining patterns of movement in the arena.[7] A sonic patterning through the course of each day and night is generated by Yankwa's musical routines; by the sounds of axes, graters and mortars; the buzz of talk during men's meetings; the laughter and chatter that prevail after the flutes have been put to rest in the evening; and the periods of quiet around noon and midnight. Batatakwayti and the events surrounding it draw attention to the sonic and visual qualities of this highly structured everyday life. It is perhaps the shared soundscape, more than anything else, that provides every person with constant evidence of the synchronicity of their own and other's activities, since it allows women to know that other women are also grating or pounding manioc, even though they cannot see into their houses. Stephen Feld (1996: 97) has argued that anthropological accounts have a visual bias, neglecting acoustic experience, although 'sound, hearing, and voice mark a special bodily nexus for sensation and emotion because of their coordination of brain, nervous system, head, ear, chest, muscles, respiration, and breathing'. This applies to rhythmic, coordinated work as much as it does to chanting. The parallel between musical expression and coordinated work is therefore experiential as well as symbolic. When men play flutes and sing, the movement of their breath is always coupled with rhythmic stepping and swaying motions, emphasising the degree to which their music is embodied. Women's manioc work involves similarly rhythmic movements and breath and it affords a holistic sensory and aesthetic pleasure to women as they strive to harmonise their movements in their huddle around the pile of tubers and inevitably end up participating in a village-wide daily round. If this were not so, why would women dress and paint their bodies to grate manioc? And why would they array themselves around the pile of tubers so that they are almost touching, in order to grate them all together?

Participating almost daily in manioc gardening and processing alongside women in my own and other households, I had taken the physical exuberance of the manioc round for granted. It occurred to me that Enawenê women's work was something to think about more closely when I found photographs of Matis and Chimane women grating and sieving manioc in a book dedicated to the topic of beer-making in Amazonia (Erikson 2004a: 54,79). These women appeared to be working quite placidly and were seated casually on the ground. They were clearly not demonstrating vigour or striving to coordinate their gestures as Enawenê women habitually did. It is nonetheless a commonality across Amazonia that women's days are largely devoted to the time-consuming processing of bitter manioc into food and drink, and this gendered division of labour has received sustained attention from Amazonianists. In a useful summary, Griffiths (2001: 247) notes that there have been three distinct lines of questioning: what does the division of labour say about the relative status of men and women? How efficient are these subsistence strategies in providing for people's nutritional needs? And what is the cultural significance of work? Griffiths notes that the three approaches have not received equal weight, with "'supposedly real" issues of gender conflict, local politics, prestige and power' taking precedence (ibid.: 258) over local conceptions of work.

The argument advanced here touches on the first question, about the extent to which gendered work can be said to be complimentary or exploitative, as well as exploring the cultural significance of work for the Enawenê. Amazonian women's time-consuming manioc work has repeatedly been cited as evidence of male domination. The argument goes that Amazonian men sustain their dominance by constraining, controlling and domesticating women by tying up their time in low-status manioc work.[8] Given Enawenê women's enjoyment of manioc work, it annoyed me to see this line of argument repeated, always by male anthropologists who had never participated in women's work. It was mind-boggling, for example, that Thomas Gregor (1985: 80–83) persisted in characterising manioc processing as 'unending drudgery' despite noting that 'in this drudgery, the villagers see a symbolism of sexual relations'. Gregor did not entertain the idea that this symbolism could be grounded in women's experience of pleasure in work. Unsurprisingly, it has been female anthropologists who have contradicted these arguments, on the basis of evidence about women's experience of work and its high cultural value.[9]

In the Enawenê case, the pleasure and vigour of manioc work is dependent on togetherness and synchronicity. Women chivvy each other to come back to grating around the pile, and when others drop out of the group, those left grating or pounding slow demonstrably. Overing and Passes (2000) have written about the sociability of work in their book celebrating mundane forms of conviviality and experience in Amazonia. Among the Pa'ikwené's of Northeastern Amazonia, Passes (2000: 99) writes that 'communality, amicability and high spirits' in work generate physical exuberance. Overing comments that Piaroa people choose to work with those with whom they have an easy bantering relationship because shared joking and laughter are considered essential to collaborative work (2000: 69). This all rings true of the many kinds of work Enawenê men and women collaborate in, but it also misses the performative, public dimension of Enawenê work, which is heightened during Batatakwayti. Overing and Passes are at pains to distance themselves from considerations of ritual and structure (which in their view have received disproportionate attention in Amazonia) in favour of mundane activities and subjective experience. But this is a problematic analytic divide from the point of view of this ethnography. Everyday life is experienced as highly structured and transformational such that working, living and relating are aestheticized and choreographed to take on poetic qualities, become public performances, and bring about altered subjective states. At Batatakwayti, the conviviality of collective work is transformed when it becomes a spectacle, and joking and gossip – which are indeed the stuff of everyday sisterhood – are replaced by conscientious absorption as elements of technique and self-presentation come to the fore, with the presence of affines, listeners and furtive male onlookers. In short, Enawenê work is highly ritualised so that 'ritual' singing and dancing with flutes in the arena cannot be strictly separated from the 'work' that goes on around the arena's edge to support it. Both kinds of activity have a common experiential base and both draw people together around their arena and auditorium.

The Enawenê's use of work to expand social relationships and create communitas finds the most obvious parallel in ethnography of collective work parties, which often occur in Amazonia and elsewhere during the felling and planting of new gardens. Commonly, the gardens' owner enlists other members of the community to open a new garden and he provides food and beer as an incentive. Consideration of work parties is particularly prominent in Andean anthropology (e.g., Good 2005; Harris 2007), and the scene Olivia Harris paints of Northern Potosí people 'dressed up in their best clothes to go out to work together … the yoke of the plough [decorated] with willow fronds' is very close to the Enawenê's joyful festivals of work for Yankwa. My argument is that the Enawenê are doing this every day – every day is a collective work party. Yankwa is an eventful routine in which different kinds of work are necessary to continually regenerate good relations with other people and with spirit beings (cf. Griffiths 2001: 249).

Now I want to add another dimension to this argument by showing that this continual intensive work effort is energised by, and in turn generates, sexual desire. In doing so, I extend Gow's (1989: 574) insights on the 'systematic connections between sexual desire and the construction of the person as a producer in the subsistence economy'. Amazonian subsistence economies generally follow a pattern of marked sexual division of labour in which men prepare gardens, hunt and fish and women do the bulk of the harvesting of staple crops and the gathering of forest foods. A proper meal invariably pairs 'male' and 'female' foods and can therefore only be produced in the context of marriage. Gow (1989: 579) demonstrates that Piro food 'is produced in relations of demand between adult men and women related as sexual partners' and that, reciprocally, gender identity is closely linked to peoples' capacities to produce specific foods within a heterosexual division of labour. It is easy to see how mutual demands for food become linked to demands for sexual gratification. As Siskind (1973) was the first to notice, in 'the hunting economy of sex' men had to win sexual gratification from women by satisfying their hunger for game. This assimilation between two kinds of satisfaction is most obvious in joking, which is invariably sexual in theme and often plays on metaphors between food and sex. Gow's argument is as relevant to the Enawenê as it is to the Piro. We have seen in previous chapters that men at the dam joke about their girl-friends' vaginas being akin to different flavours of honey; that women go to the supposedly exclusively male dams 'seeking fish and seeking penis'; and that returning fishermen are the bringers of the kinds of goods, foods and masculine bodies that women desire. These are examples of the way 'sexuality and food are made analogous at the level of desire', just as Gow suggests (1989: 567). In addition, I want to argue that productive capacity is suffused by desire, as women and men work to satisfy one another not only with the products of their efforts but also with their performances of bodily vigour in work.

Desire in Work

In my description of Batatakwayti, I left out a bawdy detail. As women pounded, groups of young men went sneaking around the outside of houses, spying in at the illuminated women. They revealed themselves by poking pestles in and out through the thatch. This was pretty obviously a ribald gesture that played on the suggestive pounding of pestle into mortar, and the up and down movement of women's bodies. Women shooed them away. I know that when men watch women pounding and grating manioc they are put in mind of sex because with a regularity I found annoying and embarrassing, men interrupted my manioc work to teach me about Enawenê sexual preferences. They congratulated me on my pounding proficiency, which, they said, reminded them of the best kind of sex, in which women moved their hips rhythmically. Above I mentioned Thomas Gregor's incongruous determination that Mehinaku women's manioc work was drudgery despite his awareness of its explicitly sexual connotations. Gregor (1985: 82) expands with relish on the analogy Mehinaku make between sex and the action of grating phallic manioc tubers. In contrast to Enawenê women's upright grating stance, Mehinaku women squat on a low bench with their knees apart, pushing tubers up and down the grating board, which they hold firm between their thighs. They say that the grating board is like a vagina which eats the penis-like manioc tuber. Moreover they employ a special rhythmic breathing technique, pushing their breath out through closed teeth, to ease their efforts. Gregor concludes: 'Above all other ordinary activities, grinding manioc replicates the sounds, movements, and standard seating position for sexual relations ... the Mehinaku themselves ... describe it as a "picture of intercourse"' (ibid.).

While the Enawenê are not quite so explicit as the Mehinaku, there is an Enawenê myth that links manioc work and sex and celebrates the sexualised quality of women's work while warning of the risks of unbridled desire. In the myth, every stage of women's manioc processing round becomes the opportunity to copulate with a giant penis, until the day when a jealous son severs the penis, following which the women abandon their son, steal men's flutes and run away from the village. The myth associates manioc work with intercourse, making the same connection that Mehinaku people make overtly and which Enawenê men suggest via their jokes. At a more general level the myth is about the Janus face of gender relations, whose sexual and maternal nature can come into conflict.

> Okoyoli saw a beautiful woman at the bathing pool and he wanted to have sex with her, despite her warnings that she was not a human but a Yakairiti woman. As he withdrew his penis after intercourse it grew longer and longer. It was so long that he had to carry it coiled up in a basket on his back. The woman told him to carry his penis into the flute house and to stay hidden there. Every day Okoyoli listened from the flute house until he heard the 'ta-la, ta-la' sound of calabashes clanking together in their bundles as women brushed past them with their laden baskets upon their return from the manioc gardens. Then he knew it was time to extend his penis into their houses. The giant penis had sex with the women as they bent over their manioc graters, and again when they bounced up and down pounding in the mortar, and again at the bathing pool as they squatted over the shallow water, thrusting their bodies up and down over the water's surface. The women took turns with the magnificent penis and Okoyoli had all the women indiscriminately.
>
> One day, as he rested in his hammock behind the woven partition next to where the women worked, a son saw all of this through a gap in the

weave. The next day, while the women were still away at the manioc gardens, he himself shook the calabashes – 'tala-tala' – to trick Okoyoli into thinking they had already returned. He chopped the penis off when it crossed the threshold and tied the severed part above the entranceway so that the women would see it upon their return. When they did see it they gasped, fearing it to be Okoyoli's penis. They shook the calabashes – 'tala-tala' – to see if Okoyoli would come as usual, but he did not. Then they went to bathe but no penis came to the pool either. All the women mourned the loss of the penis. They knew their son had severed the penis and so they abandoned him in the night, taking the flutes and pursuing Okoyoli as he fled up to the headwaters of Olowina River.

After this, the orphaned son pursues his fleeing mothers, always arriving at their overnight camp just after they have left it. One of the fleeing women takes pity on him and waits behind to give him a flute and to advise him to fish himself a new wife. At the end of the myth the women and their son have a divergent destiny; Okoyoli and the pursuing women enter the rocks at the top of the River Arimena, completing their transformation into Yakairiti, while the son is given a flute and a wife with which he will be able to restore proper village life.

I was told this myth by the women with whom I lived in gleeful detail, complete with vivid examples from our shared everyday routine – our eagerness to return from the gardens, our pleasure in owning a mass of calabashes, the joys of pounding together in the mortar and then bathing away the sweat afterwards. There was no moralising tinge to their account of the transgressive excess brought on by a mythic sex fiend with a gigantic penis. Similar myths about penises elongated through intercourse with a spirit-woman are widespread in Amazonia. Gregor (1985: 132–37) interprets the Mehinaku version as a warning about the dangers of excess desire and an expression of men's fundamental castration anxiety. Gregor does not provide a full enough version of the Mehinaku myth for me to be able to dispute his interpretation, but in the Enawenê myth, at least, Okoyoli's castration is less important than the penis's loss to women. According to Overing, the Piaroa version of the giant penis myth is ostensibly about the origins of menstruation, which women gain when they have sex with the bloody stump of the severed penis (Overing 1986: 143). Unlike Gregor, Overing gives a female perspective on the myth, noting that when women lost the giant penis 'they moped and refused to work' (ibid.). Like the Enawenê myth then, the Piaroa one brings into focus the relationship between work and sexual desire. In this sense it is celebratory: with the penis the women work with energy and make their calabashes 'sing'. On the other hand this is a story about a dangerous excess of desire: Okoyoli's penis is over-erect after he gives in to his immoderate desire for the Yakairiti woman, and women become excessively sexualised in response to his giant penis such that they renounce motherhood because they can think only of sex. The women of my household laid this on thick when they narrated the myth to me. When it came to describing the women's desertion of their son they said 'they showed him their anuses so that he saw the beads hanging down around their vaginas'. Enawenê women never show their genitals outside of sexual encounters, so this is a highly transgressive image of sex trumping motherhood. It is clear that excessive sexualisation is associated with Yakairiti in the myth, just as we also know that women were known as 'Yakairiti women' during Batatakwayti, when marauding men poked pestles in and out through the thatch. Indeed, both men and women are said to become Yakairiti when they break out of routine relations of production. These moments tend to be associated with direct, sexualised contact between them. In particular, the equivalent of women's night-time transformation into supercharged and other-worldly Yakairiti women occurs when men act as pet flutes during the final frenetic days of the returning sequence. I want to suggest that the tension between maternal and sexual gender relations in the myth, and in the two tempos of female activity, correspond to a contrast in men's performances when they play two kinds of flute: civilised, melodic flutes and bawdy pet flutes. These flute personages, with their contrasting modalities of performance – predictable order, and chaotic outbursts of energy; containment (calabashes of ketera) and overflow or spillage (libations of oloniti) – define two energetic registers within Yankwa that bring an alternate cast to relations between men and women, from respectful distance to sexualised contact.

Pet Flutes and Melodic Flutes

The pets' relationship to women is tricksy, flirtatious and direct. Women enjoy watching the rousing performances of the transfigured spirit-men and the sexual joking that is their speciality. Whereas hosts habitually mediate between Yankwa's melodic flutes in the arena and women in houses, the pets bypass the hosts to come into direct contact with women, entering houses to raid drinks from women's hearths, or beating and poking through the house thatch to tease the women inside. When Yankwa's pets come into the house to spill oloniti or maraud around kicking the thatch, young women and girls hide inside sleeping compartments (older women do not bother). We have already seen how avidly women watch the pets at Ioho, Halokwayti and at the fire-wood distribution. The pet flutes always announce and accompany the melodic flutes onto the arena (the same men carry both), but when the pets take centre stage independently of the melodic flutes, they fully evince the ludic vitality, bordering on aggression, which is their defining characteristic. Women say the pets are 'like scarlet macaws', birds defined by sexual arousal, and they are described as 'swarming' like angered honeybees. Whereas the melodic flutes have the character of elders, the pets are most often impersonated by young men in their teens and early twenties who relish the chaotic clowning, running and ululations that go with the pet role. Thus, just as there is a tension between maternal and virile female roles, which is explored in Yankwa's course, so is there a tension between civilising and aggressively sexual aspects of masculinity.

Whereas the melodic flute players wear the insignias of true human-ity (headdresses and cooked palm silks), the pets are disguised with mud or clay and with green palm fronds. And whereas the melodic flutes drink ketera from calabashes in moderate quantities, the pets spill oloniti and lick potassium salt directly from hosts' palms. In short, the pets' voracious style of consumption and excitation explicitly feeds the Yakairiti, since drinks are spilled for them, but more than this it generates performative consubstantiation with them, because men and women become Yakairiti-like as they feed, entertain and satisfy each other and the spirits. On the other hand the melodic flutes belong to the disciplined, routinised ceremonialism, which falls under the guid-ance of venerable song masters, who lead the rigorously ordered chants, coordinated movements, voices and instrumental melody.

The pets are said to be at their most aggressive and dangerous when they plant the collective manioc gardens for prospective host clans. People say that, in truth, these gardens are planted by the Yakairiti themselves. Just as they hide from pets in the village, women stay away from the gardens while they are being planted, but I was curious to see the planting of Mairoete clan's garden commence in 2009 and so I fol-lowed the men there. I saw all the adult men of the village barring the host clansmen – thus some eighty men – work in a swarm on the same patch of the vast expanse of burnt ground, moving across it together so that all were enveloped in clouds of dust, working with frenetic energy, joking loudly and uttering high-pitched ululations. Some men had palm fronds attached to their heads, partly for the wild and clownish effect and partly for shade. At mid morning, the men of Mairoete clan arrived to serve the workers with pans of oloniti and ketera. They had covered their bodies from head to toe in a thick layer of annatto dye, which has protective qualities, and had attached plastic children's toys as comical charms to themselves. They went bombastically around inviting the workers to drink. As they did so, some of the workers jumped on them, smearing dirt on their faces. Just as they had at the port side on the day of the fishermen's return, and then during the pets' firewood distributions, the hosts submitted entirely to these aggressions. As if to warn me that this behaviour should be understood within a frame marked as playful, one man told me: 'don't be upset, Yankwa has always been this way!' Even so, it was very hot as midday approached and I was quite overwhelmed by Yankwa's extreme boisterousness, so I returned to the women back in the village. I found them in an eager state of expectancy for the pets' return. At 1PM, when cries were heard on the path, women knew 'the pets were returning' and they hurried to bring mats covered in drying annatto seeds and manioc starch inside the house, since they expected the pets to come kicking the thatch and upsetting whatever was in their path – which they did.

The analogy between the Yakairiti's work of planting and the pounding work of Yakairtiti women, which both draw in the opposite sex even as they exclude them, is further underscored when we learn that the planting of collective gardens used to happen 'miraculously' under the cover of darkness – just like Batatakwayti. The pets would begin

Figure 3.3 Calabashes piled with yams are put outside the front door by the wife of a Kairoli clansman for the pet-flute *Tawado-kwase*.

planting at nightfall and then work throughout the night and on until noon. I was told that this had simply ceased to be necessary, because a growing population and plethora of steel tools now allowed planting to start after dawn and still be finished by noon. Nonetheless, the analogy between women and men's sexualised work remains: when the pets achieve work, they do so in a state of excitation that is risky and transgressive and which is, for that reason, exciting and energising for women.

While planting gardens is the work for which the pet flutes or workers are most famous, the pets also take centre stage after Batatakwayti, when men playing trumpets and whistles, disguised in wild palm fronds and behaving in an unruly manner, produce basketry for women and enter their hearth spaces to raid oloniti. In fact, this giving and taking has an effect on an economic level: the pets ensure that resources are expended publicly. They spill oloniti and lick salt and they make tools that women want and thus induce them to put stored garden surpluses into circulation publicly and dramatically. All this serves as evidence to the Yakairiti that people are willing to forego their attachment to food. Yankwa's return is complete when the Yakairiti have been completely satisfied.

Quenching the Killer's Thirst

The morning after Batatakwayti during Kairoli clan's returning sequence, *Tawado-kwase* entered the arena from the port. Tawado-kwase is one of Kairoli clan's pet flute personages, named after a species of bird and, like other pets, described as Yankwa's 'employee' or 'worker' *(wakanale)*. About twenty men entered the arena dishevelled and covered in fresh palm fronds, with newly made manioc-carrying basketry and drying mats attached to their bodies. As we watched, the women of my house commented that there were many mature men among the Tawado-kwase contingent and not only teenage jokesters. The playfulness of serious elders animated everyone to the spectacle. The wives of host clansmen instructed their husbands to 'go and take a woven mat, mine is full of holes!' and pushed calabashes full of surplus manioc starch and fibre, dried fish or Brazil nuts into their husbands' hands. The hosts then ran up to Tawado-kwase with these payments and divested the pets of the baskets. One of the hosts, Bailitero-ene, took twenty baskets and six mats from the incomers. I asked about this apparent greediness and learned that Bailitero-ene had taken manioc starch and yams into the flute house on the previous day to solicit this appearance from his clan's pet flute, Tawado-kwase. He was able to do so because his wife had just harvested an uncommonly large crop of yams. After they had taken the twenty baskets, Bailitero-ene's wife and daughter placed twenty calabashes roundly piled with raw yams outside their front door for Tawado-kwase. The basket-makers then took these yams back to their wives and children (see Figure 3.3).

Meanwhile, in our house, the resident host Kawalinero-ene had been among the basket-makers but had kept one of the baskets back for his teenage daughter, who had pleaded her desperate need with him. However, when her mother saw the yams and sweet potatoes that were being offered to Tawado-kwase, they cajoled their daughter to give up the basket and sent her father out with it after all. One of the boys of the house no sooner came struggling back with a basin full of sweet potatoes. By this time Tawado-kwase had run out of new baskets but some of the men indicated that they were now 'taking orders' for baskets, which they would later make. I wondered what they were doing carrying out old, brittle baskets riddled with holes, but everyone understood that they were offering IOUs. At this point my adoptive mother, Kawalinero-asero, dragged a whole basket full of the dried manioc discs that are always plentiful in storage in the rafters of the house and threw them out of the front door ostentatiously for Tawado-kwase. She then put out two basins full of dried manioc starch, and again fetched down from the rafters twelve more manioc discs. When more baskets were proffered, she dragged down more discs and threw those out of the front door too. Her lavishness amused us all since she usually guarded her stores conservatively.

This extravagant display took place on the same day that young men marauded around the village in teams uttering shrill cries of warning. They entered hosts' houses to raid calabashes of oloniti placed ready inside their doorways by hosts' wives. These pets poured the calabashes' contents out onto the ground, often right outside the hostess's front door, muddying the entranceway and exciting lively protestations. Three days later, on the very last day of the returning sequence, hosts would evidence over and again that the manioc gardens had been exhausted – that every last drop of oloniti to come from the host clan's collective garden had been shared with the Yakairiti. On this day known as *Ewakoneda* (which means 'the spilling') the pets entered the hosts' houses again, but this time they seized the whole pan of oloniti and spilled its contents onto the ground, where it was said to seep down into the Yakairiti's underground pans. This was the oloniti made at Batatakwayti four days earlier and which had been left to sit and sour.

In the centre of the arena, palm frond shades had been erected to protect the dancers from the sun as they played the melodic flutes without rest through the heat of the day. The pets' raids went on around them. In the afternoon, Yankwa's pets came together for one last time, now smeared in clay and donning green branches. They chased after the hosts, kneeling to receive salt into their cupped hands and to drink and spill oloniti. It was explained to me that on this day 'all of Yankwa come together' in the arena

> to eat and drink well. The pets will retire first, once they have licked the salt. They are no longer angry; they have eaten their fill. It will be many years until Aweresese clan's flutes emerge from the flute house again. The Yakairiti like to drink and drink and drink; now their pans have been filled. In the future, when they consider that their pans are dry, they will look to drink again ... it will not be too long ...

The returning sequence for Aweresese clan definitively ended that day at dusk when Yankwa's melodic flutes paraded out towards the dwelling circle and returned to the flute house, coming to a stop at its front door to indicate their preparedness to put the flutes to rest. Next, the four separate instrumental groups each entered houses belonging to host men and danced around their large central hearths, announcing their intention in song to put the flutes to rest. The host responded by handing a single calabash of oloniti to the song master who headed the line. The hosts' words and the song master's replies echoed one another:

> Here is the manioc you planted with your own hands, dangerous ones, from the second harvest, and here is the container, you have drunk from it with your pets and now look, it is just an empty calabash.

Once the oloniti had been spilled with these words, the hosts took back the empty calabash and spoke once more to each flute player in turn to ask them to put the flutes to rest. This they did by falling silent at the front door of the flute house, returning the flutes to their hanging places within, and taking off their headdresses and silks.

Conclusion

Yankwa's archetypal sequence structures not only economic activities but also the moods and energies of the community through time. Over the course of Yankwa there are phases of build-up and of release, so that conservative storage allows for lavish display at a later time, creating energetic ebbs and flows in collective life. In each phase there is a play off between routine and events that break it. While the melodic flutes uphold this routine – because their nightly drinking motivates women's daily labours with manioc and occupies the arena with predictable hours of flute play, which gradually intensify through the course of each clans' sequence – the pets are responsible for carnivalesque interruptions, which transgress gendered spaces and disturb the village soundscape.

At the centre of my analysis of these temporal and relational dynamics has been a sequence of choreographed work events, which unsettle the conventional division between male musical ceremonialism in the arena and female provisioning activities in the dwelling circle. At Batatakwayti, rather than awaking to play flutes in the night while women are still asleep, men remain dozing in their hammocks while women pound giant pestles in standing hollow log mortars. During this night-time pounding and over the course of the following day, relations of production are transfigured, habitual temporal rhythms are broken, and the organisation of space and sound are reconfigured. These events have all the markers of a topsy-turvy world, one created to allow people to reflect on their ordinary reality. They highlight the aesthetic and performative qualities of everyday subsistence tasks, which already have musical and dance-like qualities by virtue of being accomplished in synchrony at predictable times of day. The Enawenê seem to say that there is embodied pleasure; first, in the experience of absorption in collective work, and, second, in the spectacle of others' work, which is both aesthetically pleasing and sexually arousing. Women together perform feats of productivity for men, and men collectively perform feats of productivity for women. During their intercalated festivals of work, men's and women's activities are suffused with desire and energetic enthusiasm to an exceptional degree, drawing attention to the assimilation of sex and work as alternative means of expending energy while vitalising the body. Simply stated, work, like sex, is always both about giving and taking pleasure and about generating life. Women and men work to satisfy one another both with the products of their efforts and with their demonstrations of bodily vigour. As they do so they are said to be 'like Yakairiti', the distinction between people and spirit is blurred by Yakairiti women and pet flutes. This sexual merging of person and spirit is the theme of a myth about a magically elongated penis, which turns women's work into an orgy. It remains mysterious to me why the Yakairiti should be associated with heightened sexuality, but the effect is that the Enawenê become like their aggressive spirit adversaries through the holistic expenditure of breath, energy and food, which is designed to satisfy them.

When I wanted to stay in my hammock rather than go to the manioc gardens, women would warn me, 'if you are lazy, the Yakairiti will strike you down, but if you are eager to work the Yakairiti are happy'. Yakairiti are said to call the Enawenê *mae nawe*, which means 'the dead people' and also slips into the adjective 'lazy'. If people lie in hammocks and refuse to work it is a sign of illness or menstruation. Passivity is thus bound to sickness and vulnerability. Intensive work, which is ideally collective and joyously undertaken, is a moral good and helps to turn back the debilitating agency of the Yakairiti, who prey on people when they are stingy and lazy, failing to work and sing, or withholding food from public circulation. While metaphysical sanctions may be threatened to recalcitrant teenagers and lazy anthropologists, on the whole Enawenê people enjoy both their musical and provisioning work despite their relentless regularity. Work is necessary to generate an economy of plenty and the vigour of an eventful life; the evidence from myth and life suggests that work channels virile energies so that through accelerated activity and circulation of its produce people hold off their mortal condition.

I want to end by revealing a perplexing dimension to the story I have told. The myth about Okoyoli and his giant penis was not told to me by the women of my house to explain Batatakwayti, but rather on the last day of Kairoli clan's returning sequence, after the pets had finished rampaging, licking salt and spilling oloniti. The song masters were sat playing drawn-out notes on a low toned flute by the extinguished ashes of a fire. As we watched from inside the front door women said that they were 'crying for the loss of Okoyoli's penis'. I never overcame the oddity of venerable elder men enacting women's tears for a severed penis. Perhaps, though, it is not so strange that the loss of a penis should symbolise the end of Yankwa. While Okoyoli was around, women worked desirously and the three pillars of Yankwa were in place: manioc, village life and flute playing. The severance of the penis was the loss of vigorous production and the end of Yankwa. The mood was perhaps even more sombre on the day of that lament on the 23 June 2009. Kawali, the paramount leader of the Enawenê people and their most knowledgeable song master, had been fatally bitten by a snake a few days previously. There had been anger, confusion, acrimony and acute grief when his body was found and during his burial on the same evening. So I was surprised when later that night, at the usual time of 3AM, all but the closest mourners emerged onto the arena to play Kairoli clan's flutes and to drink ketera. I knew that there was no special rite of commemoration for the death of leaders, but on this day the significance of this lack struck me for the first time as an extreme orientation to time, one which makes no allowances for the vagaries of individual human lives. Yankwa's rigorous sequencing imposed its own emotional and energetic temporality; its repeated action sequences contained occasions for anxiety, for sadness and stasis, for euphoria, silliness, and extravagant clowning, and for opposition, aggression and antagonism; and every night commemorated ancestors who had once drunk ketera in the arenas of past villages.

Notes

1. Haira is the name of the handmade rubber ball that, in the game by the same name, is struck with the head across a line that bisects the arena. Men strike the ball with the head, after a maximum of one bounce, from one side of the arena to the other, often diving forwards so that their chest hits the ground and flicking their heads back to catch the ball before it bounces a second time. The aim is to propel the ball beyond the reach of the other team. Hosts and Yankwa are mixed together and there is no discernible order or regularity to the team division. Men wager prized possessions (such as arrows, radios, items of clothing or fishing equipment), which they lose or win back over successive rounds (see also Mendes dos Santos 2006: 154). Versions of this ball game are played by Paresi, Nambikwara and various Tupi-speaking peoples of the region (see Melatti 2001).

2. A degree of turn-taking makes this intensive schedule bearable. Each flute group has maximum intensity days when they lead the chanting, followed by days of comparative rest. For example, the lead group would begin playing in the flute house at 2PM, have a break between 3 and 5PM while the other groups rehearsed, and then resume playing in the arena from 5 until 9PM. On the next day this group would be the last to enter the flute house at around 5PM, and then the first to leave the arena at about 6:30PM.

3. Star-woman becomes the wife of Datamale. Either her miraculous regime is lost when he insults her so that she flees back to the sky or, in an alternative rendition, when Datamale's trickster younger brother (the same brother who fatally tricks Dokowyi into the river) pronounces that work should be arduous. Comparable Amazonian golden-age myths are presented by Lévi-Strauss (1964: 173–75; 1966: 259–60; 1971: 528).

4. Even in the mid 1980s when the Enawenê had only the few items of clothing they had raided from their Myky and Nambikwara neighbours, Vincent Cañas recorded that they wore clothes for this firewood distribution (Cañas, 25 May 1981). The most compelling explanation is that Yankwa are emphasising their workmanlike role in provisioning hosts by wearing the shorts and T-shirts that they habitually wear for garden work and fishing expeditions but do not usually wear when they appear in the arena. They also emphasise their distinction from hosts, who have a responsibility to beautify themselves with annatto when they appear in the arena.

5. I received no explanation as to why flutes were decorated and dressed at this particular moment, but I was told that the flutes were dressed as men would be for Yankwa, so feathers and silks were attached to the flutes' homologous body parts and received the same name as men's adornments.

6. Anthony Seeger (1987: 132) has made this point in the context of musical ceremonialism in the Xingu region of Amazonia, where dance and song are explicitly valued for the creation of communion.

7. Feld (1990: 267) coined the term soundscape. See Graham (1995: 92) and Ewart (2013: 42–43) for other Central Brazilian examples of regularised soundscapes.
8. For example, Rivière (1987); Goldman (1963); T. Turner (1979).
9. See Overing (1986); Heckler (2004); C. Hugh-Jones (1979: 279).

Figure 4.1 Women 'do the rounds' of others' houses to reclaim their set of calabashes after approximately 4,000 litres of *ketera* has circulated on the day of the fishermen's return. In the foreground a bunch of women stop to inspect calabashes carried by others. In the background, another line of women walk between houses with their own bundles.

4

Affinal Diplomacy in a United, Egalitarian Society

Every night from December through to February, and then again from April through to June, the men of the incumbent host clan lit fires in the arena at about 3AM and then one of Yankwa's leaders sounded a single flute from inside the flute house. All around the dwelling circle, men awakened and dressed in their ceremonial garb, dipped out of their front doors, and made for the flute house to take up their flutes and then their places at one of three or four fires just lit by the hosts. The hearths were set aflame as an invitation for men to play the host's flutes and they were continuously stoked by the hosts, who stood by to watch, listen and serve. At around three or four in the morning, when the dancing and song were well established, women associated with the host clan awoke to stir their pan of ketera, which they had made on the previous day, starting with a trip to the manioc gardens at dawn, grating and pressing the fibres through the morning, boiling the juice through the afternoon and thickening it with corn and manioc flour at dusk. They had set out their finest, largest calabashes in the evening and they now filled these with the steaming drink, as one of the hosts – most often their husband, but sometimes a son-in-law or a daughter's future father-in-law – entered to take the full gourds from their hands. A full to brimming drinking gourd holds five litres, but for ease of distribution, each contained about half that. Leaving a trail of steam in their wake, hosts carried four calabashes at a time out to the lines of dancers, leaving with full hands and returning with empty ones, to-ing and fro-ing many times until nothing but sticky remains were left in the bottom of a

125-litre pan. Between them the hosts served each of the dancers several times, and the song masters (*sotakatale*) and leaders of Yankwa (*honerekaiti*) most plentifully of all.

Once they had been served the dancers broke off and sat down to drink and banter. A collection of full calabashes gathered at each man's feet as they drank from only one. When they had had enough and there was a move to resume playing, the dancers ferried all these untouched leftovers back to their wives, who immediately poured them into a clean pan, handing the empty calabashes back to their husbands, who would, in turn, convey them into the hands of one of the hosts. During phases when the leading clan (called Aole or Aweresese) hosted in 2008 and 2009, ketera would be carried out from ten of the fifteen houses in the dwelling circle in which the seventeen adult men of this clan lived dispersed. Since the men of the remaining eight clans all danced for Aweresese and thus received several gourds-full, this ketera then re-entered all fifteen houses, where mixed pans of ketera stood ready to be drunk by all of the village's inhabitants throughout the next day. So this nightly drinking was a performance of mixture – imagine a flurry of calabashes and men, criss-crossing back and forth in the movement from dance arena to dwelling circle and back again. I represent this centripetal movement in Figure 4.2 in which each dot in the numbered houses represents one of Aweresese's hosts (in their real dwellings) and each unbroken line represents a calabash being taken to a dancer at one of the flute hearths. Dotted lines show the passage of the calabash back into the houses of the rest of the men. The diagram is drawn as if each host distributed just three drinking gourdes, but the number of lines going in and out can be multiplied by ten, since each takes out at least thirty gourdes.

After they had given the leftovers to their wives, Yankwa's dancers returned the empty but sticky calabashes to whichever of the hosts they intercepted first – they did not try to keep track of which calabash had come from which host. This meant that each host returned a mixture of calabashes to their wives or betrothal partners, who would have to go in search of her own set of calabashes, which had ended up around the other houses. I came to think of this redistribution as the nightly 'calabash round' because of the way women circulated around the dwelling circle, dipping in and out of houses to locate their missing calabashes. While the flutes were played most intensively, just before the first signs of dawn, and while most women and children still slept, or dozily drank ketera in their hammocks, I would follow my adoptive mother Kawalinero-asero, lighting our way with my torch and carrying bundles of miscellaneous calabashes in each hand.

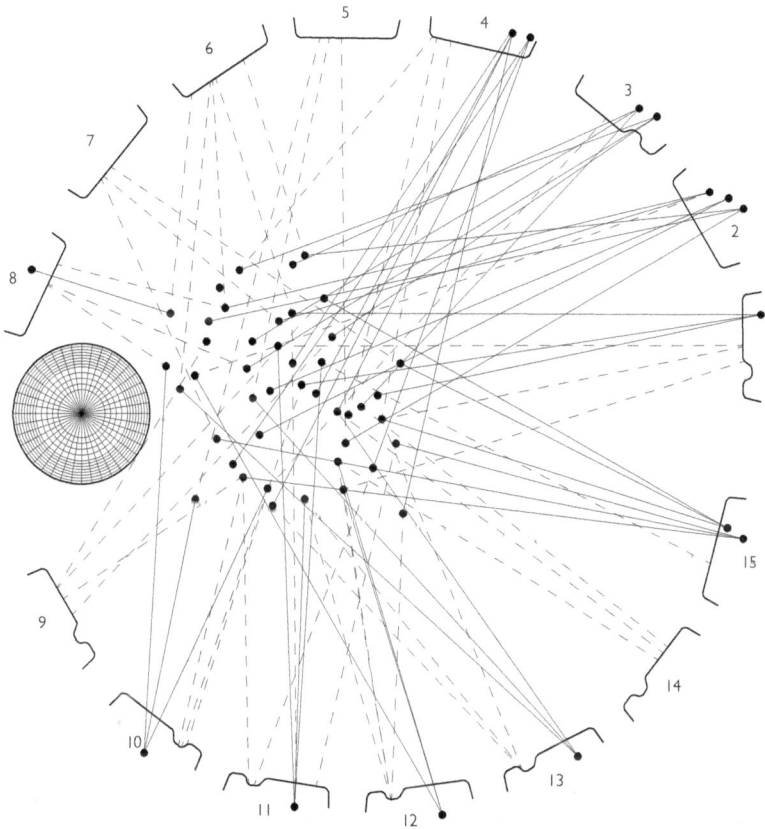

Figure 4.2 The movement of calabashes from the dwelling circle to the arena and back again. Illustration by Kate Altman.

We entered each house from which ketera had emerged to identify any of our own calabashes and to allow those we carried with us to be scrutinised by their potential owners. Women recognised each of their calabashes, identifying them by shape, density, by the colour or texture of the thread used to hang them, and sometimes by extra pieces of torn cotton or string that had been attached to their hanging loops in order to facilitate identification. After taking our own calabashes and leaving behind any that had found their home, we moved onto the next house. Women from all around the village did the same round so that bunches of women tended to form doing the rounds together (see Figure 4.1). Because houses are arrayed around the circular arena like radial extrusions from a wheel, the image I have of this round is of the dwelling circle in motion, turning and in the process mixing and circulating people, as women walked their circuits around it.

This was a favourite time of day for me because I was useful with my head torch and willingness to carry; because we walked in the darkness, out of sight from the men in the fire-lit centre; because the round relied on the exchange of few words, which suited me in the early days; because this was one of the few contexts in which I could visit other houses in a casual way (rather than as a guest); and because by following the calabash round I discovered the way people were knitted together by the dyadic relationships between pairs of couples, who betroth one or two pairs of offspring, often in their infancy, and who exchange gifts and services with increasing intensity as their children mature. These betrothal partners (*enatunawene*) avoid familiar, everyday interactions and observe name avoidance, so women were sometimes reluctant to reveal who their betrothal partners were. But on the calabash round, I could discover these partnerships without asking intrusive questions, because once I knew the identities of the host clan's male members, if there was a woman making ketera who was not married to one of them, I would know that one of her daughters must be betrothed to one of the host's sons and I could ask anyone to tell me who her future son-in-law was. Thus by following many calabash rounds, I discovered the lines of alliance that criss-crossed the arena just as the calabashes did.

The Enawenê drink rather than eat most of their daily nourishment, and ketera is the calorific porridge that keeps them going every day and on which babies are weaned. The movement of calabashes and the mixed pans of ketera that result are therefore a concrete and nightly realisation of the community's unification. A fundamental dynamic between containment and extension, between ownership and circulation, and between the outer circle of dwellings and the central arena, is made visible by the movement of drinking gourds. These movements and mixtures are contingent on the separateness of gendered lines. On the one hand, uxorilocal houses contain lines of female kin, and their manioc work fills these houses every day. The groups of women who pool their labour to harvest manioc from gardens and produce ketera are defined by their verticality, being made up of a mother and a string of daughters, or sets of sisters – always described in birth order. On the other hand, it is a line of men, related to one another patrilineally, that serves the ketera in the arena and on whose behalf the rest of the men of the community gather to sing, dance, play flutes and, of course, drink ketera. They gather together in the arena to host, whereas they live in separate houses dispersed around the dwelling circle, with their fathers-in-law and sons-in-law rather than their brothers and fathers. The men of the remaining eight clans who dance and play flutes also do so in birth order and thus the lineage-like lines in the centre of the arena. The calabashes pass between the representatives of these different lines – of women, hosts and Yankwa – realising relations of affinity of various kinds: that between spouses and betrothal partners; between host and Yankwa, who are temporarily one another's most important alter egos; and finally between unrelated women in the calabash round, who are the members of various clans but are connected to one another in this context via their separate marriages to the men of the host clan. Principles of lineality and affinity thus systematically cross-cut so that a stylised dance creates temporary mixtures of people and drinks; mixtures that are always premised on the maintenance of separate lines.

This chapter is about the spatial arrangements and social principles that are institutionalised through Yankwa and generate a centripetal and egalitarian social dynamic, one that unites people as equals, because it maintains their separation into opposed lines. My aim is to demonstrate that this dynamic is based on a thoroughgoing commitment to affinal diplomacy by the Enawenê, who are a self-consciously civic-minded people, devoted to living together peacefully with their affines in a large, united society. Yankwa is the public, performative expression of this imperative to live through affinal diplomacy. First I argue that the Enawenê's circular village plan is the essential spatial scaffolding for this egalitarian affinal diplomacy, disputing the claim that concentric spatial arrangements are inherently supportive of gender inequality or chiefly rank. Where neither one sex nor one group monopolises the central space, the village's circularity serves a unifying, centripetal, equilibrium-seeking dynamic, which works by means of the distribution of power rather than its concentration. This is the case despite the recognition of chiefly clans and men within them, and of a continuous hierarchy among the village's nine constituent clans. I argue that this hierarchy, though recognised, is contained within the walls of the flute house, where the clans' flutes remain in positions that were established when separate, culturally-distinct and unequal peoples came together to form a common society. Outside these walls, there is no pragmatic context in which one clan or one individual within it could assert their position in their hierarchy, because the principle of surrogacy that underlies every aspect of Yankwa's organisation makes self-assertion impossible.

Before elucidating this claim, I explain the likely historical genesis of this heterogeneous polity that the Enawenê strive, through the performance of Yankwa, to maintain united. I show that it depended upon a compromise between hegemony (in matters of dietary mores and language) and syncretism (in matters of dress and ceremonialism), and on certain essential social principles that enshrine affinal diplomacy, such as uxorilocal residence, which scatters clansmen among their affines, and the use of valuables to negotiate alliances. By showing that Enawenê society is the outcome of deliberate spatial arrangements and aesthetic and dietary pacts, which institutionalised affinal diplomacy historically, I connect this story of ethnogenesis to the major and minor acts of affinal diplomacy, which constitute the work of Yankwa every day and which thus continually re-found Enawenê society. In every act that constitutes Yankwa, men and women work with or for their affines, either to make plenty to drink, to gather for an impressive performance or to plant a massive garden, achieving scale by decentring their efforts. The same principle of surrogacy is realised across diverse activities: clansmen always play others' flutes, wear others' headdresses, celebrate others' spirits and drink others' manioc – and never their own; manioc fields are prepared and planted by the whole community, except the men and women who own them, and will serve their harvest. This principle of surrogacy, which is both abstract and grounded in space, is an 'institution' in the sense that it is a regulative principle that serves society as a whole and therefore exists in a paradoxical relationship with human volition. One of its effects is to quash the expression of hierarchy in this nonetheless 'chiefly', 'priestly', Arawakan temple polity. Power can never be concentrated in one clan or individual because the expression of a clan's identity is always contingent on the work of everyone else, which is affinally motivated. The everyday realisation of this centripetal, egalitarian social dynamic is elucidated through the analysis of the building blocks of Yankwa: the planting and harvest of collective manioc fields; the organisation of women's work to produce drinks; the giving and receiving of gourds of drink between men in the central plaza; and the playing of a clan's flutes that always accompanies this drinking.

The Affordances of Circular Space

> Their sages had elaborated a grandiose cosmology and had inscribed it in
> the layout of their villages and in the distribution of their dwellings. The
> contradictions confronted by all human lives they had seized again and
> again, accepting one opposition only to negate it with another, cutting and
> dividing their groups, alternately associating and opposing them such that
> they had made of their whole social and spiritual life an image in which
> symmetry and asymmetry were in balance.
> —C. Lévi-Strauss, *Tristes Tropiques*

Lévi-Strauss wrote the lyrical passage from which the above part is extracted as he strove to understand the 'ballet' of reciprocity he had seen unfolding in a Bororo village. He went on to analyse commonalities between circular plaza settlements across the world, not only in Central Brazil, but also in North American, Indonesia and chiefly parts of Melanesia. He asked: what is it about circles that offer such potential for sociological complexity? I am going to sketch the answer he developed in two essays of the volume *Structural Anthropology* (Lévi-Strauss 1958a, 1958b) that elaborate on his germinal insight about the potential circles provide for the balancing of symmetry and asymmetry, egalitarianism and hierarchy. Despite Lévi-Strauss's initial emphasis on the equilibrium between these two principles, he later came to understand circular plazas as inherently supportive of hierarchy. I want to explain why he and others thought this should be so in order to demonstrate why this potential, though recognised by the Enawenê, remains unrealised.

First, circles invite segmentation, if you draw a line down the centre of a circle you get two equal and opposite halves in a balanced dichotomy or 'diametric dualism'. This is a potential the Enawenê make use of when they draw a line in the sand from east to west and divide themselves into two teams to play their traditional ball game *haira*, in which a rubber ball is struck by the head from one side of the line to the other as both teams attempt to put it beyond the reach of the other side. Lévi-Strauss saw that the virtue of the circle was that it lent itself to multiple such oppositions and thus to continual dialectical rearrangements. His major insight was that this kind of equal and opposite dualism existed alongside 'concentric dualisms', which were asymmetrical and dynamic. This is also the case for the Enawenê. As we know from Chapter 2, the diametric east-west line that is drawn in the sand for games of haira becomes an orientation for movement, action and change along its axis during other phases of Yankwa, rather than a line designed to support an opposition. The fishermen follow it to depart to the waterways and then retrace it when they return the flutes to their central house. It is a line that connects periphery to centre, and wild, spirit other to the human self. Just so, Lévi-Strauss observed that asymmetrical values tended to be ascribed to such concentric oppositions as inside and outside, centre and periphery, male and female, such that they became lines of movement rather than fixed contrasts.

When Lévi-Strauss wrote this analysis of the relationship between space and social categories and dynamics, he was aware of the archaeological view of the plaza as an architecture of power proper to chiefly polities, whose concentric pull was put to the ends of reproducing hierarchy. This may be why, in a rationalising mood that was quite different to his poetic reflections on the Bororo's 'labyrinth of institutions' (1958b: 172), he expressed a Roman certainty about the superiority of the sacred, political, male forum over the profane, domestic, female periphery, implying that circular formations were by their nature hierarchical, since although they allowed everyone to live equidistant from the centre – an index of their equality – some (men or chiefs) had greater access to that centre than others. The idea that the concentric dualism of the circle supported symbolic and material inequalities of gender influenced a generation of scholars who followed in Lévi-Strauss's footsteps to conduct research among speakers of Gê languages closely related to the Bororo, like the Xavante, Timbira, Suyá and Apinayé.[1] In the Xingu region, where circular villages also predominate, but are associated with the dominant Arawak cultural heritage, it has been argued that the plaza upholds distinctions of class rather than gender. It concentrates power in the hands of chiefs, who dominate the public space, where they exhibit their specially decorated bodies and monopolise public speech-making (Heckenberger 2005: 292–98). Chiefly households also have the means to produce more and thus to sponsor prestige-building activities (ibid.: 199), notably the major rituals that animate the plaza – rituals that also commemorate chiefs.

In the Enawenê case, neither of these affordances of concentric dualism (the support of male domination or inherited chiefly rank) is realised. First, although men dominate the centre to play flutes during Yankwa, in the contrasting season of Kateoko it is women who wear the sun diadem feather headdresses to dance and sing as they are served drinks by men, while in the paired season of Lerohi both men and women dance in long chains that link them arm in arm. Nor does Enawenê concentric dualism support class distinctions. Although among the Enawenê as in the Xingu, chiefly status is inherited patrilineally and vested more completely in elder sons than in their younger brothers, there is no context in which chiefly individuals or lineages are celebrated. As I commented in the previous chapter, the death of the universally respected leader of Yankwa's first clan, Aweresese, was not ritually commemorated – he was buried just like anyone else and Yankwa danced for Kairoli clan later the same night. He had spent his life serving Yankwa by leading other clans' rituals on their behalf and exercising his memory of the chants so that he could lead everyone else in singing them, but there was no performance in which his chiefly status, or that of his clan, was marked. Rather than supporting stable hierarchies, the Enawenê's circular plaza is a spatial architecture for the 'systematic recursion of numerous dualities' as Mosko has argued for the Trobriand village of Omarakana (Mosko 2013: 483). Oppositions between host and leader, male and female, dwelling circle and arena, are contextual and temporary and thus dynamic and reversible, just as

Lévi-Strauss intuited in his original reflections on the Bororo case. It is not that hierarchy does not exist, or that it is not inscribed in space. In fact, as we will see now, the nine Enawenê clans are ordered hierarchically and this order is enshrined in the layout of the central flute house. Nonetheless, everything that goes on outside the flute house seems to be about keeping this hierarchy enclosed under that house's domed roof.

Clan Flutes around the Central Pillar

Inside the flute house the clans' ensembles of aerophones are ordered around a rail circling the central pillar (see Figure 4.3) in positions that enshrine the separate origins of the peoples who converged at a central place to form a heterogeneous polity. Before I speculate about the likely timing and circumstances of this convergence I want to look at what we can glean from the flute house about the ancestors of the people who compose the nine Enawenê clans. As I mentioned in this book's Introduction, in the decade after first contact in 1974 it was believed that the Enawenê were the descendants of one Paresi subgroup who had become separated from the extensive nation of which they had

Figure 4.3 Inside the flute house the flutes belonging to nine clans are arrayed around a central pillar.

once been a part. The assumption was that because the contemporary Enawenê ate fish and made canoes from the bark of the Jatobá tree, their ancestors must have shared these characteristics of material culture and diet. In fact, what emerges from Enawenê oral history is a complex and overlapping set of correspondences between several ancestral peoples who had varied customs, territorial origins and linguistic affiliations (Arawakan, Tupi-Mondé and Nambikwara), and the nine present-day clans who today live together in a single village. These distinct peoples are said to have occupied clusters of villages concentrated along different tributaries of the River Juruena in former times, when their populations were much more numerous. Sorcery killings, enemy attacks, disease and upheavals caused by foreigners invading the region pushed the remnants of these peoples to seek refuge and strength in a village called Kawekwalikwa, which is located at the centre of Enawenê-nawe territory at the confluence of the Arimena and Juruena Rivers. Thus, according to Enawenê oral history, their single polity is a fairly recent creation, the outcome of the agglomeration of separate peoples who sought strength and refuge during a period of drastic upheavals connected, directly and indirectly, to Luso-Brazilian exploration. They brought their flutes together around a single pillar as if to seal this unification.

The flute house has a circular floor plan and a tapering, domed thatch roof. It is supported by a tall, central, hardwood pillar that is much sturdier than what would be required to support its light roof. Around this trunk each clan's ensemble of aerophones is arrayed in positions that are said to have been established at Kawekwalikwa, when incoming peoples placed their flutes at their clan's position in the central house before entering the dwelling houses of their new affines. This order of priority is reaffirmed every time a new village is founded, since the flute house is the first structure to be built, and the flutes are brought over and housed within it before work begins on the houses of the dwelling circle. The arrangement of the flutes seems to simultaneously express opposition, hierarchy and equality: some of the clans are opposed on a diametric east-west axis, which seems to index simultaneously their contrasting territorial origins and cultural orientations, whereas this opposition becomes a continuous hierarchy if you move around the house anticlockwise, starting from the front door.

The flutes of Aweresese clan, whose ancestors were the original inhabitants of Kawekwalikwa, the place at the confluence of the River Arimena with the Juruena where unification occurred, have pride of place at the eastern side of the flute house, closest to the door and the arena, and facing the ceremonial pathway. They are the leaders, or first clan, of Yankwa, and are closely followed by Kairoli clan, whose ancestors are said to have shared their pescatarian diet and language. These two leading clans are also said to be the source of the dam-fishing technology that is so central to Yankwa and whose place par excellence is still the River Arimena (Mendes dos Santos 2006: 87). It was the pescatarian diet, riverine way of life and the language of these people that the most foreign of the incomers had to adopt in order to settle with them at Kawekwalikwa. The senior man of Lolahese clan who guided me around the flute house emphasised the dualism between the east and west sides of the flute house by speaking of the two leading clans as belonging to the wide, straight stretch of the Juruena River at its middle course, which is flanked by buruti palms and is the place where the Yakairiti held Yankwa in mythic times. This stretch of the river is called the Yakairiti's 'arena' (*beteko*) and is spoken of as the natural counterpart of the open, public space of the village. My guide pointed out that the flutes of his own clan, Lolahese, together with those of Anihale clan, were at the back of the house, a position he associated with the setting sun and with the tall forest (*kaira*). This was the first time the contrast between these two pairs of clans had been so explicitly posed as a series of dualisms to which unequal values were attached: between river and forest, rising and setting sun, front and back, centre and periphery. My guide gave no comparable explanation for the relative positions of the five other clans, whose flutes sit on the south and north sides of the flute house, although he did circle anticlockwise around the pillar, indicating that they fell between the two poles of centrality and alterity, with the Kawekwalese and Mairoete clans following on from the leading clans at the northern side, while Kawinalili, Kaholase and Hotakanese were at the southern side and came last in our circuit. Given my guide's focus on the dualism between two pairs of clans, it seems likely to me that rather than divide all the clans neatly into two status groups, as Silva (1998) suggested in his pioneering analysis of the Enawenê clan system, the east-west axis is the vital, orienting one, with the other clans pulled to either pole depending partly on demographic factors.

This interpretation fits with what we know about the heterogeneity of the Enawenê's ancestry, in which there are two different kinds of alterity; that associated with an ancestral people akin to the Enawenê's former enemies, the Tupi-Mondé speaking Cinta-Larga, and that associated with people who are considered inferior but with whom it is possible to share a territory, the Nambikwara. The east-west opposition would correspond thus to the contrast between an Arawak heritage associated with the river, a pescaterian diet and with hegemonic centrality to the polity, and a Tupi-Mondé heritage associated with the upland forest, terrestrial hunting and meat-eating. This first kind of dualism intersects with that between Arawak and Nambikwara, which finds expression in the pairing of leading and subordinate clans during any biennial of Yankwa. Only Kairoli, the largest clan, hosts alone, but usually there is a first, 'leading' clan (*aole*) and a second, subordinate clan referred to as both *kahene*, which means 'Nambikwara', or as *ekanokwahale*, which means 'the arm' or 'support'. Lolahese, Kaholase and Hotakanese clans are unambiguously of this latter status, judging from pairings recorded by Vincent Cañas and Marcio Silva over the decades since 1974; while Kairoli, Aweresese, Anihale and Kawekwalese are always in the position of leading clans. Mairoete and Kawinalili have hosted in both leading and subordinate positions over the last thirty years, possibly in response to demographic factors.[2] Note that Anihale is a leading clan despite its position at the back of the flute house and its consistent association with alterity. Anihale clan plays a leading role, I suggest, both because it is populous and because its 'Tupi-Mondé alterity' is constitutive of the polity. This is an inference I draw from this clan's central place in Enawenê foundation stories, which focus on the incorporation and moderation of the alterity of a people called the Towalinere, who came from the Aripuana River basin and are said to be relatives of the Enawenê's most redoubtable former enemies, the Tupi-Mondé speaking Cinta-Larga.[3] It seems likely, then, that the flutes' positions are guided by a symmetrical opposition between Arawak hegemonic centrality and Tupi-Mondé constitutive alterity, while the pairing of host clans is oriented by an asymmetrical opposition between Arawak and Nambikwara.

However helpful they may be, these convenient linguistic labels are misleading if they imply that discrete populations were thrust together in a single historical event. Just as today's Enawenê live in a syncretic polity, it is likely that they also did so in the more densely populated landscape of the past, when regional integration of peoples across linguistic divides is likely to have been the rule rather than the exception (Hornborg 2005). There is also specific evidence for longstanding Arawak-Nambikwara hybridity in this region. We know that the Paresi nation incorporated mobile, hunting people, whom they considered fundamentally different from, and inferior to, themselves. Schmidt noted during his stay among a Paresi subgroup called Koláilil on the Rivers Cabaçal, Jaurú and Juruena that Nambikwara people (known then as Cabixi by colonists and as Waikwakoré by Paresi) had been captured and incorporated as a dependent, labouring class by the Paresi (Schmidt 1917; see also Métraux 1942: 161). This points to the likelihood that hybrid Paresi-Nambikwara groups formed one or several strands of the Enawenê populace, and highlights a difference between two kinds of alterity that has been incorporated into Enawenê society

– the one encompassed and inferior, the other equal and opposite. Enawenê historical narratives about unification focus on the incorporation of Tupi-Mondé speakers called the Towalinere into a village belonging to the ancestors of the first clan Aweresese, an emphasis that suggests the normalcy of the unequal Nambikwara-Arawak alliance. The way the Enawenê tell this tale of fusion is revealing of what they consider to be the necessary conditions for the creation of a unified society. As we will see now, it is a tale of syncretism in which elements from contrasting cultural repertoires are added together to make a new whole, which is spoken of first in aesthetic terms as a perfection and completion of the decorated body; second in terms of hegemonic dietary mores and language that are imposed upon incomers; and third in terms of the social arrangements that allow formerly separate peoples to become interdependent clans, intermarrying and sharing a single panoptic space.

Fusion and Social Reform at a Central Place

Located on the River Arimena, close to its confluence with the middle course of the River Juruena, Kawekwalikwa is the majestically sized village where incomers gradually joined the ancestors of the Aweresese clan, the Kawali-nawe, who were its original inhabitants. It is likely that this agglomeration occurred during the mid-eighteenth century, when gold miners and slave raiders rushed up from Mato Grosso state's capital, Cuiabá, decimating the Paresi population (Price 1983: 131). The story about Kawekwalikwa fits colonial reports of large villages in the central reaches of the Juruena; with what we know about the operation of slave raiders in this region in the eighteenth century; and with the confused mêlée in colonial reports of 'tame' Arawakan speakers living alongside, and sometimes mixed together with, others whom colonists considered 'wild' and threatening (ibid.). The arrival of firearm-wielding foreigners bent on taking slaves also forms part of Enawenê narratives about the events that led to the Towalinere's incorporation. Supported by these convergences of written and oral histories but in the absence of rigorous ethnohistorical research or archaeological or historical-linguistic evidence, I provide a speculative reconstruction of how the Enawenê's ancestors created an enduring identity out of the mixing of distinct peoples. In fact, the full story must be much more complex than the one I tell here, if only because the most recent reduction to a single village probably occurred only in the last century – elder people today remember a more recent history in which their grandfathers lived across more than one village (Lima-Rodgers 2014:

115–16). Nonetheless I focus on the fusion in the distant past that the Enawenê represent as originary and see as the outcome of a violent history. This section is thus about what Hill terms (1996) 'ethnogenesis': a process of identity formation that is rooted in the Enawenê's historical consciousness, though they were buffeted by global histories beyond their control.

To illustrate their long-held knowledge of non-indigenous foreigners, of the state capital city Cuiabá, and of metal tools like fish hooks, the Enawenê tell a story about a man called Maitoa who was abducted in a raid and taken to Cuiabá. There he was made to hunt and garden for his masters, working from dawn to dusk and obliged to shoot down several birds each day without wasting a single bullet. As he aged and became less sure in his aim he began to displease his masters and so he escaped and eventually found his way back to his people, where he told his tale. This story melds with the events that led to the Towalinere's arrival at Kawekwalikwa, because it is said that during this era of attacks by non-indigenous foreigners (whom the Enawenê call *iñoti*) many people were left wifeless. It was a marriage alliance in these conditions that bought the Towalinere together with the Kawali-nawe. Since they lacked wives, two men from Kawekwalikwa travelled to the village of the Towalinere to find women, overcoming their fear of these tall, strong people. They encountered two fit young women at a bathing pool near the village and asked them to accompany them secretly away. Sometime later the father of the two stolen women, who was a Towalinere leader, arrived at Kawekwalikwa to see his daughters and to collect payment from his presumptuous sons-in-law. This was not a revenge mission, since he brought clubs and arrows with him only as gifts and was invited by his hosts to sling his hammock in the flute house. The two sons-in-law responded by collecting wealth from everyone in the village and hanging it on a palm fibre rope, which they suspended all the way across the central arena. This was their way of publicly presenting a generous payment to their father-in-law. With this retrospective bride-wealth payment in hand, and after seeing his daughters' were content, he is said to have returned to his own village. It was later, when the Towalinere suffered enemy attack and were left diminished in number, that they arrived at Kawekwalikwa to seek refuge with their affines. Thus the coming together of these unlike people was forged in a period of violent upheaval and demographic collapse, initially through bride capture, then through an amicable event of affinal diplomacy, and finally with the establishment of a permanent covenant based on dress, diet and social arrangements that were designed to create solidarity between unrelated men.

Enawenê people say that before the Towalinere arrived, the Kawali-nawe looked just like the peoples of the Upper Xingu, who wear only palm nut bead chains. They did not yet know about the beautiful palm fibre silks that they today wear to dance for Yankwa, Kateoko and Lerohi. These were introduced by the Towalinere along with the manner of containing the penis by tying the foreskin with a palm fibre tie; the annatto-dyed band of rubber all women wear wedged tightly between their calf muscles and knees; and the distinctive Enawenê haircut with a deep fringe extending behind the ears. The original inhabitants of Kawekwalikwa eagerly adopted these beautiful items of dress. The Towalinere's diet, however, was rejected. While the incomers formerly ate terrestrial game – monkeys, wild pigs, deer and tapir, among them – they had to conform to the superior diet of the fisherfolk at Kawekwalikwa. A shared, perfected body ensemble was thus coupled with an ascetic dietary pact that allowed for the circulation of nourishing foods and drinks drawn from a dietary repertoire centred around fish and manioc.

It seems likely that as well as abandoning meat-eating, the Enawenê's ancestors outlawed other risky practices and substances associated with supernatural communion and social disharmony in the course of the tumultuous history through which their heterogeneous polity emerged. These are the cultivation and smoking of tobacco; beer-drinking; and the internal aggressions of poisoning, all of which have been enduring practices among Paresi, Nambikwara and Tupi-Mondé speakers. I want to suggest the hypothesis that these dangerous substances were rejected in order to hold discord and schism at bay. The Enawenê's rejection of these practices may have been a self-conscious effort to found a polity upon affinal civility. Enawenê people explicitly stated that they had decided collectively to outlaw the use of poison, although there was always the risk of its revival, since people still knew how to make poisons. As for tobacco, I was told that its cultivation and smoking by shamans had ended only when the Enawenê were forced to leave behind their gardens in their flight from the Cinta-Larga's attacks in the mid-twentieth century. The rejection of beer-drinking mostly passed under silence as an eternal moral dictum. Only once in the course of our joint manioc processing did a woman mention that in the past women had left drinks to ferment in huge hollowed-log troughs, but that this custom had been lost. I now wish I had probed this particular silence with more direct questioning: when and why did the Enawenê give up drinking inebriating beer? Without direct answers I can only suggest a likely scenario based on the few researched cases of Amerindian teetotalism and ascetic dietary practices. This evidence points to the conscious rejection of fermentation because of its well-known social and cosmological effects.[4]

Erikson characterises Amerindian teetotalism, which is fairly rare, as a conscious 'prophylactic ascetic policy' (Erikson 2004: 47). The Matis renounced inebriating drinks at the same time that they rejected powerful substances like chilli, tobacco and hallucinogens in response to the trauma of post-contact epidemics (ibid.). In the Upper Xingu the rejection of meat-eating, cannibalism and other 'savage' customs that define peoples at the margins of its ceremonial exchange system are foundational to the self-conscious identity of those who belong to this regional ritual polity (Basso 1995: 17). Like Upper Xingu people, the Enawenê are very aware that their neighbours imbibe huge quantities of beer and vomit the excess. This spectre lives on in the habits of the Yakairiti, who are commonly characterised as drunken. The Enawenê also comment of the moral depravity of drunks they see lurching around the streets of nearby towns and identify the fits of two epileptic community members with the state of drunkenness. In fact, the association the Enawenê make between drunkenness, uncontrolled alteration and ultimately death is widespread in Amazonia – what differs is people's orientation to it. Most in the region embrace this risky transformative power with periodic bacchanalian beer-drinking, copious vomiting and, inevitably, outbreaks of violence, while a minority repudiate drunkenness for its incitation of supernatural danger, aggression and the loss of thoughtful regard for others.

It seems likely that the Enawenê's ancestors abandoned beer and tobacco, and attempted to outlaw poisoning, just as they had abolished carnivory, in favour of a shared, ascetic dietary pact that fostered people's harmonious coexistence and mixture. Whereas these are inferences I have had to draw in the absence of Enawenê commentary, the social organisational contract that facilitated the incomers' incorporation is quite clearly enunciated by Enawenê people. It amounts to the organised mixture of separate peoples in a single panoptic village space, which becomes a theatre for the performance of egalitarian affinal civility. As I mentioned in the previous section, incoming peoples to Kawekwalikwa placed their flutes together at the centre of the village as if to fix the coordinates of their separateness and their simultaneous unification in that microcosmic space. They themselves, however, were invited to join the houses of their new affines. I see this concrete image of incomers installing their flutes at a central place and then dispersing to separate houses as the expression of a diplomatic covenant that is based on the decoupling of gendered forms of lineal continuity and affinity. The ideal, self-perpetuating aspect of clanship is embodied by flutes, whose hierarchical arrangement in their house persists immutably. The arena is the place where these clans and their members are put into alliance and opposition, and where their members mix and circulate. The dwelling circle is the setting for the processes of social reproduction, which puts individual couples – partners to their children's betrothal – rather than whole clans, into opposition and alliance (see Nahum-Claudel 2018). In the next section I want to elaborate the argument that the organisation of Yankwa depends on the counterpoint between paradigmatically 'male' and 'female' principles of lineality, the one expressed in clanship, the other in residence. Female lines are gathered in uxorilocal houses while male lines are reconstituted in Yankwa's collective gardens, in the arena when they host, and to some extent, at fishing dams.

'Female' Houses and 'Male' Clans

Why does Yankwa depend on principles of male and female lineality being opposed? The one expressed in clanship, and the other in houses? Anthropologist Robert Murphy, who worked with the Tupi-speaking Mundurucu of the Tapajos River in the 1950s, was preoccupied by the 'disharmony' he found in their social organisation, which, like that of the Enawenê, dispersed the members of patrilineal clans across uxorilocal households and, in the Mundurucu case, even separate settlements. Murphy (1956) saw this arrangement as an aberration among the known kinship systems of the world and he was convinced that the residential scattering of Mundurucu men must have been the outcome of colonial upheavals that had 'obliterated' the corporate character of their descent groups. Murphey's argument is based on his certainty that clans should be corporate groups sustained by the fit between principles of filiation and locality. Of course, Enawenê historical narratives attest that previously corporate groups had precisely to lose their tie with locality and their corporacy in order to form a common polity. Clansmen gather together not to dance and sing themselves but to serve the mixed members of all the other clans. A clan's flutes are played in the arena by all the men except those of the owning clan; likewise the drinks that are served to them are produced by women who are related to the clan by affinity, rather than by women who belong to the clan. In both cases work is accomplished by lines of people, but these lines are not those of clanship: fathers and sons come together at the same hearths to play the flutes of the hosting clan; mothers and daughters work together not on behalf of their own clans (though all women are lifelong members of their fathers' clans) but for other clans to whom they are related by affinity. Rather than being an illogical aberration in kinship systematics, the Enawenê suggest the productivity of rendering clan corporacy contingent upon affinal relationships of various kinds. I start with affinity that crosses gendered lines, namely that between men who host and women who work inside houses to provision their distributions of food and drink. This gives the house an ambiguously gendered character. It appears as an icon of a 'male' clan when a man carries ketera out of its front door to serve in the arena, while when a grandmother, her daughter and a gaggle of grandchildren are immersed in the work of producing that ketera, the character of the house as the container of a female line comes to the fore.

To underscore the enduring importance of uxorilocality, at the time of my fieldwork there were fifty-one married men and only four of them lived patrilocally. Looked at from the inside, houses are places of close female kinship in which men principally figure as affines. Men start out their married lives as outsiders; they are thrust into the company of other in-married men who come from various clans and have no pre-existing solidarity. Even once these men become friends who regularly fish together, and once relationships with their wives' parents become warm and quasi-filial (after a formal, distanced and respectful start), it is still the case that men tend to come in and out through the day and are almost always outnumbered and individualised compared to the solidary women whose shared work fills the common areas of the house every day.

The fundamental nature of the house as a place of female kinship, whose open space is occupied by manioc-processing tasks at which the women pool their labour, is reflected in the architectural dominance of the collective hearths (*berakwa*) at which pans of drinks simmer away and discs of manioc fibre dry. The open space of any house is dominated by one, two or three sturdy wooden hearths, which are anchored to a house's two or three supporting pillars, depending on the house's length. Halataikwa's fifteen houses are each around eight metres wide and six tall, but vary in length considerably, stretching back from their front doors, which open onto the arena, for twenty to thirty metres. These houses contain family compartments (*waxelako*), which are walled off from the public hearth and social spaces with panels woven from palm fronds. The smallest house I observed in 2009, composed of a senior couple and the families of their married daughters, had only four such family compartments, while the largest had ten, its front and back halves each occupied by separate uxorilocal clusters related by past or antici-pated marriage alliances. Whatever the size and internal complexity of the house, though, a central corridor always runs its length, in places narrowing to a squeeze between two compartments, in others opening out to accommodate the collective hearths, each of which is shared by three or four women, who are usually sisters, or mothers and their married daughters, each of them with their own sections of the drying racks, and spaces for their pans of drink. These lines of women also share the giant hollow log mortars, which usually stand just inside the front and back doors of the house, to benefit from the light.

But although houses thus join lines of women and are animated by, and architecturally defined by, their daily manioc work, the houses are places of mixture and contrasting gendered characteristics come to the fore depending on one's perspective. Looking out from the flute house, houses stand for patrilineal clans because there is an ideal that the senior man of each clan should establish his house in the position in the dwelling circle that corresponds to the position of his clan's flutes around the central pillar of the flute house.[5] As such, a clan's position at the 'wheel's hub' should match its position on its 'rim'. Although not all senior men had managed to establish their household in the ideal position during my fieldwork, houses did stand for clans: a house was commonly referred to as 'X man's house', after any one of the senior men who inhabited it and, during periods when any one of these men hosted, their house stood as an icon for their whole clan. We saw this on the night of the fishermen's return, when Yankwa gathered in a huddle at the doorways of the lead hosts' houses to sing of their humble offering of fish, and also at the culmination of the returning sequence, when Yankwa's dancers entered the hosts' houses to circle their central hearths in order to offer the very last drop of oloniti to the Yakairiti. More prosaically, since the flute house is the place of Yankwa, the house of the senior host becomes a hub where other clansmen plan and discuss their common tasks. They inspect the headdresses they will use to crown Yankwa and hang up flattened baskets of fish they have received from Yankwa in the eaves of this meeting house.

Nonetheless, as we know from the description that opened this chapter and its accompanying diagram, the food and drinks that this line of male hosts serves to Yankwa are not made centrally, in the lead man's house by his wife and daughters, but rather at the many dispersed hearths of women married or betrothed to men of the clan. In many separate houses simultaneously, lines of co-resident female kin work 'for Yankwa' (*Yankwa oana*), as they say. Mothers and daughters, and groups of sisters, pool their labour to provision the host clan's nighttime distribution of ketera, when any of their husbands (or daughters' future husbands) host. This collective work is usually led by the women whose husband, betrothal partner or son-in-law is to host that night.

Just after dawn she leads her sisters to one of the individual gardens he has planted for her or to his plot in his clan's collective manioc field. In 2008 and 2009, the aim was always to make a 125-litre pan of ketera, since this was the conventional amount said to go around the populous village – and no doubt because it was also the largest-sized pan that could readily be purchased in catering supply stores in Cuiabá. These expensive pans were prized possessions, since they allowed women to abundantly supply Yankwa. To fill the pan, groups of three or four women harvested baskets of manioc weighing around forty kilos each, often assisted by a couple of young girls with miniature baskets.

When the seventeen adult men of Aweresese clan hosted over the course of approximately three-week long departing and returning phases in 2008 and 2009, the wives of about eight to ten of the clansmen made such pans of ketera on any night. Because Aweresese is a large clan, only the wives of senior men provisioned ketera every night. This amounted to a daily production of around 1,250 litres and represented the labour of about forty women, at least half the adult female population. This work to make the nightly ketera is affinally motivated in just the way men's activities are. Since clans are exogamous and since women usually provision not their own clan but those of their husbands and betrothal partners, most of these women would not be Aweresese clanswomen themselves, just as none of the men playing Aweresese clan's flutes are its clansmen. There is thus a distribution of efforts on behalf of the singularised clan, so that producing plenty is not achieved by the concentration or centralisation of efforts in a single, localised clan but rather by the collected efforts of women throughout the dwelling circle.

In my own small house, I joined the manioc work of four sisters most days, and this one line of women (who belonged to Kairoli clan) was a productive hub for all nine clans. We cooked most often for their husbands, who belonged to Aweresese, Anihale, Kaholase and Kairoli clans and for their father of Kairoli clan.[6] We also made ketera on some days when Kawinalili, Kawekwalese and Hotakanese clans hosted, since their daughters were betrothed to boys from each of these clans. Over any clan's approximately twenty-day hosting sequence, women made ketera roughly every other night when their husbands hosted, compared to about twice for their betrothal partners, although this increases in frequency when the betrothed couple are nearly mature enough to become co-resident. Occasionally, I and this line of sisters also assisted their mother and maternal grandmother, who were both marked female members of their respective clans, Mairoete and Lolahese. As I will explain shortly, this gave them hosting obligations for their own clan on top of their affinal obligations. The women of one small house thus worked at varying intensities 'for Yankwa' when any one of the nine clans hosted.

This is the case because my adoptive mother and father had spread their betrothal alliances widely in what is both an ideal and a fairly typical distribution. For nine children they had betrothal partnerships with five different couples, with each of whom they had betrothed one, two or three children. The village is a mesh of such dyadic alliances created through each couple's multiple, reciprocal infant betrothals. It is prevented from becoming 'knotted' – with large clusters of alliances coalescing – because marriage into any of an ego's four grandparental clans is avoided, and because in a single generation preferential marriage alliances between pairs of clans are also rejected (Silva 2012: 204). Both of these norms, which favour alliance between people who have become maximally distant, rather than the repetition of alliances, prevent clusters of clans from becoming disproportionately solidary; assure that clansmen are scattered rather than re-united in uxorilocal houses; and that women's work to produce on behalf of any one clan will be distributed throughout the dwelling circle. In short, because of this even distribution of marriage alliances, each uxorilocal household is a node of widespread affinity that is set to become a knot of productive effort on behalf of every clan.

In order to more forcefully demonstrate why uxorilocal residence is a fundamental support to the affinal diplomacy that is staged at Yankwa I want to briefly entertain a thought experiment: what would happen if there were a universal shift to patrilocal residence? The problems this would enchain are already apparent in the predicament of the wife of a man of Lolahese clan who had chosen to live with his father in defiance of the uxorilocal residence norm. He was able to do this because his wife's brother is married to his own sister and both men agreed to opt out of living with their in-laws when Halataikwa was founded in 2007. Their situation reflects an egalitarian ideal in Enawenê betrothal partnerships in which two couples exchange a daughter and a son with another couple's son and daughter, so that each family loses a son but gains a son-in-law under their roof.[7] In the case of these two defiant brothers-in-law, each couple has instead kept a son under their roof and lost a daughter. This solution, while pleasing to the two men, creates difficulties for their wives. The wife of the man of Lolahese clan has a particularly difficult task. She should ideally be producing ketera every day when his small clan hosts in order for there to be enough to go around in the nightly distribution. Of course, she lives with her mother-in-law, who has the same obligations to produce ketera for Lolahese clan. These two women, because they have the same obligations, could never pool their labour, unlike sisters, who have different affinal obligations and thus can do so. This reality was evident architecturally in the small house; the two women had separate pans of ketera, sets of calabashes, mortars and hearth spaces. During the time when the younger woman had a newborn to care for and could thus not harvest manioc, she relied on the willingness of her mother and sister to cross the arena in order to help her.

This counterexample illustrates the fact that female kin work together because they have different affinal obligations, whereas a woman and her daughter-in-law work separately because they have the same obligations. If everyone lived patrilocally, when any one clan hosted, all of the women of the 'clan house' would have to provision their husbands simultaneously. They could invite their sisters in to make up their work groups but the house would become impossibly full of piles of manioc and pans of boiling juice. The house would be a factory of productive effort when the clan hosted and it would be idle for the rest of the time. And while a single house exploded with effort the rest of the houses in the village would be dormant, their members departing to work at others' hearths. The consequences would not only be pragmatic, they would threaten the equitable performance of Yankwa by clans of vastly different sizes. In the uxorilocal arrangement, even when a small clan like Lolahese hosts (with only six adult male members in 2009), the amount of ketera it can produce will not be drastically less than that produced by a large clan if the men's wives produce ketera nightly assisted by their sisters, and if men's betrothal partners also make separate pans. In a patrilocal arrangement the equalising effect of the distribution of efforts would be lost and house size and differential productive capacity would become visible signs of clans' relative stature, just as they are in Upper Xingu villages, where populous chiefly houses sponsor festivities. Thus the 'disharmony' between clanship and residence, which perplexed Robert Murphy, can be seen as a way of equalising the clans' stature. It ensures that every clan is equal to the whole community.

Having established that women's work 'for Yankwa' is affinally motivated just as is men's work singing and dancing in the arena for the host clan, I now want to introduce an exception. Each clan has a few female members known as *wayato*, which means 'female owners', or more colloquially as *halikalo*, 'female hosts'. These women harvest gardens and provision cooked foods when their brothers host, in addition to the work they must undertake for the clans of their affines. Strictly speaking the title is exclusive to women who receive special clan names at birth and whose status as owners of Yankwa is activated when a plot of their clan's collective manioc field is marked out and planted for them by Yankwa's leaders. The special status of these female hosts is also recognised on specific days within the ceremonial calendar, when they cook foods made from their own plot's harvest. Occasionally, I also saw female hosts appear in the arena alongside their brothers and fathers. Such was the case in 2009 at the firewood distribution that followed Batatakwayti, when the two female hosts also received clownish abuse and great heaps of firewood from Yankwa's pets. I suggest that this fairly exclusive wayato role is a place-keeper for women's clanship in general; it is a reminder that as lifelong members of their father's clans all women are owners of Yankwa alongside their brothers. In addition it serves as a reminder of women's overall ownership of Yankwa as the chief audience to men's flute playing. Many of Yankwa's chants are addressed to *nowayto*, 'my female owners'. Men said that these chanted dedications addressed both the official wayato (the few women named at birth) and 'all women' *(ouiro makale)*. Women's place within Yankwa is therefore dual: within a relational matrix in which women predominantly figure as affines, the wayato role serves as a reminder of women's clanship and thus of their ownership of Yankwa. In the next section I turn to the men of Yankwa, who work to realise another clan's identity through performance in the central arena and bodily exertions at the fishing weirs and in gardens.

Performing Mixture and Singularity

When I first arrived in the village of Halataikwa in January 2008, I was busy making lists of all five hundred or so community members' clan affiliations. I saw the men of Aweresese clan serving drinks and soon learnt their names and their filial and brotherly relationships to one another. Then there were the lines of men – arranged in birth order, just as Aweresese clansmen were always described – who played different wind instruments around four separate hearths as they prepared to go fishing. Since these lines looked lineage-like and often joined men and their sons, I assumed that the eight clans that opposed the hosts were parsed out two clans per hearth – or something of that nature. I soon learnt that my misunderstanding was fundamental. I would learn that whether singing, planting gardens or going on dam-fishing expeditions 'Yankwa' was always composite; clan affiliation was irrelevant within the mixed multitude that worked for the host clan. Although men often joined the same hearth as their father and learned to play its particular instrument from him (just as they more often than not followed him to his favoured fishing dam), men of different clans were mixed together at each of the four flute groups that dance around separate hearths, just as they were mixed at the five fishing dams. Yankwa is the 'superclan', the whole community that works, sings, dances and drinks for the host clan and its spirits, thereby embodying and ennobling it. This is quite tangible in the relative passivity of the host clan, who offer fire, ornaments, food and drink to the rest, who perform energetically on its behalf. We could say that Yankwa places people in the position of spectatorship and service to their own identities.

As Lévi-Strauss observed in his fascination with Bororo dialecticism, such a system confronts European ideas about embodied identity and about selfhood as interiority. Crocker (1977: 136), who worked with the Bororo after him, also struggled to convey this inversion of his readers' 'common sense' notions: 'the crucial point is that never do the members of a clan act out the representation of their own *aroe* [soul or name]. Instead, they invite members of clans in the other moiety to be such actors, and they paint and ornament them'. However, beyond the evident similarity, there is also an instructive difference between Enawenê and Bororo performances on behalf of other clans. In the Bororo case the ornaments worn and the body designs painted on others were, as Crocker put it, 'nominative emblems' of a clan's unique patrimony (ibid.: 135). Among the Enawenê this is not the case. As I noted above, the suite of ornaments worn by Yankwa's dancers are the result of a historical hybridisation, whose goal was to create a perfect synthesis. Regardless of the hosting clan, Yankwa's dancers are clad in this perfect attire and the identical headdresses they wear are each emblems of the shared humanity of their wearers, since they are icons of the life-giving sun, which was domesticated by the cultural hero in mythic times. And, even though there would be no visible difference if dancers wore their own headdresses, they do not do so but rather allow themselves to be crowned by hosts with others' headdresses. What this convention of swapping identical headdresses seems to stress is the use of dialectical counterposition as a pretext for circulation and mixture, rather than in quest of the mirroring effect sought by the Bororo. Rather than see their individual destiny realised by another individual, the Enawenê see a shared, collective identity realised by everyone.

What happens is that when a clan prepares to host Yankwa, sons gather in their father's house to examine and count out the senior man's headdresses, which he keeps folded away like retracted fans in bamboo tubes that are sealed with wax. They open them out, smooth the feathers, secure them in their diadem form and hang them ready on strings suspended from the rafters, ready to crown all the rest of the adult men of the village. However, the men of any one clan do not own enough headdresses to crown the men of the remaining eight clans, so extra headdresses have to be borrowed by prospective hosts from some of the senior men who will shortly be crowned with them. In 2008 and 2009 this was the case because of two factors: a fast-growing population and the catastrophic loss of valuables occasioned by a spate of house fires. For any phase of Yankwa (or indeed during seasons of Lerohi or Kateoko, which use the same headdresses), upcoming hosts therefore borrowed headdresses, returning them to their owners at the end of the hosting sequence. In fact, even without the recent extenuating circumstances, it is an explicit moral dictate that one cannot be stingy and possessive with the things that belong to Yankwa – essentials such as headdresses, clay pots and large calabashes or mixed pans of ketera belong to the whole community even if they are held by individuals.[8]

So Yankwa looks the same whoever is hosting, since identical ornaments are worn, but how does it sound given that the ensemble of three or four instruments played for a clan is particular? For example, Kairoli's giant gourd trumpet with its long bamboo duct produces a singularly low-toned sound while Lolahese's rattles, worn at the knee, bring a rhythmic beat. The singularity of the sound produced for any clan is softened by the permanence of one instrument, which is shared by all the clans and which produces the melodic baseline that is archetypally Yankwa's sound. This is the bamboo duct recorder with four stops, whose generic name is *lolohe* and which is said to be as ubiquitous and essential to Yankwa as calabashes are. In addition to this instrument, the orchestral arrangement of the separate instruments also minimises the singularity of performances on behalf of any one clan. At each hearth the players alternate independently of the other hearths between phases of chanting, playing instruments, and resting by sitting down on the logs that jut out from their fire. The cumulative effect is an intercalated mixture of sound that occasionally reaches peaks of flute or vocal intensity. It is both differentiated and harmonic (cf. Hill and Chaumeil 2011: 33) and differs only quite subtly depending on which clan is hosting. Clans' distinctiveness is thus only subtly manifest in visual and sonic media. Where it is most strongly manifest is in the invisible realm of discourse, and particularly in esoteric nomenclature.

Much of the information I gathered about clanship consisted of long lists of names: living clansmen in birth order; ancestors; and pantheons of celestial and subterranean spirits. This esoteric nomenclature and the spirit world it indexed lay behind any particular performance of Yankwa. The instruments had generic names, which referred to their physical properties and did not vary from clan to clan; for example, the pair of cashapona palm trumpets, 'belonging under the water'; an end-blown round gourd trumpet with a bamboo duct, 'bamboo'; the oval gourd trumpet, 'gourd'; an oval gourd trumpet played by blowing over an opening at the top of the gourd's curved stem, 'curvy'. However, alongside these generic names, each instrument also had clan-specific names, which referred to the spirits whose presence they personified. Confused by the proliferation of esoteric names, I tended to use the generic names and people would correct me with a series of other names, which referred to the invisible, spirit qualities of the instrument. My notebooks are full of these lists, which to me have remained mysterious representations of the differentiated pantheons of Yakairiti that lie behind any particular performance of Yankwa. But just as the Yakairiti are frequently evoked as a class opposed to humanity, rather than as a series of individualised spirits, so the overall emphasis in the performance of Yankwa was on mixture above singularity, and uniformity above particularity. A concomitant is that no clan's Yankwa was considered superior to that of any other; what varied was the quality of the performance on any one day. This was down to the quality of leadership from song masters and the willingness of everyone else to emerge from their houses, decorate and gather in the arena. A bad performance was a poorly attended one or one in which the chants were incomplete or uttered in an incorrect order. To underscore the lack of distinction between clans, those large and small, or leading and subordinate in a pairing, also hosted for an equal duration and followed the same ideal ceremonial sequence, which included the same chants. The scale of the performance was also equal whatever the size or importance of the host clan, since it was always the mixed members of the other eight clans who performed, and always the same small number of song masters who presided.

In all these ways, the hierarchies and oppositions that are fixed in the layout of the flute house and expressed in the pairing of host clans find little expression in the arena's performances. There is thus no pragmatic context in which a clan's particularity is celebrated; in which competition can emerge between clans; or in which a clan can affirm its position in the status hierarchy. In the next section I want to show that the principle of surrogacy by which the whole community acts on behalf of any individual clan is a contract upon which Yankwa is re-founded every time a collective manioc field is planted for a new host clan. Hosts are defined by their ownership of this field whose harvest they serve in the arena but they play no role in siting, clearing or planting it themselves. Rather, hosts are made when others do this work for them. The founding of collective fields is the responsibility of senior men, who reciprocate over the years, and their reciprocal planting is the key to the

Figure 4.4 On 28 June 2009 women enter the arena after cleaning Kawinyalili clan's manioc field. They have stopped on their way for a collective beautification.

eternal cycling of hosting obligations between the nine clans through the decades.

The Clan as 'The Whole Community'

Others site new collective gardens and thereby 'plant' future hosts. I express it this way because the collective manioc field, called *Yankwa ikiyakakwa*, is the condition of a clan's public recognition; first because the layout and expanse of the collective gardens reflects the size and structure of the host clan; and second because it is when the men of a clan serve drinks made from this field's harvest that they appear together in the arena. The idea that manioc gardens were 'like white people's contracts' was introduced by an Enawenê man in a conversation we were having about infant betrothal. He wanted me to understand that once a man had planted a manioc garden for his son's future wife and her mother to harvest, the betrothal was firmly established. The to and fro of gendered foods between the two families – fish from a boy's father to a girl's mother, and cooked garden foods the other way – led up to this garden contract. Subsequently, every time a woman harvested from the garden planted by her betrothal partner, she would carry a large and very full calabash of ketera made from that day's harvest to her future son-in-law and his father. She would also go expressly to this garden to make ketera for her betrothal partner when his clan hosted. A mother thus anticipates the work that her daughter will perform for her husband when they become a productive unit. On a larger scale, Yankwa's collective manioc fields are contracts that anticipate future obligations. When leaders site a new garden so that a clan can host in the distant future, they are undertaking to clear and plant this garden over two years and then to dance for the host clan and lead dam-fishing expeditions for them over two more years. Through all of these activities they will drink the host's manioc. In this section I want to show why it is that collective manioc fields are such good 'contracts' on which to found Yankwa. This has to do with the dissociation between labour and ownership at every stage of the field's making; and also with the field's layout and expanse; the clonal properties of manioc; and the lifecycle of the manioc plant itself.

Collective fields are sited years in advance by the senior men, who envisage leading Yankwa on another clan's behalf. The leader sites the patch of virgin forest that will be cleared and then he invites others to view it. The next morning he announces that in future Yankwa will drink for the clan. We could say that the field founds the clan since it becomes the ground and condition for its recognition as host. This recognition grows gradually over about a five-year period, as the garden comes into existence. In 2009 there were already murmurings that Kairoli clan would host in the future, although their field would not actually be cleared until 2012 or planted until 2013, and they would only host in 2014 and 2015. The real work starts two years before the clan will host the central phases of Yankwa, the lead up to and return from dam-fishing expeditions. At this point, the work of clearing, burning and planting is accompanied each day by the playing of the flutes of the garden-owning clan and the singing of chants, which, through their symbolic associations, speed the felling of trees or the action of fire. As during every other phase of Yankwa, the men of all eight clans play the hosts' ensemble of wind instruments in the hours before dawn. The hosts crown the dancers with sun diadem headdresses and serve ketera to the flute players in the arena, and refreshing oloniti to the workers in the field. At this stage, drinks are made from manioc harvested from each host's individual manioc gardens.

In 2009, when I saw Kawinalili's manioc field planted over five days, followed by that of Mairoete, it was once the field had been subdivided, one plot for each clan member, that hosts crowned Yankwa's dancers with headdresses. At dawn, once the night's musical routine and ketera-drinking was over, the leaders (*honerekaiti*) amongst Yankwa's multitude – the same senior men who took the initiative in siting the gardens – were the first to take up their axes and machetes and to walk in the direction of the site. To facilitate the transition from beautified work in the arena to dirty garden work, the hosts set up a rail for them on the side of the arena that was nearest the garden (it was the north side) so that they could hang up the flutes on their way to work (see Figure 4.4). Having hung their flutes at around 7AM, the workers took them up again at around 10AM, as soon as they had bathed in the stream to clean off the dirt and sweat on their walk back from the garden. They played through the hottest part of the day until around 3PM, when they sometimes returned to the gardens to continue working. Unsurprisingly, men spoke of this short phase of planting as Yankwa's sweatiest and most gruelling one.

Once the field had been burnt so that it resembled a mass of charcoal with severed, fire-ravaged logs and branches littering it, the leaders divided it into transects (*eheko*) for each of the adult members of the clan, planting tall sticks as markers between plots. This resembles the division of the fishing dam into trap positions, which become the responsibility of individual owners. Just so, each plot has its owner and in 2009 some young literate men wrote names on pieces of paper and taped these onto the stakes that divided the plots. Once they were washed away by the rain, everyone remembered the order of the transects and this is probably because the transects are hierarchically arranged with the senior men of the clan in the middle of the garden and younger men and marked female members – the wayato – towards the outside, so that the layout and expanse of the field reflects the size and structure of the host clan. Its thoughtful subdivision by leaders is an act of recognition of each of the clan's mature members. For example, when I visited Kairoli clan's newly planted field with a senior man of the owning clan in July 2013, he named each of the thirty-six transects as we walked from the garden's entrance to the forest, which marked its far boundary. All the wayato and young men who were close to coming of age were represented with small transects, in anticipation of their maturing in time for the harvest. The separate lineages that compose this large clan were represented, since sets of brothers had their transects side by side and in birth order. The overall hierarchy of the clansmen was also recognised, since the large, central transects belonged to the clans' leaders, who were also its song masters. Halfway down each of these central transects a few mothers of manioc, which stood iconically for the whole field, had been planted and fecundated with offerings of smoked fish and drinks.

As well as acting as a guide to the composition of the host clan, the field's shape acts as a guide to harvest. My Kairoli guide explained that when women harvested from their husbands' plot in order to make ketera for the hosts to serve, they would start harvesting at the end of their transect nearest the field's entrance. Through the hosting sequence they would gradually work their way down, aiming to reach the far end when Yankwa finished returning in around June. The shape of the garden thus supports Yankwa's temporal progression each year as hosts attempt to quench the thirst of the Yakairiti over the course of the returning phase. Time and progress will be measured out in harvests and will be visible in the contrast between long, leafy manioc branches and the short sticks recently replanted following a first harvest.

Founded and made by others, this manioc field establishes the host clan as a corporate body. This is clear both in the recognition of every member and their status in the subdivision of the ground, and also in the provenance of the manioc that is subsequently planted. Manioc is clonally propagated from the stems of existing plants, so that in order to make a 'new' field, the leaders and men of Yankwa had to cut stems from existing plantations. It is significant that the manioc Yankwa plant is host men's own, which they go to considerable lengths to gather. Because men tend to site their manioc gardens down paths that lead out from the backs of their houses, and since the men of any one clan are dispersed around the dwelling circle, their manioc gardens are dotted around the wide and intensively cultivated ring, of patchwork ownership, that surrounds the village. Playing the flutes of the host clan, the men of Yankwa go to raid manioc stems from individual gardens belonging to each of the host clansmen and they carry them back to the cleared and subdivided field, amassing them in heaps at the entrance, ready for a frenzied planting early the next morning. When the time comes for planting, no attempt is made to plant individuals' stems in their own transects. What this effort to fetch the stems suggests is the importance of reconstructing clan unity in a field that becomes a kind of vegetal realisation of the clan's self-contained and self-perpetuating aspect.

The garden's genesis thus simultaneously establishes the self-sufficient unity of the clan and asserts that it could not exist without others. The clan is dependent on the will, initiative, knowledge and enthusiastic work of everyone else who establishes the clan as host. They do so via the field whose harvest will nourish Yankwa – that is, it will feed the same men and spirits who planted the field – over the coming years. This is why, when I went to see the new Kairoli garden in 2013, my guide emphasised to me that the garden 'was Yankwa' because it belonged to 'the whole community' and not just to Kairoli clan. He used the Portuguese word *comunidade* to ensure I understood the meaning of 'Yankwa', in which the individual clan realises the whole community and vice versa. Indeed the ownership of this unified body of land is dispersed throughout the whole community, female and male, because women also play an important role in preparing the garden for planting. It is also projected beyond the realm of human relationships, since both women and men's work in the garden is animated by Yakairiti.

In 2009, on the morning after the garden had been subdivided, the leader invited all the women of the village to help clear the field of remaining wood. All except the wayato of the host clan, to whom the garden belonged, set off for the field to work as Yakairiti-women *(Yakaloti-nero)*, with the leaders' wives *(honerekaiti-nero)* in front, just as they were at Batatakwayti, when supernaturally energised women pounded manioc for the hosts. They uprooted stumps, piled up branches and set light to these half-burnt remnants of forest, working in a festive mood and enjoying the opportunity to survey the massive, fertile expanse of ash, which most of them would return to harvest the next year. On their way back to the village, they stopped for a conscientious, collective beautification at the bathing pool and then re-entered the village arena, passing underneath the hanging flutes (see Figure 4.4). To mark their status as Yakairiti on this day, the hosts met them in the arena with handfuls of potassium salt and their wives had set out calabashes full of oloniti, which the entitled spirit-women went and took directly from their hearths. Through work, beautification and consumption they thus participated in incarnating the spirits of the host clan, the ultimate owners of this collective manioc field, which is planted with them so that it may later quench their thirst. As I mentioned in Chapter 3, when the men of Yankwa planted the field on the next day, they did so as Yakairiti, wielding their hoes and attacking the soil with stylised ferocity.

Planted in June 2009 this field would be ready to harvest in time for the fishermen's return with the Yakairiti from the fishing dams in 2010. Perhaps a little would be harvested even before their departure. The lifecycle of the field then determines the duration over which the owning clan hosts by serving drinks made from its plentiful crop. During the two years in which a collective garden yields plentifully, smoked fish is returned to the host clan in recognition of the manioc they have served and in anticipation of all that the fishermen will drink upon their return. Over two further years, as these gardens wane in productivity, the clan retains a residual hosting role, leading intercessional phases of the ceremonial sequence called *Edaytiri* and *Amamaneda-hwale*, in which hosts and Yankwa swap places, the former dancing and the latter serving them.[9] These intercessional phases thus remind everyone of who has hosted more recently or more long ago, but a clan must nonetheless wait for others to decide that its 'turn' has come around again on an imaginary Ferris wheel, in which clans rise to become host over two years, host fully for a biennial and then host residually for two further years as they fall downwards on the other side of the wheel. However, this wheel image suggests more order and predictability than is necessarily in evidence in the cycling of hosting obligations through the nine clans. It would be too artificial to say that the clans 'obey a rigorous system of circulation' as Silva suggested in his analysis of the Enawenê ceremonial system (1998: 8), because not all clans host with the same frequency and not all pairings are stable over the long term. On the other hand, host pairings are often repeated and there are some long-standing reciprocal relationships between the senior men of two clans, who become leaders and hosts to one another in turn. These men install one another as hosts by planting gardens for one another and then serve their harvest to one another over the years. This was the case during the two years of my fieldwork in 2008 and 2009, when senior men of Anihale clan led Yankwa for Aweresese clan; Aweresese clan having just led Yankwa for Anihale in the previous biennial. In fact, the reciprocal relationship between the senior men of these two clans had a long history and the pairing of Aweresese and Lolahese clans as hosts was also long-standing.

In sum, the endurance of at least some of these oppositions and pairings ensures a degree of predictability to the cycle. However, the Enawenê never listed a conventional rota in their explanations to me; instead they focused on the planning of future gardens, always forecasting the biennial after next, or the one after that, and they did this from their present position in time, with their fail-safe memories of past pairings and host-leader oppositions, which stretched back over many decades. Thus Yankwa's temporality is grounded in the planning, siting, burning and planting of manioc fields, and then their waning productivity. It is a temporality that is detached from events of the lifecycle or the will of men. However, just as women figure primarily as alhnes but retain the position of hosts and owners through the wayato role, so there is a dual and asymmetric route to becoming a male host, either as owner of a collective field planted by others, or as owner of individual gardens planted by one's own labour. This path nonetheless rests on the bestowal of recognition from the rest of the community.

Humbly Seeking Recognition

Clans can also put themselves forward to host Yankwa when no field has been planted for them. In Portuguese, the Enawenê contrast these two paths to hosting by explaining that one is based on the *roça coletivo* – the subdivided field sited and planted by others – while the other is based on the *roça individual*, the gardens men clear and plant annually for their wives and daughters, which are usually called simply manioc gardens (*ketekwa*). Whereas in the first case, as we have seen, the agency of the clan's Yakairiti is embodied by all the rest of the community, in the second, clansmen are compelled to present the will of their own Yakairiti for recognition by the rest of the community. This occurs in response to serious illness within a clan, which is said to be caused by the rising thirst of its Yakairiti. However, although the hosts thus put themselves forward they do so in a way that foregrounds their passivity. First they stress that the Yakairiti demand to drink; second, in the way the brief inauguration ceremony unfolds, they present themselves as vulnerable; and third, the rest of the community affirm this powerlessness by withholding their acceptance of the host's invitation to drink.

In May 2009, I looked out from the front door of our house with the recently married husband of one of my younger sisters. It was 4PM, during the period every afternoon of Yankwa's returning phase, when flute groups took turns to circle the central post of the flute house in preparation for their evening emergence into the arena. On this day, the habitual pattern was interrupted by a brief ceremony called *Etayxwalalo*, named after the lines of drink that are placed in the arena by expectant hosts. The men of the smallest clan of the village, Hotakanese (which was, in 2009, composed of just four fit, mature men: a father and his three young married sons – the father's father was alive but too infirm to participate) all carried calabashes or metal pans of oloniti out of their houses and placed them on the ground in arced lines, each thirty or so containers long. My sister's husband told me 'watch, this is a difficult moment, the men will not emerge quickly from their houses'. Indeed, the four men stood very still, exposed to the scrutiny of the panoptic dwelling circle and displaying a solemnity and stillness that occurred quite rarely in Halataikwa. Compared to the flurrying simultaneity of distributions of fish soup, which was occurring almost daily during that period, it felt like a long interval before a senior man of Aweresese clan emerged in the arena. Even then, he did not walk directly towards the lines of drink but rather headed straight towards the flute house. The senior man of Hotakanese had to step forward to intercept his path. He stopped still a few paces away and stood at right angles to his addressee staring into space and uttering a formal dialogue that invited the Aweresese clansman to take the drink, after which the future host took a calabash from the line and handed it to him. Next to emerge in the arena was a senior man of Kairoli clan. My young companion told me that these first recipients of drinks would be the 'true leaders' (*honerekaiti kaxata*) of Yankwa, while the stream of men who came out of their houses more quickly after them would only be 'minor leaders' (*kixixi honerekaiti*). Ultimately all the men of the village – the whole of Yankwa – emerged from their houses to drink the oloniti and to join in the discussion about the new shape of Yankwa's season in the coming year, when there would now be three clans hosting every phase in turn: Kawinalili, Mairoete and Hotakanese.

The acceptance of drinks was thus both a promise to provide leadership and a general show of recognition; by accepting to drink from one calabash, the men of Yankwa effectively promised to drink from many more the following year. Thus, although the contract between the host clan and the rest of the community is established via the offering and acceptance of drinks rather than the making of gardens, everything about this tense, testy offering suggests hosts' submission to the will of others and underplays their initiative. The usually almost simultaneous offering and acceptance of drinks is slowed down and thought-out, because the taking of this drink implies the taking of many more. All hosts are not equal and just as women's responsibility to work for their affines trumps their responsibility to their own clan, individual gardens are not equal to collective ones. Hosts that emerge from the acceptance of drinks will always come after the single clan or pair of clans whose position as hosts has long been established by the siting and planting of collective gardens, regardless of their position in the clan hierarchy.[10]

Conclusion

I began this chapter with a description of Yankwa's nightly routine, in the course of which the whole community works for one clan and in the process reinvents itself. The aesthetic, dietary and social covenants that are at the origin of the Enawenê's unified but heterogeneous polity are thus realised every night in the hosts' offering of ketera to the men who play their flutes: that men should live among their affines and be compelled to exchange substance and identity with them; that nourishing, non-alcoholic drinks should circulate daily to be drunk by everyone from mixed pans; that the garden I harvest and the fish I catch are not owned by me but rather are owed to my affines and to the Yakairiti. A mundane performance can thus be understood to re-found the social contract. Enawenê society is the outcome of deliberate spatial arrangements, institutions and aesthetic and dietary pacts, but its foundation is never complete and stable, rather it is re-founded everyday through major and minor acts of affinal diplomacy: a leader takes the initiative to site a new garden, a host lights the fires or hands a calabash of ketera to a dancer.

I sought to explain why a circular village plan was an essential spatial scaffolding for this polity because of the paradoxical potentials of circular space to simultaneously unify, oppose and hierarchise. Having presented the pacts and institutions that are its historical anchorage, I turned to the ways in which this egalitarian, affine-focused mode of relating is organised through Yankwa's basic ceremonial organisation. Men and women work for their affines collected in lines around flute hearths or at household hearths. Nonetheless there is a difference in character and emphasis between the way women and men live with their affines and within lines of kin. Male lines tend to be virtual (names, lines of men in a lineage-like flute group) and temporarily constituted, whereas female lines are substantial and permanent – sisters usually live together for their whole life and work together every day. For men, affinity is the everyday norm of relating, both in the house and in the arena, where they are mixed together with unrelated men, whereas for women, events in which they meet female affines, though frequent (the calabash round, Batatakwayti, and work in the garden as Yakaloti-nero), are laden with excitement.

In terms of the musical, decorated performance of Yankwa itself, I have argued that it is always a compromise between typicality and singularity, such that every clan is represented as one refraction of the unified identity of the Enawenê people. That is why Yankwa sounds and looks more or less the same to an outsider whichever clan hosts, and why no clan's Yankwa is considered inherently superior to any other, even though the nine Enawenê clans vary greatly in size and are ordered hierarchically. In each Yankwa the same number of men dance, the same songs are sung, the same orchestral music results and comparable quantities are eaten and drunk. A performance is good and true when it draws in the whole community and faithfully reproduces ancestral patterns. Why then do the Enawenê bother to celebrate Yankwa separately for each of the nine clans if it is not a matter of celebrating the unique patrimony of a clan, its origins or its position in the hierarchy? The answer, I think, is that the clans must continue to exist in their separateness in order to continue to perform their mixture and interdependence through the exchange of manioc gardens and their harvests, headdresses and ornaments, and fishing dams and their smoked catch.

Without Yankwa there would be no need for a flute house in which the clans' origins are permanently fixed at the centre of the polity; no manioc fields in which the clans' subdivided unity is recognised; and there would be no occasion for men to gather together in patrilines to light fires, bestow headdresses and serve drinks.

Collective manioc fields are the ideal contracts on which to found Yankwa, because they are living embodiments of this dependence of the one on the many. Planting a field is a many-faceted act of recognition of an individual clan on the part of the whole community. The field resembles the clan in structure, size and in its vegetal makeup – it is a clan body realised as a fertile field but crucially one that is made without the participation of the bodies of the clansmen or women themselves. This decoupling of ownership and labour is the bedrock of Yankwa's affinal diplomacy. It is spearheaded by individual senior men, who are motivated by reciprocal obligations, past and anticipated, to other senior men. By opposing one another stably and being ready to assume new responsibilities, these men assure the perpetuation of Yankwa over the decades. By these means, Yankwa's temporality is assured whatever the vicissitudes of human lives. At the same time, Yankwa also provides an opening to life's events, since clans can offer themselves as secondary hosts without the temporal and spatial anchorage of a manioc field.

I have shown that social diplomacy is an everyday art among these self-consciously civic-minded people, devoted to living together peacefully with their affines in a single polity. Of course, we also know from the first half of this book that every act of social diplomacy is always also an act of cosmological diplomacy, since by serving other persons, people are always also serving the Yakairiti. In the next chapter I turn to this cosmological diplomacy, which is not only socially but materially mediated. Whereas I began this chapter by tracing the circulation of calabashes and drinks through various oppositional relationships, in the next chapter I focus on the physical and metaphysical properties of calabashes, manioc drinks and persons. It is through cookery, curing, care of the body, and craftwork that the Enawenê negotiate with their invisible alter egos, who are the occupants not of other houses or clans, but of other levels or dimensions of the universe.

Notes

1. See T. Turner (1979, 1984); Melatti (1979); Seeger (1981); DaMatta (1982).
2. The clan in the supporting role tends to be the less numerous of the two. The members of Lolahese, Kaholase and Hotakanese clans made up just 4%, 3% and 5% of the

population respectively in 2011 compared to Kairoli, Aweresese and Anihale, which have always hosted as leading clans in the decades since contact and which composed 28%, 15% and 15% of the population respectively in 2011 (clan population data from Silva 2012: 101).

3. The Cinta-Larga have no memory of non-bellicose relations with the Enawenê, so it is likely that the Towalinere refers to one of the other Tupi-Mondé-speaking groups of Brazil's Rhondonia State who are now extinct as independent peoples (see Lima-Rodgers 2014: 151–156).

4. The literature on beer-drinking in Amazonia far outweighs that on teetotalism and it has been particularly focused on Tupi-speakers. See, for example, Stolze-Lima (2005: 311); Vilaça (1992: 189); Viveiros de Castro (1986: 354), and for a synthesis, Sztutman (2008).

5. In Halataikwa only four clan leaders' houses are positioned in the dwelling circle position corresponding to their flutes. The ideal seems to be especially salient for the two leading clans, Aweresese and Kairoli. Looking out from the front door of the flute house, the two houses that appear straight ahead (either side of the ceremonial pathway) are those of Aweresese and Kairoli although the head of Aweresese clan, Kawali, moved out of his clan house in 2007 to create his own small house on the opposite side of the village. He said he was tired of living in a big, populous house. Based on Santos' (2006: 225–26) valuable record of household composition we know that Kawali inhabited the 'correct' house from 1984 to 2007. The head of Kairoli clan, a man called Ataina, lived in his clan house, on the south side of the ceremonial pathway until his death in 2007. Hi son, who is Kairoli's leader after him, still occupies the back pole of that house, while his son-in-law (of Anihale clan) occupies the front, where once Ataina lived. Kawekwalese and Hotakanese clan's leaders also live more or less in line with the position of their flutes. The heads of Anihale and Towalinere-kase clan, whose flutes are on the western side of the flute house, also live on the western side of the dwelling circle, although not in positions that directly correspond to those of their flutes. Overall then, Kairoli and Aweresese clan leaders appear to be most anchored and there is a partial correspondence in the position of some of the other clan leaders and their flutes.

6. Note that one of the sisters was married to a man of her own clan, Kairoli. This marriage occurred in 2008 and was the first clan-endogamous marriage recorded in the village. However, during my stay I heard of two further incipient betrothals within Kairoli clan, and so it thus seems likely that Kairoli people are deliberately flouting the ideal of exogamy to further a process of segmentation within their clan, which is by far the largest of the nine clans.

7. Based on computational analysis of 170 marriages, Silva has shown that 59% involve the repetition by a male ego of an alliance made through his sister. Taking the female ego's viewpoint, 51% repeat an alliance made through a brother. Nonetheless, when betrothal partners establish a relationship, if one has two daughters of the appropriate age and the other two sons, this gender replication (which joins brothers under the same roof) is also a fairly common compromise (Silva 2012: 203–208).

8. The same kind of borrowing and circulation occurs with names that are very definitely nominative emblems, since a clan's stock of personal names expresses its lineal continuity with new generations conceived to directly replace ancestral ones. Typically children are named after great grandparents whose death has ceased to be a painful memory. Names are also 'lent' between clans and 'returned' in the next generation, such that the most common names in the village, Kawali, Bayakoli and

Bailitere for boys; and Menakalose, Marekerose and Kawalinero for girls are ubiquitous. These names retain a reference to an owning clan but have ceased to function
as emblems of that clan's identity.

9. There is also an important and more extended intercessional phase between the end
   of Yankwa's return for both of the incumbent clans and the gardening phase for the
   next pair of clans. It is the occasion to have a 'little drink' *(edaytiri)* from the waning
   gardens belonging to the previous biennial's hosts. These two clans take back the
   hosting role briefly, over two days each, and in an attenuated fashion. In 2009, the
   flutes were played for no more than half an hour before ketera was offered by the
   hosts and they were put away.

10. The emergence of third or even fourth host clans seems to have become an almost
    annual occurrence in recent years. Kairoli was as a third host clan in 2009, followed
    by Hotakanese in 2010. Although these extra clans host for equivalent sequences
    before and after dam fishing, they do so for a single year, as opposed to a bien-
    nial and, as I explained in Chapter 2, their primary responsibility is to fish for the
    true hosts (the owners of collective manioc gardens). Furthermore, the distinction
    between the two kinds of host, which is defined by the individual or collective nature
    of the gardens from which they harvest, is marked at every transfer of drinks from
    host to Yankwa. When a hosts gives foods or drinks made with the harvest from
    the collective field they speak a metaphorical formal address, which translates as
    'here is that which is from your own hand' *(noaka hewesekowointale)*. Although my
    interpretation of this esoteric formula must be tentative, since it is not based on rig-
    orous linguistic analysis, it seems likely that this address refers to the displacement
    of agency, from the host-owner who gives, to the affine-spirit who plants and also
    later receives. The host himself had no hand in planting or tending the manioc that
    he now offers. The 'hand' *(weseko)* that receives is also the hand that planted. Since
    the fingered leaves of manioc are also known as its 'hands', perhaps the hand in the
    address also refers to manioc woman herself. When hosts serve drinks made from
    the harvest of individual gardens, the formal dialogues spoken by hosts reflect the
    garden's individual status: 'from your own hand' is replaced by *noaka emanaywale*,
    which people described to me as indicating the 'individual' nature of the garden.

5

Cosmic Diplomacy

Cooking, Curing and Crafting Human Life

This chapter is about fire and transformative cookery, which are central to the definition of Enawenê identity during the agricultural seasons of Yankwa and Lerohi. The argument is that cookery, which here encompasses not only the use of fire to transform food, but also material things and bodies, is the everyday activity of forging a living position in a dangerous cosmos. Because of its central role in sustaining life, cookery can be understood as the curative transformation of bodies (both human and non-human) that encompasses cuisine, the crafting of objects, shamanism, and forms of bodily care – most notably seclusion mores. The aim of the chapter is to account for an aspect of Enawenê life that was so obvious – so apparently merely material – that it quickly came to seem unremarkable to me: the many fires that burned at Yankwa and the intensely cooked life of the community during this season. Every afternoon during Yankwa blazing fires burned under pans of manioc milk in every house, since huge amounts of heat are necessary to make sweet porridge from the poisonous milk of bitter manioc; all through the day and night logs smouldered under drying manioc breads, flour and starch, which were arrayed on huge hearths so that they could later be stored away; the constant embers of these hearths also served to harden clay pots that sat in the ashes and to slowly dry out calabashes that hung above the hearths. Not only foods and containers but also people were constantly warmed by fire. Before sleep, small hearths were lit in the triangular spaces created between slung hammocks in every sleeping quarter of every house; at about 3AM every night hosts lit three

Figure 5.1 A typically laden hearth.

or four fires in the arena around which dancers circled; fishermen lived in sturdy smoke houses and took care to avoid the reckless mixture of fire and water; hosts boiled and dried palm fronds to create palm silks and they also burned palms and furiously boiled their diluted ashes in order to create a small residue of potassium salt. On the first evening after the fishermen's return from the dams, hosts laid a pyramid-shaped bonfire of tree trunks in the centre of the arena, around which the other-worldly fishermen's reintegration to human life was staged. This thoroughly transformed village in which the Enawenê dwell is matched by the burning of vast manioc gardens and a diet of laboriously cooked foods.

The counterpart to this passion for fire was a dislike of rawness, which ran even to water, which was never drunk unadulterated unless an individual was savagely thirsty. This rarely happened, because people packed well for even short journeys, taking either honey to mix with stream water or bottles of oloniti, a drink made from manioc that has undergone several stages of fermentation, drying and boiling. An elderly woman known as Hoanaytalo by everyone, after her role as a prominent blessing shaman, once told me that in the distant past, when the Enawenê knew neither cooking fires nor manioc, they had lived like tapirs, eating only raw leaves. Rawness was always associated with a pre-cultural and prehuman state in this way, so that I had to learn not to eat sweet and crunchy raw peas and lima beans as I picked them in the gardens, and to pick kernels of corn off the cob one by one and to chew them individually. When I bit into the cob or ate the sweet, crunchy, peas as I picked them from the tree, I was called a peccary with less humour than disgust.

As I commented in the previous chapter, it is often in terms of food – staple crops, definitions of edibility and styles of cuisine – that the Enawenê reflect on their contemporary identity, on the alterity of their neighbours and on their own past. Thus when people commented on their past unification at Kawekwalikwa they first mentioned the adoption of a common pescatarian diet. In fact, it is a staple observation in Amazonian anthropology that eating together and eating alike produce shared identity and kinship, and that diet is diacritical of social and cosmological alterity as well.[1] This reflects Amazonian peoples' particular emphasis on corporeal production as the locus of identity.[2] Beyond the specificities of Amazonian identity construction, it must be recognised that cuisine plays a central role in the embodiment of culture worldwide as a key medium for social learning and inscription. Yamin-Pasternak et al. (2014) have argued that this is so because it is embodied through the five senses simultaneously. This rings true in the Enawenê case. As I showed in Chapter 3, the Enawenê's manioc-dominated cuisine fills the house, patterns time through each day, regulates women's techniques of the body, and shapes the village soundscape. It also generates sweet, smoky, perfumed and musky smells so that olfaction is another channel through which the Enawenê economy generates pleasurable sensation.[3] In fact, the first two Enawenê adjectives I learned upon my visit to the former village of Matokodakwa in 2006 were beautiful (*awale*) and fragrant (*ayadé*). Beautiful referred to the decorated bodies of dancers and the sound of their flutes. Fragrant referred to the musky smell of fermented manioc drying out on mats in the sun and billowing up from the mortar when it was pounded into a flour; to the sweet smell of annatto dye exuded by decorated bodies or carried on the breeze from mats covered in drying seeds; and to roasting fish or detoxified manioc juice.

Precisely because cuisine quickly becomes part of embodied experience it is easy to forget to analyse it. It was a visit to the Nambikwara that prompted me to start to think carefully about the Enawenê's pyrotechnic bent and their emphasis on smoking, drying and extensively transforming foods, as well as bodies and things, and it is with this journey that I begin this exploration of how the Enawenê cook, craft and cure a human life in a cosmos that perennially puts it in threat.

The Raw and the Cooked

In April 2009 I walked across the savannah with five Enawenê men with whom I was living at the fishing dam. We were going to visit the Nambikwara village of Camararé. The men had with them the smoked meat of a couple of peccaries, which they had come across and killed while searching the forest for the special bark used to make fish traps. As I mentioned in Chapter 1, they wanted to exchange this meat for tucum palm-nut bead chains made by Nambikwara women and thereby add to their stock of gifts for their wives and lovers. This would be a profitable expedition, since the peccary was worthless to the Enawenê whereas the Nambikwara tended to give their valuables to the Enawenê for little or no return, partly because they feared them.

In the Nambikwara's savannah village I noticed the scarcity of firewood – not a single hearth was lit in the daytime. There was no evidence of dry stores and calabashes had been left 'raw' rather than sealed to become watertight containers. An Enawenê woman, who had also been to visit the Nambikwara in the previous year during her stay at her husband's fishing dam, enthusiastically told me about her impressions of the Nambikwara village, also focusing on their cookery:

> Their food is ugly. They boil up tapir blood and drink it, they roast crickets, they eat fish that is full of maggots, they roast lizards, they eat frogs, they roast meat and eat it raw – while the middle is still bloody they eat it! They have no hearths, they have no manioc loaves in storage. They put manioc in a basket lined with leaves and when it has soured they make manioc bread with it. They just throw away the manioc's milk!

Her low estimation of these exotic habits matched the Enawenê's view of the Nambikwara's lowly status as people who sleep on the ground rather than raised up in hammocks, and it epitomises Edmund Leach's observation that cultural discriminations of edibility are everywhere taken as signs of moral discernment and are the wellsprings of cherished superior feelings (Leach, Hugh-Jones and Laidlaw 2000: 326). In other words, cuisine is embodied but it is also objectified, reflecting judgements of character and value. In 1938 Lévi-Strauss lived with the Nambikwara of the same region I visited, and although he did not share the Enawenê woman's prejudicial tone or my implicit contrast with Enawenê habits, he was nonetheless impressed by the immediacy of Nambikwara cuisine (1948: 107–8):

> the tayra and bat have no sooner been passed through the flames to burn their hairs than his wife puts herself to the task of – for the first time

– cleaning and grating a small quantity of sweet manioc, from which she hastily presses a bread directly into the ashes of the fire. At the same time she breaks the lizard eggs directly into the ashes as well and takes them out barely cooked; she no sooner shares them between herself and the baby... All these operations unfolded very rapidly, with a kind of urgency, and have finished within a half hour.

Subsequently, Lévi-Strauss would become intrigued by the way that cognates for 'raw' and 'cooked' became idioms for naturalness and cultured civilisation worldwide (1964: 344), examining a series of Gê and Tupi myths from Central Brazil about humans' appropriation of fire from various animal species, which allowed them to overcome their original bestial condition. He would also expand upon the close association made in Amerindian mythology between control of fire and the arts of civilisation (1966: 60). Lévi-Strauss lamented that ethnographers had usually neglected people's culinary practices (ibid.: 406). He thought that the analysis of a people's 'system of recipes' could tell us a great deal about their logic and sensibility as well as about their relationship to others (1968: 496).

Here Lévi-Strauss's insight into the encoding of relative values in the sensory matter of cuisine – what Marshall Sahlins (2010: 374–75) has called his culinary 'infrastructuralism' – provides the foundation for my analysis of the fabrication of Yankwa's key items of material culture: calabashes that are used as containers of drinks, sun diadem feather headdresses worn by dancers, and the transformation of manioc into the various foods and drinks that circulate in the arena. In Lévi-Strauss's terms, through all of these processes, the Enawenê's preference for the supremely cooked apex of the culinary triangle is manifest.[4] Their exclusion, or very careful circumscription of, natural states of rawness and natural transformations induced by rotting or fermentation is very striking (Lévi-Strauss 1968: 403, 408). As we already know from the analysis of Batatakwayti in Chapter 3, the Enawenê usually re-boil the manioc and corn 'beer' they make, excluding the possibility of fermentation. It is such concrete choices about how to transform foods and constitute bodies that I chart. The argument, to state it in Lévi-Strauss's terms, is that this emphasis on the supremely cooked corner of the culinary triangle in Enawenê cuisine, craftwork and in the constitution of healthy Enawenê bodies is 'curative', contributing to the project of sustaining human life in a cosmology that places the human in peril. I use the term 'cure' in the dual sense of the original Latin 'cūra' which is also retained in the English meaning: to heal the body and to prepare/preserve foods for keeping. The word's assimilation of two processes we usually separate fits well with the analogy Enawenê draw between creating good, durable and safe foods and things by means of cookery and crafting, and strengthening and protecting the vulnerable body through seclusion practices and shamanism. This formulation is also consistent with Lévi-Strauss's understanding of cuisine, which he decoupled from a necessary link to consumption. This is most evident in his exploration of the regulation of the bodies of adolescent girls in menstrual seclusion (1968: 417–421), during which, as he notes, what is at stake is simultaneously the health of the body and the order of the cosmos.

In developing this argument I also draw on more recent Amazonianist anthropologists, who have argued that definitions of identity in an animist cosmos are about life or the human condition, rather than 'culture' defined in relativist terms in opposition to a universal 'nature' (Viveiros de Castro 1998a). In particular I draw on Carnerio da Cunha (1978) and Viveiros de Castro (1992), who have explored the consti-tution of Amerindian persons in dialectical reference to both animal-ity/nature and also death/supernature. In Viveiros de Castro's usefully pithy phrasing, there is a 'dual contrast of the human condition with the beasts and the gods' (1992: 304). Like the Krahó and Araweté, the Enawenê are defining themselves not only as cultured and civilised in opposition to their pre-cultural bestial selves or their relatively 'raw' neighbours the Nambikwara, but as living in opposition to invisible others – 'enemies, gods and the dead' (Viveiros de Castro 1992: 140). This emphasis on the metaphysical dimensions of cookery and eating is shared in much Amazonianist anthropology, and the second half of this chapter explores the Enawenê version of this entailment, which involves two major actors: the subterranean killers whom we have met many times before, the Yakairiti, and the animate manioc plant (kete). The Yakairiti are represented as demonically opposed to Enawenê mores in every way, whereas manioc is represented as an Enawenê woman who is vulnerable just as other women are and must be secluded, fed and shamanised in order that she may grow healthily. In contrast to the Yakairiti's predatory alterity, it is paradoxically manioc's kindredness to humans – and especially women – that is the ground for her threat to their vitality.

It is my contention that curative cookery is the means by which the Enawenê constitute themselves as living people vis-à-vis these threat-ening others so that diet, cuisine, the control of ingestion and feasting become key technologies for cosmic diplomacy. I will begin with an ethnographic elaboration of Enawenê curative cookery, which shows that the treatment of bodies and valuables, in particular calabashes and

Figure 5.2 Applying layers of ash and blood-like dye to new calabashes.

headdresses, is based on highly mediated and phased curative cookery. I will then move onto the recipes followed in the preparation of food, principally manioc-based foods, since these are the mainstay of the diet during Yankwa. Given that people eat food, wear headdresses and use calabashes to extend themselves towards others, all of these processes of cure are mutually reinforcing, generating a supremely cooked human position.

Cooking as Curing: Parrots, Calabashes and People

As we know from the previous chapter, the circulation of both large calabashes full of ketera and sun diadem headdresses works to mix and unite the Enawenê population. Both headdresses and calabashes are also paramount Enawenê valuables – they are among the few items that are kept by descendants after their owners' death. In this section I demonstrate that both of these items of material culture are assimilated to human bodies; headdresses are made from the feathers of parrots, who are people's pets and similars, and calabashes resemble women's bellies. The processes involved in manufacturing both these valuables is also akin to the treatment of vulnerable bodies, so that fabrication is also cure.

Parrots (*kokwi*) and scarlet macaws (*kalo*) are the only pets Enawenê keep. They spend most of their time on perches outside the back of the house, coming down to the ground to eat the chewy, swelled corn-seed that is scraped out from the bottom of pans of ketera for them. They are brought into the house to sleep at night, sometimes after a lengthy search by their owners in the branches of nearby trees. Parrots sing, eat cooked garden produce, and live in and around houses, so that it is unsurprising that people say they are 'like us' (*wixo ikali*). Like most people who keep sociable birds, Enawenê talk to the scarlet macaws that are their pets alongside yellow-fronted Amazon parrots, and the occasional parakeet.[5] Parrots are buried under their sleeping perches when they die (Mendes dos Santos 2006: 119–20), just as people's graves are dug underneath the spot where their hammock formerly swung. They are also said to have a human post-mortem destiny, entering their owner's clan house in the huge, perfected celestial village (*enolekwa*).

The feathers taken from these similars are worn by Enawenê people in many artful ways, the most important of which is the sun diadem headdress (*daweriyti*) worn by men at Yankwa and Lerohi, and by women at Kateoko. This headdress is an icon of the moderate, life-giving sun, a mythological personage called Kaxi, who was directed to occupy the sky by the cultural hero Datamale in one of his first world-making gestures. As I was told many times the world was initially in darkness. Datamale gave his Uncle Kaxiyi a scarlet macaw headdress (large and red) and sent him to the sky. Kaxiyi took his nephew's gift and rose up to the top of the sky, where he sat fixed at noon, emitting a fierce heat that caused all the Enawenê's drinks to evaporate as soon as they were ready, so that people were perennially parched.[6] Datamale thought about what he would do. He called Kaxiyi down on a false premise and then trapped and buried him in a big hole he had dug. It was dark again. Again he called upon his Uncle Kaxiyi, only this time he gave him a headdress made from the tail feathers of the yellow-fronted Amazon parrot, which he had fabricated just as Enawenê people do today, putting pure yellow feathers towards the outside and arranging increasingly red-flecked ones towards the middle. Taking this yellow-red headdress, Kaxiyi rose up in the east, reached the top of the sky at noon, and fell westward in a cooling arc. Datamale thus tamed an initially cannibal sun to create the conditions for human life.

Enawenê people wean and nurture parrots captured from their nests. The concept of nurture and weaning (*enawetene*), which applies to breastfeeding infants and weaning parrots with cooked and sometimes masticated foods, has the same root as the Enawenê's self-designation and is also used to describe the acts by which Datamale went about 'becoming human' (*Enawenêtwa*), such as acquiring the embers of a cooking fire with which to warm himself. This suggests that by weaning parrots the Enawenê are self-consciously humanising them so that they will be able to live in Enawenê houses and give up their feathers to serve their owners' humanising project. Sun-diadem headdresses are made with the carefully transformed, moderately 'cooked' feathers of parrots who have undergone a process of cure at the hands of their owners, who subject their parrots to a series of therapies, inserting powerful substances into their tail feather follicles so that the feathers, which are naturally green, grow back yellow and yellow streaked with red. This process is known as 'tapirage' in the literature and is documented with varying recipes across Amazonia (Métraux 1928, 1944). I never witnessed this process but recorded one Enawenê man's explanation, which suggested that this process of changing coloration works by means of the balancing of hot and cold humours, which create the perfect feathers from which to construct an icon of the moderate sun.[7] This treatment is far from cosmetic; the parrot undergoes a kind of shock treatment and has to be nurtured back to life, much like a sick kin member who has been struck with fever and must be helped to cool-recover (*maka*).

A tail feather is removed, and a solution made from three substances – red annatto dye (*ahete* latin. Bixa orellana), an unidentified 'medicinal tree bark' (*baraiti*) and the glandular secretions of a poisonous toad called *watala* (possibly the cane toad, Rhinella marina) – are poked into the parrot's uropygial gland at the base of its tail with the extracted feather. This causes the 'green to dissipate' (*hoira tekwa*). Hoira is a colour property denoting raw, new and green and is used to describe young foliage or shiny, new aluminium pans. Yellow, orange and red, which form a colour property that shares the name of annatto dye (ahete), replace it.

Annatto bushes proliferate outside the backs of houses, where people discard seeds after they have applied the dye to their bodies to define the musculature and frame the face. Used in moderation, annatto has curative properties, but women also warn their daughters not to decorate with it too often, since it 'burns' *(kera)* the skin. Annatto is thus hot whereas tree bark medicine is always described as cold *(tiha)*. The properties of the third component of the solution applied to the tail follicle is less clear. The watala toad's name possibly derives from the word for hot *(wata)*, although this is speculative. I was told the toad's secretions caused the follicle to 'sneeze'. The parrot's tail thus goes from cold/green/ raw to warm/red-orange/moderately cooked through the application of a combination of powerful substances that together rebalance the parrot's humours. The parrot is said to 'fall down' *(edowata)*, as its pulse weakens and it pants for breath. After this shock treatment the parrot's recovery is helped along by feeding it with cooked corn. The concept of recovery coincides with that of 'cooling down', which indicates the association of sickness with excessive heat or fever, such that the parrot, just like a feverish person, therefore cool-recovers (maka). About a month later the parrot's new yellow-red feathers can be plucked to contribute to the making of a new headdress. These headdresses worn by lines of identically attired dancers are therefore the iconic symbol of the moderate sun that has been made by working a mysterious chemistry of hot and cold humours on a human-like bird.

Just as headdresses are icons of the sun and indexes of moderate cookery, calabashes are concretely womb-like and are produced through an involved transformative process involving rotting, drying and sealing to manipulate the properties of these natural containers. This is women's work and calabashes, in contrast to headdresses, are also quintessentially women's valuables: they relate to women's bodies; they are concretely used by women in payments made for shamanic services or in exchanges they make for male goods; and they contain foods and drinks produced through women's labour. Calabashes *(xixase* or *xixawe)* are as ubiquitous in Enawenê houses as mugs, glasses, bowls, plates and cutlery are in many kitchens. In my small household alone there must have been over a thousand calabashes, split between the house and the storage shelter some thirty metres away out the back.[8] Everyone from small girls to old men owned their own calabashes, which ranged from the tea and tablespoon sized ones that are made by expectant mothers for babies to play with, to the five-litre giants used to hold the generous portions of drink carried to betrothal partners. I noticed that in Enawenê households people always ate from the same few, chipped calabashes, while hundreds of pristine ones hung unused in the rafters, becoming nesting places for mice, and hiding places for girls' vanity supplies of annatto seeds, mirrors and combs. The big calabashes – the 'fine china' – were taken down from their hanging place, dusted, inspected and admired by groups of women, calabash by calabash, before the start of a new season's hosting obligations, when they would be used nightly. Some of the most prized calabashes – large, sturdy and darkly smoked – had escaped the destruction of personal property that occurs at death and were proudly brought out and shown to me as very old and prized possessions.

In January and February 2008, as Yankwa prepared to leave for the fishing dams, much of my time was occupied harvesting and making calabashes with women. The gourds *(hitiri)* from which calabashes were made grew in the chaotic and varied swampy gardens, which lie beyond the immediate circle of pristine manioc fields, and women carried them home on sporadic day trips that broke their routine manioc work. From an outsider's perspective the miracle of gourds is the speed with which they grow and their hardness, durability and boundedness, despite their growing in contact with the wet earth. Fatness and strength are the main compliments paid to human bodies (the worst thing is to be skinny and frail) and these are also the qualities desired of calabashes. The Enawenê's aim was not to decorate the outer surface of calabashes with patterns (as many other peoples do), but to grow them fat *(agotiri)* and strong *(kiñata)*, and then to seal them so that their inner surface became black *(kia)* and shiny *(berakwa)*. This involves a process of controlled rotting out, washing, drying and sealing, which I repeated many times with women of various households, who called on me for gourd-harvesting trips, because they knew I was keen on having my own bundle.

Gourds grew quickly as soon as the rains began, and when they reached a good size around February they were cut from their vines and left on the ground to rot from the inside. Though left in such humidity, as long as they were not cracked their outer casing only hardened and strengthened as their pithy innards rotted away. They were then cut in half with a small saw, and their contents – which stank of vegetal putrefaction – were cleaned out before they were piled into worn-out carrying baskets and submerged in a river or stream so that the rotted interior could dissolve away with the help of the flowing water. The cleaned, empty gourd halves, with their vein-patterned, creamy-white interior surfaces were then placed above the house's central hearth to dry thoroughly. Once dry, their inner surface was sanded with dry corn husks or sandpaper until it was very smooth. It was then sealed by the application of a viscous solution made from a sticky, brown tree bark called *hemaiti*, which has the dark red colour and adhesive texture of congealing blood. This blood-like substance was painted onto the inner surface of the calabash and then ashes made from a lightweight, fast-burning bark were rubbed in to soak up the dye. Layers of dye and ash were alternately applied many times over the course of a few days, until the calabashes' inner surface became shiny and black. Finally, a pebble was rubbed over the inside surface to harden it further and then the calabashes were hung up, near to the hearth (but not too near, or the inner surface would crack into an eggshell pattern), to dry again.

The transformation is obvious enough: a porous, pithy, white, veiny inner surface becomes sealed, shiny and black through a process of assisted putrefaction, dissolution, treatment and drying. All the women emphasised the achievement of qualities of strength, smoothness and shine through the patient application of layers of dye and ash and the slow drying of the calabashes. They also noted the blood-likeness of the dye. However, no one directly commented on what seemed obvious to me: the likeness of calabashes to pregnant bellies or the resemblance of the calabash-making process to the tattooing of girls' bellies and breasts upon their first menstruation, which prepares them to become mothers. Girls' profusely bleeding wounds are sealed with ash just as calabashes are. The association between women's bellies and calabashes was emphasised by at least one woman, who had decorated the outside of her largest calabashes with the simple motif that is tattooed onto girls' bellies. There are a few reasons why the association lacked discursive elaboration, in stark contrast to the sun diadem with its charter myth. First, calabash-making is habitual whereas headdress-making is periodic and specialised; second, the calabash's qualities of roundness, speedy growth, hardness, their containment of multiple seeds, and their veined, placental appearance are self-evident. Third, the dye is patently blood-like; it is both viscous and smells metallic. Finally, the processes of calabash-sealing with 'blood' and ash and the tattooing of girls' bellies is obviously similar. I will now briefly describe this process, which is an aspect of Enawenê seclusion that is unique to a girl's first menstruation and occurs on top of the other practices associated with 'lying down to rest' that I introduced in Chapter 1 and will elaborate further later in the present chapter.

When a girl first menstruates she is secluded in a walled-off section of her parent's sleeping compartment, where she lays in her hammock by a moderate fire, undergoes shamanic blessings and baths and eats a bland diet that excludes fish and manioc. Once her first menstrual bleed is over, tattooing is undertaken by a practised female affine. It takes several hours, usually spread over two days. The girl makes the needles herself during her seclusion as part of the craftwork that occupies her hands during this time of otherwise quiet passivity. She uses cotton threads to lash thorns onto small sticks to make what look like tiny pick axes. The tattooing was done by repeatedly pricking the skin with these dainty instruments as the girl lay down flat on her back, still and quiet. As blood flowed from the prick wounds, it was wiped off and black ash (from the underside of a cooking pot) was rubbed in its place in order to blacken the wounds so that the pattern would stand out boldly against the skin. Annatto dye, which has antiseptic properties, was then applied to the wounds daily. The tattoos were considered healed when they had turned shiny and black. This process of wounding and healing also imposed the temporality of seclusion, since a girl was ready to begin the sequence of shamanic blessings and baths that prepare her for emergence once the tattoo wounds were healed, which took approximately one month. Just before emergence she also drank an intensely bitter/cold (*tiha*) emetic to purge her belly of impurities – especially salt – that had gradually accumulated. The girl had also been cooked by the constant hearth in her compartment and she had replaced all of her old ornaments with newly fabricated ones. With the bland diet and the emetic, her body was purified of any residue of toxicity. The black marks that accentuated the curve of her belly and shape of her breasts when she emerged drew attention to this preparedness of a newly fertile body for maternity.

In summary, the elaborate operations involved in crafting the two key items of Enawenê wealth, which are also Yankwa's key media for social diplomacy, is one of curative cookery. They are akin to processes of making healthy human bodies and restoring them from sickness and vulnerability. I need now to explain why it is that the human position should need to be fortified in the ways I have described. This takes me into an exploration of the Enawenê's position in the cosmos and how they strive to mitigate their vulnerability through cuisine and feasting.

Feasting with Killers

Fausto (2007) has synthesised a wealth of data on Amazonian people's food practices to argue that eating always has a cannibal potential where plants and animals have subjective capacities themselves or are owned by spirits that do. This potential can be promoted or contained through various means and for diverse ends. People can eat 'cannibalistically' to acquire capacities, accumulate potency or trigger transformations in themselves. Among the most obvious ways they do this is by ingesting powerful substances like ayahuasca, tobacco, beer and jaguar bile, or simply by eating foods in their raw state of maximum potency, which is usually indexed by the presence of blood. Cannibalism in this expanded sense tends to be about escaping the human position in some way; most commonly by bringing hunting prowess or shamanic insight. On the opposite end of the spectrum are everyday cookery and food-sharing practices, which must exclude this cannibal potential in order to constitute the bonds of kinship. People process foods physically and metaphysically to extinguish their transformative potency; for example, by boiling meat very thoroughly to remove the trace of blood or by shamanising foods to disarm their spirit owners (see also S. Hugh-Jones 1996).

Using this schematic sketch we can already say a few obvious things about the tendencies of Enawenê cookery and commensality. The Enawenê tend to exclude the cannibal tendency and the triggering of transformation. Beasts (*kinase*) are rivals to be ambushed and killed if they invade corn gardens to steal crops, or opportunistically killed to provide meat for Nambikwara, but they are not food for Enawenê people. When people wanted to stress to me that the Enawenê were fearless warriors (*hwalekayti*), they boasted of having eaten 'peccaries, monkeys and people' in the past, which reveals the relevance, for them, of the conceptual equation between carnivory and cannibalism, highlighted by Fausto. Today's Enawenê have excluded bloody game all together, denying the possibility that it could ever be possible to remove such foods' potency. Coupled with this they avoid raw or even swiftly cooked vegetable foods and have eliminated tobacco and beer. As you might expect, then, the Enawenê prefer the extreme 'anti-cannibal' pole of Fausto's continuum: elaborate cuisine, lengthy cooking, and the routine shamanic treatment of foods – even, and as we will see, especially vegetable foods like manioc, which most Amazonians consider relatively inert.[9] So even for pescatarian ascetics like the Enawenê, who seem to have excluded the sharp end of food's cannibal potential, eating remains dangerous. This is the case, because all harvested foods and every catch of fish brings the risk of counterpredation from the Yakairiti, who are in a diffuse sense the owners of all the resources that sustain human life, not only food crops and fish but also palms and waterways. Everything must be shared with them. I will show that the Yakairiti are enemies imagined as raw and wild travesties of the cooked and civilised people. The everyday necessity of eating is a commensal diplomacy with these perverse alter egos. What interests me here is not only defining this oppositional relationship but also charting how these purely imagined opposites become entangled in a commensal diplomacy that rests on the satisfaction of appetites for the same cooked foods and the upholding of shared values of generosity and industry.

As we have learned over the course of this book, the Yakairiti are a constant presence in Enawenê village life. They are spoken of in a totalising way as a perverse subterranean race; or individualised as spirits belonging to landmarks in Enawenê territory; or listed by knowledgeable people as named members of a clan's pantheons; or referred to as the owners of fish and palms. In a way that was never entirely clear to me, to become Yakairiti was also one post-mortem destiny for Enawenê people. The Enawenê vital principle (*hiyako*) is said to take three different invisible forms upon death: the celestial ancestor, the wandering spectre and the subterranean Yakairiti. The face, the breath and the heart's pulse (my interlocutor breathed in deeply to demonstrate the unified, central life force) become the superhuman celestial ancestors (*Enole-nawe*), who are bigger, stronger and more beautiful than earthly humans; they are eternally youthful and are endowed with supreme shamanic power, which they can use either to help or harm their earthly descendants. Their celestial sphere (*enolekwa*) is like other paradises, a perfected copy of human society but one that is impossible, since it is free of affinity.[10] In it, male and female ancestors alike live in their clan houses around an immense plaza that is animated by constant ceremonial life. The Enole-nawe are sometimes referred to as the 'grandparents' of the living, and Enawenê shamans also call on Enole-nawe 'spouses' to assist them in retrieving patients' life force when it has been robbed by the Yakairiti. In all these ways the Enole-nawe remain related to the living as similars.

This celestial journey is the story the Enawenê like to tell when they speak of post-mortem destiny, focusing on the reacquisition of a youthful body and evoking a spatial map of the celestial world. The destiny of the body's weaker pulses who become enemies to the living received less commentary in all of my informal interviews on this subject. I learned that the wrist's pulse became the wandering, shadowy spectre of corporeal corruption called *dakoti*, who is skinny and weak like the shadow-pulse it is born from. Dakoti sometimes manifests as the sound of wailing children heard in the forest and its presence is also felt in rainbows, strong winds or upon looking into the setting sun. Monkeys and armadillos, which are a source of fright and ill omen when encountered on forest paths, are also instantiations of dakoti.

Compared to the omnipresence of the Yakairiti in everyday Enawenê talk, the Enawenê had very little to say about the connection between themselves and the Yakairiti when we discussed eschatology, except to state that a third weak pulse became Yakairiti upon death. Nobody described a post-mortem journey of transformation into Yakairiti, nor was there a relationship terminology that applied to Yakairiti. The focus of both everyday and mythic discourse was on antagonism between the living and these dead. This kind of relationship of negation and predation between enemy-spirits and humans was described by Carnerio da Cunha (1978) in her work among the Krahó, in terms that are apt for the Enawenê case as well. These dead 'incarnate maximal alterity, living in an anti-society to the extent that their society negates in its fundamentals the society of the living and is hostile to it, robbing it of its members' (ibid.: 3). There is a very clear confirmation of this in the description Enawenê people make of the mutually exclusive perspectives that Yakairiti and Enawenê hold of one another. Yakairiti literally means 'those who kill with arrows' and the Yakairiti are said to call the Enawenê the 'dead people' *(mae-nawe)* in their language, negating their self-designation as 'living people' *(Enawenê-nawe)*.

In addition, like the Krahó, the Enawenê seem to imagine a mirroring relationship with the Yakairiti, typically describing them in terms of their subversion of Enawenê aesthetic and dietary mores. For example, Yakairiti are said to ornament themselves with living snakes, which are their pets, just as parrots are the Enawenê's pets. Whereas Enawenê people have short, deep fringes, and frame their faces with lines of annatto across the forehead and down in front of the ears, the Yakairiti's unruly hair covers their eyes and obscures their faces. Whereas Enawenê wear flowing palm silks when they dance and thick buruti silk belts, Yakairiti have live snakes at their limbs and an anaconda wrapped around their hips. And whereas the Enawenê diet consists of elaborately prepared drinks, the Yakairiti's various kinds of oloniti are made by mixing water with different kinds of clay, red or black earth, or with raw palm fruits. These inversions epitomise the Yakairiti's rawness vis-à-vis their own transformed, civilised bodies and habits. The Enawenê thus seem to echo the dialectical cast of mind Carnerio da Cunha (ibid.: 145) evoked for the Krahó: 'I am that which what I am not is not ... And this *I* is to be alive'.[11]

During the seasons of Yankwa and Lerohi the Enawenê affirm and stabilise a human, living position in the context of this agonistic, oppositional relationship with the Yakairiti. However, as we have seen in previous chapters, the relationship is not only agonistic but collaborative and imitative as well. Humans and spirits 'cross the mirror' not only at the point of death and during serious illnesses when human souls are taken by Yakairiti captors, but also when men incarnate Yakairiti inside the village of the living so that the hosts can satisfy them with foods, drinks and salt. Furthermore, the living have a hold over the Yakairiti because they share the same values – abundant manioc gardens, fish to eat, a lively arena filled with music and clowning – and also hunger and thirst for the same foods and drinks. Yakairiti covet all the foods proper to Yankwa, manioc, fish and potassium salt above all, but also all other agricultural produce and some gathered foods as well (particularly Brazil nuts and palm fruits). As we know from Chapter 3 Enawenê cuisine is overwhelmingly oriented to catering for everyday feasting: the public display, distribution and consumption of food in the arena, which assures sharing with the Yakairiti. More immediate forms of cookery and consumption are limited to small family snacks. Women roast a small catch of fish to share within the house or quickly bake yams, taro or sweet corn directly in the ashes of the fire to eat with their children; and they sometimes make pure manioc starch breads (*makehero*) and boiled manioc milk (*makerenyali*) as sweet treats for their children's breakfasts, but any sizeable catch or harvest is always destined for public circulation, and people work to build up a storable surplus to allow for large-scale distributions at a later date. Yakairiti are thus enemy-others who are also participants and beneficiaries of all Enawenê economic activity: they plant manioc gardens and they drink the oloniti and ketera that are made from their harvest; they lead shoals of fish into the traps so that they can later share the smoked catch; drinks are poured into the ground in order to fill up the Yakairiti's pans; and the Yakairiti enter the bodies of Yankwa's dancers to imbibe through them; everyday everyone drinks ketera that has first publicly circulated for Yankwa and thus for the Yakairiti. The Enawenê thus cook for and feast with their killers on a daily basis during Yankwa and Lerohi. Their subsistence strategies, processing methods and preferred recipes are oriented to this public commensal diplomacy with these omniscient and omnipresent others.

To illustrate the all-seeing nature of the Yakairiti, women told me that the spirits took frequent inventories of household stores, counting the sacks of manioc flour and piercing them to check their contents remained muskily fragrant (ayadé) rather than musty and mouldy. Neglectful housewifery was said to anger the Yakairiti, just as laziness and stinginess did. Not only do the Yakairiti uphold social values but their defining traits are also defining human weaknesses. The Enawenê's most persistent affirmations about Yakairiti are that they are stingy (*madi*), thirsty (*lalu*) and attached (*ahakawetene*) to human foods, which is a term that can imply both loving affection between kin and also covetous retentiveness. Stinginess and excessive attachment are the same shortcomings that Enawenê people accuse each other of. Indeed, it is because people and Yakairiti share attachments to the same foods that eating with Yakairiti assures people's health, while eating in private is an opening to pain and illness (*kawê*). Most deaths are attributed to the Yakairiti's dissatisfaction as a result of their perennial thirst, of individuals' laziness in producing for the Yakairiti or specific instances in which people ate selfishly within the house. Atolole-neto, a female shaman (*sotailoti*), explained to me,

> Yakairiti go to the manioc gardens and they see you there taking manioc and they are angered, so they put a fever in you, they take away children and their mothers. The Yakairiti are angry because they are attached to corn, manioc bread and manioc flour and white people's corn seed too.[12] Only when they drink Yankwa's drinks are they happy.

The pathogens (*ehwale*, literally 'eaters') that Yakairiti insert into people's bodies to get their revenge commonly take the form of manioc skin, grubs, fish skin and bones, which are exhibited to onlookers when they are removed from the mouths of shamans who have sucked at the patient's skin. This indicates the role of the foods of Yankwa – manioc and fish – in mediating the relationship between humans and spirits.

Sucking therapy can be a fairly routine treatment for minor pains and complaints but when a person is gravely ill, limp and feverish in their hammock, their pulse (*hiako*) is considered to have been captured and hidden by the Yakairiti, and shamans attempt to retrieve it. In a delirious state the patient acts as a medium for the Yakairiti, saying 'I am thirsty, I want to drink oloniti'. Shamans and specialists in a specific genre of chants called *dakotia* surround the patient, the former divining the illness's cause and prognosis and treating the patient by sucking on their skin, and the latter chanting. Around this nucleus are a crowd of onlookers, and occupying the nearest hearth space are the patient's female kin, busy preparing whatever dishes they can muster from current stocks: usually manioc and corn porridge (ketera) and fish soup (*holokwale*), but also honey-water (*mahla*); frozen chickens (*omao*) brought in specially from town; individual portions of fish and manioc bread set out on banana leaves; portions of rice, and a kind of fish-cake called *werowerohi* made from mashed taro or arrowroot, lima beans, fish and salt. Whatever there is is laid out for the shamans to eat and share with their celestial spirit auxiliaries, who assist them in countering the Yakairiti's predation by revealing to the shaman the place where the captured pulse has been hidden – often a sack of manioc flour stored up in the eaves or distant manioc gardens – which is another indication of the directly food-mediated relationship. Along with payments of clay pots, calabashes, feather ornaments, bead chains, jaguar teeth or peccary tooth necklaces, the food induces the shamans and their auxiliaries to do their curative work. While cooking and eating, curing and divination continue inside the house, one of the patient's clansmen lines up calabashes of ketera or fish soup in the arena and invites the men of other clans to accept the food and to eat it with the Yakairiti. To the eye, these distributions are indistinguishable from those made by one clan to all the rest in the course of Yankwa, which indicates the life-affirming purpose of all food distributions.[13] Just as stinginess was the original cause of the Yakairiti's predation, the food-giver's generosity is said to urge the Yakairiti to loosen their hold on the pulse they have captured, allowing it to return to the patient's body.

The Enawenê thus make the everyday necessity of eating into a commensal diplomacy with enemy spirits, whose character undermines the supremely cooked and civilised values of living people. It is perhaps not surprising that people who define the civilised as cooked and transformed, imagine the agents of death, who would steal them from this life, as raw and wild travesties of themselves. What is interesting is their entanglement via a commensal diplomacy whose efficacy rests on the humans' and their killers' shared appetites and values. In the next section I detail the transformation of manioc into the foods and drinks that are good for both Enawenê and the Yakairiti to eat. This will take us into other ways in which these recipes make food safe to eat: physically, because poisonous manioc must be detoxified, and metaphysically, because manioc is the other omnipresent threat to the vitality of living people.

Manioc: The Supremely Cooked

Bitter manioc gardens (*ketekwa*) surround the Enawenê's village in a wide circumference. Large, thriving manioc gardens are the prime focus of collective and individual pride for the Enawenê as they are for the Paresi (Ramos Costa 1985: 130). Upon visiting Paresi gardens and hearing their owners' horticultural wisdom, Mendes dos Santos (1994: 74), who later worked with the Enawenê, remarked that he had 'the sensation of visiting manioc's "centre of origin" and the place of its first domestication'. Indeed, manioc is the staple crop of most Arawakan-speaking peoples, including all those who live along the southern periphery of the Amazon drainage (Heckenberger 2005: 190–95). The plant (*Manihot esculenta*) was domesticated between eight and ten thousand years ago in the southwest Amazon (Rival and Doyle 2008: 1119–120), where humans 'taught' it to reproduce clonally (Rival 2001). Cultigens were selected for preferred traits like large, toxic, juicy tubers (Dufour 1993: 583), and techniques were developed for making these tubers, whose milk is full of potentially deadly cyanide, into staple foods and drinks. Many anthropologists before me have been fascinated by the variations in manioc cookery found across Amazonia and in speculating about why different peoples prefer the recipes and techniques they do.[14]

I will start my own description of the Enawenê's system of recipes with ketera, the drink I have mentioned over one hundred times in the course of this book so far because of its ubiquity in Enawenê life. Ketera is one of a family of drinks called *manicuera* in Portuguese, which are made across Amazonia from the boiled juice of manioc. Its name in the Enawenê language is an elision of 'manioc' *(kete)* and 'milk' *(eda)*, indicating that this is the primary product of manioc for the Enawenê – that which is most closely associated with the living plant, and which is the paradigm of nourishment for Enawenê people as a substance assimilated to breast milk *(toto eda)* and on which babies are first weaned. As we saw in the previous Chapter, ketera-making defines Enawenê women's daily round; it is everyone's most constant source of nourishment, and it is the substance whose daily circulation and mixture realises the community's unity.

I will show that ketera is an intensely cooked product, both because a huge amount of heat is necessary to detoxify the juice and because it incorporates sun and fire-dried elements. It is also a complex product, because it entails the separation of manioc's different components (starches and fibre) from the juice, their drying and then their recombination; finally, it is standardised, since milk from the two kinds of tubers, and from a first pressing and a diluted second pressing, is mixed to make a ketera that is a compromise of plentiful and sweetly concentrated. This responds firstly to the imperative to make a large quantity of a consistent quality – a panful that is equal to all the others with which it will become mixed when it circulates at the night-time distribution. Secondly, ketera's quality of recombinant mixture allows for the separation and stocking of manioc products for other uses.[15] This recipe and the constancy with which it is followed allows for the amassing of storable surplus and its subsequent expenditure in the dynamic explored in Chapter 3. As such it can be thought of as not only the Enawenê's primary source of nourishment but also as the infrastructure for Enawenê cuisine, because every other manioc-based food (breads, oloniti) is made from the stores of starch and flour that are amassed as by-products of its making. As I was told at the start of my fieldwork in January 2008, 'there is no manioc bread before Yankwa depart, just *ketera, ketera, ketera*; no one "eats" [*hakahetene*, which refers to the pairing of manioc bread and fish] at the moment; we just drink ketera, dance and sing'. Intensive drinking of ketera allowed women to amass the ingredients with which they made the dry breads that would sustain Yankwa's fishermen during their two month absence and then to make the satisfyingly complete meals of fish coupled with manioc bread that followed their return. This essential quality of recombinant mixture requires processing in multiple stages from harvest to drink as I will now detail.

During planting, harvesting and processing, Enawenê focus on a pragmatic dual categorisation of manioc, distinguishing between 'dry' and 'juicy' tubers.[16] The former kind makes higher quality bread but gives little juice, while the latter makes low quality bread but expels a lot of juice when grated. Of the two, the juicy kind is planted in much greater quantity, reflecting the dominance of ketera in the Enawenê diet. Once they have been peeled and washed, the tubers are sorted into a smaller pile of dry tubers and a larger pile of juicy ones. Typically, between three and five women grate all the tubers at the same time, one of them grating the denser, dry tubers (which are much harder work) into a separate basin, since the mash from these will be used to make the high-quality flour that is used for making flatbreads. Like many Amerindian women, Enawenê use graters (*timali*) made from the sharpened aerial roots of a buruti palm set in horizontal grooves on a rectangular piece of hardwood to grate the tubers to a watery mash (Dole 1978: 218). This technology is essential because grating makes the poisonous cyanogenic glucosides soluble (bound cyanide is stable up to 150°c) so that the prussic acid can be boiled off leaving the glucose (see Dufour 1999). This is the magic of ketera; the toxicity of the tubers accounts for the eventual sweetness of the drink.

Once all the tubers are grated, one of the women presses the mash on a fine sieve, squeezing most of its moisture into the pan below and forming a disc of starchy fibre between her hands. These disc or oval-shaped *xaokwase* are placed to dry and smoke on the bottom shelf of the hearth. After a few days during which they mildly ferment as they dry and smoke above the fire, these can be broken up over a sieve and pressed onto a griddle to make high-quality breads called *malosero*, which accompany meals of fish. Some of the loaves are used fairly immediately in this way, while others are left to smoke for weeks until they are completely dehydrated and can therefore be stored for months. Women build up stocks of these darkly smoked xaokwase, whose flour, once pounded and sieved, makes a chewy brown bread called *malaitihi*. However, these are not only food stores, like bundles of calabashes the dry discs are a source of pride for women and a store of currency.[17] I was once told that to be 'a woman without xaokwase' (*maxaokwanero*) is to be poor like Nambikwara women. Sacks of xaokwase are stored in order to celebrate plenty for its own sake – recall from Chapter 3 my adoptive mother's public lavishness on the culminating day of Yankwa's return when she threw xaokwase out of her front door for one of Yankwa's pet flutes. This fairly immediate usage or dry storage is the predominant method used with dry tubers. With juicy tubers, the pressed mash is dropped into a pan of water to be further leached of starch and then pressed again. The thoroughly leached fibre is then discarded or perfunctorily dried on the hearth and then griddled to make grey, sour-tasting 'rotten bread' (called *detero*, 'rotten woman'), to whose significance, as a food favoured by the Yakairiti, we shall return.

The solid component of the tubers is destined for bread in these ways, while the liquid from the juicy and dry tubers is a combination of concentrated and diluted liquids. Before it is boiled another component is separated off. This is the valuable starch, most of which is in suspension. The juice is left to sit in containers so that by the early afternoon the starch will have fallen to the bottom of the pan, forming a solid, white layer. At this point the manioc milk is poured off and put to boil, while the starch is put outside to dry under the sun so that it can be removed in lumps, further dried on a woven mat above the fire, and then stored in sacks. It will be used to make pure starch breads (make-hero), which are an occasional breakfast food or added to pounded xaokwase to make complete breads. The manioc juice boils ferociously through the afternoon, until the fumes coming off it have become fragrant (ayadé), having lost the acrid smell (*ahwe*), which indicates the lingering presence of cyanide.

What results is a thin, grey and very sweet juice from which all the starchy and fibrous components have been removed. Drunk like this it is called makerenyali. In order to become ketera, the complete drink, it must then be thickened with dry stores of manioc and corn. Women take down dry ears of corn from the eaves of the house, where they are suspended following harvest, and pound these in the standing hollow log mortar to make coarse flour. They do the same with two old, dry xaokwase. Thickening the simmering juice is the final task of the day and it falls to an experienced woman who knows how to achieve a thick and even consistency. Sometimes supplements are added: a few handfuls of starch adds glutinous jelly lumps to the drink, while chopped yams or sweet potatoes add sweetness and texture. Once thickened at dusk the ketera is ready to be cooled and tasted and the burning embers under its pan are removed to kindle sleeping hearths. Most of the ketera is to be served to Yankwas dancers in the night, but an amount is drunk in the evening by the women who made it together with their husbands and children. Women typically sit down with a large calabash resting in a small hollow in the ground in front of them and, taking a smaller calabash that fits into the other like a Russian doll, repeatedly lift full cups of it into the air to pour their contents down. Recalling the earlier discussion of balanced humours, ketera is never drunk hot; it must cool-recover (maka) first.

Ketera's quality of recombinant mixture allows for the stocking of manioc products for other uses. It makes a lot more xaokwase and starch than it uses up; however, its making only dissipates the corn stocks, whose dwindling is an index of the passing of the season of Yankwa into Lerohi, when new corn gardens are planted. Indeed the combination of a trio of corn, manioc and fish is the ideal of all the foods that circulate at Yankwa. Fish is always eaten with manioc bread, and fish soup (holokwale) is made by combining fresh or smoked fish with both corn and manioc flours, mixed into a base of either boiling water or boiled manioc juice. The soup is then served with a pair of breads, one yellow corn one and one grey-white manioc one, which rest on top of each clay pot or calabash.

The reason my host Kawalinero-ene insisted that there was 'nothing to eat' before the fishermen's departure was that these complete foods were not part of the diet. Because fish was scarce, corn was being conserved and women focused their energies on amassing stores of ketera's by-products to allow them to make the starch-rich breads that the fishermen would take to the dams. These breads, in which all the ingredients have been separated, dried and recombined, baked and then dried once more, are supremely cooked in Lévi-Strauss's (1968) terms and in a manner that mirrors the process by which fishermen smoke the fish that they catch in their traps – with great care so that it arrives for the hosts in good condition. To make them, women harvested a larger proportion of dry tubers in January and early February to build up a stock of high-quality xaokwase, which were left to thoroughly dry before being pounded and sieved to obtain a fine flour. They sprinkled a layer of pure starch onto clay griddles (which distribute heat better than the steel ones used nowadays for other kinds of bread) followed by a thick layer of the fine flour and then another of starch. The breads then cooked for about twenty minutes each side – much longer than other kinds of bread. They were then placed on a high shelf above the hearth to dry completely (they are visible in Figure 5.1). By the time they were packed into waterproof baskets on the eve of the fishermen's departure, they were rock solid and bone dry and the fishermen would take care to keep them that way during their wet journeys to the dam-fishing encampments.

Enawenê culinary style thus places great emphasis on the careful, staged mediation of fire, which is necessary to detoxify manioc milk, and to transform perishable tubers into an array of durable stores for future use. Out of the everyday plenty of ketera, there is the constant creation of future plenty, which allows people to go on sharing proper, complete foods throughout Yankwa and into Lerohi, when the manioc gardens and corn stocks are shrinking. A self-consciously civilised ethos is imposed through this elaborate cuisine and its attendant ideals of delayed, moderate consumption and durable wealth creation. By these means people distinguish themselves from the raw, wild, voracious consumption habits of the Yakairiti, at the same time as they satisfy the Yakairiti by publicly sharing large quantities of proper foods and consuming in their houses only the initial taste separated out from the larger pot and the plentiful leftovers that return to them through various affinal pathways.

Entertaining and Containing Drunkenness

This is not the complete story of the Enawenê's commensality with Yakairiti however. If storage and future-orientation, and containment and self-restraint, are the everyday order – especially in the period before Yankwa leave for the fishing dams – feasting and excess periodically overtake this regime (as we saw in Chapter 3), especially after Yankwa return from the dams. The Yakairiti's favourite fare is put into circulation and is consumed in a frenzied, uncontained way – oloniti is spilled, salt is licked directly from the palms of hosts, pungent or 'rotten' breads are discarded to litter the ground and gluts of fish soup go uneaten.[18] The Yakairiti are said to 'desire' (*ésané*) this superfluity. Enawenê cuisine therefore caters specifically to the perverse tastes of the Yakairiti, entertaining a subversive counterpoint to dominant Enawenê values of moderation and budgeting. As we saw in Chapter 2, feeding spirit-men with heavy ketera calms and disarms them, while offering salt and soured oloniti excites, dramatising the opposite, cannibal potential of food.

It is worth pausing for a moment on the nature of oloniti, which can be thought of as the fulcrum of this dialectic in Enawenê cuisine between foods that are properly human (cool, sweet, complete, fragrant) and are consumed according to an aesthetics and morality of containment and moderation; and those that satisfy the tastes of the Yakairiti, either because of their intrinsic properties (rotten, pungent, sour) or because of their exuberant superfluity. Oloniti is at once the drink that satisfies basic human thirst every day and that which provides the ferment that assimilates Enawenê to Yakairiti. This is most obvious in the habitual gesture of Yankwa's men as they drink a gulp from a calabash and then spill the rest to the ground with an ululation. At specific moments libations of soured oloniti are also poured into the ground to quench the Yakairiti's thirst. In Chapter 2 we saw that hosts left pots of oloniti souring under a special shelter on the path for the returning fishermen to spill for the Yakairiti on their way up from the port to the arena, and in Chapter 3 we saw that the oloniti made during women's night-time pounding was left to sour and was then spilled for the Yakairiti during the final day of Yankwa's returning sequence. In Chapter 4 I argued that the Enawenê's rejection of fermentation is likely to have been a fairly deliberate social reform, since the basic features of Yankwa resemble the beer-drinking parties of their nearest neighbours, namely the opposition between drinkers and servers, and the offering of beer to familiarise or dominate others. During Yankwa it is the Yakairiti who are the ultimate drinkers and unlike Enawenê people they are said to like 'oloniti that is like *cerveza*' and are often described as drunk in their aggressiveness, voracity, thirst and unpredictability. Yankwa's 'decisive behavioural code' is thus equal to that of other Amazonians' beer festivals – to drink until there is nothing left (Sztutman 2008: 12) – and it also involves a blurring of subjective boundaries between men and spirits, since men perform the Yakairiti's aggression and voracity as oloniti-raiding pet flutes. Furthermore, if we look at the oloniti-making process we see that it is made in the same way as weakly fermented beers, across Amazonia, by the addition of a masticated starch element to a bland base. This sweetens the drink and promotes its fermentation if it is left alone to develop. However the Enawenê reboil their oloniti a few hours after they have added pre-masticated breads so that fermentation does not have time to occur and any trace of alcohol disappears through prolonged boiling. Enawenê women recognise that oloniti becomes *katala* ('sour like a lemon' and 'fermented like beer') if it is not reboiled in this way and they apparently find the taste of fermentation disgusting; I often saw women toss soured oloniti to the ground and exclaim 'Yuck, it has already soured!' (*awere, haita katala!*). So, from what is this key drink in Yankwa's commensal diplomacy made?

Oloniti is the final by-product of ketera, made entirely from the ends of tubers that were too small or fibrous to grate without grating one's fingers off. It is the last task of each morning's manioc work to roughly pound these leftovers in the mortar. The small pieces are then piled in a basin and sit inside the house until the following day, long enough to become sour smelling and to be covered in fruit flies – a sign that they are mildly fermenting. The following day, the bits are squeezed with the hands and spread out on mats to dry under the sun. Once they have become lightweight and brittle, these accumulated odds and ends are pounded in batches, and women are covered in the fragrant powder that billows up from the mortar. The resulting fine flour, called *makalahi*, is stored in sacks in the eaves above the hearth. It is the Enawenê's most essential dry store and that of which the Yakairiti are most covetous. Because the manioc is fermented before being dried, makalahi has a perfumed, musky fragrance that people and Yakairiti alike find delightful. Oloniti is made by adding this fragrant makalahi to boiling water, usually along with a smaller quantity of corn flour. It can be drunk as soon as it cools, but the solid part will be in suspension, making it bitty and cloudy. In this form the drink is not only bitty but also 'bland' (*manena*) and is considered drinkable but unpalatable. In order to sweeten it women masticate breads made from coarsely pounded manioc and corn flours and then add this saliva-mixture to the cooled oloniti. Because of the action of the saliva in converting the starches into sugars, this causes the solid parts to fall to the bottom of the pan and sweetens the drink.

Across Amazonia, this mastication method is used to promote the process of fermentation in the production of corn and manioc beers. However, when we compare Amazonian fermentation practices, it becomes clear that even if it were not reboiled, oloniti would only ever become a very mild beer. Stronger beers are produced through a combination of the Enawenê's ketera and oloniti-making processes, with masticated starches added to a base with an already high sugar content; for example, boiled and cooled manioc juice (e.g. Stolze-Lima 2005: 282–83). I suggest that the Enawenê's strenuous separation of oloniti and ketera-making recipes and procedures is further evidence of their self-conscious rejection of beer. It would only take a small modification of the Enawenê's system of recipes to produce vast quantities of inebriating beer instead of great pans of warm, nourishing ketera.[19] This is why I consider oloniti to be the fulcrum of the culinary system, the fragile, porous boundary that separates and connects Enawenê and Yakairiti mores. Rather than drink beer themselves the Enawenê moderately imbibe two kinds of 'anti-beer', drinking nourishing ketera and thirst-quenching oloniti throughout each day while occasionally allowing pans of oloniti to sit and sour so they can be spilled for the drunken Yakairiti. The men of Yankwa thus perform the drunkenness of the spirits while staying on this side of the mirror that separates them from their others.

As we have seen, the invisible Yakairiti present us with the mirror opposite of Enawenê ethos, appearance and culinary mores, although on closer inspection these enemy spirits take Enawenê lives because of the values and tastes they share with Enawenê people and which they therefore uphold. We now need to meet another agent who is intimately involved in Enawenê cookery and commensality, in order to account for the intensively cooked character of Enawenê cuisine from an alternative perspective. This is manioc herself or rather 'blood-woman' (*Tiolero*) or the 'mother of manioc' (*Kete-neto*), who is directly present in the plant from which the Enawenê draw most of their sustenance. The Yakairiti and the mother of manioc provide inverse perspectives on the problem of human commensality with potentially predatory alter egos. Unlike the perverse Yakairiti, manioc is human in the same way as Enawenê people are: she flourishes by growing big, fleshy tubers according to the same principles of shamanic care, seclusion and feeding that Enawenê people observe in order to grow healthily. Whereas Yakairiti cause acute sickness in response to individual and collective moral failings (failings to promote a beautiful and productive collective life based on constant feasting and performance); manioc causes chronic but low-level ill health in individuals who come into contact with her when they are with blood. This contact implies that they have flouted seclusion taboos, which are designed to keep people and manioc apart. The final part of this chapter thus takes us full circle, reapproaching the themes of cure and care of the body that came to the foreground in the analysis of Yankwa's material culture. This introduces the question of restrictive diets, which are based, precisely, on the exclusion of the foods of Yankwa: manioc, fish and potassium salt.

Blood-Woman, the Mother of Manioc *(Tiolero, Kete-neto)*

Manioc robs men and women of their vigour when they are careless during their own or their sexual partner's postpartum or menstrual phases, causing chronic ill health rather than acute, life-threatening sickness, by taking from vulnerable people the robustness and vitality that characterise the plant's own body. When people talk about the risks associated with being careless in the observance of seclusion restrictions they invariably exemplify this by referring to one of a handful of people in the village who have been 'taken by manioc' (*kete yone*). Most often cited are the two epilepsy sufferers in the population, who are said to have been 'taken' in their infancy. Epilepsy is considered an extreme form of chronic affliction, the more usual symptoms are a generalised degradation of vigour, including persistent headaches, frailty, listlessness and weight loss, together referred to as *momenasena*.[20] The lifelong and incurable nature of epilepsy is explained by the parents having eaten manioc or visited their gardens during the most vulnerable days of their infants' life. It was my impression based on a few cases I followed that people generally suffered from manioc affliction for periods ranging from several months to a few years. My adoptive mother was one of manioc's victims in 2008 and 2009, and during the time when I lived with her she never harvested or processed fresh manioc or drank ketera. Instead, she ate old, smoked manioc breads together with beans, fungi and corn. In fact, her diet resembled that of a new mother or teenage girl in seclusion. When she sought the treatment of shamans (*sotailiti*), who work by sucking pathogens from the body, they invariably extracted manioc skin, leaves and grubs, which were presented as evidence of manioc's depredations from inside her body.[21]

The action of fire, coupled with shamanic incantations, reduce the predatory potency of manioc, just as they do that of game in meat-eating societies in Amazonia. The risk manioc poses thus decreases along a spectrum from raw to cooked: gardens are more dangerous than raw tubers and ketera, which are in turn more potent than oloniti; and fresh breads are much riskier than breads made from old, heavily smoked discs of flour (malaitihi). At the most dangerous end of the spectrum is sweet manioc (*mamalakali*), whose tubers are low in toxicity and can therefore be eaten, feebly transformed by fire – merely boiled or roasted. Some women said they never ate mamalakali, menstruation or no menstruation. This spectrum of potency and danger conditions the rhythm of patients' emergence from postpartum and first menstrual seclusions. First they eat manioc foods made from dry stores like oloniti and dark breads, later fresh breads and ketera, still later they resume processing raw manioc, and finally they return to garden work. Emergence from seclusion is thus coextensive with the progressive reintroduction of manioc foods and work according to a hierarchy of animacy, from cooked foods through raw tubers to living plants. Each phase of reintroduction is presided over by a blessing shaman, who utters incantations into the food or garden ahead of the patient's contact with it, thus mediating between humans and manioc. This brings new salience to the extensive use of heat, separation, prolonged drying and smoking, which characterise manioc cuisine. These can now be understood not only as a means to remove manioc's poison or generate a storable surplus, but also as means to reduce the metaphysical power of manioc to harm, in order that it may fulfil its proper role of bringing health to the human body.

As I mentioned above, it is typically the meat of bloody game animals that receives such thorough treatment in Amazonia. For the Enawenê on the other hand, it is clear that the 'bloodiest' foods are manioc and fish. That fish has an affinity to blood carried by its scent is a common observation and one that is elaborated by the Enawenê and by other pescatarians in Amazonia, as we saw in Chapter 1.[22] However it is far more unusual in the region for manioc to be perceived as dangerously bloody. How is manioc's bloodiness imagined and represented by Enawenê people, such that it motivates herculean avoidance and transformation efforts?[23] As I will now describe, the ritualised planting of the symbolic 'first' manioc and the general care taken to attend to gardens suggests the plant's symbolic status as a teenage girl who is in the prime of vitality but also at the peak of vulnerability.

Enawenê people always reminded me that manioc was an Enawenê woman called Atolo or Tiolero, the latter version of her name translating as blood-woman. I will paraphrase a part of the myth about Tiolero, which is a story about manioc's original identity as the daughter of the cultural hero Datamale and his star-wife Kokotero. This myth provides the charter for the way the plant should be treated today. Tiolero begged her mother Kokotero to bury her up to her chest in cool, loose, ashy soil and then to leave without looking back. She told her to return only after the first rains fell and to bring fish caught in the traps of her father Datamale's dam.[24] Tiolero's desire for fish is an often repeated refrain in Yankwa's chants, as well as in the incantations of blessing shamans. I transcribed one of these chants. In it the fish are named in sequence, each bringing Tiolero some tool or quality that is a transformation of their own defining characteristic into something Tiolero desires to make her into a proper Enawenê woman. In this chant, manioc is imagined as an ideal human woman: strong, decorated and fragrant, mobile and endowed with the tools she needs to work manioc. The first fish is the pike characin, who brings her menstrual blood and strength so that she will not die; the next is the Leporinus fish, who brings her its sweet fragrance; the following two fish bring her orange and red annatto dyes; from the next four she acquires essential woman's tools, such as a stick to help her walk, a manioc grater, a woven fan she uses to kindle her hearth and a water carrier. The ninth fish is the voracious wolffish, who makes her strong, tall and gives her the ability to walk. The tenth is the largest fish of all, the giant catfish, who makes a sturdy carrying basket for her manioc crop. Other episodes from the mythic repertoire surrounding manioc focus on the plant's physiology, which is directly equated to the female body, rather than its womanly attributes. Tiolero is said to be present in the fingered leaves of the plant (her hands), its tubers (her feet), its petioles (her arms), the bud notches on its stalks (her breasts) and the resin that leaks from them (breast milk).

Manioc's ritualised planting, which occurs just before the men of Yankwa start their frenzied planting of the whole collective field, supports Tiolero's symbolic status as a teenage girl and provides further hints that her planting in the cool earth is akin to a girl's first menstrual seclusion. In the centre of Yankwa's collective manioc gardens two or three 'mothers of manioc' are planted in larger than usual mounds of earth and they are propitiated in a rite that is a transformed version of Tiolero's mythic burial. Unlike the majority of Enawenê ceremonialism, which is public and collective, only Yankwa's leaders and the blessing shaman are present. These participants ate and drank some oloniti and smoked fish from the dam and they sprinkled the rest on the mounds where the stems had just been planted. According to Mendes dos Santos (2001: 120–22), the incantations that the blessing shaman utters over the mounds follows the same long path as that administered to a girl on the night she enters her first menstrual seclusion.[25] Once the field has been planted no one should enter the collective garden until the onset of the rains, when the manioc stems have reached shoulder height, respecting Tiolero's mythic request that her mother should bury her in the cool soil and then leave 'without looking back', only returning with the start of the rains. At this turn of the seasons, Yankwa's leaders and the blessing shaman again visit to feed and bless the mother of manioc's central mounds. Since the collective gardens are planted around June and the rains generally return in September, the duration of manioc's 'seclusion' from human company closely matches that of a teenage girl.[26] We can see that manioc's symbolic status as a teenage girl undergoing puberty seclusion conditions the rhythm in which gardens are planted, tended and harvested, just as they condition Enawenê women's own alternating rhythms of seclusion and contact with the plant, which are dictated by menstruation and childbearing. So too, following Tiolero's dictates promotes the high yield of the garden – its health and fertility – just as dietary restrictions and shamanic blessings undergone by Enawenê persons when they are with blood ensure that they remain fleshy, strong, energetic and productive in the future.

We can now appreciate that it is manioc's kindredness to healthy humans – her large, fleshy, juicy tubers – that is the source of her danger to them during periods of blood. The story of manioc's relationship with people, and especially with women, is thus one of similarity and codependence, in which people have the responsibility to ensure that mutual growth and health is not stymied by mutual depredation. The two species' interdependence is symbolised by blood. Manioc and women's blood are simply incompatible. To abstract a little from Enawenê discourse and practice it is as if contact between them caused blood to seep away from each, leeching both of vitality. As we know, both men and women avoid manioc gardens, raw tubers and ketera during periods when they are with blood, to avoid the risk of being 'taken by manioc' and suffering long-term ill health. But this risk is reciprocal; either side can wither and blight the other. If a man visits his manioc gardens when his wife is menstruating, not only will he grow skinny and fleshless himself, but his manioc tubers will grow shrivelled and lightweight too. Beyond these negative precautions, which set up barriers between bloody manioc and people, cultivators also take positive steps to promote manioc's growth. The quasi parental and shamanic treatment of manioc is most explicit in the case of Yankwa's collective gardens, since it is the job of Yankwa's leaders to ensure that the mother of manioc is fed with fish, shamanised and then left alone to grow during a period of seclusion.

In order to complete this story of mutual entailment between manioc and human fertility, which depends on the control and mediation of contact between plants and persons, let us turn now to human seclusion. This will allow me to tie the material presented in this chapter with the analysis in Chapter 1, where I showed that Yankwa's dam-fishing endeavour involved Yankwa's fishermen in a collectivised version of life cycle seclusion. The striking parallelism between the father-son myth of dam fishing and the mother-daughter myth of manioc agriculture is matched by the central role played by seclusion in mediating human relationships with both fish and with manioc. Recall that as the fish's blood was shed by traps, which were closely identified with their makers, contact between the encampment and the dam, men and traps, trap owners and their own fish, was subject to a set of restrictions. In the same way Enawenê peoples' – and especially women's – contact with manioc is carefully disciplined in ways that I will now detail. In fact, the annual cycle of Yankwa, which synchronises fishing and agricultural activities as I noted in Chapter 1, is defined by seclusion above and beyond the male collective seclusion at the dams. I will demonstrate that Yankwa's different phases (leaving, away, returning) can be understood as an intercalation of mutual seclusions and exposures of fish, manioc and people, which assure the fertility of these three interdependent species.

Seclusions for and from Manioc

Fundamentally Enawenê men and women are conjoined rather than separated by their subjection to blood: there are no restrictions on contact between the sexes; both are mutually subjected to women's blood. Instead, restriction is on contact between the couple or nucleus (in the case of birth) and other species – principally fish and manioc.[27] As I mentioned in Chapter 1, seclusion is always a response to the presence of blood and is simply referred to as 'lying down' (*aoxikya*), which implies restorative rest. The strictest seclusions are those observed by teenage girls and boys and they share the same central features: manioc foods, fish and salt – the foods of Yankwa – are excluded from the diet in favour of small quantities of inert foods, including honey mixed with water, corn drinks, boiled legumes, gathered fungi, Brazil nuts, softened palm fruits and unsalted rice. Girls are secluded for two to three months upon their first menstruation and women and infants' postpartum seclusion is of a similar duration. These long seclusions comprise a first month spent inside a partition put up in the household for the purpose, resting quietly in their hammocks by a constant hearth without body ornaments. This strict period ends when postpartum bleeding has ceased or a girl's tattoo wounds have healed.[28] During a second month the patient keeps to the house and gradually reintroduces foods to the diet. Teenage boys' seclusion when their first sexual partner menstruates or gives birth is strict in terms of diet, physical segregation and the regime of blessing shamanism undergone, but it is much shorter in duration than that of a teenage girl, lasting for approximately one week. During monthly menstrual seclusions, men and women stay around the house rather than fishing or gardening, do little work and restrict their diet but they do not lie down in a compartment.

The chief imperative of seclusion is withdrawal and hiddenness in order to avoid exposure to the predatory potential of a cosmos that is hyper-animated relative to the patient's vulnerability and porousness. Thus, regardless of the duration of seclusion, proper conduct involves remaining indoors to avoid the sun's rays, which would penetrate the vulnerable head like arrows, as well as a few 'table manners' (Lévi-Strauss 1968: 418–20), such as boiling food in uncontaminated pans (small aluminium cauldrons are ideally brought from town for girls in their first seclusion) and never baking foods in the ashes of fire. In addition to the physical separation of the patient and their special diet and cuisine, patients are subject to the incantations of blessing shamans (hoanaytale/o), whose efficacious words and breath are directed onto the tops of their heads and onto the foods they eat.[29] These strings of metaphor play their part in setting up a barrier between the patient and their potential predators and then in making their contact safe once again. As the brother of one secluded teenage girl explained to me when I went to keep her company and found her very reluctant to talk, she was silent lest the hearth, hammock, hammock posts, house posts, the structure of the cooking hearth, the pestle and mortar, the fish and manioc on the hearth, the corn and so on and so on, should hear her. The house and all that was inside it was bearing down on her with its arrows, ready to 'take' her.[30] Blessing shamanism not only protects those in seclusion but also prepares them for emergence and ingestion. This occurs through a conventional series of blessing sessions, which are administered by one of the village's specialists in return for payment in the usual items of Enawenê currency: smoked fish, smoked manioc loaves, calabashes, palm-nut bead chains and feather ornaments. Each of these sessions is accompanied by a bath in a purifying tincture made from the same *mehkali* vine that was used by men at the dam to cleanse themselves of lingering blood or bad dreams.[31] The series of blessings and purifying baths controls the patient's gradual re-emergence into the cosmos.[32] Once this series is complete, it remains for foods to be reintroduced into the patient's diet: each new species of fish is blessed before it is eaten as well as every form of manioc in the order: oloniti, ketera, raw tubers and finally gardens. This ensures that re-entry into the workaday world and household commensality occur very gradually. For example, in the first menstrual seclusion I observed most closely, on the morning after the last blessing session, oloniti was blessed for the girl to drink so that she could now take from her household's pan freely. On the same day the pestle and mortar were blessed so that she could participate in pounding dry foods, but it was another month before raw tubers were blessed so that she could help her sisters and mother to grate manioc daily and it was a further month until she was reintroduced to the first manioc garden. The gradualness of this re-entwinement with manioc was further ensured because tubers originating from different gardens, and also the gardens themselves, needed to be blessed separately, constraining how often and how far a woman could venture.

In sum, women's re-emergence into the cosmos and the social world is coextensive with the establishment of contact with manioc, so that we can say that Enawenê life cycle seclusions are first and foremost seclusions for and from manioc. This was reaffirmed for me as I observed the repetition of the same repertoire of blessings for each patient; saw the measures taken to prevent contact between manioc and secluded patients; was warned weekly that I should never risk manioc gardening during menstruation; and witnessed the shamanic treatments and diets of those who had been 'taken by manioc' as a result of past carelessness. And as I have described, it is manioc's fertility – indexed by her womanliness – that imposes this rigorous and effortful avoidance. This is especially marked in the Enawenê's young and fast-growing population, in which there are many new births and young people reaching adulthood. The population's prodigious fertility implies that while 'the whole community' drinks ketera nightly with Yankwa there are numerous people abstaining from this commensal circuit because they are with blood. At the same time, a high birth rate and growing clan numbers require that men plant more manioc gardens for wives and betrothal partners and that Yankwa plan ever bigger collective fields for Yankwa's host clans. This mutual flourishing of people and manioc requires vigilant care to assure the continuation of this virtuous cycle of fertility.

This discussion of the symbolisation of manioc in mythology, in her ritualised planting and in the incantations of blessing shamans, as well as the evidence of how this impacts on everyday subsistence activities, reveals the sharing by humans and their staple crop of principles of fertility, growth and health – principles that are embodied by blood and are shared by beings the Enawenê consider to be endowed with blood – fish, manioc and humans. The reproduction of these three species is assured by Yankwa's temporality. Human reproduction, fish migrations and spawning, and the growth and harvest of manioc gardens, are entwined and intercalated in Yankwa's cycle. When manioc enters seclusion, Yankwa ends for the year and she emerges at the onset of the rains, which is also when the fresh corn sprouts and grows rapidly, and the leafcutter ants take their dramatic nuptial flight in a sudden eruption of fecundity. While the Enawenê leave the manioc gardens to grow, the flutes of Yankwa also remain hidden in the flute house, which is allowed to fall into disrepair through the seasons of Saluma and Kateoko. During the period of manioc's rapid growth, as the river levels rise, Yankwa begin to dance in preparation for departure and to drink ketera. At this point the fish are faraway upriver fattening and spawning; they are absent in the flesh while they are omnipresent in men's talk and songs. There follows the dam-fishing period, during which men are in an intense identification with fish via their traps, but are separated from women, from manioc gardens and ketera, and also from their flutes. When the fishermen return, fish, manioc and people all come together in feasts in which fish and manioc foods are paired. Once all of the host clans have finished returning, people look ahead to the next year, and the last of Datamale's trap-caught fish fecundates the new manioc gardens and then Datamale's daughter, Tiolero, enters her underground seclusion again. One woman hinted at the human dimension of this fertility calendar – the transposition of human, fish and manioc reproduction – when she explained 'supposing you become pregnant when Yankwa returns, then the child will be born when Yankwa is ready to leave',

Conclusion: Fortifying Humanity

This chapter has been about finding the Enawenê's cosmological entanglements in apparently unremarkable processes like manioc cookery and calabash-making, rather than in shamanic rituals and esoteric lore (C. Hugh-Jones 1979:181–82). The ethnography has comprised recipes for staple foods; the sensory properties of fabrication processes (e.g. stench, bloodiness, shine, wet, dry); labour sequences (e.g. makalahi flour: pound, ferment, sun dry, smoke dry, pound, sieve, store); the physiology of living organisms (e.g. parrots, calabashes, women's bodies, manioc plants); and practices involved in nurturing the vitality of human bodies and plants. It is such deceptively basic material-semiotic processes that constitute the stuff of everyday experience. In the Enawenê case this experience is ideally characterised by the beauty of healthy human bodies; houses filled with an abundance of dry stores, sun diadem headdresses and bundles of calabashes; the air carrying the fragrance of drying annatto and fermenting manioc; mouths tasting the sweetness of proper, complete foods; and daily and longer cyclical rhythms propelling life onward. As well as generating aesthetic and sensory pleasure I have suggested that it is through these processes that the Enawenê exert control over their place in the universe, ensuring the perseverance of proper human life, which, they tell us, is a life founded upon the control of fire, heat and humours.

First and most simply, Enawenê cuisine, fabrication work and bodily care all involve a high degree of pyrotechnic mastery and the absorption of a lot of heat. This is partly a necessity because toxic bitter manioc is the staple crop but even then it must be understood as a necessity that the Enawenê choose by selecting toxic cultigens for their culinary value. You can boil taro and eat it, put an ear of fresh corn in the ashes, grill small fish to eat, but this kind of food has an ephemeral availability and does not go round. Very little of Enawenê cuisine is of this simple or immediate kind, which is the stuff of indulgent individual snacks rather than shared meals. Since these are private and not shared with the Yakairiti or with ones affines, eating them is always a risky pleasure. The overwhelming emphasis in Enawenê cuisine is on everyday feast foods, and their recipes involve the creation of complete foods that combine manioc with a smaller quantity of corn and fish and involve a long series of operations. The Enawenê are thus very clear about the values they attach to the culinary triangle: the raw is depreciated as tending towards a bestial, prehuman condition, or the poverty and the lowly status of the Nambikwara, and it is almost entirely excluded from the diet during Yankwa. What a 'state of nature' is to the raw, supernature is to the rotten/fermented ('nature's cookery' in Lévi-Strauss's terms). These processes of natural transformation are carefully circumscribed by the Enawenê as if they wished to entertain, without ever occupying, the perverse and drunken position of the Yakairiti. Fermentation is deployed in recipes but it is confined to the early steps: oloniti is left to ferment a few hours and then reboiled; manioc odds and ends are left to ferment but are then thoroughly dehydrated; xaokwase ferment only as they are simultaneously smoke-dried. Fermentation brings an appreciated scent to makalahi flour and gives rise to the slightly sour-dough taste of fresh breads cooked from moist xaokwase, but to allow these natural transformations to run their course would be to entertain communion with the Yakairiti. This is indeed what we find occurring when pans of oloniti are left to sit and sour especially for the Yakairiti, and 'rotten' breads are made from sour manioc pith. These deliberate culinary abominations occur within the context of choreographed performances of other-becoming, subversions of human mores that are conventional rather than intoxicated.

This is distinct from the courting of self-transformation from the inside out that we find in so many Amazonian contexts. To become 'translucent' is an Araweté idiom translated by Viveiros de Castro (1992: 219) for the effects sought from inebriating tobacco. Unlike the Araweté, the Enawenê are not Tupian dionysiacs thirsting for self-alteration and escape from the confines of human life. In fact, this contrast between 'conservative' Gê people and 'anarchical' Tupi-Guarani ones frames Viveiros de Castro's magisterial book on the Araweté (1992: 3–6; 304–5). The Araweté are figured against the Gê; they are not dialectical, not conservative, do not put difference to the service of identity. For them the human condition is intercalary and precarious, but this does not make it 'a bastion to be fortified, but, rather, a passageway, an equivocal and ambivalent place' (ibid.: 305). I have read these words again and again and each time I have been forcibly struck by their eloquence in describing what the Enawenê, in turn, are not. For the Enawenê, the human living condition is precisely a bastion to be fortified. If Enawenê people become other they do so from the outside-in, through disguise (wild palm fronds, mud), bodily exertions (the changes to the body during dam fishing) and performance (the boisterous clowning of pet flutes, the licking of salt and spilling of pans of oloniti). But all of this is possible against a backdrop of an effort to stabilise and conserve their unified identity as a living community.

Curative cookery is a key medium through which human life is assured and moulded. It maintains and restores the body and the cosmos to health and balance, and it blocks the backsliding into death and illness, which Enawenê people are always anticipating. Preventing acute sickness, chronic ill health, frailty or listlessness, and aspiring to corpulence, strength, vitality and productivity are their goals. They pursue them through mundane cookery that is oriented to making the daily fare safe and good to eat (sweet, fragrant, complete) and by means of the fabrication of important adjuncts to human personhood, such as dried, hardened and sealed calabashes, and moderately 'cooked' headdresses, which alongside food and drink are the major media for Yankwa's social diplomacy. This cuisine and craftwork is matched by the purging, sealing and definition of women's bellies at puberty; the careful control of their body and skin temperature via the constancy of the low hearth during their seclusion and the application of moderate amounts of annatto dye to the skin; and the choice of inert (rice, corn, fungi) or pre-cured foods (old and smoked manioc) for their diet.

This project of stabilising the human condition is a predicament that is peculiar to cosmologies that place the human at a level with or slightly below other existents in the cosmic pecking order. Living with the Enawenê through the seasons of Yankwa and Lerohi, it often seemed as if the Yakairiti's perspective on the Enawenê-nawe – that as the 'dead people' they were destined to become the killers' prey – was the ground against which Enawene self-conceptions as 'living people' figured. Similarly striking was the intensity with which Enawenê women lived with, and in a sense for, their staple crop during Yankwa, which was the season in which the community was most intensively involved in cultivating, processing and eating manioc. As I have described, the effort to control contact with manioc, for one or another household member, rarely slipped from attention, with proper relations with the plant oscillating between complete avoidance and intense involvement.

As the privileged medium for the negotiation of life, I have argued that cookery, understood in an expanded sense to include fabrication and care, is an everyday cosmological diplomacy that is curative first at a literal or economic level because food is preserved for the future; and second at a more abstract, cosmological level because the control of fire, heat and humours is a key therapeutic principle for maintaining the body and the cosmos in health and balance. These literal and abstract levels cannot be separated because the preservation techniques that are central to Enawenê cookery are the condition of possibility for the amassing of storable surplus for the sacrificial feasts that ensure the community's continued health. This is not a 'political' economy in the sense that surplus is not put to the service of supporting distinctions within the human community, as it surely could be if labour relations were differently configured. Here the 'economic' matters of growing, harvesting, cooking, distributing and consuming food are encompassed by cosmology because they mediate the relationship between the living and the dead, between embodied agents (living people, living plants, birds – souls within bodies) and disembodied agents (spirits – souls without bodies).[33] We could call this a diplomatic economy, since its aim is to mediate between potential enemies who threaten Enawenê life, either through zero sum game of life/death (stealing souls) or via the erosion and depletion of life force (blood). Choice of diet, cuisine, restriction and expansion of the commensal sphere, as well as the quantity and kinds of foods circulated and ingested are all technologies for this diplomacy.

In the next chapter we shift from this every day, materially mediated micro-diplomacy with invisible others, which takes place in gardens and houses, to political negotiations, which take place at roadsides, works sites and in urban meeting rooms, and whose media are speech, documents and collective presence. This foreign diplomacy is also about the perseverance of a life of health, plenty and prosperity, which is threatened at simultaneously pragmatic and cosmological levels by the state's appropriation of riverine resources.

Notes

1. See, for example, Gow (1991, esp. 150–78); Fausto (2007: 502); Lagrou (2000: 159–67); McCallum (2001: 96–108); Rival (1998: 621); Viegas (2003); Vilaça (1992, 2002).
2. See, for example, Seeger, Da Matta and De Castro (1979); Taylor and Viveiros de Castro (2006); T. Turner (1995); Rival (2005).
3. In my experience the Enawenê's cuisine is immediately palatable to newcomers, just as the aromas contained by the circular village are inviting and seductive. It was reading Yamin-Pasternak et al.'s (2014) wonderful article on contemporary Bering Strait Inuits' odour etiquette (eating wearing latex gloves to keep the hands odour-free) that led me to consider the importance of the Enawenê 'smell-scape'. Yamin-Pasternak et al. (2014: 630) point out that mammalian engagement with smell is uniquely direct: 'the odor signals spurt directly from the environment into the cerebrum as they travel through the nasal passage with inhaled air … odor evades all mediation, gushing to provoke an emotional response'. This makes olfaction a particularly powerful and emotive embodiment of culture.
4. Lévi-Strauss's triadic code (the raw, cooked and rotten) emerged from an analysis of myths of the origin of fire from central Brazil, among speakers of Gê and Tupi languages. In both ensembles of myths, fire was won from an animal and in each case the species was defined by its diet. But the Gê won fire from the jaguar, who devours raw flesh, and the Tupi from a vulture, who eats rotting flesh. While a triangle of raw-rotten-cooked operates in all myths of the origin of fire, the decisive contrast was between raw and cooked in the first case and rotten and cooked in the second. Thus the values associated with cookery were different in each case (1964: 152). His ideal-typical exemplification of the culinary triangle was intended to inspire ethnographers to discover the relevant contrasts in any particular cultural context. He noted the widespread association of roasting with primitiveness and boiling with

evolutionary advancement (the invention of pottery), but, perversely he said, boiling clearly induced a process akin to rotting because food decomposes, breaks up and becomes mushy in water more quickly than it does in air. Boiling was thus not unambiguously cultured. Slow, steady cookery techniques in which foods are slowly baked and then dried, or carefully smoked on specially made racks, are those which fully approximate the abstract category of the cooked (Lévi-Strauss 1964: 403, 408).

5. These birds are considered civilised. Others, for example the blue and yellow macaw is captured for its feathers but is killed rather than kept because it squawks loudly and is said to have an angry temperament.

6. This myth belongs to the trope of the mishandled diadem, which stretches throughout the Americas (Lévi-Strauss 1964: 298).

7. The curative combination of hot and cold humours is a general feature of Enawenê cure that is widely shared in the Americas, see, for example, Butt Colson (1983), Ariel de Vidas (2004: 160–165), Belaunde (2005).

8. People had built these storage houses after headdresses and other ceremonial valuables (as well as pots, pans, tools, hammocks and calabashes) had been destroyed in cooking fires that lit the thatch and razed the village during the dry season in 2007.

9. Work on eating in animist Amazonia has tended to focus on the problem of consuming game mammals, because bloody-fleshed species are commonly taken to have the greatest subjective potency. At the bottom of the food chain and the hierarchy of animacy, plants and relatively bloodless fish are considered – both by most Amerindians and by their ethnographers – to be relatively unproblematic. See, for example, Fausto 2007; S. Hugh-Jones (1996); Vilaça (1992, 2000); Crocker (1985); Århem (1996).

10. On this theme, see Lévi-Strauss (1969: 497–98); Carnerio da Cunha (1978:122–26, 145); Viveiros de Castro (1992: 66).

11. Carnerio da Cunha worked among the nearby Gê-speaking Krahó of Central Brazil, but similar spirit mirror worlds are found in societies around the world; for example, Ariel de Vidas (2004: 142); Lévi-Strauss (1988: 117–26); Schieffelin (1976: 99–101); Stasch (2009: 217–24).

12. In readiness for Yankwa and Lerohi men buy sacks of corn seed from an animal feed supplier in Juína to supplement their own harvest, this reflects the Enawenê perception that, however good the harvest, there is never enough to satisfy the Yakairiti (this was also the case ten years earlier, according to Mendes dos Santos 2001: 137–38).

13. These distributions can occur at any time of the year; the host is always of the sick person's clan (which is not necessarily the incumbent clan of the ritual at the time) and they have a specific name, *hesailiti*. Particular formal dialogues accompany the encounter between the donor and recipient.

14. See, especially, Wilson and Dufour 2002; Carneiro (2000); Erikson (2004a); C. Hugh-Jones (1979: 174–80); Stolze-Lima (2005: 293); Sztutman (2008).

15. There are many simpler recipes possible. For example, it is possible to simply boil the grated manioc mash to a thick paste without prior separation of liquid and solid parts, as the Umotina apparently did (Oberg 1953: 107), or to separate out only the fibre, boiling the milk with the starch still in suspension as Xinguanos do on ceremonial occasions (Dole 1978: 227).

16. Dry tubers are called *iowsero* (iow means 'dry', 'ero' is a feminine suffix). The juicy tubers are called *kalalo* and described as *kalonê*, which means 'full of drink'. Mendes dos Santos found the same wet/dry division among Paresi (1994: 76). This classification sits alongside the common bitter/sweet distinction, which refers to manioc that

is high in toxicity versus that which can safely be eaten simply roasted and boiled. In fact there is a bittersweet continuum within a single species. In line with Mendes dos Santos' findings (ibid.: 180 n. 69), I recorded Enawenê names for fifteen varieties of bitter manioc, whereas sweet manioc went by a single name, mamalakali, and was planted in small quantities and eaten fairly rarely.

17. Women poked eyes and noses in xaokwase and named them after land animals, perhaps they did this because they 'lived on' as exchange media.

18. Sour-tasting bread called detero is made to accompany large distributions of fish soup because the Yakairiti are said to like it. Another chewy and pungent bread called *makalaia* can also substitute it and is made simply by pressing moistened manioc flour (the kind made from the fermented odds and ends of tubers, described below) onto the griddle. Although people stressed that these breads were 'food' (*hanini*), no one ever took more than a bite before discarding them to the floor.

19. Separation (*hololo*), which occurs upon the addition of the sugars is the desired state of oloniti whereas ketera has to remain thick, with the solid parts in suspension. When my sister Yokwali-neto discovered that her ketera had separated during the night, becoming 'like oloniti' she said, she threw away all 125 litres and the paddle that she had stirred it with and made another batch of ketera the next day for her husband's clan distribution, to compensate the loss. There was much consternation in my house about the ketera's separation; I was asked if I had woken in the night to drink furtively from the pan, breaking the skin that forms over the ketera and introducing some element that could lead to fermentation. Oloniti and ketera production are also separated temporally and spatially. I never saw women chewing toasts for oloniti and thickening ketera at the same time. Oloniti's ferment is chewed through the morning and added around midday, while ketera is thickened at dusk. The emphasis on sweetness that should not be allowed to topple over into fermentation also applies to Enawenê adoration of honey, which they never allow to ferment. This means keeping stored honey dry and drinking it immediately once it has been diluted to make the honey water that is oloniti's dry-season replacement.

20. In fact the symptoms resulting from the long-term consumption of inadequately processed bitter manioc ('konzo', as it is known in Africa), among which are unsteady weakened limbs, dizziness and headaches, are akin to the package of chronic weakness and neurological affliction that Enawenê associate with untimely exposure to manioc. As we have seen, Enawenê cuisine is extremely rigorous in ensuring manioc's thorough detoxification. Perhaps there is a trace here of a collective memory of cyanide poisoning and its associated neuropathy.

21. In 2013 I was surprised to see that she had begun to eat and harvest manioc and, at the same time, to practise as a blessing shaman like her elderly, highly respected mother, whom the whole village called Hoanaytalo after her special role as a blessing shaman. I received no explanation for this change, but the most likely one is that through her exposure to the incantations and her discussions with her mother around the subject, she had not only learned the secret formulae that render manioc safe but also, by mastering them, had overcome her vulnerability.

22. The smell of fish, blood and sexual fluids are covered by a single olfactory term *ede* from which the term *ka-ede-na*, which describes anyone in a seclusion state, must derive, translating as 'smelling blood' or 'with blood'. The avoidance of fish thus seems to correspond to the logic that to eat something bloody while a person is with blood would lead to a dangerous excess. This is supported by the fact that Enawenê women avoid certain fish species like the pike characin fish and an unidentified

species called *ewehe* (which has razor-sharp teeth) because their ingestion was said to cause excessive bleeding. Xingu people share the Enawenê conception that the bloodiness of fish is transmitted through its smell and also proscribe fish to secluded persons (e.g. Crocker 1985: 56; Viveiros de Castro 2002: 55; Vanzolini Figueiredo 2010: 192–93).

23. The avoidance of manioc is effortful to maintain for the whole household because houses are full of manioc and everyday involves handling the crop. For example, when a newborn had been born into the household in which I lived, every manioc harvest had to be blessed outside of the house before it could be bought in and grated; alternatively we decamped to grate manioc under the hot sun or our resident blessing shaman grandmother created a smoke screen by burning bits of cotton between the piled manioc and the compartment in which a newborn and its mother lay.

24. Starring mother and daughter, this myth is the agricultural counterpart to that starring father Datamale and son Dokowyi, which provides a guide to men's relationship with fish. Like the latter, as well as being known by all Enawenê people and being frequently narrated, episodes from this myth are the matter of Yankwa's chants.

25. Mendes dos Santos (2006: 190–95) offers a fuller version of the charter myth for manioc's ritual treatment as well as a valuable comparative analysis of the Tiolero and Dokowyi myths as models for Enawenê gender complementarity. He has also suggested (ibid.: 191–92) that the Enawenê conceive of manioc as vampiric, as has been reported for the Achuar (Harner 1984: 70–76; Descola 1994: 192–209). He proposes that the Enawenê blessing shamans' incantations to Tiolero are akin to the songs (*anent*) Achuar women murmur to assuage the bloodthirsty tutelary spirit of their manioc gardens. The fish and oloniti offered to the mother of manioc upon her ritual planting would thus be 'a means to compensate her lost blood by other means … so that it does not become necessary for her to seek it among people' (2001: 123). While I agree that this is a logical inference, which fits my own analysis of manioc planting as the symbolic seclusion of a girl in her first menstrual seclusion, nobody ever spoke directly to me of manioc's thirst for blood, as they did routinely talk about the Yakairiti's thirst for manioc drinks. What seemed prominent in people's representations of manioc woman was her kindredness to human women rather than the perversion of nurture represented by vampirism. I am not denying the elegance of the symbolic shorthand that accounts for all this in terms of manioc's vampirism, or the probability that the Enawenê might explicate it to others in this way, but what seems to me more profound is what this vitality vampirism implies at an abstract level about the relationship between people and their staple crop.

26. I was also told that the mother of manioc is blessed again on the eve of her uprooting the night before the last day of Yankwa's returning sequence, when the Yakairiti drink their fill, the chants are finished, the flutes are put to rest and Yankwa's headdresses are returned to the hosts.

27. I stress the mutualistic aspect of seclusion practices, which are foremost here (see Overing 1986: 146). This is a question of women's greater vulnerability to blood and does not imply that women's blood is polluting to men. Men must take care to avoid fishing and manioc gardening while they are exposed to the blood of women with whom they have sexual contact but women are not themselves dangerous to men. This is clear in the fact that Enawenê women can cook and serve food for ceremonial distribution, have sex, and dance in the arena during their menstruation. On the other hand, semen is dangerous to children before they can walk, so women are

supposed to avoid sex (which would penetrate the baby via breast milk) until their baby is walking.

28. After birth a woman drinks a bark tincture (called *hétale*), which hastens the cessation of postpartum bleeding along with a bland drink of corn flour boiled in water (*madalio*) to induce milk production. Menstruating girls also drink this bland corn drink and eat little else at first.

29. Hoanayti is an esoteric poetic language, which is obscure to non-specialists. What I could glean from my limited enquiries was that the shamans' incantations evoked the mythic origins of beings throughout the cosmos as if to remind them of their originary personhood, and in repeated refrains they asked them to 'lower their gaze' and 'put down their arrows' of harm, which they brandished towards the patient. Each blessing followed a specific path through different dominions; for example, from the stars, through tree species, to fish species, the manioc encircling the village, the flutes in the centre of the village and back to the nearby house posts. What I gained was only this vague sense of an effort to weave the patient back into relation with the known world through a concentric movement outwards and inwards in both time (connecting origin times and present) and space (bringing the whole landscape of the cosmos into relation with the patient).

30. People explained that these things were all *kahale wayate* or *atahale wayate*, which I would tentatively translate as 'owned by (unspecified) owners' and 'owned by the masters of the trees' (*atahale* is an elision of *ateira-hale*, 'tree-master').

31. It is prepared in advance by the blessing shaman, who whisks the solution with a stick as they speak into it, as if catching their words in the growing head of foam. I saw my adoptive grandmother preparing this tincture many times. She would sit hunched over the calabash for about half an hour, uttering incantations into a solution made by rubbing the foaming vine into the water. By the time she finished, a big head of foam stood above the rim of the calabash. The patient would rub this foam and liquid first into their hair, and then all over their body, once the incantations on their own head were complete.

32. The first blessing session occurs at noon or dusk on the day menstruation begins or the baby is born and is called 'blowing the head' *(ixiwiri hoene)*. The patient lies still and silent in their hammock with the blessing shaman perched behind them and bent close so that their mouth nearly touches the passive head. They oscillate between utterances and blowing, projecting their incantations into the patients head over approximately five hours. The patient's limp body is supported by the hammock and generally they doze. Later, in the lead up to emergence from seclusion *(ainyakwata)*, patients take a sequence of four nightly baths in mehkali inside their seclusion compartment after dusk. The sixth blessing session is called 'getting up' or 'throwing off the basket' *(ainyakwata, tohé halatene)* and takes place after nightfall on the eve of their emergence, outside the back of the house and under the stars. The patient sits with a woven basket over their head (an aluminium basin will do) in front of the shaman, who murmurs incantations that repeat the 'path' *(awiti)* of the initial head blessing. The seventh session is called *mitikwata* and reintroduces the patient to the water, so that they now emerge from the house for the first time in the light of day. It occurs about two months after the onset of seclusion for a woman, and allows her to bathe at the public bathing pool instead of inside her compartment. The shaman leads the patient along the path to the pool they habitually use, uttering incantations as they go. When they arrive the patient first bathes in mehkali, before taking a bath in the water of the pool itself. In general a youth or new father

undergoes the same three major blessing sessions (the head, the basket, the water) in quicker succession. Men emerge from seclusion after just four or five days, and can begin to eat manioc and fish as soon as the foods are blessed for them. Boys are also introduced to the bathing pool at dawn on the morning after throwing off the basket and are reintroduced to the manioc gardens whenever they next need to visit them.

33. I am implicitly responding to Goody's critique of Lévi-Strauss' attempt to develop a culinary heuristics for anthropology. Goody (1982: 37) claimed that Lévi-Strauss stripped cuisine from its infrastructure: its tie to biological needs, questions of production and distribution, and class interests.

6

Yankwa's Foreign Diplomacy and Saluma's Defiance

They have lied to us, the fish are dying and the water is dirty so we want
to be rid of the dams. All the Enawene Nawe are agreed about this, we all
want to throw away the dams. We do not want the money anymore. The
water is very dirty, what if the fish die out? We do not eat meat at all so we
do not want the dams. We are not joking. You can help us, we must not be
alone. Do you understand us? We are very serious. We know about dams
because we too build dams for Yankwa. The Yakairiti will be angry with us;
that is what the Enawene Nawe think and worry about – what if Yankwa
ends and Saluma as well? Do you understand? We are not joking.
— *Halataikwa Enawene Nawe*, 21 September 2008

This statement was written in September 2008 to affirm the community's rejection of the compensation offer made by the hydroelectric dam
consortium Juruena Participações e Investimentos S.A. It was drafted
by a handful of men who were in the municipal seat of Juína to see
what could be done to halt the dams' construction, now that there was
no further judicial recourse. Brazil's Supreme Court had overruled a
restraining order temporarily imposed by Mato Grosso state's Public
Prosecutor and construction work on the Telégrafica dam, located less
than 30 kilometres from the southern border of the Enawenê's demarcated territory and upstream of their fishing waters, was underway
again. With this statement the community representatives reached out
to the London-based NGO Survival International, who were eager to
campaign on the damming issue, but would only do so on the condition

that the Enawenê rejected compensation outright. Over the previous months there had been a series of tense meetings with the consortium, FUNAI, and the four other indigenous groups who would be affected by the dams in order to come to a compensation settlement. At this point the Enawenê had abandoned these negotiations in response to obfuscation by consortium representatives and their patronising, disrespectful attitude, and underhand attempts to bypass political processes by buying off the Enawenê's opposition.

In the statement, the Enawenê attempt to express, in terms that had become conventional to them by 2008, why the substitution of their temporary wooden dams for these permanent concrete ones represented a crisis in both subsistence and existence: not only malnourishment but cosmic catastrophe – the ire of the Yakairiti and their predation against the Enawenê community. As we know, the Yakairiti belong in the courses of rivers, and especially in waterfalls, odd rock formations and palms and they are considered the ultimate owners of all the riverine resources on which the Enawenê depend for their livelihood, most importantly fish. This binds people in a continual obligation to share the resources they appropriate throughout the human community and with these invisible owners. Whether we privilege the Enawenê's cosmological or practical discourse, it is true that these dams pose a drastic threat to the health and prosperity of the Enawenê. The response of the Brazilian government, for whom expansion in the hydroelectric sector is a major policy objective, has been to attempt to recover the Enawenê's economy and cosmology with a cocktail of economic and ideological substitutes – money and goods on the one hand, and cultural patrimony projects on the other. Steadfast arguments that reject money and technology on the basis of traditional beliefs and environmental stewardship could thus only be one element in the Enawenê's diplomatic armoury. In 2008, when five dams were already under construction, it made sense for the Enawenê to maximise compensation from the consortium while aiming to limit the proliferation of dams. As Kirsch (2007: 314) has argued, indigenous movements against resource capture and extractive industry face complex situations, and cannot be expected to conform to the ideological purity required of anti-development campaigns. The Enawenê's statement is thus both prophetic in nature and legible in a pragmatic register as a temporary retrenchment to a position of pure opposition.

In this chapter I chart the Enawenê's negotiation of this textbook case of conflict of interest: the development of resources for international trade at the expense of local livelihoods. In a political and economic situation in which outright opposition to the dams is doomed to failure because of the alignment of corporate and government interests in the expansion of Brazil's hydroelectricity sector, the Enawenê succeed to a remarkable degree in forcing the government to recognise their stake in the River Juruena's resources. This efficacy depends on the maintenance of an adversarial positioning, by which I mean that they assume a position of rival sovereignty in relation to the state, so that compensation negotiations became diplomatic in nature. On the Enawenê's side, negotiation strategies were deliberate, strategic and measured with the other's response in mind; they took place between parties who, although they belonged to a single national territory, had fundamentally opposed interests and were each mutually excluded from the political space and discourse of the other. The Enawenê assumed this separation and they worked to cross divides of autonomy, language and divergent priorities, rather than to break them down. Thirdly, as the claim to rival sovereignty implies, negotiations were diplomatic because the Enawenê were prepared to back up their position by force with confrontations, road blocks, occupations, boycotts of meetings and acts of political warfare. Seeking recognition from the government, they oscillated between negotiation and confrontation, cooperation and autarchy, and the incorporation of goods and their refusal.

In October 2008, soon after they had drafted the above statement for Survival International, fortified by the warrior dances and chants of Saluma, the Enawenê invaded and burned the construction site of the nearest dam causing millions in damages and stalling construction for six months. This act of aggression was highly controlled: great care was taken not to harm the powerless construction workers present at the site, since the aim was to target the government – this was a political gesture designed to force the government to apprehend the Enawenê as a power to be treated with and thus an invitation to resume compensation negotiations on a more equal footing. It was necessary because the government had persistently refused to treat with the Enawenê as significant interlocutors in matters that affected their livelihood. This political reading of the situation is clear in one man's retrospective of events leading up to the invasion and burning of the construction site:

> We closed the Juína road at the bridge [in May 2007]. It's a federal road, it belongs to the government. And the government did not respond. Later, we occupied the dam [in December 2007], and the government did not respond. We again closed the bridge [in May 2008] and the government did not respond. For these reasons we became angry … The government is the owner, 'let's burn' we decided.[1]

My overarching claim in this chapter is that the Enawenê forced the government and the dam consortium to treat them as diplomats, to some degree overturning an initial situation of disregard for their claim to the river's resources, their knowledge of the environment and indeed their very status as important interlocutors. Of course, from the perspective of governance of national territory, negotiations with the Enawenê should not be diplomatic in nature. First, Brazil's indigenous citizens are conceived as vulnerable wards of state who require a paternalistic attitude of protection and provision of benefits, and FUNAI, the government body that has a tutelary role over Amerindians, is supposed to mediate in all matters of governance that touch their lives.[2] Indeed, in this case, FUNAI had effectively given permission for the dams' construction ahead of any consultation with the Enawenê. This order of events reveals the lack of meaningful participation of indigenous people in developments that affect their livelihood. In fact, Brazil's constitution has been routinely ignored to enable a rapid proliferation of hydroelectricity plants across the Amazon drainage. In this situation the Enawenê's relative success in extracting material benefits and in forcing the state to negotiate with them is owed to their skill in foreign diplomacy.

As I explained in the book's Introduction, this argument is inspired by Lévi-Strauss's proposition that people whose social dynamics are oriented to diffusing antagonisms in ways that, although aggressive, do not result in total warfare are likely to be particular adepts in the art of foreign diplomacy (Lévi-Strauss 1949: 151). After all, the Enawenê's blockades, occupations and their attack on the dam infrastructure caused disruption in the lives of other Brazilian citizens but, during the time of my fieldwork, nobody was physically harmed. I and many of the Enawenê's other allies thought their objective fair: to compel the government to include them in matters that concerned their existence. Their means were proportionate to the devastation of their livelihood that would be caused by these dams.

In this chapter I take several steps to advance this argument, building on my previous publications on Enawenê relations with Brazilian government agencies (Nahum-Claudel 2012, 2016a). First I provide an overview of the small hydroelectricity centres that immediately effect the Enawenê, and I place these developments in the wider political and economic context of Brazil's policy of rapid expansion in the hydroelectricity sector. This policy places the Enawenê and many other Amazonian peoples suddenly in a situation of conflict over vital resources, and compels them to negotiate with multiple outside agents in a unevenly weighted struggle in which dams are a fait accompli by the time consultation begins; assessments of environmental impact are either neglected or disregarded; the judiciary has proved unable to protect affected people's constitutional rights; transnational NGO support for indigenous resistance has been ineffective; and the relevant government bodies have been unable to stand in the way of projects with such high-level backing. Given all of these conditions the pattern has been that indigenous people are constrained to accept the only redress that is on offer: money and goods. Next I ask what the Enawenê do with this new income, which far outweighs other sources. I show that money and goods are channelled into Yankwa's egalitarian, collectivist economy of plenty, funding fishing expeditions and communal feasts. The Enawenê avidly incorporate these new resources, which they see as their due, and this does not quiet their pursuit of recognition at a political level. It is the oscillating dynamics of this pursuit that I subsequently detail, focusing on the events leading up to and following on from the burning of Telegráfica dam in 2008.

Hydroelectric Dams in Amazonia

Once completed, the Juruena Complex will comprise nine 'small' (under 30 megawatt) and two large hydroelectric dams distributed over a 110 km stretch of the Juruena River's upper reaches (Almeida 2011: 36 cit. AAI 2007). These dams lie upstream of the Enawenê and Nambikwara's contiguous territories, and downstream from the demarcated lands of the Paresi, on a stretch of the river that is increasingly flanked by soya fields. The Enawenê say that Telegráfica, the furthest downstream of the string of dams, is located at a place called Yokwalikwa, where the ancestors of the Enawenê and Paresi split. This indicates these dams' location in an area that the ancestors of the Paresi, Enawenê and Nambikwara lost first to Rondon's famous telegraph line, which is the dam's namesake, and then to new towns, cattle farms and soya fields. According to Souza, who worked for a time for the Enawenê's long-time NGO allies, OPAN, the Enawenê began to hear rumours about the planned dams in 2003, and had begun debating whether they would accept compensation, at what value and what the environmental impacts might be (Souza 2011: 31), but they were only officially notified about the dams after the construction licenses had been granted and the works begun in 2006 (Galvão 2016: 57). At this point, the community started protesting actively. By this time however, FUNAI had already authorised the construction of the five small hydroelectric centres.[3] Consultations and studies of environmental and social impact in which the Enawenê were asked to participate from 2006 onwards were therefore retrospective legitimation exercises. However, the Enawenê did not assume their disempowerment; indeed, in September 2007 they considered that discussion and consultation about the dams was only just beginning. Thus when a group of Enawenê fishermen saw the advancing construction of Telegráfica dam with their own eyes, they were dismayed to find that the dams had already become a reality.

Their assessment of the precipitous and unaccountable construction of the Juruena Complex is an accurate one. Legislative changes introduced in the early 2000s waived the usual requirements for full environmental impact assessment for plants generating less than 30 megawatts. This has allowed these so-called small hydroelectric centres to pass under the radar of social concern and environmental monitoring. However it seems to make little difference whether the dams are small, numerous and hidden from public scrutiny as in the Enawenê case; or gigantic, singular and famous as in the case of Belo Monte, a mega-dam that began operation on the Xingu River in 2015 and is the largest and most expensive piece of infrastructure in the country. In both cases the contemporary situation is reminiscent of Brazil's military dictatorship, when large-scale infrastructure projects were also central to the government agenda and when, just as today, affected people's claims were ignored until all decisions had already been made (Baines 1999: 215 cit. Viveiros de Castro and Andrade).

With hydroelectric dams proliferating across the Amazon drainage and the wider world in the name of clean energy and national prosperity (Millikan 2014), the Enawenê's situation at the start of this century is emblematic rather than exceptional. Hydroelectric frontiers are multiplying apace in Brazil, as harnessing the hydroelectric potential of the Amazon drainage has become the central tenet of national energy policy. There are twenty-five large hydroelectric dams and hundreds of smaller plants that are in various stages of construction and licensing across the watershed (Athayde 2014: 81). According to one estimate these dams will impact at least 30 per cent of the Amazon's indigenous territories (Ibid.). Devastating riverine ecologies, causing deforestation, water pollution and loss of fisheries, dams are ruinous to the livelihoods and freedoms of people who depend upon rivers for both subsistence and navigation. Dams also bring with them a package of secondary effects, which damage ecosystems and fragment territories, such as road networks, industry, logging and urbanisation.

This kind of critical scrutiny of the green credentials of hydroelectricity has been largely ignored in the fervour to profit from this free resource, as has the protest of affected peoples.[4] The best known example of this resolute, blinkered pursuit of hydroelectric development in contemporary

Brazil is the Belo Monte mega-dam, which began to operate in the Xingu indigenous reserve in 2015, despite years of well-organised and high-profile indigenous opposition and despite its location in the place that has served since the 1950s as the icon of Brazil's commitment to give sanctuary to indigenous peoples. Belo Monte will divert 80 per cent of the Xingu River's flow, devastating 1,500 square kilometres of forest and affecting the livelihood of 25,000 indigenous people, who live in the Xingu indigenous reserve (Irigaray 2014: 129). That this should be occurring in a country with a robust court system and constitution is due to the alignment of interests between government policy and elite political patronage groups linked to mining, logging and agribusiness industries.

When the ink dried on President Lula's large-scale infrastructure programme known as the 'PAC' in 2007, harnessing the hydroelectric potential of the Amazon drainage became a cornerstone in Brazilian economic policy. [5] The priority given to energy in this plan reflects the increasing reliance of the national economy on the export of raw materials. Extracting and transforming these materials profitably relies on a cheap and abundant supply of electricity (Fisher 2014: 138). Hydroelectric dams create the conditions in which primary industries can prosper. Through the PAC, the concessionaires who build and run hydroelectric dams benefit from fiscal incentives set up to support sustainable energy generation (such as 'PROINFA', implemented in 2002), and subsidised loans from the Brazilian National Development Bank (BNDES). By directing public investment into private initiatives the ruling party secures the patronage of industry (Galvão 2016: 94 cit. Sampaio Jr. 2007). In the case of the Juruena Complex, the consortium has effectively received every possible benefit and guarantee for their investment, such that the initial high costs of construction and the investment risk posed by indigenous opposition is far outweighed by the dams' long-term profitability. This is guaranteed by the government energy company Eletrobrás, which buys the dams' electricity for the first twenty years of operation. In one estimate the first five of the River Juruena's dams will generate an annual profit of 110 million reals for the consortium (Galvão 2016: 97).[6]

This meshing of vested interests puts projects effectively beyond the law or the constitution. Blairo Maggi, a Mato Grosso soya impresario, who branched into the energy sector in order to build the Juruena Complex (the dams neighbour his soya fields) epitomises this interlocking of public and private interests. He has been well known to the Enawenê since 1998, when he and his father bribed the Enawenê with their first aluminium boats and outboard motors so that they could build an illegal road cutting through the Enawenê's recently demarcated territory (Dal Poz 2006). The public prosecutor successfully halted that road, but in 2001 Maggi's entrepreneurialism brought him into the Enawenê's life once again, when his new offshoot company, Maggi Energia, commissioned viability studies for dams on the Juruena River. In 2003 Maggi was elected governor of Mato Grosso, a position he was able to use to ease the dam licensing process (his political status has since risen; in 2016 he became Minister for Agriculture in Michel Temer's government). In April 2008 the public prosecutor ordered the suspension of construction works on the Juruena Complex because of shortcuts taken in the environmental licensing process. Four months later this ruling was overturned in the Supreme Court on the grounds of a grave risk of 'rupture in the order, economy and public health of the nation' (Minister Gilmar Mendes cited in Galvão 2016: 59). This reflects a wider pattern in which restraining orders placed on the licensing and construction of dams on the grounds of human rights violations or non-compliance with environmental legislation are nullified by generic invocations of threat to the national economy or security. The Executive has even invoked state of exception legislation remaining from the military dictatorship era (Millikan 2014: 136). Concessionaires act with awareness of this total government backing, while the government agencies who should ensure environmental standards and indigenous participation, IBAMA and FUNAI, also become resigned to the inevitable. In this context of effective impunity, both public consultations with effected populations and environmental impact assessments are 'essentially theatrical exercises' (ibid.: 135).

In this situation of false consultations, environmental assessments funded by concessionaires, the corruption of bodies charged with environmental regulation, the impotence of the judiciary, and the unwillingness of the relevant government bodies to stand in the way of projects with such high-level backing, Amazonian peoples like the Enawenê lack effective allies. In their struggles, neither foreign nor national NGO interventions have been effective. They are easily dismissed as imperialist meddling in affairs that concern regional and national governance and prosperity (see e.g. Ramos 1998: 117; Conklin 2002: 1052). In 1989 a transnational show of charismatic protest was effective in halting the Kararaô dam (the predecessor of Belo Monte), because a newly democratised Brazil was seeking legitimacy on the international stage and depended on World Bank finance. Today funding for the dam is national (indeed, Brazil is also exporting its hydroelectricity ambitions by financing dams in neighbouring countries), and foreign intervention tends to delegitimise rather than strengthen local causes. Thus the anti-Belo Monte publicity provided by the director of *Avatar*, the sensationally popular sci-fi adventure film, had no similar impact to that of international celebrities such as Sting in 1989 (see Fisher 2014: 135 and T. Turner 1992), nor did Survival International's web-based campaign for the Enawenê, or the excellent feature written by Christina Lamb for the *Sunday Times Magazine* (Lamb 2009).

The upshot is that indigenous people like the Enawenê have to rely on their own political skills to negotiate a vastly expanded new political arena. There is no doubt that Enawenê foreign relations took on a new degree of complexity and intensity with the whole state apparatus aligned in the goal of exploiting hydraulic resources on the Juruena River. By 2008 their 'Who's Who' list included FUNAI personnel at the local, state and national level; the consortium's environmental and social representatives, its workers and Blairo Maggi; members of the office of the Public Prosecutor (MPF) in Cuiabá; and high level agents from environmental agencies (IBAMA, SEMA), the Ministry of Mining and Energy, and the National Institute of Cultural Patrimony (IPHAN). Besides this there were local mayoral authorities in the municipalities of Sapezal, Comodoro and Juína, with whom they negotiated the receipt of conservation incentive funds called ICMS Ecológico.

Whereas up until 1998 the Enawenê's peaceful relations with outsiders had been entirely mediated by the NGO OPAN, which had provided culturally informed assistance and healthcare provision, delivered in the village and in the Enawenê's own language, in the hydroelectric era they suddenly had to engage with multiple government agencies located in urban centres nearby and distant, with whom negotiations were conducted in Portuguese and in a foreign bureaucratised logic of meetings and documents. During the time of my fieldwork, the dams were the primary mover for meetings in town and the primary source of income in the form of out-and-out bribes, ill-defined acts of company and government largesse and, eventually, official compensation for environmental damages.

Both for the peoples of the Xingu, who are affected by Belo Monte, and for the Enawenê the status of such official or unofficial payouts – what the money compensates for – has been blurry. This is the case because information about the scale of damming and its impact is fragmented and contradictory (e.g. Cului 2014: 265). Compensation is officially justified as a mitigation for environmental impact under the rubric of 'Basic Environmental Plans', but the consortia deny, minimise or gloss over the impacts. In the Enawenê case this amounted to a farce in which the consortium repeatedly denied that the dams would have any impact on the Enawenê, Paresi, Nambikwara, Myky and Rikbaktsa at all because of the dams' location outside of demarcated indigenous territories and the small size of their reserves. These assurances contradicted the results of their own studies, and the Enawenê's observations of environmental degradation.[7] This inconsistent position enabled the company to use the official logic of mitigation to buy off opposition under a mountain of valued goods, which were not tied to environmental mitigation objectives. Of the six million reals of compensation paid out to the Enawenê, Rikbaktsa, Myky, Paresi and Nambikwara, only 150,000 reals (2.5%) was set aside for environmental monitoring (Almeida 2011: 61 n.53). The Enawenê and Xingu cases suggest that concessionaires have an interest in maintaining this obscurity so that environmental protection plans can be more easily used to buy off indigenous opposition.[8] The government has totally failed to prevent this cynical perversion of the consortia's responsibilities to mitigate environmental damages.

In the Enawenê case compensation was manifestly a payoff, taking the form of a shopping list of goods valued by the community, such as outboard engines, aluminium boats, vehicles and gasoline provision. Quite clearly compensation is designed to quash protests that pose an obstacle to the smooth operation and profitability of these developments. So what do the Enawenê do with these payoffs? And to what extent does receiving them suppress their will to oppose and obstruct developments?

Foreign Goods and What They Are Good For

From the American Northwest to Hawai'i and Highland Papua New Guinea, foreign wealth has been incorporated into local sumptuary economies like Yankwa, which have served as a powerful means to assimilate world historical change (see Nahum-Claudel 2016b). Marshall Sahlins (1985: 138) is the author most prominently associated with the argument that people assimilate the circumstances of history through their own world-making acts, although they unavoidably run new empirical risks in the process and thus become burdened with a world that imposes its own logic. The purchase of farmed fish for Yankwa's feasts in 2009, the ambivalent event with which this book opened, was one such attempt to accommodate constraining forces and to exert some control over agencies that determine human flourishing. Feeding the Yakairiti now required a diplomatic relationship with dam-building outsiders, who by damming the river and stopping the fish's migrations appropriated resources that belong to the Yakairiti. The Enawenê have been very explicit about this, always appealing to state agents and consortium

representatives for resources necessary to stave off the Yakairiti's predation. When the Enawenê eventually accepted the compensation deal in
a meeting held in March 2009, they immediately used it to buy fish for
the Yakairiti's feasts.

Whereas the Enawenê considered motorised navigation to be an
unambiguously positive development because it allowed men to fish
more regularly and further afield, and to arrive at their dam sites in
one day rather than two weeks of painful paddling, the purchase of
farmed fish was a gloomy necessity. Although novel, experimental and
thus tinged with a certain degree of excitement, it was an uncomfort-
able compromise, just a way of doing Yankwa in a compromised era.
The lack of fish put into question the fishermen's ability to master the
boundary between land and water, traps and fish, men and Yakairiti.
They were forced to seek out this mastery at the frontier between the
Enawenê community and the outside world (Nahum-Claudel 2012).
Anxious to feed the Yakairiti, whose alliance at the fishing dams had
failed to bring the fish shoaling into the traps, the Enawenê enrolled
outsiders in their project to continue Enawenê life via the satisfaction of
the Yakairiti. They sought communal payments or large quantities of a
single necessary resource to accomplish specific tasks in the ceremonial
calendar. Demands, always urgent, were thus made in the name of 'help
for the ritual'. Many other foreign goods are now taken for granted as
part of the Enawenê economy, but these individually acquired goods,
bought with pension or maternity benefits, or the salaries of healthcare auxiliaries, are separate from communal payments sought out from
institutions.[9]

A few examples of these payments in recent years demonstrate their
large scale as well as the Enawenê's entrepreneurialism in seeking out
new sources of support. In 2008 and 2009, in advance of the signing of
the final compensation deal, the hydroelectric dam consortium was the
main source of funds for gasoline to fuel the fleet of boats that would
carry the men to their encampments, offering 9,000 litres in 2008 and
6,000 in 2009 (Almeida 2011: 57, 84). In 2011, Yankwa's gasoline was
purchased with 55,000 reals from municipal environment funds (ICMS
ecologico), whose receipt the Enawenê had newly negotiated with the
mayoral authorities (Souza 2011: 32). In 2012 The National Institute of
Cultural Patrimony (IPHAN) purchased seventy tonnes of farmed fish
after being petitioned by the Enawenê to help. The agency was no doubt
happy to have seized on a tangible and immediate means to fulfil its
responsibility to safeguard the intangible cultural heritage of Yankwa.[10]

These appeals to different governmental agencies generally succeeded, first because they were made with such persistence and urgency,

and second because they chimed with the value outsiders place on ritual life as a sign of exemplary cultural vitality. The most urgent requests were for gasoline to enable Yankwa's departure and fish to enable its return, but gasoline was also requested to enable Lerohi and Saluma's fishing expeditions and for the amassing of palm fronds to thatch houses on the occasion of building a new village. In advance of Kateoko hundreds of balls of red cotton were requested from FUNAI to enable women to dance in newer, brighter red skirts. In advance of Lerohi large quantities of corn seed were sought with which to make the special corn oloniti that distinguishes the season. The final compensation package was also devoted to goods valued for their contribution to the ritual economy.

The Enawenê's list consisted of vehicles, boats and engines, and kitchen equipment for the large-scale catering that Yankwa required. Except for the communally owned trucks these goods would be owned by individuals who had proved that they needed them in order to fulfil Yankwa's relational duties. I witnessed the collective process of deliberation about how they would be distributed in the last week of my field-work in July 2009, when news came through the village payphone that the compensation was ready to be paid out. A microphone and amplifier, powered by a petrol generator, was set up in the arena. Someone called out: 'Women, teenagers, adults come; the dam's money has emerged, let us all talk together!' In this meeting and others held over two subse-quent nights, the procedure was to circle the village, allowing members of each household to make claims in turn. I saw that distribution was to be egalitarian, because claims were consistently made by individuals based on the prerogative to work for others and because, within the new technological baseline, the effort was to furnish everyone with the same tools. These extra goods would enable what the Enawenê con-sider to be the good life – that is, they would expand the production of plenty for Yankwa and the whole complex of values associated with it that I have explored in this book: the generation of desire and vitality through energised work; egalitarian, centripetal social dynamics based on affinal sociality; and the stabilisation of a human position in a pred-atory cosmos.

On 4 July 2009 the meeting grew gradually and people in each cat-egory took turns to take the microphone and make a case for why they should receive a particular good. As I understood it from listening to this meeting without having set eyes on the official plan, an original quota of thirty five boats and engines had been defined within the compensa-tion package. These had already been assigned to senior men who still lacked their own craft. Now additional claims were being put forward by men in their early twenties and even late teens. These men proved their eligibility by verbally filling their own boats with their dependent kindred. The new claims added up to a new total of fifty-one outboard engines. So that every adult man could have his boat, it was decided that two four-wheel drive vehicles would be forfeited from the existing project inventory.

For their part, women made equally ardent claims to the equipment that they needed for their daily manioc cookery, no matter that it was of much lesser monetary value; thirty-nine 125 litre pans, one hundred aluminium basins and one hundred water carriers had been listed. Again, in each house, senior women had already been named in the existing list but younger women now argued their case repeating similar pleas: their girl children needed a water carrier so that they could participate in manioc processing, and they needed pans of their own now that they had x number of future sons-in-law for whose clans they would need to make ketera. In short, claims were made via the evocation of Yankwa's relational duties, senior men and women taking precedence in line with their greater responsibilities, and younger people making claims based on their maturing responsibilities to fish and cook for others.

In order to continue to exact goods in the quantities desirable for a fast-growing population, the Enawenê needed to continually revive outsiders' recognition anew with trips to and from town to make claims 'for the ritual'. Although the consortium became an important source of resources for their ritual economy, the Enawenê also resisted the consortium's attempts to win their support for the dams through such largesse. They view the dams as the government's responsibility and they sought to sit at a table with high-level government officials and consortium representatives for a genuine consultation process. This opportunity was never offered to them because, as I have already explained, they were called to perform their participation only once the dams were under construction. Because of this disregard, the Enawenê were compelled to force the government to listen by disrupting regional traffic or delaying building works on the construction site. They learned that through such disruptions they could partially and temporarily overturn the government's indifference to their cause. I now turn to this dynamic in which defiance is a premise for diplomatic engagement.

'No Longer Time to Talk'

As we have seen, one aspect of Enawenê diplomacy is the incorporation of boats, gasoline and other tools (as well as the relationships that are their channels) into Yankwa. The other aspect is political warfare: road blocks, occupations, the nonviolent taking of hostages, and the burning of property. While the incorporative move belongs to the Yakairiti-oriented Yankwa, warfare is the preserve of Saluma. In this section I describe chronologically the lead up to Saluma's most drastic act, the attack and burning of the worksite of Telegráfica dam by the warriors of Saluma and the women of Kateoko, who accompanied them to gather the spoils from the raid. My aim is to show that there was no inevitability to this act, nor was it a spontaneous outburst of anger; rather it was the outcome of diplomatic breakdown over several months and it was strategically planned and calculated with the government's likely response in mind.

As I explained in the book's Introduction, Saluma, like Yankwa, refers at once to a season of the year, the form of ceremonialism associated with it and the temporary but absorbing identity it confers on the people who celebrate it. During Saluma, men dance in a circle around a single fire, lit by women, in the centre of the arena. Age and clan distinctions around this fire are irrelevant, since there is a global opposition between Saluma (men) and Kateoko (women). Every married couple in the village also has dyadic partnerships with other couples, with whom they reciprocate with gendered gifts and services along cross-sex lines: a man provides fish and honey (or spoils from town such as biscuits, pasta or soap) to between one and five other women with whom he is paired (called his *wakanalo*), while his wife receives the same from those women's husbands (who are called her *wakanale*) and in return gives them woven adornments made from cotton, which she has spun herself. Unlike Yankwa, Lerohi and Kateoko, who all wear sun diadem feather headdresses that are icons of humanity and are bestowed by others, the men of Saluma wear their own black curassow or eagle feather headdresses; and instead of playing flutes they carry bows, arrows and clubs.

Saluma and Kateoko take place seasonally but Saluma also danced and sang when events required it 'out of season'. Thus Saluma always danced on the day before Yankwa were to depart for the fishing dams, in order to seek the protection of the celestial ancestors, both for those who remained short on defences in the village (with most of the men away) and for the fishermen who exposed themselves to illness and injury in their arduous dam construction task. In 2008–2009 Saluma also danced as men prepared to burn the worksite of Telegráfica; for the conciliatory meetings the Enawenê attended in Brasilia a month later; and in preparation for municipal meetings about land use reform, which pitted the Enawenê against powerful landowners, who wished to see less land protected and more of it classified for agricultural use. On all these occasions, Saluma danced before departure and upon return. Its verses were improvised to describe the events envisaged, and the happenings that occurred, while choruses evoked the predatory potencies of the harpy eagle and jaguar, and of war clubs and enchanted arrows animated by blessing shamans to strike fear in the enemy.

Incorporative and defiant moves in Enawenê diplomacy are thus to an extent given by the Enawenê's annual calendar, which requires everyone's energies to be focused on Yankwa's orchestration from January through to June, and frees and readies men to travel to meetings and road blocks most intensively in September and October. However, there is also flexibility within the annual calendar, with switches occurring between ritual modalities to allow men to block the road in protest in May, or to build a new flute house for Yankwa at the height of Saluma in October. The events surrounding the burning of Telegráfica demonstrate this seasonal temporality of defiance and cooperative incorporation.

On 4 September 2008, I returned to Halataikwa to start my second stint of fieldwork, having left towards the end of Lerohi a month before. I found Saluma dancing throughout the night and the community talking of the threat posed by damming with great singularity of intention, with long men's meetings in the arena, which doubled as collective arrow-crafting sessions and battle-strategy discussions. These continued as Kateoko took over the arena in the middle of September. On 2 October 2008, Saluma interrupted Kateoko to burn the flute house that had served Yankwa in the previous season in order that a fresh flute house could be constructed. This was a response to the warnings of one of the village's shamans, who communicated the Yakairiti's growing dissatisfaction, and their eagerness to drink again. Many people grumbled that the house should be replaced only at the time of the fresh corn harvest, which was still two months off. There were also worries that the corn harvest would never materialise, since there had been so little rain. Perhaps because of the general anxiety and ferment in the air at this time, Yankwa arose to build a new flute house nonetheless. Over three days, a bigger and better flute house was constructed in the place where the other had stood, and the flutes of Yankwa and the routine of nightly ketera-drinking briefly resumed. Once this work was complete, Kateoko danced briefly, just for a couple of days, and then Saluma interrupted once more on 9 September for the final preparation to burn Telegráfica. The warriors, accompanied by some of the women of Kateoko, left early on 11 October to attack, burn and loot the dam's worksite. Throughout their day's absence, the rest of the women of Kateoko animated the plaza with their song and dance, ready to gather the spoils of the attack that evening.

Like other warrior collectives, Saluma cultivate solidarity, focus and ancestral potency through self-decoration, shamanic incantations, song, dance and arrow-making (e.g. Harrison 1993: 114; Gordon 2006: 212–17). While Saluma danced, preparing for the raid, my adoptive mother, Kawalinero-asero, told me to stay inside the house: 'Enawenê men are tough Chloe, Yankwa and Saluma too; they don't feel anything for you, they'll beat you, they don't feel pain for you'. She was warning me of the men's suspension of understanding to which all women should be sensitive, but to which I, as a foreign woman living among them during a time of fervent enmity, should be especially mindful. When they returned from the raid, those who had gone seemed satisfied, and somewhat impressed, with the degree to which this subjective cultivation had been effective. They commented that construction workers at the dam had been 'struck dumb' *(makanase)* and had 'cried in fear' *(tiyina, merena)*. They also observed that these workers had been willing to leave behind their most treasured possessions. Family photographs, mobile phones and identity documents had all been abandoned in their rush to escape. The workers' fear confirmed the efficacy of Saluma and the potency of the Enawenê's celestial ancestors. For their part, the workers, who had left their families to earn a wage working under precarious conditions at a remote construction site, must have responded to what they would have apprehended as an attack by 'isolated Indians' *(indio isolado)*, Indians who were still 'fierce warriors' *(indio guerreiro, indio bravo)* to repeat some of the stereotypes available in the Brazilian public imagination. One young Enawenê man told me about a confrontation he had with the boss at the site. Since he spoke fair Portuguese, it had been decided that it would be his job to command all the workers to board buses in order to leave the site so that they would not be harmed by the fire. He was realising a strategy that had been planned in advance to ensure that there would be no fatalities (another such strategy was to immediately topple the radio communications tower to prevent a counter-attack and subsequent escalation). As he was issuing this order to the frightened workers, the boss had pleaded with him, 'Wait', he had said, 'let's have a meeting, let's talk!' The boss asked to speak to a specific Enawenê man with whom he had become friendly during the latter's reconnaissance trips to the dam to check the advance of construction as well as to procure gifts of gasoline from the on-site pumps. The young man described the boss as a pitiable figure. He was well aware that the boss felt betrayed, because a former relationship of bantering approximation had been suddenly replaced by deaf resoluteness. Despite his sensitivity, the young man ignored the boss's plea, simply repeating his order that he should call on the bus drivers to evacuate the workers immediately, before more warriors arrived to set the site on fire.

This young man's recollection reveals his self-awareness about Saluma's purposeful recasting of subjectivity. The approximately 120 warriors had continued to cultivate this resoluteness right up until their invasion. As well as dancing throughout the night of 10 October they had also stopped on their approach to the site to don their black curassow feather headdresses, smear their bodies with mud, blacken their faces, and bind bark ropes around their torsos and arms. The man who told me about these final preparations concluded that they had made themselves 'dangerous' (*kiwini*) and looked just like Yankwa's fishermen do when they meet hosts for the first time on the bank of Halataikwa's special port. On this occasion they similarly stopped for last minute self-decoration to ensure their other-worldly wildness. As we know from Chapter 2, the returning fishermen brandish 'spears' tipped only with smoked fish, and their clash with the hosts allows for the venting of worldly jealousies but contains this aggression within accepted bounds. Recall also that the clash between fishermen and hosts is but the first encounter in a choreographed series of confrontations and speeches that draw the wild incomers back into the centre of the polity, assuring their surrender and their taming. The incomers wear their curassow feather headdresses so that these can be removed by hosts and replaced with sun diadems, just as they smear mud and black genipap dye, so that these can be gradually substituted with red annatto. Although the attack on Telegráfica was not equivalent to Yankwa's elaborately staged ritual of diplomatic incorporation, it was nonetheless an act of contained aggression that remained within the limits set by the community in the previous months, during which the decision had been made that no one should be harmed, since the aim was to burn the construction site and not to start a war that would bring reprisals. This act was not an end in itself, but was the premise for conciliation with the government, who the Enawenê construed as the ultimate owners of the burnt infrastructure.

As the retrospective statement cited in the opening pages of this chapter makes clear – 'The government is the owner, "let's burn" we decided' – the attack was necessary because the government 'did not respond' to their repeated attempts to participate in the planning process. This act of destruction was the outcome of a painfully ambivalent relationship with the other parties involved in negotiations, not only the consortium representatives and the various government agencies, but also the other indigenous groups who had patronised their less-worldly Enawenê neighbours with accusations of ignorance and troublemaking. This concrescence of angry frustration had been channelled into singularity of purpose through Saluma's dawn and dusk meetings, its dancing and chanting, and arrow-making sessions. By burning cars, gasoline, urban infrastructure, motors and machinery, the Enawenê 'threw away' (*halatene*) the dam and the goods that abounded on the construction site, but which had still failed to materialise in their own village. The dominant idiom of burning, trashing and laying waste suggests that this act was a redress for the state's unmet obligations to the Enawenê.[11]

Before I turn to the sequel to this act of political warfare, which did make the Enawenê essential interlocutors, if only because of the loss of profits they could cause, let me review the significant events leading up to it over one year. What I aim to show is that the Enawenê see themselves as the government's necessary interlocutors rather than as disempowered subjects. The government and consortium, on the other hand, tend to act on the basis that the Enawenê occupy a powerless position. I rely on Juliana de Almeida's thorough chronological narrative of Enawenê negotiations surrounding the dams, both for events that occurred prior to the start of my fieldwork in January 2008, and for clarifications of the content of meetings held and documents sent in 2008 and 2009, which Almeida, through her role as OPAN representative, often witnessed first-hand, while I more often gleaned events in a murky but revealing third-hand from people who remained back in the village.

Almeida's report agrees with my own impression that the dams only became a palpable reality in September 2007, when a group of fishermen came upon the worksite of Telegráfica. Even though the Enawenê had heard about the dams from FUNAI in 2003 they seem to have been confident up until this point that construction would not begin without their consent. When they received a visit from a consultant whose company had been hired to conduct an anthropological survey for the dam licensing process in 2006, they sent her away because they rejected the dams and thus had no interest in discussing details with this stranger. In December 2006 they attended a meeting at a Paresi village, where they heard about a compensation deal and were taken to see a hydroelectric centre in operation in an effort to convince them of the dams' minor impact (Almeida 2011: 47–48). After this meeting, the Enawenê drafted a document to explain their position to the consortium. It was translated by a man who had worked with the Enawenê for years (as an employee of OPAN and then FUNAI) and who was now employed by the consortium, who hoped his insider knowledge would smooth negotiations with the Enawenê. Like their actions up to this point, the letter's closing words show that before they saw construction progressing with their own eyes they believed that their stand against the dams would be heeded.

> We are here – we are the Enawenê nawe. We have been thinking, we want very much that compensation should be permanent. We are not joking. We do not want to eat from fish farms, this is difficult for us. If you build a dam, the dam is forever [i.e. the money should be forever as well] ... Do not build the dams alone, we want to be present, we do not want to be tricked. (cited in Almeida 2011: 52)

Once the fishermen had seen the dams, the community faced the destabilising realisation that they would be ignored, and the following community letter was sent to the public prosecutor and to government agencies responsible for environmental protection.

> We do not agree with the initiation of dam construction works. We have not yet finished discussing the subject. We have not had any response from the document that we sent, yet the works have begun. It would be a big problem for us if the fish ran out. We have already sought out Blairo Maggi in Cuiabá and he told us that he would come to our village to converse but he has not come. ... We wish there to be a big meeting before works begin.[12]

In this dignified discourse, addressed to the relevant authorities, the Enawenê present themselves as necessary partners. This is a clear expression of the Enawenê's belief that their point of view potentially could be taken seriously by the consortium, and also that they consider it desirable and possible to engage in negotiations. In the silence that reigned afterwards, and with the absence of any indication that they were being listened to, in December 2007 the entire adult male population occupied the worksite of Telegráfica for the first time, holding the 350 workers there hostage (Almeida 2011: 54). As their official statement said, they did this because the works had unjustly begun without their knowledge and because they had received no response to the protest letters they had sent (ibid.). The result of this occupation was a meeting on 11 January 2008 at which all the government entities they had previously addressed were present, in addition to representatives of the Nambikwara, Myky, Rikbaktsa and Paresi peoples (ibid.: 55). At the meeting they were appeased with the promise that independent studies would be conducted to assess the dams' environmental impact (they never were), and they were sent away with nine thousand litres of gasoline, which was enough to secure Yankwa's departure for the fishing dams the nout month. It was at this point, at the end of January 2008, that I arrived in Juína to begin my fieldwork and met twenty Enawenê´men ready to return to the village with their cargo of gasoline. This placatory gift effectively solved an immediate problem for Yankwa's leaders, who now focused on their obligations to fish for the hosts.

However, by May 2008, once the fishermen had returned laden with fish and had danced for the first of the two host clans, the Enawenê, along with representatives from other indigenous groups, immediately returned to the task of overturning the government's indifference. They blocked the bridge over the Juruena River just as they had done at the same point in 2007. The collective protest statement began: 'We have already sent documents to all the authorities to resolve our problems, but nobody has resolved them or paid any attention'. It goes on to list diverse community problems that are failures of governance related to healthcare assistance, the need for impact studies and compensation for the dams, and the lack of redistribution of municipal environmental protection funds to indigenous communities. The statement ends by listing the relevant authorities whom the Enawenê, Rikbaktsa, Cinta-Larga, Arara, Myky, Irantxe, Kayabi, Apiaca and Mundurucu people wished to meet with in order to resolve the blockade (ibid.: 59). The outcome was another meeting held in June 2008 in the nearby town of Brasnorte.

Twenty Enawenê representatives attended this meeting, where the consortium's Enawenê-speaking representative offered to renegotiate the benefits the Enawenê would receive through the Basic Environmental Plan, so that it was more favourable to them (Almeida 2011: 60–61). The Enawenê refused to negotiate privately, in the absence of the other affected groups, thus resisting the consortium's attempts to transform negotiations into a depoliticised, 'under the table' deal (ibid.). Days later, on 11 July, they were called to a meeting, which, this time, did involve high-level government agents, both from the planning and research arm of the government energy sector (Empresa de Pesquisa Energética, EPE) and from Brasilia's FUNAI offices. However, to their dismay, rather than being a resolution of the current crisis – namely, the advancing construction of the Juruena Complex of dams, which was still without Enawenê agreement – the government presented an entirely new threat. They were seeking permission to enter Enawenê territory in order to conduct viability studies for further dams, one of which was located at some rapids right at the centre of the Enawenê's demarcated territory. According to Almeida (2011: 64) and in keeping with what I heard upon the delegation's return, the Enawenê representatives were presented with a map pinpointing sixty-six sites for future hydroelectric plants, all across the Juruena and Aripuana River basins. They were suddenly confronted with the damming of their entire river system. Using promises and threats, EPE attempted to cow them into agreeing to allow the viability studies. It was implied that there was hope for the land demarcation process the community had been pursuing for years if they allowed the researchers access, but if they did not the process would not advance and they would additionally lose the right to receive any compensation for the existing dams of the Juruena Complex. The Enawenê refused to submit to this intimidation and returned to the village, angry, disgusted at their treatment and panicked about the scale of the damming.

After this meeting the Enawenê decided to accept compensation for the five dams that were already under construction upstream of their territory on the Juruena River, but to reject the rest of the dams of the Juruena Complex (at this point, a further three were licensed and three more were envisaged) as well as the many more revealed by EPE's map. However, at the beginning of September 2008, in a meeting held by FUNAI with the five indigenous groups who stood to be compensated for the Juruena Complex, the thirty Enawenê representatives present were pressured into signing their names to the meetings minutes, which stated their acceptance of a compensation package of six million reals for all eight dams, of which the Enawenê and Nambikwara would receive shares of one and half million each, and the Paresi, Myky and Rikbaktsa shares of one million each. It was after this turbulent and decisive month in which Enawenê representatives had been pressured, tricked and bribed in a string of tense meetings that I returned to the village to find Saluma in full swing. The sense I gained was of confusion about the number of dams and the status of studies and licenses, and revulsion at the way the terms of the discussion continually shifted, undermining the community's attempt to position themselves firmly in relation to the proposals. It seemed to the Enawenê (and it was indeed the case) that the payment of compensation was ever deferred to the next meeting, while the number of dams increased. It was this sense of having been routinely disrespected that led to a community decision to boycott further meetings, and embrace a purely oppositional stance. What I hope to have made clear in this narrative is that this positioning was not only a principled rejection of the dams on the grounds of the importance of riverine resources; it was also a moral response to the quality of their interactions with consortium representatives, government agents and other indigenous groups.

Even after this closure, one further attempt was made to open dialogue. Ten Enawenê men who were in Juína to vote in municipal elections defied the boycott to travel to a meeting scheduled by the consortium in Cuiabá on 6 October. As they said upon their return, they had gone to 'hear what the company had to say' in case they 'spoke well'. In other words, this was a final opportunity to turn the tides. Instead it strengthened their resolve because of the accusatory and patronising treatment they again received. When they refused to agree that the compensation would be for eight dams rather than five, the company's environmental and social representative spoke rashly and aggressively, accusing the Enawenê of being dupes to the environmental rhetoric of OPAN representatives, who were also present at the meeting. As the Enawenê delegation walked out of the meeting room, members of the other indigenous groups repeated the insult. As one Enawenê man later told me, they had responded that they were wise and knew that the dams would cause the fish's death. They thus positioned themselves as alone in holding fast to a principled, far-sighted position. Almeida's interpretation (2011: 76–77) has prompted me to reconsider this self-affirming stance as not only a proud self-affirmation but also as an ambivalent, defensive response to their exclusion from the emerging consensus, which allied the other indigenous groups with the consortium and government and isolated them as the delinquent faction. Almeida suggests that the divisiveness of compensation, both internal to the community and interethnic, was an important factor in the Enawenê's eventual acceptance of the compensation deal for all eight dams in March 2009. For a people whose internal political life stresses collaborative and consensual deliberation and thoughtful, measured speech, being positioned as the ignorant party responsible for persistently derailing negotiations, and being subject to ostracism, must have been troubling. Nonetheless, at this point in September 2009, the effect of this final humiliation was that the whole community was galvanised in the decision that it was no longer time to talk. Now, at last, there was complete unity in the community and total singularity of intention.

The Enawenê's discursive emphasis on listening for beautiful speech – on wanting to be heard and understood – and their clarity about times for talk and times for silent withdrawal resonates with Simon Harrison's pioneering work on traditional warfare in the middle Sepik of Papua New Guinea. Among Avatip people warfare is part of a dynamic inter-relationship between communicative exchange and its withdrawal. Talk implies a degree of self-other identification, empathy and cooperation, while the cessation of communication is an active closure and implies covering up all these qualities that are basic to human relationships (Harrison 1989, 1993). This chimes with the Enawenê's affirmation that they went to war when 'it was no longer time to talk' or – and it comes to the same – that they ceased talking when they decided that it was time to go to war. Talk had to be founded on some measure of mutual recognition. This had been denied over and over again. Harrison's analysis appeals to me because it treats aggression as a form of relationality – as a way for 'political actors to affect and be consequential to one another'

(Harrison 1993: 21). Just so, the Enawenê's blockades and occupations, and finally their well-planned attack, confronted and sought to overturn the government's indifference to their own position.

A Diplomatic Reopening

In the days following the warriors' return women feared aggressive retribution from the government (bombs being dropped on the village) but men quietened their fears. The raid had been calculated with the likely response in mind and, given what the Enawenê had learned in recent years about the government, they expected to be called to another meeting. They were met with a disquieting silence: no visits and no calls on the solar-powered village payphone, which had just been installed. Eager to know how their acts were registering on others, a group of men went to spy on the dam, remaining hidden and using looted handheld radios to listen in on what was being said by consortium officials and police, who were surveying the site. Then, having still received no solicitations, five men went to Juína to hear what the 'iñoti were saying and thinking'. They returned with printouts of regional news reports, which estimated that the raid had caused fifteen million reals in damages, and with the promise that eighty-four community members would go to Brasilia for a high-level meeting with the authorities. At the time, I understood that this meeting had been called by FUNAI, but Almeida (2011: 80) reveals that the Enawenê themselves requested it and demanded the attendance of certain high-level officials, including the presidents of FUNAI and IBAMA, and the attorney general. It was also they who stipulated the large size of their own delegation. This represents a familiar strategy on two fronts; first, the Enawenê always attempted to send the maximum number of representatives to any meeting or road block, which they justified according to the need to assert themselves by sheer force of presence. Second, they had been adept at manipulating the geography of power and they knew that encounters with powerful officials based in Brasilia could be immediately fruitful, circumventing the usual bureaucratic channels – the documents they always sent and which got no reply (see Nahum-Claudel 2016a).

It is clear that when it occurred this meeting was conceived by the Enawenê as an encounter between equal powers, which took place, appropriately, at the centre of the nation. Almeida (2011: 81), who participated in this meeting in early November, recorded several interesting details, which were unknown to me in the village and confirm the Enawenê's conciliatory intention in orchestrating this meeting. First, the Enawenê wore their sun diadem feather headdresses, whose significance as icons of civilised human life I demonstrated in Chapter 5. They were also unarmed, whereas at various meetings with the consortium, which they expected to be adversarial, they had carried bows and arrows. Secondly, they refused to allow the consortium representative to enter the meeting room. He was forced to wait ignominiously outside, despite having funded the Enawenê's coach travel, luxurious hotel accommodation and ample personal spending money. Just as they had previously blocked the consortium's attempts to use money and goods to depoliticise negotiations, now also they insisted on the political rather than pecuniary nature of what was at stake – it was a matter of the government's responsibility.

From the reports I heard upon the delegation's return it seems that those in the meeting room acquiesced to all their demands, some of which were not directly connected to the dams: they would get a FUNAI 'chief of post', whose sole job would be to attend to their administrative needs, as well as a house in Juína, so that they would no longer have to sling their hammocks in communal shelters in the field behind the FUNAI office. The president of FUNAI had personally promised to do everything in his power to stop the dams' construction. Clearly what mattered was that they had been listened to and also hosted. This alone was evidence that the position they commanded with respect to FUNAI, and in relation to the dam-building impresario Blairo Maggi, had shifted in their favour. They had sat at the table in Brasilia and Maggi had received a smaller Enawenê delegation personally in Cuiabá. It seemed less important that he had made them no promises. What seemed crucial in Enawenê discourses was that the government would now work for them. Whereas the dams had been the Enawenê's problem, a burden that had consumed the community's energies intensely since June, they now believed – or certainly wanted to believe – that they now shared this burden. 'Now FUNAI has a big problem' as one man put it. The dams had now become a shared problem and they would no longer be isolated and ostracised in their opposition. People were noticeably light, full of a relief that had been too long in coming.

Those who had travelled to Brasilia told stories about the luxurious farmstead-style hotel in which they had been housed and taken their meals, and of the money they had been given to spend: three 100 real notes each – large denomination notes that are rare, blue and crisp. However, after a few days of much needed relief, misgivings began to be voiced. People said that FUNAI had deliberately covered up their conquest by hiding them away at the out of town hotel, far from media attention. Their cynicism was well placed. The meeting was a performance of acquiescence intended to impress the Enawenê. The promises made were immediately disavowed; the attendees claiming that they had been made under duress, even though the Enawenê had been unarmed and dressed for diplomacy.[13] Soon after this meeting the regional FUNAI office in Juína did contract an employee dedicated to Enawenê needs, but the town house, the impact studies and the commitment to apply pressure to halt the dams' progress were all empty promises. Although the Enawenê voiced their doubts about the meeting's efficacy they did not do so with much commitment, since the focus of life was now back in the central arena.

The remaining women had continued to dance Kateoko while the mixed delegation was in Brasília. Upon its return Saluma had danced for one night, tying soaps, bags of pasta and biscuits to their bodies for the women of Kateoko to take. The strong winds, rain and thunder that inaugurate the rainy season had begun during their absence, so the community's energies turned to the nuptial flight of the delicious leafcutter ants and the profitable fishing with the live queens as bait. The catch was good and the Enawenê said that, though it was early for Yankwa to begin, the Yakairiti were eager to drink. With the new flute house already constructed in the ferment that preceded the attack on Telegráfica, everything was ready in mid November for Yankwa's flutes to be played for Kawinalili clan, the first of the new hosts for the 2009–2010 biennial. Everyone was saturated with iñoti concerns after the months of anxiety and mounting tension, and all were enjoying resting, bathing and, in short, resuming day-to-day life. In any case, while Enawenê men had been free to concern themselves with iñoti matters while Kateoko danced, it is quite simply impossible to actively sustain such intensive foreign relations during Yankwa, which requires the whole community to be oriented inwards. Whereas Saluma and Kateoko are made for travel, for the assimilation of unexpected events and the incitement to assertive, outward-focused action, Yankwa draws the community into their own plaza and into the diplomacy between clans, and between humans and Yakairiti, which is staged there.

Conclusion

On 30 March 2009, in the middle of their fishing expeditions, the Enawenê attended the meeting at which they finally accepted 1.5 million reals in compensation for the eight dams of the Juruena Complex. The consortium's standing as the single dependable source of fuel for Enawenê fishing expeditions was an important factor in their acceptance.

The ritual economy now assumed the availability of resources that were most readily acquired from the hydroelectricity consortium. I travelled to this meeting along with some of the fishermen at Maxikyawina's dam at the point when we still held out hope that the fish might shoal into the traps. I have analysed the strategic skill shown by Enawenê representatives at this meeting, where they signed to accept the compensation deal on the condition that a permanent compensation agreement would be negotiated in the future (Nahum-Claudel 2016a: 489–92). This had been their consistent demand since 2006, on the logical grounds that if the dams were to permanently impact upon Enawenê livelihood then compensation should also be eternal, returning every month like the salaries that support iñoti livelihoods. In 2012, the one-off payment of a million and a half having run out, the Enawenê indigenous association began to receive a regular monthly income of 20,000 reals. Upon my visit in 2013 I learnt that this had been a compromise figure: the Enawenê had asked for 100,000 while the consortium had wanted to offer just 8,000, on the logic of a thousand per dam. This long-pursued goal of permanent compensation had been secured via familiar means. At the end of Yankwa in July of 2012 they had occupied the construction site of the sixth dam (the first five dams had begun generating electricity), occasioning a meeting in Brasilia in which permanent compensation was promised.

In the end, the Enawenê are consistently successful in exacting money and goods from the government and consortium, while they fail in the underlying political goals that motivate them to demand this recognition from foreigners. The pattern has been set at this frontier; money is available while political participation is denied. The letters written by the Enawenê in 2006–2007 suggest that they began with the assumption that their position would be of importance to the government. Their actions in 2008–2009 suggest that they learned that indifference is the default position. Recognition must be coerced. They have also learned that expert research on environmental impact is a sham, and they have come to see all research as a vanguard for exploitation. If there is no political will to protect the environment, or their economy which depends on it, then they must make the best of the situation and share in some of the enormous wealth that these dams bring.

Given the extremely constrained outcomes of these negotiations, the use of the term diplomacy might seem utopian, glossing over the reality of domination and internal colonialism, and talking as if the Enawenê could exist outside the state that has demarcated their territory and determines the viability of their livelihood. I use the term because it captures something of the Enawenê's side of the equation, namely their own empowerment and their implicit claim to sovereignty, which to some extent they manage to impose on those who treat them as disempowered subjects (albeit with an unpredictable, 'warlike' nature). This begs the question: what would it take for Amerindians to be recognised as diplomats, to be consulted in genuine negotiations over national interest? Under what conditions could the meeting that the Enawenê called in Brasilia have been a genuine negotiation undertaken in good faith, rather than a simulation of diplomacy on the part of government officials? How obvious it should have been to a government with decades of experience negotiating with Amazonian leaders painted with black genipap dye and wielding clubs and bows that the Enawenê attended this meeting not as intimidating warriors but as receptive, conciliatory diplomats. And how tragic that the state prefers to manage crises with cowardly acquiescence and the demonstration of largesse, rather than include people like the Enawenê in the political process. While the Enawenê strive to understand the Brazilian political system in order to manipulate it for their advantage – this is after all the diplomat's aim – the Brazilian political system shows no such reciprocal interest.

When it emerged in the late 1980s with such force in Latin American nations, the discourse of indigenous rights intended to open a space for the negotiation of identity and sovereignty within nation states. The identity part has grown while the sovereignty part has not; in Brazil today there is relentless resource exploitation, the demarcation of indigenous territories has all but ceased, and constitutional protections for Brazil's indigenous minority prove to be meaningless in the face of development prerogatives, which are a mask for elite enrichment. Meanwhile film and heritage projects multiply. The National Institute of Cultural Patrimony was busy inventorying Yankwa in the very year that the hydroelectric dams rendered its essential technology ineffective. To speak of the diplomatic artfulness of a tiny population of Brazilian Amerindians seems optimistic in such times and yet the boldness of the men who act as emissaries for their community seems to warrant it, as does the performance of civility in Enawenê collective life.

Epilogue: History Repeats Itself

Just before I left Halataikwa in July 2009, every man, woman and child in the village had signed or fingerprinted a community letter requesting that a road be built linking their village to the region's main road. This would alleviate the stress of acquiring gasoline for the long river trip to reach town, allow sick patients to reach treatment more quickly and provide access for farmed fish to be delivered directly to the village. By chance, when I next returned to Juína in May 2010, I found the leaders of all but one of the nine clans at FUNAI headquarters for a meeting about the road. They told me that Yankwa had been put on hold so that each of the clans could be represented in this systematic way. I was tutored in the changes that had been made to the way foreign relations were managed: 'the young men are not in charge. We clan leaders are in charge today. Can you see any young men here?' In 2008–2009 it was men in their twenties and thirties (those who had made particular efforts to learn Portuguese) who attended meetings on behalf of the community. Their clan affiliations were irrelevant. Elder men denied that this work made them true leaders. They said that these young men were only sent as 'little leaders', *(aolexi)* or 'employees' *(empregado)*, to enable Yankwa's song masters to continue orchestrating everyday cere-monial life. This was based on the decision that Yankwa should not be interrupted by foreign concerns.

In 2010, by contrast, Yankwa had been put on hold to allow clan heads to attend a meeting about the desired road. The implication was that foreign affairs were to be managed with the same gravitas as cere-monial life, by the same judicious, elder leaders. This policy change had been enabled by the recent deaths of two elderly leaders. The men who now stepped into their shoes were in their forties and fifties – they were rising song masters and also had some grasp of Portuguese and of the machinations of government. As such, they bridged the gap that had formerly existed between men in their twenties and thirties, who had been delegated foreign affairs, and elders in their sixties and seventies, who had led ceremonial life. This shift in policy and personnel indicated the extent to which foreign affairs were now considered to be of central concern to Yankwa.

Three years later, in July 2013, when I again returned to Halataikwa, it was by chance that I arrived just two weeks after the long-awaited road had been completed. The new road starts from the opposite bank of the Iquê River and runs approximately 40 km in a north-westerly direction to join up with the regional road that links Juína with Vilhena in the neighbouring state of Rondonia. The Enawenê were eager to tell me about the long process through which the road had been acquired. It now felt like a familiar story. The road was the outcome of long dip-lomatic struggle, and ultimately of Saluma's defiance. I had seen the community petition for the road signed and fingerprinted just before my departure in 2009. It had never received a response. The Environment

Ministry (IBAMA) had refused to license the road. Although the Enawenê did not say so, I knew that IBAMA could not legally sanction this road, since it cut through the Iquê Ecological Reserve, which lies adjacent to the Enawenê's demarcated territory on its northeastern side. As a federal ecological reserve it is, at least in principle, inviolable. When the Enawenê got to a pitch of frustration with IBAMA's perceived inflexibility, they 'threw away' IBAMA by burning down its dilapidated brick research base inside the reserve, and then began to clear a road using their own chainsaws. Ten Enawenê representatives were then flown to Brasilia for urgent meetings. In those meetings they reported arguing that the reserved land was their own to build gardens and pathways on as they chose, and that IBAMA had in any case neglected its duty to protect the land, which had already been invaded by loggers and settlers. Upon their return from Brasilia, the mayor of Juína provided funds and heavy machinery for the road's construction (I do not know whether he did so with IBAMA approval), while Enawenê men provided much of the labour for free.

One of the young men of my household showed me a video he had shot on his new smartphone of Juína's mayor and his councillors in Halataikwa to inaugurate the road just the previous week. In the clip the local politicians were surrounded by Enawenê men as the mayor attempted to boast of the 80,000 reals he had spent on the Enawenê's road. The cluster of men around him were neither listening attentively nor celebrating the achievement of a long-awaited goal as the mayor must have wished; rather they were already complaining of the poor quality of the unpaved road.

At the end of my visit I left in a truck that was taking patients to town for medical treatment. On the same day, the new possibilities afforded by the road were being tested by two men who were going to Sapezal to buy 200 sacks of young corn for Lerohi's special oloniti, spending 3,000 reals' of the communal funds held by the Enawenê indigenous association. On the same morning, two large, open trucks filled with excited women were leaving to pick cotton from a farmer's fields in the municipality of Sapezal. They looked forward to the adventure and also to having ample cotton to spin during the upcoming season of Kateoko, which would begin after the end of Lerohi. In October 2014, I read an online news report about the urgent start of maintenance and gravelling work on the Enawenê's access road, which would put an end to a nine day road block and toll station that the Enawenê had mounted (Maia 2014).

Notes

1. Interview with an Aweresese clan member held on 31 October 2008 (see Almeida 2011: 79).
2. See Ramos (1998) for an overview of FUNAI's role.
3. The dams are called Cidezal, Parecis, Rondon, Telegráfica and Sapezal.
4. The claim that these dams are a sustainable source of electricity rests on the limited calculus of greenhouse gas emissions, which are calculated by comparison to the burning of fossil fuels. Even according to this limited calculus, dams' green credentials have been challenged on the grounds that, first, flooded reservoirs act as methane factories (Millikan 2014 cit. Fearnside and Pueyo 2012) and, second, dams' long-term productivity depends on the maintenance of river levels, which are vulnerable to climatic change.
5. PAC stands for Programa de Aceleração do Crescimento, Growth Acceleration Programme.
6. Based on research with social movements resisting Belo Monte's construction, Taylor Klein (2015: 1139) has argued that this neoliberal order potentially increases opportunities for citizens to make demands on the state, since they can now ask the state to force the consortium to act for the public good. This argument ignores the intermeshing of government and corporate interests, and the environmental and social degradation caused by dams, which circumscribes what he judges to be the kinds of 'public goods' that citizens can demand.
7. One of these environmental impact reports concludes that the Enawenê are rendered 'extremely vulnerable' by the works. The reports' substantive contents are ignored by the consortium, who cite them only as proof-positive of legality, social responsibility and accountability.
8. In the Belo Monte case too, little to no attempt has been made for compensation to live up to its stated aim of environmental and social protection. In 2012, when the dam's construction was already well underway, a permanent plan for compensation and mitigation was still absent. Facing urgent demands from affected communities, the consortium Norte Energia hastily launched an 'Emergency plan' to placate the solidary opposition of indigenous groups. In this plan, each group received monthly payouts of 30,000 reals to spend on shopping lists they dictated initially to FUNAI employees and later, once FUNAI's intermediation ended, directly to consortium employees. Cohn (2014) describes the Xikrin discourse in which, once they accepted the consortium's generosity, continued protest was deemed hypocritical and immoral by a majority within the community. Cohn (2014: 268) suggests that the consortium essentially usurped the protective role that the state had neglected to play. In a situation of fear and uncertainty about the dam's impact on their livelihood, the Xikrin were presented with promises of good schools, healthcare and support with their productive activities – everything they had long demanded and never received from the government. Heurich comes to similar conclusions based on his experience with the Araweté, for whom the reception of these emergency payments made the consortium appear as 'the great donor of universal and infinite gifts of merchandise' (Heurich 2015; see also Watts 2014).
9. The foreign goods that are a routine part of the Enawenê economy are as follows: machetes, axes, and hoes for garden work and firewood gathering; aluminium pans, basins, and skillets have largely replaced clay pots. Balls of red cotton, burgundy polyester, and thick white cotton are used for weaving skirts, garters and hammocks

respectively, reducing the need to grow and spin cotton; soap, mirrors, combs, scissors and tweezers are necessary for grooming; flip-flops to protect the feet, and cheap shorts and T-shirts to protect the body from gnats in the garden. Men like to have better clothes and closed shoes for trips to town; fishing tackle and varied hooks and flies have long enabled experimentation and diversification in their fishing techniques; and diving masks have helped make dam-building and spear-fishing easier. Some foods have been incorporated into the household menu: rice is good for the postpartum and menstrual diet when manioc is out, and also good for everyone to eat on meagre days; salt and oil are appreciated as a new way to cook and season foods; popcorn and black beans are good snacks; and frozen chickens are a luxury appreciated by shamans and celestial ancestors, and are purchased and roasted as offerings when a patient's life is in danger. Households might also buy sacks of corn seed from animal feed suppliers if their corn harvest is less plentiful than they would wish (which it invariably is). This will ensure that their ketera can always be a rich orange colour rather than a dull grey, and their oloniti sweetened and completed by the addition of corn. One of the most important and transformative foreign technologies has been outboard motors (generally 15 horse power) and aluminium boats. Silva (2006) clarifies the sources for the first motor boats acquired: seven boats were given to the community by the farmers associated with the illegal road; four further motors were gained from a bishop in the region; another came from an NGO; and two came from gold prospectors. In subsequent years a few more motors and boats were purchased with state pension payments. By 2001, the number of motorised boats was nineteen and by 2006 it had risen to thirty-six. Following the payment of compensation in 2010, it probably reached around a hundred.

10. This information is obtained from the report published in 2013 by UNESCO on the status of activities undertaken by IPHAN for the urgent safeguarding of Yankwa (UNESCO 2013: 6).

11. For this reason I have analysed the attack elsewhere as a potlatch of destruction (Nahum-Claudel 2012).

12. Community letter in Portuguese, sent 10.10.07, cited by Almeida (2011: 53–54).

13. Almeida (2011: 81 note 63) records that there was an official annulment of all promises made in the meeting, notably the commitment to undertake independent studies of the dams' impact. The representative from the government energy company sent a memorandum to FUNAI recording that they had been pressured by the presence of armed indigenous participants.

BIBLIOGRAPHY

Aïkhenvald, A. 1999. 'The Arawak Language Family', in R. Dixon and A. Aïkhenvald (eds), *The Amazonian Languages*. Cambridge: Cambridge University Press, pp. 65–106.

Allard, O. and E. De Vienne. 2005. 'Pour une Poignée de Dollars: Transmission et Patrimonialisation de la Culture chez les Trumai du Brésil Central', *Cahiers des Amériques Latines* 48–49, 127–45.

Almeida, J. 2011. 'Alta Tensão na Floresta: Os Enawene-Nawe e o Complexo Hidrelétrico Juruena', in A. Lima, A. Fanzares and J. Almeida (eds), *Jeitos de Fazer: Experiências Metodológicas para Elaboração de Planos de Gestão Territorial em Terras Indígenas*. Campinas: Editora Curt Nimendaju.

Andrello, G., A. Guerreiro and S. Hugh-Jones. 2015. 'Space-Time Transformations in the Upper Xingu and Upper Rio Negro', *Sociologia e Antropologia* 5(3): 699–724.

Ardener, E. 1975. 'Belief and the Problem of Women and the "Problem" Revisited', in S. Ardener (ed.), *Perceiving Women*. London: Weidenfeld & Nicolson, pp. 1–27.

Århem, K. 1996. 'The Cosmic Food Web: Human-Nature Relatedness in the Northwest Amazon', in P. Descola and G. Palsson (ed.), *Nature and Society: Anthropological Perspectives*. London: Routledge.

Ariel de Vidas, A. 2004. *Thunder Doesn't Live Here Anymore: The Culture of Marginality Among the Teeneks of Tantoyuca*. Boulder, CO: University of Colorado Press.

Arruda, R.S.V. 1984. Relatório Antropológico Sobre o Grupo Indígena Salumã (Enawenê Nawê). FIPE/MINTER/SUDECO.

Arruda, R.S.V. et al. 1987. O Assassinato do Ir. Vicente Cañas e a Demarcação da A.I. Salumã.

Athayde, S. 2014. 'Introduction: Indigenous Peoples, Dams and Resistance', *Tipití: Journal of the Society for the Anthropology of Lowland South America* 12(2): 80–92.

Baines, S.G. 1999. 'Waimiri-Atroari Resistance in the Presence of an Indigenist Policy of "Resistance"', *Critique of Anthropology* 19(3): 211–26.

Baldus, H. 1952. 'Supernatural Relations with Animals among Indians of Eastern and Southern Brazil', *Thirtieth International Congress of Americanists*. Cambridge, UK.

Basso, E. 1975. *The Kalapalo Indians of Central Brazil*. New York: Holt, Rinehart & Winston.

———. 1995. *The Last Cannibals: A South American Oral History*. Austin, TX: University of Texas Press.

———. 2007. 'The Kalapalo Affinal Civility Register', *Journal of Linguistic Anthropology* 17(2): 161–83.

———. 2009. 'Civility and Deception in Two Kalapalo Ritual Forms', in G. Senft and E.B. Basso (ed.), *Ritual Communication*. Oxford: Berg, pp. 243–70.

Belaunde, L.E. 2005. *El Recuerdo de Luna: Género, Sangre y Memoria entre los Pueblos Amazónicos*. Lima: Fondo Editorial de la Faculdad de Ciencias Sociales.

———. 2006. 'A Força dos Pensamentos, o Fedor do Sangue: Hematologia e gênero na Amazônia', *Revista de Antropologia* 49: 205–43.

Bessire, L. 2014a. *Behold the Black Caiman: A Chronicle of Ayoreo Life*. Chicago, IL: University of Chicago Press.

———. 2014b. 'The Rise of Indigenous Hypermarginality: Native Culture as a Neoliberal Politics of Life', *Current Anthropology* 55(3): 276–95.

Bird David, N. 1999. 'Animism Revisited: Personhood, Environment, and Relational Epistemology', *Current Anthropology* 40(1): 67–91.

Bond, D. and L. Bessire. 2014. 'Ontological Anthropology and the Deferral of Critique', *American Ethnologist* 41(3): 440–56.

Bonilla, O. 2016. 'Parasitism and Subjection: Modes of Paumari Predation', in M. Brightman, V. Grotti and C. Fausto (eds), *Ownership and Nurture: Studies in Native Amazonian Property Relations*. New York: Berghahn, pp. 110–33.

Brandão, A.P.B. 2014. 'A Reference Grammar of Paresi-Haliti (Arawak)', Ph.D. thesis. Austin, TX: University of Texas.

Brightman, M., V.E Grotti and O. Ulturgasheva. 2012. *Animism in Rainforest and Tundra: Personhood, Animals, Plants and Things in Contemporary Amazonia and Siberia*. New York: Berghahn.

Brown, M. 1985. *Tsewa's Gift: Magic and Meaning in an Amazonian Society*. Washington: Smithsonian Institution Press.

Busatto, I. et al. 1995. *Estudo das Potencialidades e do Manejo dos Recursos Naturais na Área Indígena Enawene-Nawe*. Cuiabá: Operação Amazônia Nativa e Centro de Estudos e Pesquisas do Pantanal, Amazônia e Cerrado – GERA/UFMG.

Butt Colson, A. 1983. 'An Amerindian Derivation for Latin American Creole Illnesses and their Treatment', *Social Science and Medicine* 17: 1229–248.

Cabalzar, A. 2005. *Peixe e Gente no Alto Rio Tiquie: Conhecimentos Tukano e Tuyuka, Ictiologia, Etnologia*. São Paulo: Instituto Socioambiental.

Cabalzar, A. and E. Candotti. 2013. *Exposição Peixe e Gente*. Exhibition catalogue. Manaus: Museu da Amazônia; Instituto Socioambiental.

Calderón-Corredor, K. 2011. 'El Cacurí entre los Cotiria', Masters thesis. Bogotá: Universidad Nacional de Colombia.

Cañas, V. 1977–1987. Unpublished Personal Diary, D.L. Pivetta (ed.). Cuiabá: OPAN archive.

Carelli, V. and F. Campoli. 2009. *Yaõkwá, um Patrimônio Ameaçado* [DVD]. Olinda, Brazil: Vídeo Nas Aldeias.

Carneiro, R. 1983. 'The Cultivation of Manioc among the Kuikuru of the Upper Xingú', in R. Hames and W. Vickers (eds), *Adaptive Responses of Native Amazonians*. New York: Academic Press, pp. 65–112.

———. 2000. 'The Evolution of the Tipití: A Study in the Process of Invention', in G. Feinman and L. Manzanilla (eds), *Cultural Evolution: Contemporary Viewpoints*. New York: Kluwer Academic/Plenum, pp. 61–93.

Carnerio da Cunha, M. 1978. *Os Mortos e os Outros*. São Paulo: Hucitec.

Chernela, J. 1993. *The Wanano Indians of the Brazilian Amazon: A Sense of Space*. Austin, TX: University of Texas Press.

Clastres, P. 1977. *Society Against the State*. Oxford: Blackwell.

———. 1998. *Chronicle of the Guayaki Indians*. London: Faber and Faber.

Cohn, C. 2014. 'O Fim do Mundo Como o Conhecemos: Os Xikrin do Bacajá e a Barragem de Belo Monte', in J.P.D. Oliveira and C. Cohn (eds), *Belo Monte e a Questão Indígena*. Brasília: ABA, pp. 253–77.

Conklin, B. 2001. 'Women's Blood, Warriors' Blood, and the Conquest of Vitality in Amazonia', in T. Gregor and D. Tuzin (eds), *Gender in Amazonia and Melanesia: An Exploration of the Comparative Method*. London: University of California Press, pp. 141–75.

———. 2002. 'Shamans Versus Pirates in the Amazonian Treasure Chest', *American Anthropologist* 104(4): 1050–61.

Constantinou, C. 1996. *On the Way to Diplomacy*. Minneapolis, MI: University of Minnesota Press.

Cornago, N. 2013. *Plural Diplomacies: Normative Predicaments and Functional Imperatives*. Leiden: Martinus Nijhoff.

Costa Júnior, P. 1995a. 'A Pesca na Sociedade Enawene-nawe', in I. Busatto, M. Silva, G. Mendes dos Santos and C. Sá(eds), *Estudo das Potencialidades e do Manejo dos Recursos Naturais na Área Indígena Enawene-Nawe*. Cuiabá: Operação Amazônia Nativa e Centro de Estudos e Pesquisas do Pantanal, Amazônia e Cerrado da Universidade Federal de Mato Grosso, pp. 101–44.

———. 1995b. 'Anexo 3: Estimativas da Produção de Pesca de Caráter Ritual', in I. Busatto, M. Silva, G. Mendes dos Santos and C. Sá (eds), *Estudo das Potencialidades e do Manejo dos Recursos Naturais na Área Indígena Enawene-Nawe*. Cuiabá: Operação Amazônia Nativa e Centro de Estudos e Pesquisas do Pantanal, Amazônia e Cerrado - GERA/UFMG, pp. 148–57.

Crocker, C. 1977. 'The Mirrored Self: Identity and Ritual Inversion among the Eastern Bororo', *Ethnology* 16(2): 129–45.

———. 1985. *Vital Souls: Bororo Cosmology, Natural Symbolism, and Shamanism*. Tucson, AZ: University of Arizona Press.

Dal Poz, J. 1991. 'No País dos Cinta Larga: Uma Etnografia do Ritual', Masters thesis. São Paulo: Universidade de São Paulo.

———. 2006. 'Os Enawene-nawe e a Estrada Sapezal-Juina'. Brasilia: MPF.

Da Matta, R. 1982. *A Divided World: Apinaye Social Structure*. Cambridge, MA: Harvard University Press.

Denevan, W. 1992. The Pristine Myth: The Landscape of the Americas in 1492', *Annals of the Association of American Geographers* 82(3): 369–85.

Descola, P. 1992. 'Societies of Nature and the Nature of Society', in A. Kuper (ed.), *Conceptualising Society*. London: Routledge, pp. 107–26.

———. 1994. *In the Society of Nature: A Native Ecology in Amazonia*. Cambridge: Cambridge University Press.

———. 2001. 'The Genres of Gender: Local Models and Global Paradigms in the Comparison of Amazonia and Melanesia', in T. Gregor and D. Tuzin (ed.), *Gender in Amazonia and Melanesia: An Exploration of the Comparative Method*. Berkeley, CA: University of California Press, pp. 91–115.

Dole, G. 1978. 'The Use of Manioc among the Kuikuro: Some Interpretations', in R. Ford (ed.), *The Nature and Status of Ethnobotany*. Ann Arbor, MI: Museum of Anthropology, University of Michigan, pp. 217–47.

Dreyfus, S. 1963. *Les Kayapo du Nord, État de Para, Brésil: Contribution à l'étude des Indiens Gé*. Paris: Mouton.

Dufour, D. 1993. 'The Bitter is the Sweet: A Case Study of Bitter Cassava (Manihot Esculenta) Use in Amazonia', in C. Hladik, A. Hladik, O. Linares, H. Pagezy and A. Semple (eds), *Tropical Forests, People and Food: Biocultural Interactions and Applications to Development*. New York: UNESCO and Parthenon, pp. 575–87.

———. 1999. 'A Closer Look at the Nutritional Implications of Bitter Cassava Use', in A. Goodman, D. Dufour and G. Pelto (eds), *Nutritional Anthropology: Biocultural Perspectives*. Houston, TX: Mayfield Publishing.

Echeverri, J.A. and O.E. Román-Jitdutjaño. 2011. 'Witoto Ash Salts from the Amazon', *Journal of Ethnopharmacology* 138(2): 492–502.

Enfield N.J. 2009. 'Everyday Ritual in the Residential World', in G. Senft and E.B. Basso (eds), *Ritual Communication*. London: Bloomsbury Academic, pp. 51–80.

Epps, P. 2009. 'Language Classification, Language Contact, and Amazonian Prehistory', *Language and Linguistics Compass* 3(2): 581–606.

Erickson, C. 2000. 'An Artificial Landscape-Scale Fishery in the Bolivian Amazon', *Nature* 408(9 November): 190–93.

Erikson, P. (ed.). 2004a. *La Pirogue Ivre: Bières Traditionnelles en Amazonie*. Nanterre: Musée de la Brasserie de Saint-Nicolas de Port.

———. 2004b. 'Bières, Masques et Tatouage chez les Matis d'Amazonie Brésilienne', in P. Erikson (ed.), *La Priogue Ivre: Bières Traditionnelles en Amazonie*. Nanterre: Musée de la Brasserie de Saint-Nicolas de Port, pp. 47–55.

Ewart, E. 2013. *Space and Society in Central Brasil: A Panará Ethnography*. London: Bloomsbury.

Fausto, C. 2007. 'Feasting on People: Eating Animals and Humans in Amazonia', *Current Anthropology* 48(4): 497–30.

———. 2012. *Warfare and Shamanism in Amazonia*. Cambridge: Cambridge University Press.

———. 2016. 'How Much for a Song: The Culture of Calculation and the Calculation of Culture', in M. Brightman, V. Grotti and C. Fausto (eds),

Ownership and Nurture: Studies in Native Amazonian Property Relations. New York: Berghahn, pp. 133–56.

Fausto, C. et al. 2011. *As Hiper Mulheres* [DVD]. Olinda, Brazil: Vídeo nas Aldeias.

Feld S. 1990. *Sound and Sentiment: Birds, Weeping, Poetics, and Song in Kaluli Expression*. Philadelphia, PA: University of Pennsylvania Press.

1996. 'Waterfalls of Song: An Acoustemology of Place Resounding in Bosavi, Papua New Guinea', in K. Basso and S. Feld (eds), *Senses of Place*. Santa Fe, NM: School of American Research Press, pp. 91–137.

Ferguson, B. and N. Whitehead. 1992. *War in the Tribal Zone: Expanding States and Indigenous Warfare*. Santa Fe, NM: School of American Research Press.

Fisher, W.H. 2014. 'O Contexto Institucional da Resistência Indígena a Megaprojetos Amazônicos', in J.P.D. Oliveira and C. Cohn (eds), *Belo Monte e a Questão Indígena*. Brasília: ABA, pp. 133–43.

Francisco, J. 2012. 'Ceia, Cânticos e Batalha Tribal Fazem Parte de Ritual Espiritual dos Enawenê' [Online Film Clip]. 20/06/2012. Retrieved 6 April 2017 from http://g1.globo.com/globo-reporter/noticia/2012/06/ceia-canticos-e-batal-ha-tribal-fazem-parte-de-ritual-espiritual-dos-enawene.html

Galvão, M. 2016. 'Pequenas Centrais Hidrelétricas, Comunidades Indígenas e Espoliação: O Projeto Juruena e os Enawene Nawe no Mato Grosso', Ph.D. thesis. São Paulo: Universidade Estadual de Campinas.

Gluckman, M. 1962. 'Les Rites de Passage', in M. Gluckman (ed.), *The Ritual of Social Relations*. Manchester: Manchester University Press, pp. 1–53.

Godelier, M. 1969. 'La "Monnaie de Sel" des Baruya de Nouvelle-Guinée', *L'Homme* 9(2): 5–37.

Goffman, E. 1967. *Interaction Ritual: Essays on Face-to-Face Behavior*, Garden City, NY: Anchor Books.

Golde, P. 1986. *Women in the Field: Anthropological Experiences*. London: University of California Press.

Goldman, I. 1963. *The Cubeo: Indians of the Northwest Amazon*. Urbana, IL: University of Illinois Press.

Good, C. 2005. '"Trabajando juntos como uno": Conceptos Nahuas del Grupo Doméstico y de la Persona', in D. Robichaud (ed.), *Familia y Parentesco en México y Mesoamérica: Unas Miradas Antropológicas*. Mexico City: Universidad Iboamericana, pp. 275–95.

Goody, J. 1982. *Cooking, Cuisine and Class: A Study in Comparative Sociology*. Cambridge: Cambridge University Press.

Gordon, C. 2006. *Economia Selvagem: Ritual e Mercadoria entre os Indios Xikrin-Mebengokre*. São Paulo: UNESP.

Gow, P. 1989. 'The Perverse Child: Desire in a Native Amazonian Subsistence Economy', *Man* 24(4): 567–82.

———. 1991. *Of Mixed Blood: Kinship and History in Peruvian Amazonia*. Oxford: Oxford University Press.

Graham, L. 1995. *Performing Dreams: Discourses of Immortality among the Xavante of Central Brazil*. Austin, TX: University of Texas Press.

————. 2012. 'Image and Instrumentality in a Xavante Politics of Existential Recognition: The Public Outreach Work of Ete´nhiritipa Pimentel Barbosa', *American Ethnologist* 32(4): 622–41.

Gregor, T. 1970. 'Exposure and Seclusion: A Study of Institutionalized Isolation among the Mehinacu Indians of Brazil', *Ethnology* 9(3): 234–50.

————. 1977. *Mehinaku: The Drama of Everyday Life in a Brazilian Indian village.* Chicago, IL: University of Chicago Press.

————. 1985. *Anxious Pleasures: The Sexual Lives of an Amazonian People.* Chicago, IL: University of Chicago Press.

————. 1994. 'Symbols and Rituals of Peace in Brazil's Upper Xingu', in L. Sponsel and T. Gregor (eds), *The Anthropology of Peace and Nonviolence.* Boulder, CO; London: L. Rienner, pp. 241–59.

Griffiths, T. 2001. 'Finding One's Body: Relationships between Cosmology and Work in North-West Amazonia', in L. Rival and N. Whitehead (eds), *Beyond the Visible and the Material: The Amerindianization of Society in the Work of Peter Riviere.* Oxford: Oxford University Press, pp. 247–61.

Harner, M.J. 1984. *The Jívaro: People of the Sacred Waterfalls.* Berkeley, CA: University of California Press.

Harris, O. 2007. 'What Makes People Work?' in R. Astuti, J. Parry and C. Stafford (eds), *Questions of Anthropology.* Oxford: Berg, pp. 137–67.

Harrison, S. 1989. 'The Symbolic Construction of Aggression and War in a Sepik River Society', *Man* 24(4): 583–99.

————. 1993. *The Mask of War: Violence, Ritual and the Self in Melanesia.* Manchester: Manchester University Press.

Heckenberger, M. 1998. 'Manioc Agriculture and Sedentism in Amazonia: The Upper Xingu Example', *Antiquity* 72: 633–48.

————. 2005. *The Ecology of Power: Culture, Place, and Personhood in the Southern Amazon, A.D. 1000-2000.* London: Routledge.

————. 2013. 'The Arawak Diaspora: Perspectives from South America', in W. Keegan, C. Hofman and R. Rodríguez Ramos (eds), *The Oxford Handbook of Caribbean Archaeology.* Oxford: Oxford Handbooks Online, pp. 1–11.

Heckler, S. 2004. 'Tedium and Creativity: The Valorization of Manioc Cultivation and Piaroa Women', *Journal of the Royal Anthropological Institute* 10(2): 241–59.

Heurich, G.O. 2015. 'Impactos Imediatos e Futuros: Os Araweté e os Executores do Plano Emergencial de Belo Monte', in P.X.-I. Socioambiental (ed.), *Dossiê Belo Monte - Não Há Condições para a Licença de Operação.* São Paulo: Instituto Socioambiental, pp. 75–78.

Hill, J. 1996. *History, Power, and Identity: Ethnogenesis in the Americas, 1492-1992.* Iowa City, IA: University of Iowa Press.

Hill, J. and J.-P. Chaumeil. 2011. 'Ouverture' in J. Hill and J. P. Chaumeil (eds), *Burst of Breath: Indigenous Ritual Wind Instruments in Lowland South America.* London: University of Nebraska Press.

Hill, J. and A. Hornborg. 2011. *Ethnicity in Ancient Amazonia: Reconstructing Past Identities from Archaeology, Linguistics, and Ethnohistory.* Boulder, CO: University Press of Colorado.

Holbraad, M. and M. Pedersen. 2017. *The Ontological Turn: An Anthropological Exposition*. Cambridge: Cambridge University Press.

Hornborg, A. 2005. 'Ethnogenesis, Regional Integration, and Ecology in Prehistoric Amazonia: Toward a System Perspective', *Current Anthropology* 46(4): 589–620.

Hugh-Jones, C. 1979. *From the Milk River: Spatial and Temporal Processes in Northwest Amazonia*. Cambridge: University Press.

Hugh-Jones, S. 1979. *The Palm and the Pleiades*. Cambridge: Cambridge University Press.

———. 1994. 'Shamans, Prophets, Priests and Pastors', in C. Humphrey and N. Thomas (eds), *Shamanism, History and the State*. Michigan: University of Michigan Press, pp. 32–76.

———. 1996. 'Bonnes Raisons ou Mauvaise Conscience? De l'Ambivalence de Certains Amazoniens Envers la Consommation de Viande', *Terrain* Online, 26: 1–22, URL: http://terrain.revues.org/index3161.html

———. 2009. 'The Fabricated Body, Objects and Ancestors in Northwest Amazonia', in F. Santos-Granero (ed.), *The Occult Life of Things: Native Amazonian Theories of Materiality and Personhood*. Tucson, AZ: University of Arizona Press, pp. 33–59.

Irigaray, M. 2014. '"Killing a People Little by Little" Belo Monte, Human Rights and the Myth of Clean Energy', *Tipití: Journal of the Society for the Anthropology of Lowland South America* 12(2): 128–33.

Jakubaszko, A. 2003. 'Imagens da Alteridade: Um Estudo da Experiência Histórica dos Enawene Nawe', Masters thesis. São Paulo: Pontifícia Universidade Católica de São Paulo.

Journet, N. 1995. *La Paix des Jardins: Structures Sociales des Indiens Curripaco du Haut Rio Negro (Colombie)*. Paris: Institut d'Ethnologie.

Kaeppler, A. 1978. 'Dance in Anthropological Perspective', *Annual Review of Anthropology* 7: 31–49.

Kapferer, B. 2004. 'Ritual Dynamics and Virtual Practice: Beyond Representation and Meaning', *Social Analysis* 48(2): 35–54.

Keane, W. 1995. 'The Spoken House: Text, Act, and Object in Eastern Indonesia', *American Ethnologist* 22(1): 102–24.

Kirsch, S. 2007. 'Indigenous Movements and the Risks of Counterglobalization: Tracking the Campaign against Papua New Guinea's Ok Tedi Mine', *American Ethnologist* 34(2): 303–21.

Lagrou, E.M. 2000. 'Homesickness and the Cashinahua Self', in J. Overing and A. Passes (eds), *The Anthropology of Love and Anger: The Aesthetics of Conviviality in Native Amazonia*. London: Routledge, pp. 152–70.

Lamb, C. 2009. 'The Tribe that Stood their Ground', *The Sunday Times Magazine*, 15 February 2009.

Lathrap, D. 1970. *The Upper Amazon*. New York: Praeger.

Leach, E., S. Hugh-Jones, J. Laidlaw (eds). 2000. *The Essential Edmund Leach*. London: Yale University Press.

Lévi-Strauss, C. 1948. 'La Vie Familiale et Sociale des Indiens Nambikwara', *Journal de la Société des Américanistes* 37: 1–132.

————. 1949. 'La Politique Étrangère d'une Société Primitive', *Politique Étrangère* 2 : 139–52.

————. 1955. *Tristes Tropiques*. Paris: Plon.

————. 1958a. 'Les Structures Sociales dans le Brésil Central et Oriental', in *Anthropologie Structurale*. Paris: Plon, pp. 140–54.

————. 1958b. 'Les Organisations Dualistes Existent-Elles?' in *Anthropologie Structurale* . Paris: Plon, pp. 154–91.

————. 1964. *Le Cru et le Cuit (Mythologiques 1)*. Paris: Plon.

————. 1966. *Du Miel au Cendres (Mythologiques 2)*. Paris: Plon.

————. 1968. *L'Origine des Manières de Table (Mythologiques 3)*. Paris: Plon.

————. 1969. *The Elementary Structures of Kinship*. London: Beacon Press.

————. 1971. *L'Homme Nu (Mythologiques 4)*. Paris: Plon.

————. 1988. *The Jealous Potter*. Chicago, IL: University of Chicago Press.

————. 1990. *The Naked Man (Mythologiques 4)*. Chicago, IL: University of Chicago Press.

Lima-Rodgers, A.P. 2014. 'O Ferro e as Flautas: Regimes de Captura e Perecibilidade no Iyaōkwa Enawene Nawe', Ph.D. thesis. Rio de Janeiro: Universidade Federal do Rio de Janeiro.

Lisbôa, T.D.A. 2010. *Os Enauenê-Nauê: Primeiros Contatos*. Cuiabá: Carlini and Caniato.

Lizot, J. 1976. *Le Cercle des Feux: Faits et Dits des Indiens Yanomami*. Paris: Éditions du Seuil.

Maia, D. 2014. 'Índios Bloqueiam Rodovia Em MT E Cobram Até R$ 200 De Pedágio'. *Folha de S. Paulo*, 7 October. Retrieved 14 March 2017 from http://www1.folha.uol.com.br/poder/2014/10/1528819-indios-bloqueiam-rodovia-em-mt-e-cobram-ate-r-200-de-pedagio.shtml?cmpid=%22facefolha%22

Marsden, M., D. Ibañez-Tirado, H. David. 2016. 'Introduction: Everyday Diplomacy', *The Cambridge Journal of Anthropology* 34(2): 2–22.

Maybury-Lewis, D. 2009. 'Indigenous Theories, Anthropological Ideas: A View from Lowland South America', *Anthropological Quarterly* 82(4): 897–927.

McCallum, C. 2001. *Gender and Sociality in Amazonia: How Real People are Made*. Oxford: Berg.

Melatti, J.C. 1979. 'The Relationship System of the Kraho', in D. Maybury-Lewis (ed.), *Dialectical Societies: The Gê and Bororo of Central Brazil*. Cambridge, MA: Harvard University Press, pp. 45–82.

————. 2001. '12a Aula: A Mangaba e o Pequi' [lecture notes]. Universidade de Brasilia. Retrieved 6 April 2017 from http://www.juliomelatti.pro.br/mitos/m12pequi.pdf

Mendes dos Santos, G. 1994. 'Caracterização das Espécies e Variedades Vegetais Cultivadas Pelos Pareci', *Gerando Dehates* 1(1).

————. 2001. Seara de Homens e Deuses: Uma Etnografia dos Modos de Subsistência dos Enawene-Nawe', Masters thesis. São Paulo: Universidade Estadual de Campinas.

————. 2006. 'Da Cultura a Natureza: Um Estudo do Cosmos e da Ecologia dos Enawene-nawe', Ph.D. thesis. São Paulo: Universidade de São Paulo.

Mendes dos Santos, G. and G. Mendes dos Santos. 2008. 'Homens, Peixes e Espiritos: A Pesca Ritual dos Enawene-Nawe', *Tellus* 14: 39–59.

Métraux, A. 1928. 'Une Découverte Biologique des Indiens de l'Amérique du Sud: La Décoloration Artificielle des Pumes sur les Oiseaux Vvants', *Journal de la Société des Américanistes* 20: 181–92.

———. 1942. *The Native Tribes of Eastern Bolivia and Western Mato Grosso.* Washington: Smithsonian Institution, Bureau of American Ethnology.

———. 1944. '"Tapirage", A Biological Discovery of South American Indians', *Journal of The Washington Academy of Sciences* 34: 252–54.

Millikan, B. 2014. 'The Amazon: Dirty Dams, Dirty Politics and the Myth of Clean Energy', *Tipití: Journal of the Society for the Anthropology of Lowland South America* 12(2): 134–38.

Mosko, M. 2013. 'Omarakana revisited, or "do dual organizations exist?" in the Trobriands'. *Journal of the Royal Anthropological Institute* 19: 482–509.

Murphy, R. 1956. 'Matrilocality and Patrilineality in Mundurucú Society', *American Anthropologist* 58(3): 414–434.

Nahum-Claudel, C. 2012. 'Enawene-nawe "Potlatch Against the State"', *Social Anthropology* 20(4): 444–57.

———. 2016a. 'The To and Fro of Documents: Vying for Recognition in Enawene-nawe Dealings with the Brazilian State', *Journal of Latin American and Caribbean Anthropology* 21(3): 478–96.

———. 2016b. 'Feasting', in F. Stein, S. Lazar, M. Candea, H. Diemberger, C. Kaplonski, J. Robbins, R. Stasch. *The Cambridge Encyclopaedia of Anthropology.*

———. 2018. 'The Curse of Suow among the Amazonian Enawenê-nawê', in P. Pitarch and J.A. Kelly (eds), *The Culture of Invention: The Anthropology of Roy Wagner in the Americas.* Herefordshire: Sean Kingston.

Nahum-Claudel, C., N. Pétesche et al. (2017). 'Pourquoi Filmer sa Culture? Rituel et Patrimonialisation en Amazonie Brésilienne (Karajá, Enawenê-nawê, Suruí du Rondônia)', *Journal de la Société des Américanistes* 103 (2).

Oberg, K. 1953. *Indian Tribes of Northern Mato Grosso, Brazil.* Washington, DC: Smithsonian Institution.

O'Hanlon, M. 1989. *Reading the Skin: Adornment, Display and Society among the Wahgi.* London: British Museum Press.

Overing, J. 1986. 'Men Control Women? The "Catch 22" in the Analysis of Gender', *International Journal of Moral and Social Studies* 1(2): 135–56.

Overing, J. and A. Passes (eds). 2000. *The Anthropology of Love and Anger: The Aesthetics of Conviviality in Native Amazonia.* London: Routledge, pp. 97–114.

Overing Kaplan, J. 1975. *The Piaroa, a People of the Orinoco Basin: A Study in Kinship and Marriage.* Oxford: Clarendon Press.

Passes, A. 2000. 'The Value of Working and Speaking Together: A Facet of Pa'ikwené (Palikur) Conviviality', in J. Overing and A. Passes (eds), *The Anthropology of Love and Anger: The Aesthetics of Conviviality in Native Amazonia.* London: Routledge, pp. 97–114.

Pires de Campos, A. 1862. 'Breve Notícia que dá o Capitão Antônio Pires de Campos do Gentio Bárbaro que há na Derrota da Viagem das Minas do

Cuyaba e seu Recôncavo', *Revista Trimestral do Instituto Histórico, Geographico e Etnographico do Brasil* 25: 437–49.

Praet, I. 2013. 'The Positional Quality of Life and Death: A Theory of Human-Animal Relations in Animism', *Anthrozoos* 26(3): 341–55.

Price, D. 1983. 'Pareci, Cabixi, Nambiquara: A Case Study in the Western Classification of Native Peoples', *Journal de la Société des Américanistes* 69: 129–48.

Ramos, A. 1994. 'The Hyperreal Indian', *Critique of Anthropology* 14(2): 153–71.

———. 1998. *Indigenism: Ethnic Politics in Brazil*. Madison: University of Wisconsin Press.

———. 2009. 'Disengaging Anthropology', in D. Poole (ed.), *Companion to Latin American Anthropology*. London: Wiley-Blackwell, pp. 466–84.

———. 2012. 'The Politics of Perspectivism', *Annual Review of Anthropology* 41: 481–94.

Ramos Costa, R.M. 1985. 'Cultura e Contato: Um Estudo da Sociedade Paresí no Contexto das Relações Interétnicas', Masters thesis. Rio de Janeiro: Universidade Federal do Rio de Janeiro.

Reichel-Dolmatoff, G. 1985. *Basketry as Metaphor: Arts and Crafts of the Desana Indians of the Northwest Amazon*. Los Angeles, CA: Museum of Cultural History, University of California.

Rezende, U. 2003. 'Fonética e Fonologia da Língua Enawene-Nawe (Aruak): Uma Primeira Abordagem', Masters thesis. Rio de Janeiro: Universidade Federal do Rio de Janeiro.

Rezende U. 2006. 'Apontamentos Sobre a Escrita Enawene-Nawe (Aruák)' [Unpublished work]. Rio de Janeiro: Faculdade de Letras e Museu Nacional, Universidade Federal do Rio de Janeiro.

Rival, L. 1998. 'Androgynous Parents and Guest Children: The Huaorani Couvade', *Journal of the Royal Anthropological Institute* 5(4): 619–42.

———. 2001. 'Seed and Clone: A Preliminary Note on Manioc Domestication, and its Implication for Symbolic and Social Analysis', in L. Rival and N. Whitehead (eds), *Beyond the Visible and the Material: the Amerindianization of Society in the Work of Peter Rivière*. Oxford: Oxford University Press, pp. 57–80.

———. 2005. 'Introduction: What Constitutes a Human Body in Native Amazonia?', *Tipití: Journal of the Society for the Anthropology of Lowland South America* 3(2): Article 1.

Rival, L. and M.K. Doyle. 2008. 'Domestication and Diversity in Manioc (Manihot esculenta Crantz ssp. esculenta, Euphorbiaceae)', *Current Anthropology* 49(6): 1119–128.

Rivas, R. 2004. *El Gran Pescador: Técnicas de pesca entre los Cocama-Cocamilla de la Amazonía Peruana*. Lima: Pontificia Universidad Católica del Perú.

Rivière, P. 1984. *Individual and Society in Guiana: A Comparative Study of Amerindian Social Organization*. Cambridge: Cambridge University Press.

———. 1987. 'Of Women, Men and Manioc', in H. Skar and F. Salomon (eds), *Natives and Neighbors in South America: Anthropological Essays*. Goteborg: Goteborys Etnografiska Museum, pp. 178–201.

Roscoe, P. 2001. '"Strength" and Sexuality: Sexual Avoidance and Masculinity in New Guinea and Amazonia', in T. Gregor and D. Tuzin (eds), *Gender in Amazonia and Melanesia: An Exploration of the Comparative Method*. London: University of California Press, pp. 279–337.

Sahlins, M. 1985. *Islands of History*. London: University of Chicago Press.

———. 2010. 'Infrastructuralism', *Critical Inquiry* 36(3): 371–85.

Santos-Granero, F. 2002. 'The Arawakan Matrix: Ethos, Language, and History in Native South America', in J. Hill and F. Santos-Granero (eds), *Comparative Arawakan Histories: Rethinking Language Family and Culture Area in Amazonia*. Champaign, IL: University of Illinois Press, pp. 25–51.

———. 2009. *Vital Enemies: Slavery, Predation, and the Amerindian Political Economy of Life*. Austin, TX: University of Texas Press.

Schieffelin, E. 1976. *The Sorrow of the Lonely and the Burning of the Dancers*. New York: St Martin's Press.

Schmidt, M. 1917. *Die Aruaken: Ein Beitrag zum Problem der Kulturverbreitung*. Leipzig: Veit & Co.

———. 1943. 'Los Paressís', *Revista de la Sociedad Científica del Paraguay* 6(1): 1–67.

Seeger, A. 1981. *Nature and Society in Central Brazil: The Suya Indians of Mato Grosso*. Cambridge, MA: Harvard University Press.

———. 1987. *Why Suya Sing: A Musical Anthropology of an Amazonian People*. Cambridge: University of Cambridge Press.

Seeger, A., R. Da Matta and E.B.V. De Castro. 1979. 'A Construção da Pessoa nas Sociedades Indígenas Brasileiras', *Boletim do Museu Nacional* 32: 2–19.

Seligman, A., R. Weller, M. Puett and B. Simon. 2008. *Ritual and Its Consequences: An Essay on the Limits of Sincerity*. Oxford: Oxford University Press.

Silva, M. 1995. 'Estutura Social Enawene-Nawe: Um Rápido Esboço', in I. Busatto, M. Silva, G. Mendes dos Santos and C. Sá (eds), *Estudo das Potencialidades e do Manejo dos Recursos Naturais na Área Indígena Enawene-Nawe*. Cuiabá: Operação Amazônia Nativa e Centro de Estudos e Pesquisas do Pantanal, Amazônia e Cerrado da Universidade Federal de Mato Grosso, pp. 19–33. 1998. 'Tempo e Espaço entre os Enawene Nawe', *Revista de Antropologia* 41(2).

———. 2001. 'Relações de Gênero entre os Enawene-Nawe', *Tellus* 1(1): 41–66.

———. 2006. 'Notícias Recentes', in M. Silva (ed.), *Povos Indígenas no Brasil: 2001-2005*. São Paulo: Instituto Sócio Ambiental.

———. 2012. 'Liga dos Enawene-Nawe: Um Estudo da Aliança de Casamento na Amazônia Meridional', Livre-docência thesis. São Paulo: Universidade de São Paulo.

Siskind, J. 1973. *To Hunt in the Morning*. Oxford: Oxford University Press.

Sofer, S. 1997. 'The Diplomat as a Stranger', *Diplomacy & Statecraft* 8(3): 179–86.

Souza, E.R.D. 2011. 'Sociocosmologia do Espaço Enawene Nawe', Masters thesis. Bahia: Universidade Federal da Bahia.

Stasch, R. 2009. *Society of Others: Kinship and Mourning in a West Papuan Place*. Berkeley, CA: University of California Press.

———. 2011. 'Ritual and Oratory Revisited: The Semiotics of Effective Action', *Annual Review of Anthropology* 40: 159–74.

Stolze-Lima, T. 1999. 'The Two and its Many: Reflections on Perspectivism in a Tupi Cosmology', *Ethnos* 64(1): 107–31.

———. 2005. *Um Peixe Olhou Para Mim: O Povo Yudjá e a Perspectiva*. São Paulo: UNESP.

Strathern, A. and M. Strathern. 1971. *Self-Decoration in Mount Hagen*. London: Backworth.

Strathern, M. 1988. *The Gender of the Gift: Problems with Women and Problems with Society in Melanesia*. London: University of California Press.

Sztutman, R. 2008. 'Cauim, Substância e Efeito: Sobre Consumo de Bebidas Fermentadas entre os Ameríndios', in B. Caiuby Labate, S. Goulart, M. Fiore, E. McRae and H. Carneiro (eds), *Drogas e Cultura: Novas Perspectivas*. Salvador: Edufba, pp. 219–50.

Taylor, A.-C. and E. Viveiros de Castro. 2006. 'Qu'est-ce qu'un corps?', in S. Breton (ed.), *Un Corps Fait de Regards (Amazonie)*. Paris: Musée du Quai Branly, pp. 148–99.

Taylor Klein, P. 2015. 'Engaging the Brazilian State: The Belo Monte Dam and the Struggle for Political Voice', *The Journal of Peasant Studies* 42(6): 1137–1156.

Tsing, A.L. 2005. *Friction: An Ethnography of Global Connection*. Princeton, NJ: Princeton University Press.

Turner, T. 1979. 'The Gê and Bororo Societies as Dialectical Systems: A General Model', in D. Maybury-Lewis (ed.), *Dialectical Societies: The Gê and Bororo of Central Brazil*. Cambridge, MA: Harvard University Press, pp. 147–78.

———. 1984. 'Dual Opposition, Hierarchy and Value: Moiety Structure and Symbolic Polarity in Central Brazil and Elsewhere', in J.-C. Galey (ed.), *Différences, valeurs, hiérarchie: Textes offerts à Louis Dumont*. Paris: Editions de l'Ecole des Hautes Etudes en Sciences sociales, pp. 335–70.

———. 1992. 'Defiant Images: The Kayapo Appropriation of Video', *Anthropology Today* 8 (6): 5–16.

———. 1995. 'Social Body and Embodied Subject: Bodiliness, Subjectivity, and Sociality among the Kayapo', *Cultural Anthropology* 10(2): 143–70.

Turner, V. 1977. *The Ritual Process: Structure and Anti-Structure*. Ithaca, NY: Cornell University Press.

UNESCO. 2013. 'Report on the Status of an Element Inscribed on the List of Intangible Cultural Heritage in Need of Urgent Safeguarding', Intergovernmental Committee for the Safeguarding of Intangible Cultural Heritage, Baku, Azerbaijan, 2–7 December 2013.

Valadão, V. 1995. *Yãkwá, o Banquete dos Espíritos* [DVD]. Olinda, Brazil: Vídeo Nas Aldeais.

Valeri, V. 2000. *The Forest of Taboos: Morality, Hunting, and Identity among the Huaulu of the Moluccas*. Madison, WI: University of Wisconsin Press.

Valeri V. and J. Hoskins. 2002. *Fragments from Forests and Libraries: Essays by Valerio Valeri*. Durham, NC: Carolina Academic Press.

Vanzolini Figueiredo, M. 2010. 'A Flecha do Ciúme: O Parentesco e seu Avesso Segundo os Aweti do Alto Xingu', Ph.D. thesis. Rio de Janeiro: Universidade Federal do Rio de Janeiro.

Viegas, S.D.M. 2003. 'Eating with Your Favourite Mother: Time and Sociality in a Brazilian Amerindian Community', *Journal of the Royal Anthropological Institute* 9(1): 21–37.

Vieira Weiss, M.C. 1998. 'Contato Interétnico, Perfil Saúde-Doença e Modelos de Intervenção Mínima: O Caso Enawene-Nawe em Mato Grosso', Ph.D. thesis. Rio de Janeiro: Fundação Oswaldo Cruz: Escola Nacional de Saúde Pública.

Vilaça, A. 1992. *Comendo Como Gente: Formas do Canibalismo Wari (Pakaa Nova)*. Rio de Janeiro: Editora UFRJ.

———. 2000. 'Relations between Funerary Cannibalism and Warfare Cannibalism: The Question of Predation', *Ethnos* 65(1): 83–106.

———. 2002. 'Making Kin Out of Others in Amazonia', *Journal of the Royal Anthropological Institute* 8(2): 347–65.

———. 2010. *Strange Enemies: Indigenous Agency and Scenes of Encounters in Amazonia*. London: Duke University Press.

Viveiros de Castro, E. 1986. *Araweté: Os Deuses Canibais*. Rio de Janeiro: J. Zahar.

———. 1992. *From the Enemy's Point of View: Humanity and Divinity in an Amazonian Society*. Chicago, Il.: University of Chicago Press.

———. 1995. *Pensando o Parentesco Ameríndio: Estudos Amerindios*. Rio de Janeiro: UFRJ.

———. 1996. 'Images of Nature and Society in Amazonian Ethnology', *Annual Review of Anthropology* 25: 179–200.

———. 1998a. 'Cosmological Deixis and Amerindian Perspectivism', *The Journal of the Royal Anthropological Institute* 4(3): 469–488.

———. 1998b. 'Dravidian and Related Kinship Systems', in T. Trautmann, M. Godelier and F. Fat (eds), *Transformations of Kinship*. Washington: Smithsonian Institution Press.

———. 1999. 'Etnologia Brasileira', in S. Miceli (ed.), *O Que Ler na Ciência Social Brasileira (1970-1995)*. São Paulo: Editora Sumaré: ANPOCS.

———. 2001. 'GUT Feelings about Amazonia: Potential Affinity and the Construction of Kinship', in L. Rival and N. Whitehead (ed.), *Beyond the Visible and the Material: The Amerindianization of Society in the Work of Peter Riviere*. Oxford: Oxford University Press, pp. 19–43.

———. 2002. 'Esboço de Cosmologia Yawalapíti', in E. Viveiros de Castro (ed.), *A Inconstância da Alma Selvagem*. São Paulo: Cosac e Naify.

———. 2004. 'Perspectival Anthropology and the Method of Controlled Equivocation', *Tipití: Journal of the Society for the Anthropology of Lowland South America* 2(1): Article 1.

———. 2009. 'The Gift and the Given: Three Nano-Essays on Kinship and Magic', in S. Bamford and J. Leach (ed.), *Kinship and Beyond: The Genealogical Model Reconsidered*. New York: Berghahn, pp. 237–36.

———. 2010. 'The Untimely, Again', in E. Viveiros de Castro (ed.), *Archaeology of Violence*. Los Angeles: Semiotext(e), pp. 9–52.

———. 2014. *Cannibal Metaphysics*. Minneapolis: Univocal.

Viveiros de Castro, E. and C. Fausto. 1993. 'La Puissance et l'Acte: La Parenté dans les Basses Terres de l'Amérique du Sud', *L'Homme* XXXIII (2–4): 141–70.

Walker, H. 2012. 'Demonic Trade: Debt, Materiality, and Agency in Amazonia',
    Journal of the Royal Anthropological Institute 18: 140–59.
————. 2013. *Under a Watchful Eye: Self, Power, and Intimacy in Amazonia.*
    Berkeley, CA: University of California Press.
Watts, J. 2014. 'Belo Monte, Brazil: The Tribes Living in the Shadow of
    a Megadam'. *The Guardian* 16 December 2014. Retrieved 20 May
    2015 from https://www.theguardian.com/environment/2014/dec/16/
    belo-monte-brazil-tribes-living-in-shadow-megadam
Wilson, W. and D.L. Dufour. 2002. 'Why "Bitter" Cassava? Productivity of "Bitter"
    and "Sweet" Cassava in a Tukanoan Indian Settlement in the Northwest
    Amazon', *Economic Botany* 56(1): 49–57.
Yamin-Pasternak, S., A. Kliskey, L. Alessa, I. Pasternak and P. Schweitze. 2014.
    'The Rotten Renaissance in the Bering Strait: Loving, Loathing, and Washing the
    Smell of Foods with a (Re)acquired Taste', *Current Anthropology* 55(5): 619–46.
Zorthêa, K. 2006. 'Daraiti Ahã: Escrita Alfabética entre os Enawene Nawe', Masters
    thesis. Mato Grosso: Universidade Federal de Mato Grosso.

INDEX

Note: An 'f,' 'm,' or 'n' following a page number indicates a figure, map, or endnote, respectively.

www.ingramcontent.com/pod-product-compliance
Lightning Source LLC
Chambersburg PA
CBHW070613030426
42337CB00020B/3777